Zenescope Entertainment Presents:

Grimm Fairy Tales

Volume 1

zenescope
WWW.ZENESCOPE.COM
ZENESCOPE ENTERTAINMENT, INC.

JOE BRUSHA - PRESIDENT
RALPH TEDESCO - V.P./ EDITOR-IN-CHIEF
DAVID SEIDMAN - ART DIRECTOR
RAVEN GREGORY - EXECUTIVE EDITOR
JENNA SIBEL - PRODUCTION ASSISTANT

THIS VOLUME REPRINTS THE COMIC SERIES GRIMM FAIRY TALES, ISSUES #1-6 PUBLISHED BY ZENESCOPE ENTERTAINMENT PLUS THE SHORT STORY "LEGACY". THIRD EDITION, MAY 2009 · ISBN: 0-9786874-0-X

Grimm Fairy Tales: Volume 1 trade paperback, May, 2009. Third Printing. Published by Zenescope Entertainment Inc., 501 Office Center Drive, Ste. 8, Fort Washington, Pennsylvania 19034.

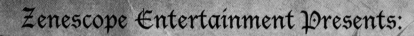

Zenescope Entertainment Presents:

Grimm Fairy Tales

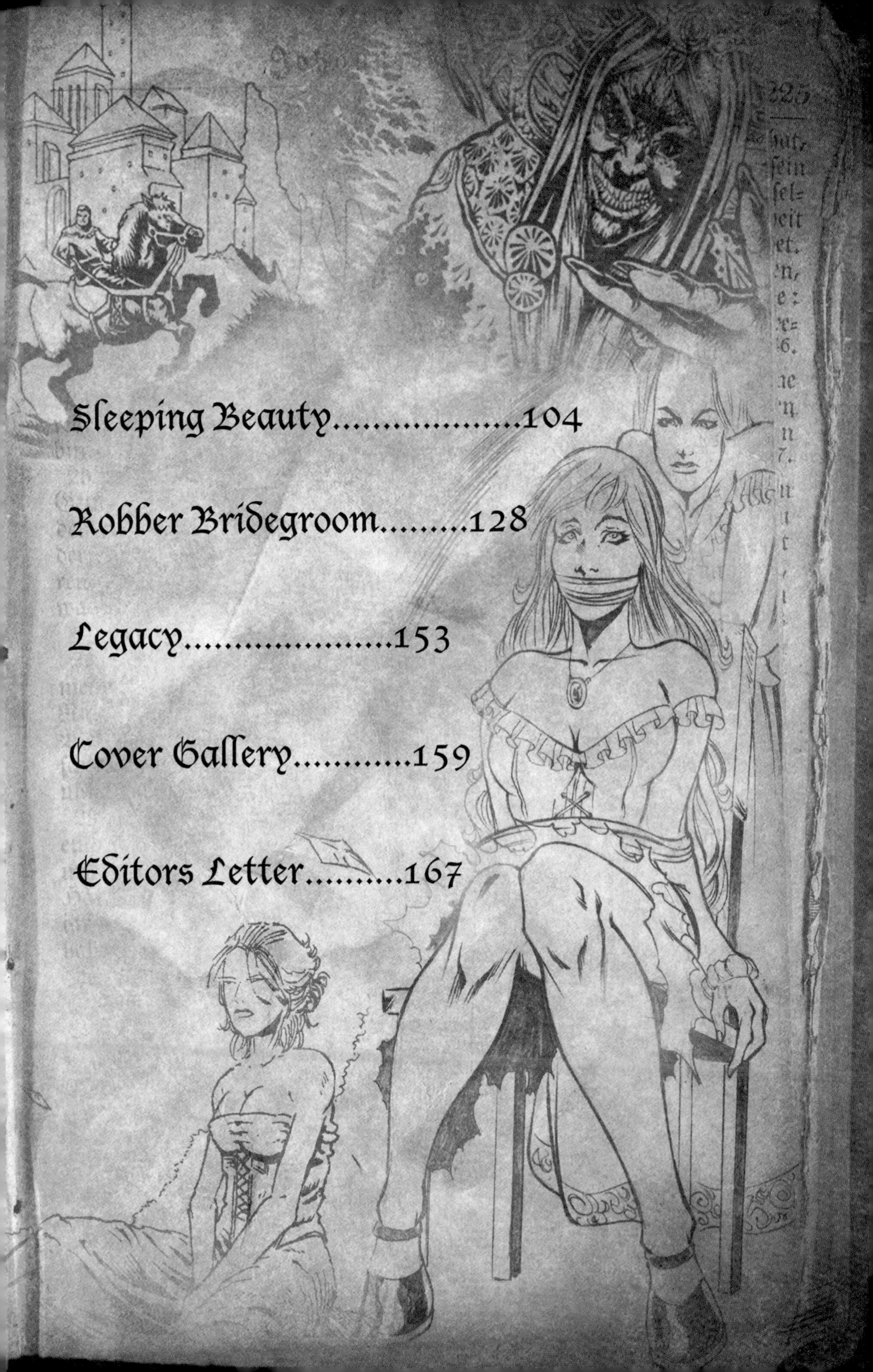

Introduction

Once upon a time, there was a boy who loved trains. Real, big, noisy trains. And if he was ever walking alone, or riding in the car with his family, and he came across train tracks, he would try to sit and wait until he could see a train go by. Needless to say, this didn't sit well with the rest of his family, who made it abundantly clear they didn't share his fascination, or his patience, with regard to said pastime.

And just yesterday, that boy, who is now deep into his adult life, was driving his own grownup car on the way to his (barely) grownup job, when suddenly he realized that he was headed toward tracks again—and for just a moment, all the feelings came rushing back—as if he was still that young boy looking at the tracks for the first time. And he wondered how this normal, everyday occurrence could stir such feelings.

As you probably guessed (if only because the story wasn't very exciting), that kid was me. And it really came to me, just yesterday, that my love of trains has endured for pretty much my whole life and I really don't know why. I just love the feeling I get. It's a feeling of endless possibilities, and just a hint of danger. And that's the same way I felt when I heard or read a fairy tale. Just thinking about it now takes me back to a different place where I wasn't worried about money or jobs or homework or loves. All I really cared about was staying awake for a few more minutes so I could hear my mom or my dad or my older sisters tell me one more story…

…One more Grimm Fairy Tale.

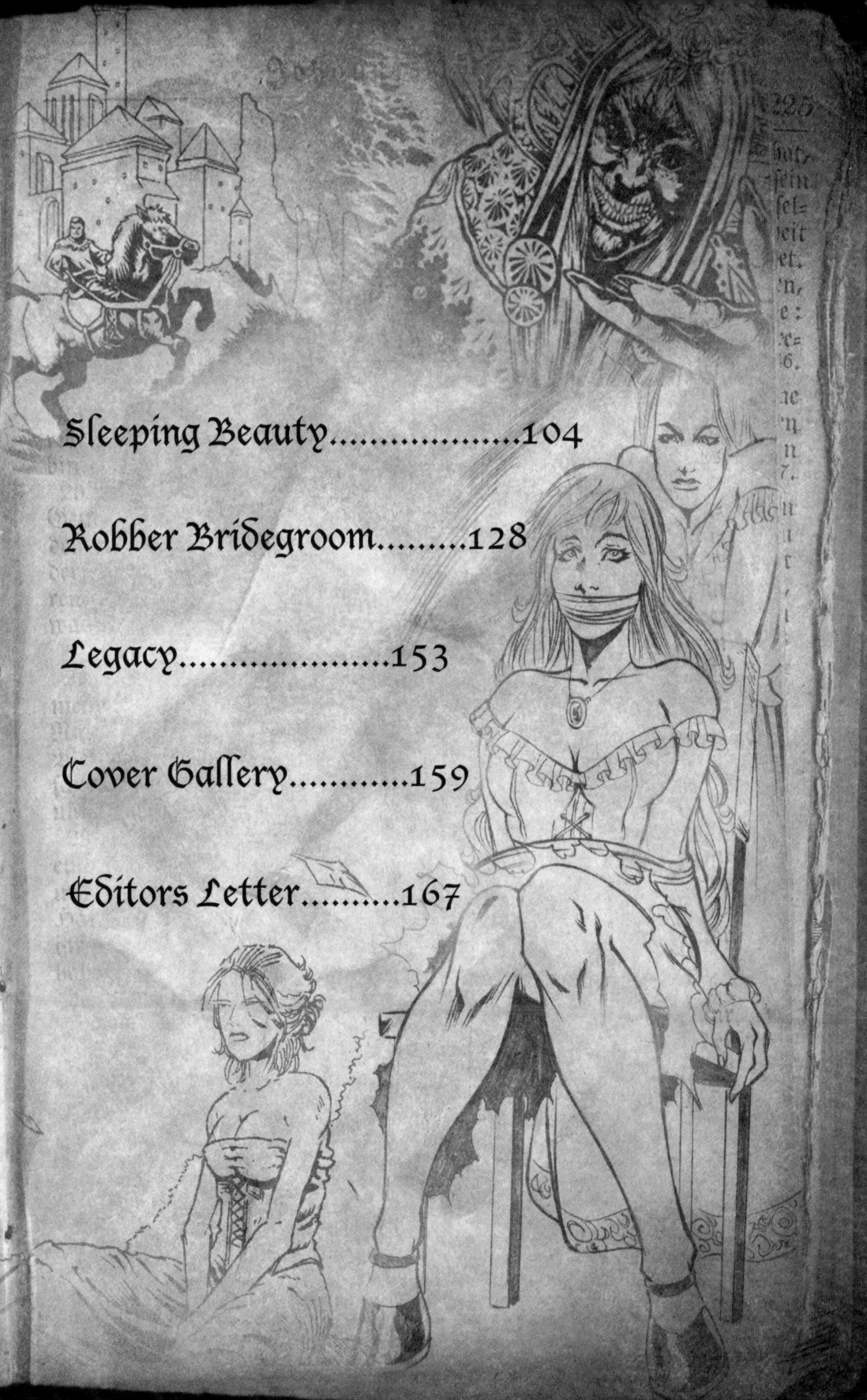

Introduction

Once upon a time, there was a boy who loved trains. Real, big, noisy trains. And if he was ever walking alone, or riding in the car with his family, and he came across train tracks, he would try to sit and wait until he could see a train go by. Needless to say, this didn't sit well with the rest of his family, who made it abundantly clear they didn't share his fascination, or his patience, with regard to said pastime.

And just yesterday, that boy, who is now deep into his adult life, was driving his own grownup car on the way to his (barely) grownup job, when suddenly he realized that he was headed toward tracks again—and for just a moment, all the feelings came rushing back—as if he was still that young boy looking at the tracks for the first time. And he wondered how this normal, everyday occurrence could stir such feelings.

As you probably guessed (if only because the story wasn't very exciting), that kid was me. And it really came to me, just yesterday, that my love of trains has endured for pretty much my whole life and I really don't know why. I just love the feeling I get. It's a feeling of endless possibilities, and just a hint of danger. And that's the same way I felt when I heard or read a fairy tale. Just thinking about it now takes me back to a different place where I wasn't worried about money or jobs or homework or loves. All I really cared about was staying awake for a few more minutes so I could hear my mom or my dad or my older sisters tell me one more story…

…One more Grimm fairy tale.

Whether I was checking under my covers to make sure the
Big Bad Wolf wasn't hiding under there or in a forest
wondering what I would do if I saw a gingerbread house
sitting there, the Brothers Grimm's tales both tantalized
and terrified me. And as I grew older, went to college and
learned about the interpretations of the stories, I developed
an even deeper appreciation for them as I realized the
underlying reasons for why they resonated so much with
me and every other child who ever heard or read them.
They weren't just entertainment;
they were archetypal tales · cautionary tales.

And now, thanks to the fantastic folks at Zenescope
Comics, we've been presented with a re-envisioning of
those classic childhood tales for a new generation. Whether
it's the self-centered narcissism of Sleeping Beauty, the
newly vengeful Cinderella, or the true consequences of
Rumpelstiltskin's tempting offer, we get to see—from the
perspective of everyday people, exactly what the brothers
intended us to be afraid of.

Great work, guys. But please don't tell me what the
train and the tracks really represent, because I'm
not sure if I can take the answer!

David Wohl

David Wohl
Los Angeles, California
June, 2006

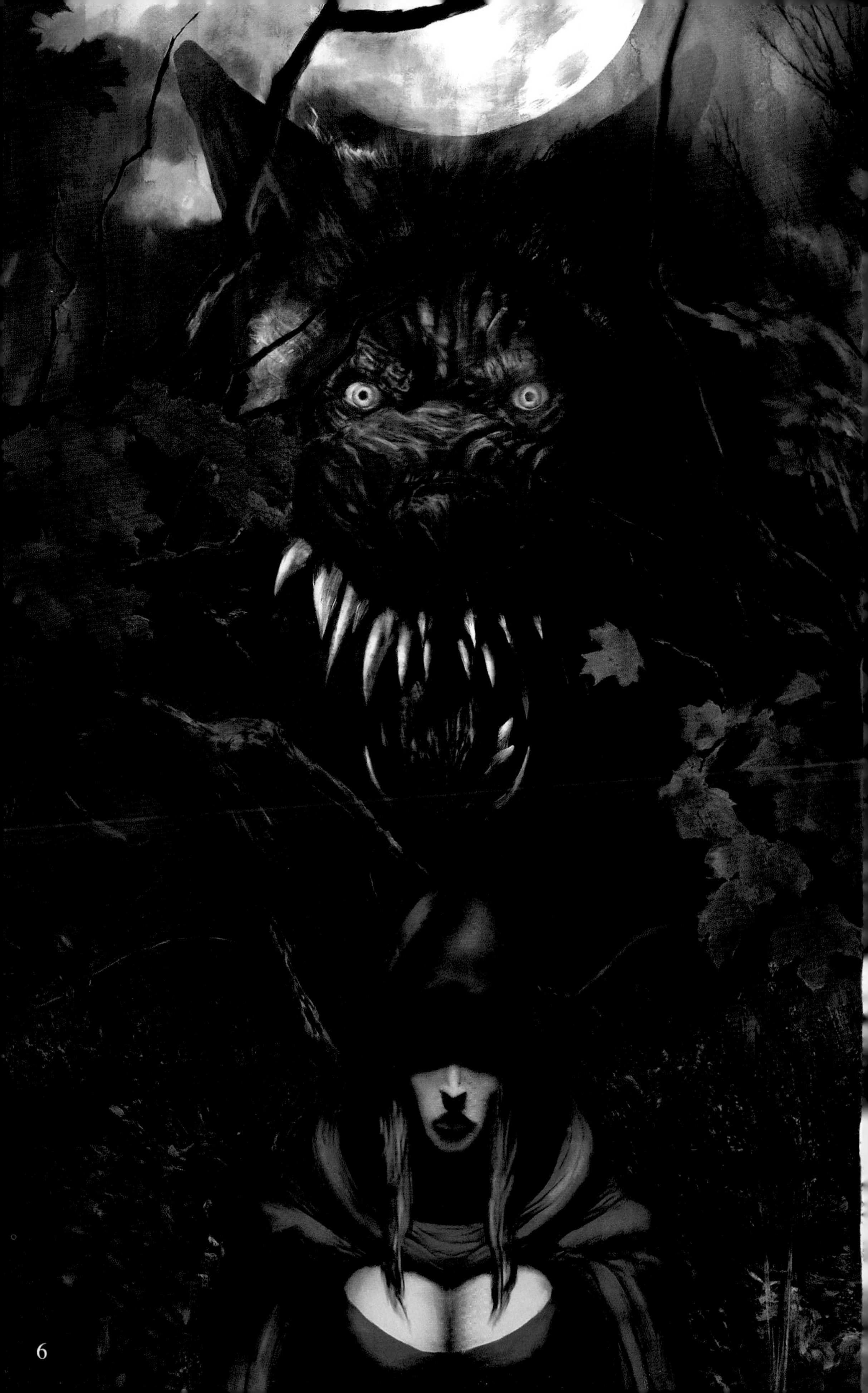

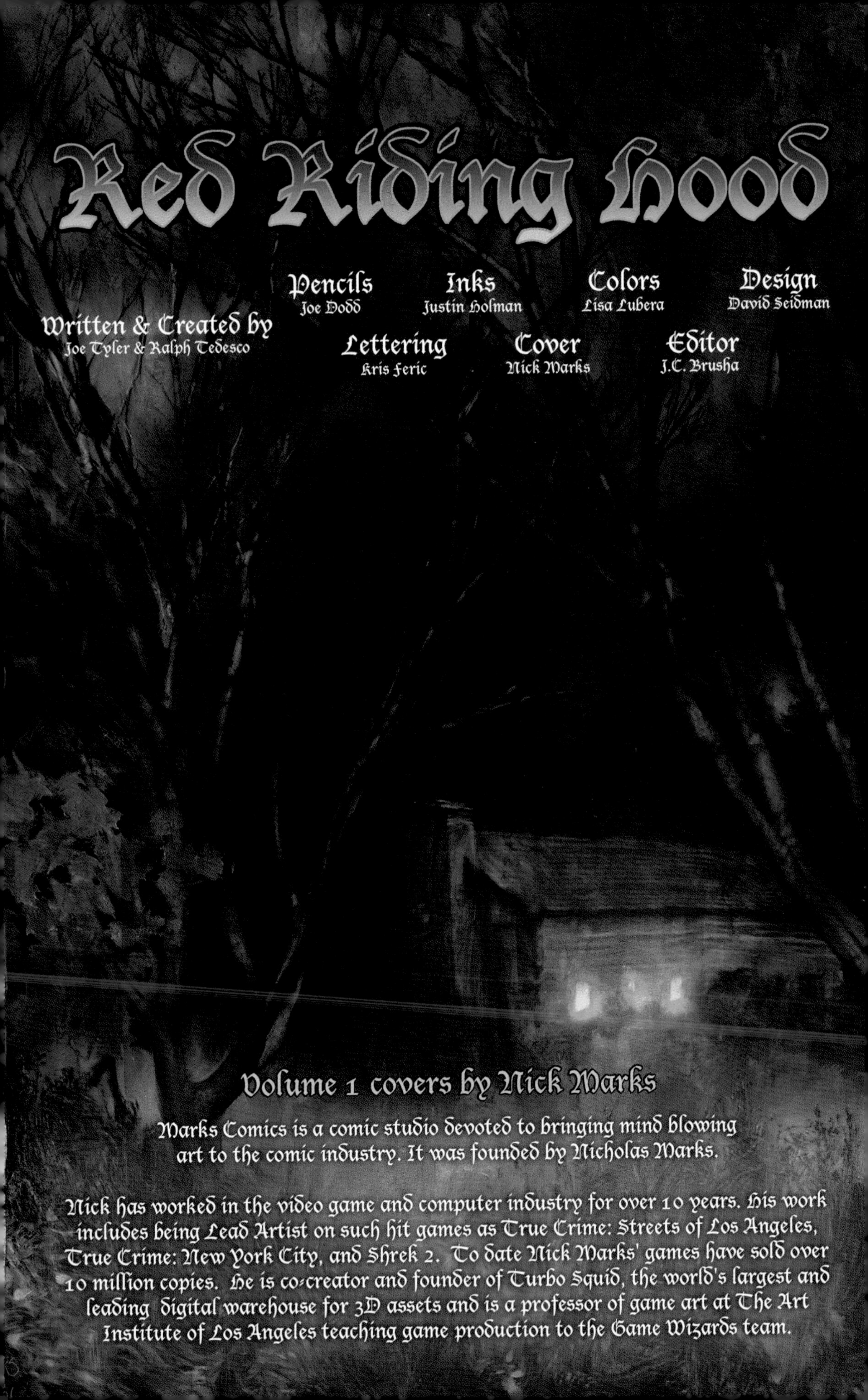

Red Riding Hood

Written & Created by
Joe Tyler & Ralph Tedesco

Pencils
Joe Dodd

Inks
Justin Holman

Colors
Lisa Lubera

Design
David Seidman

Lettering
Kris Feric

Cover
Nick Marks

Editor
J.C. Brusha

Volume 1 covers by Nick Marks

Marks Comics is a comic studio devoted to bringing mind blowing art to the comic industry. It was founded by Nicholas Marks.

Nick has worked in the video game and computer industry for over 10 years. His work includes being Lead Artist on such hit games as True Crime: Streets of Los Angeles, True Crime: New York City, and Shrek 2. To date Nick Marks' games have sold over 10 million copies. He is co-creator and founder of Turbo Squid, the world's largest and leading digital warehouse for 3D assets and is a professor of game art at The Art Institute of Los Angeles teaching game production to the Game Wizards team.

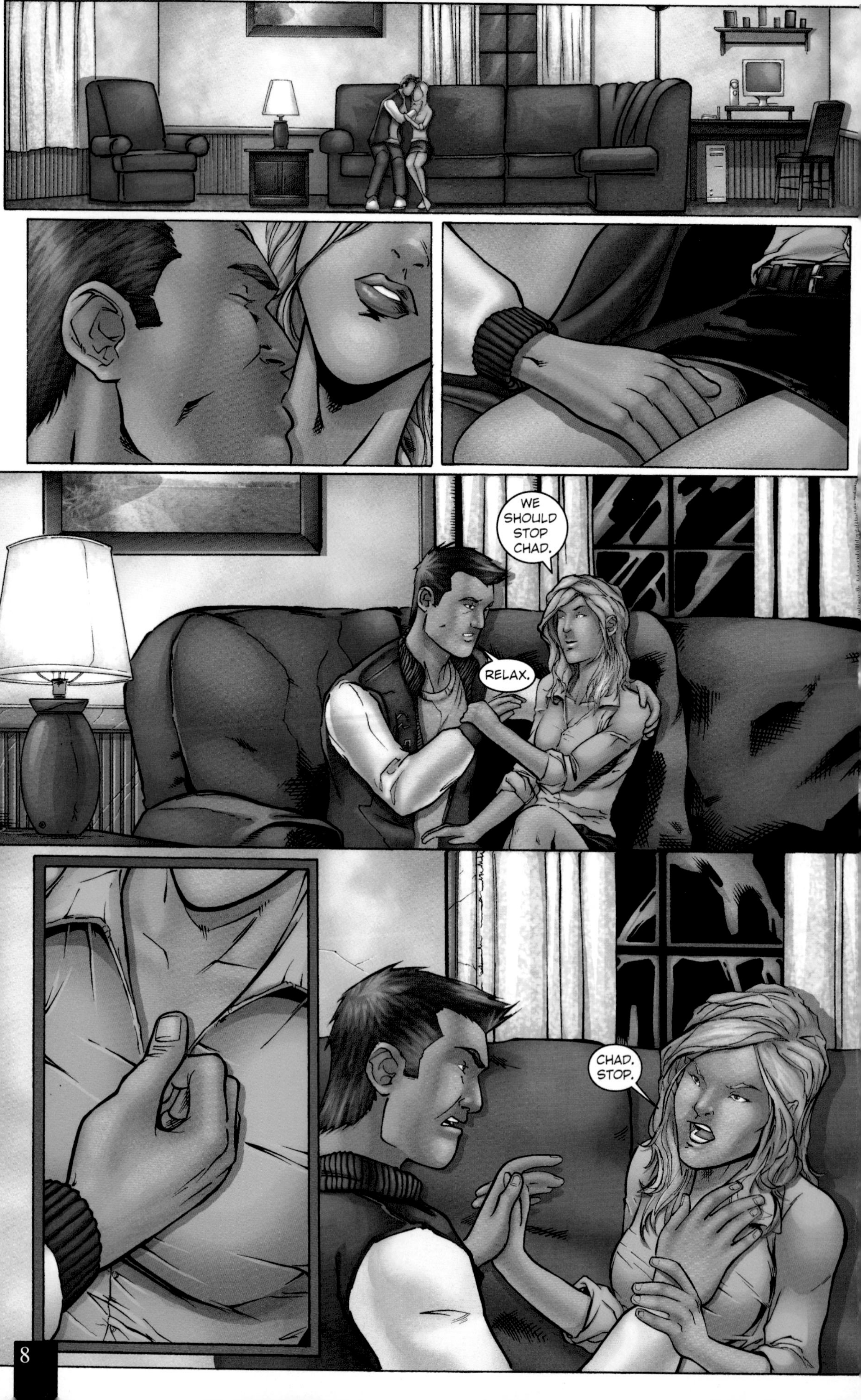
WE SHOULD STOP CHAD.
RELAX.
CHAD. STOP.

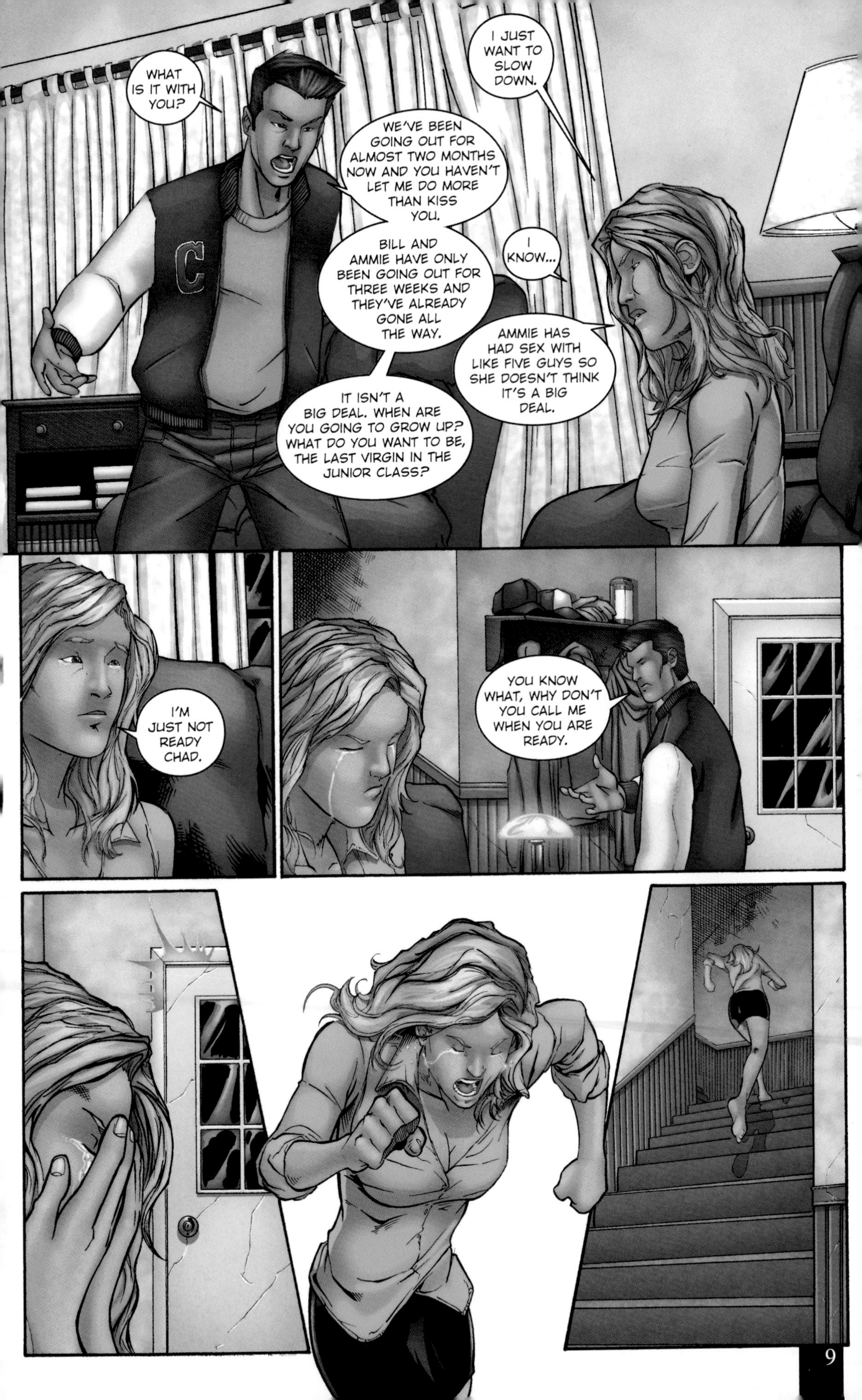
WHAT IS IT WITH YOU?
WE'VE BEEN GOING OUT FOR ALMOST TWO MONTHS NOW AND YOU HAVEN'T LET ME DO MORE THAN KISS YOU.
BILL AND AMMIE HAVE ONLY BEEN GOING OUT FOR THREE WEEKS AND THEY'VE ALREADY GONE ALL THE WAY.
I JUST WANT TO SLOW DOWN.
I KNOW...
AMMIE HAS HAD SEX WITH LIKE FIVE GUYS SO SHE DOESN'T THINK IT'S A BIG DEAL.
IT ISN'T A BIG DEAL. WHEN ARE YOU GOING TO GROW UP? WHAT DO YOU WANT TO BE, THE LAST VIRGIN IN THE JUNIOR CLASS?
I'M JUST NOT READY CHAD.
YOU KNOW WHAT, WHY DON'T YOU CALL ME WHEN YOU ARE READY.

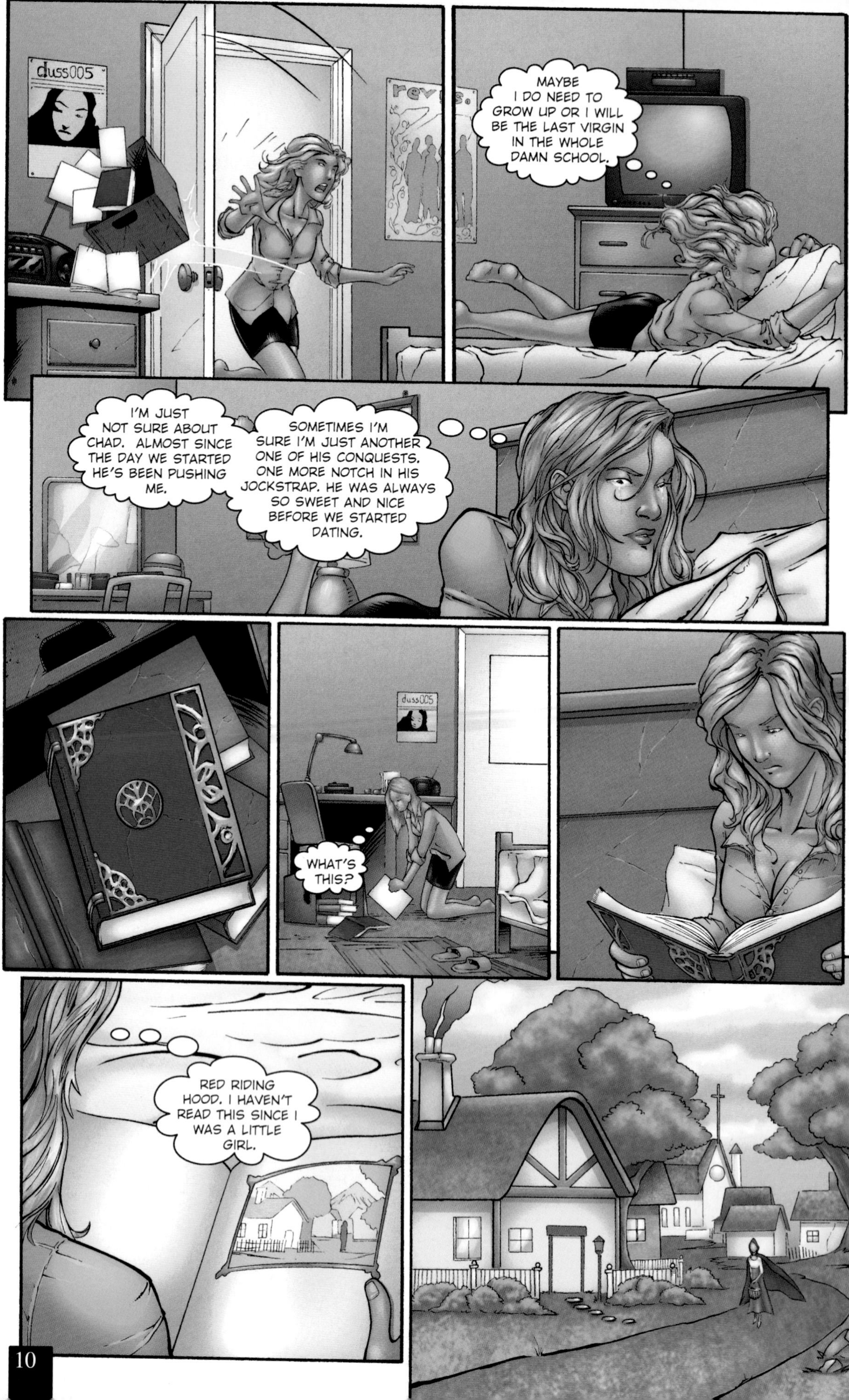
duss005
revs
MAYBE I DO NEED TO GROW UP OR I WILL BE THE LAST VIRGIN IN THE WHOLE DAMN SCHOOL.
I'M JUST NOT SURE ABOUT CHAD. ALMOST SINCE THE DAY WE STARTED HE'S BEEN PUSHING ME.
SOMETIMES I'M SURE I'M JUST ANOTHER ONE OF HIS CONQUESTS. ONE MORE NOTCH IN HIS JOCKSTRAP. HE WAS ALWAYS SO SWEET AND NICE BEFORE WE STARTED DATING.
duss005
WHAT'S THIS?
RED RIDING HOOD. I HAVEN'T READ THIS SINCE I WAS A LITTLE GIRL.

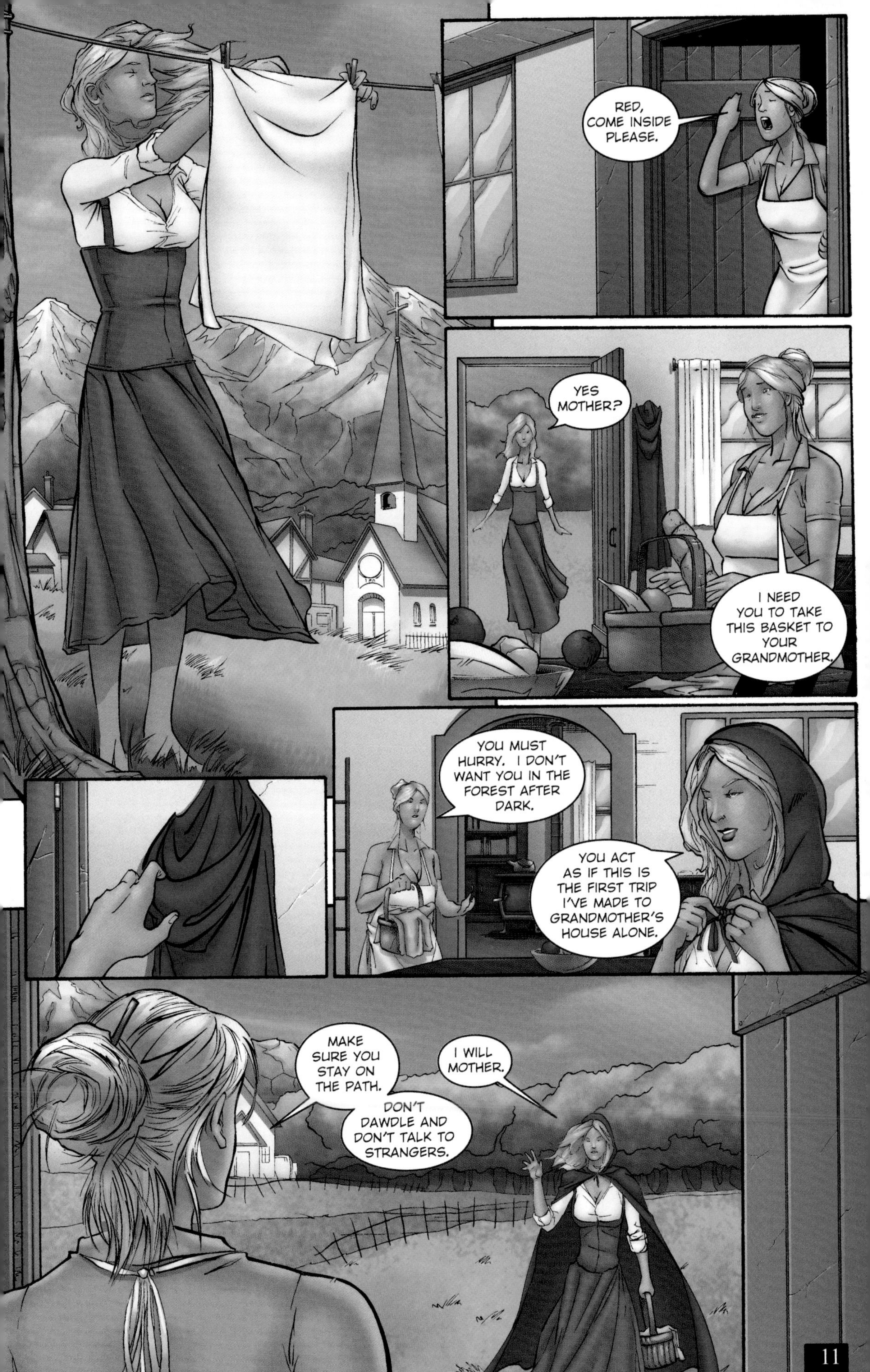
RED, COME INSIDE PLEASE.
YES MOTHER?
I NEED YOU TO TAKE THIS BASKET TO YOUR GRANDMOTHER.
YOU MUST HURRY. I DON'T WANT YOU IN THE FOREST AFTER DARK.
YOU ACT AS IF THIS IS THE FIRST TRIP I'VE MADE TO GRANDMOTHER'S HOUSE ALONE.
MAKE SURE YOU STAY ON THE PATH.
DON'T DAWDLE AND DON'T TALK TO STRANGERS.
I WILL MOTHER.

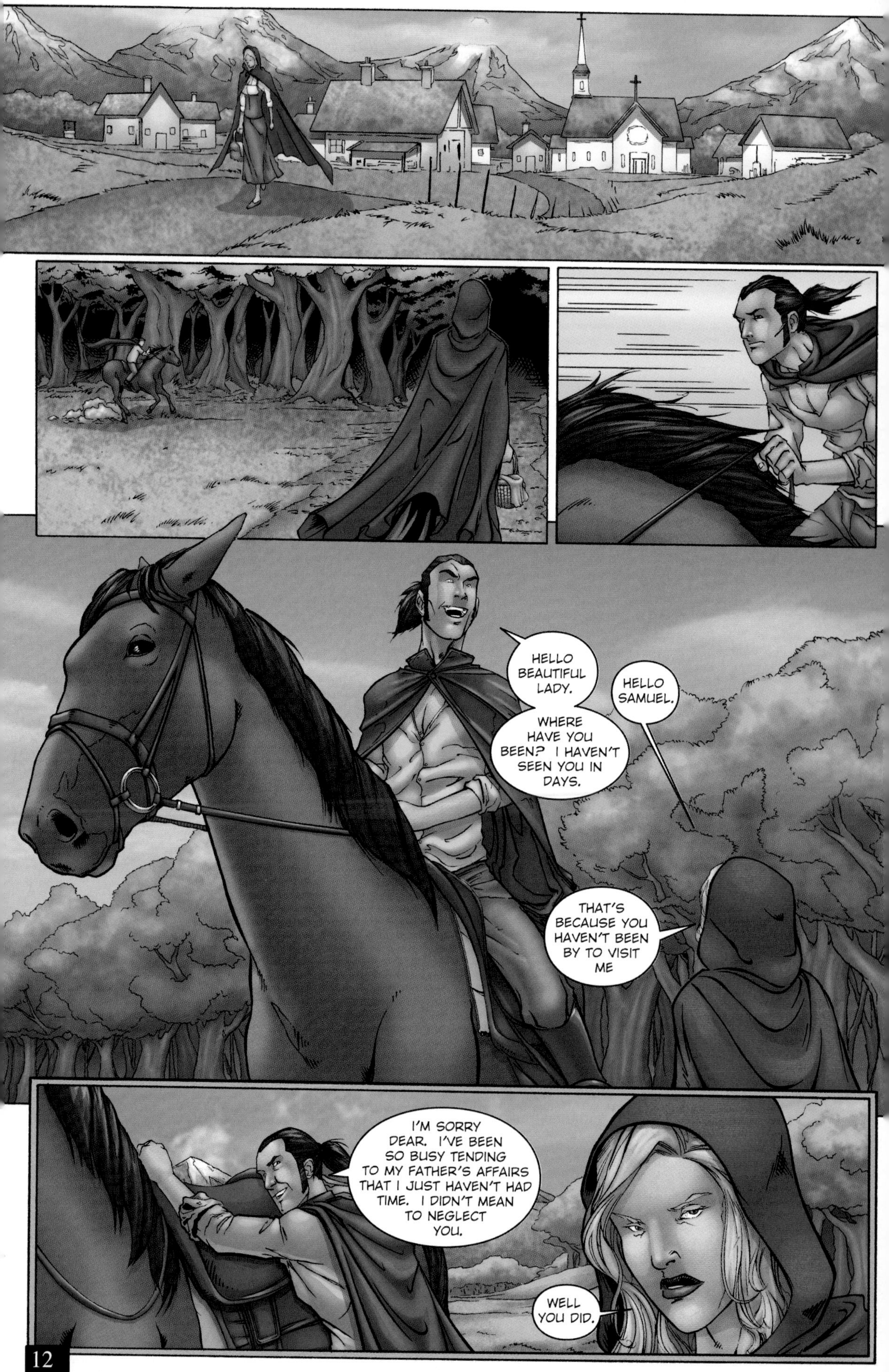
HELLO BEAUTIFUL LADY.
WHERE HAVE YOU BEEN? I HAVEN'T SEEN YOU IN DAYS.
HELLO SAMUEL.
THAT'S BECAUSE YOU HAVEN'T BEEN BY TO VISIT ME
I'M SORRY DEAR. I'VE BEEN SO BUSY TENDING TO MY FATHER'S AFFAIRS THAT I JUST HAVEN'T HAD TIME. I DIDN'T MEAN TO NEGLECT YOU.
WELL YOU DID.

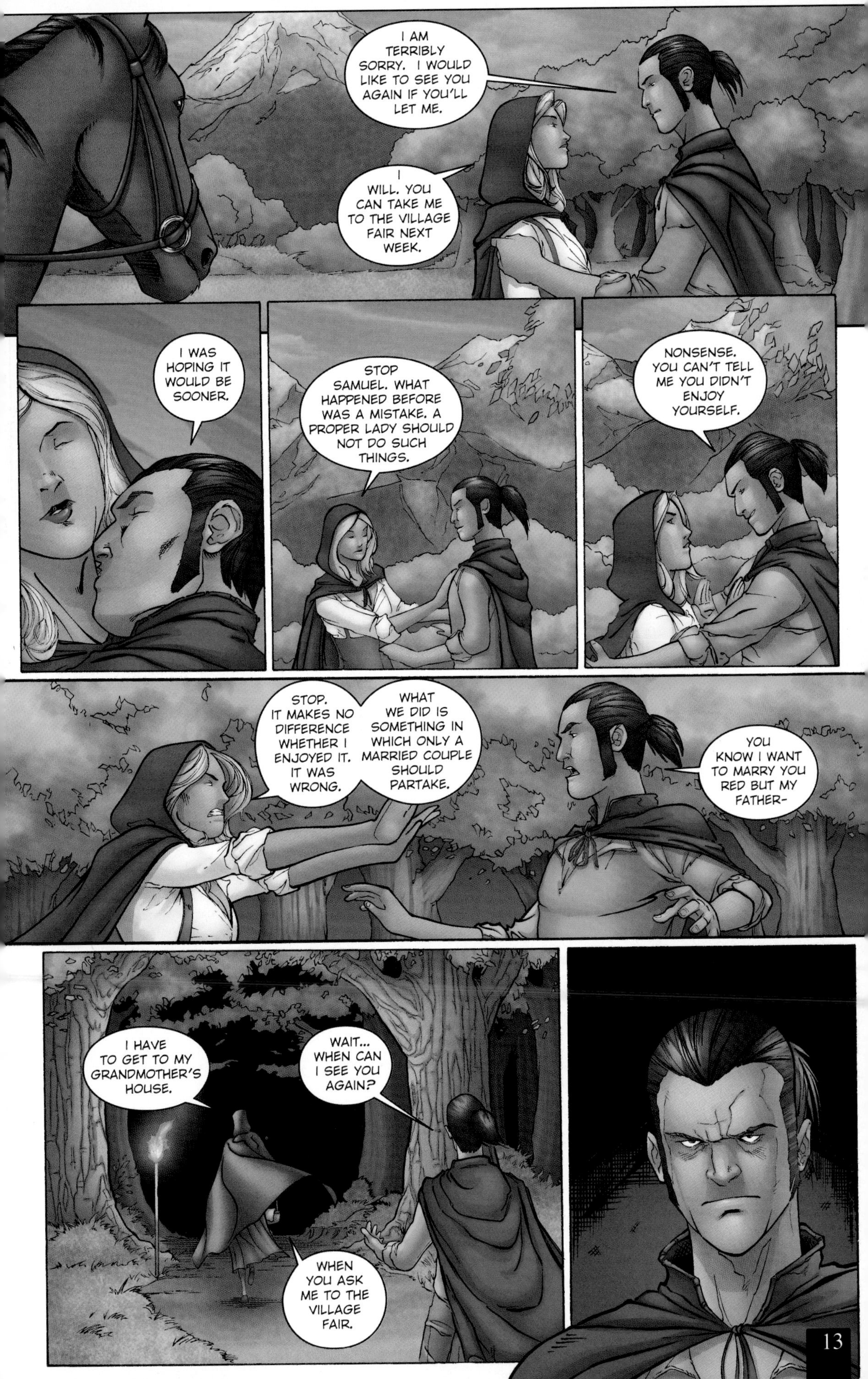
I AM TERRIBLY SORRY. I WOULD LIKE TO SEE YOU AGAIN IF YOU'LL LET ME.
I WILL. YOU CAN TAKE ME TO THE VILLAGE FAIR NEXT WEEK.
I WAS HOPING IT WOULD BE SOONER.
STOP SAMUEL. WHAT HAPPENED BEFORE WAS A MISTAKE. A PROPER LADY SHOULD NOT DO SUCH THINGS.
NONSENSE. YOU CAN'T TELL ME YOU DIDN'T ENJOY YOURSELF.
STOP. IT MAKES NO DIFFERENCE WHETHER I ENJOYED IT. IT WAS WRONG.
WHAT WE DID IS SOMETHING IN WHICH ONLY A MARRIED COUPLE SHOULD PARTAKE.
YOU KNOW I WANT TO MARRY YOU RED BUT MY FATHER-
I HAVE TO GET TO MY GRANDMOTHER'S HOUSE.
WAIT... WHEN CAN I SEE YOU AGAIN?
WHEN YOU ASK ME TO THE VILLAGE FAIR.

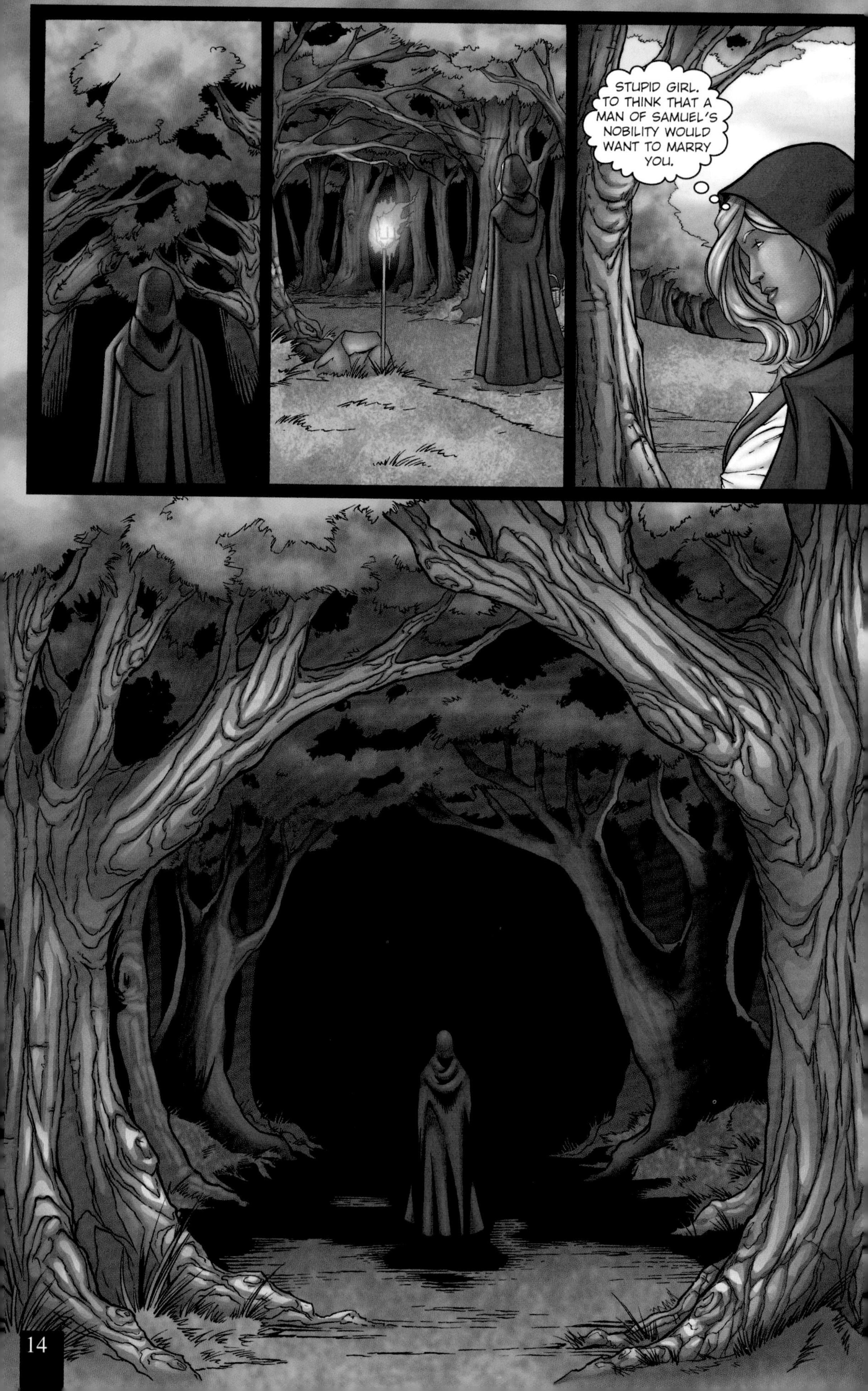
STUPID GIRL. TO THINK THAT A MAN OF SAMUEL'S NOBILITY WOULD WANT TO MARRY YOU.

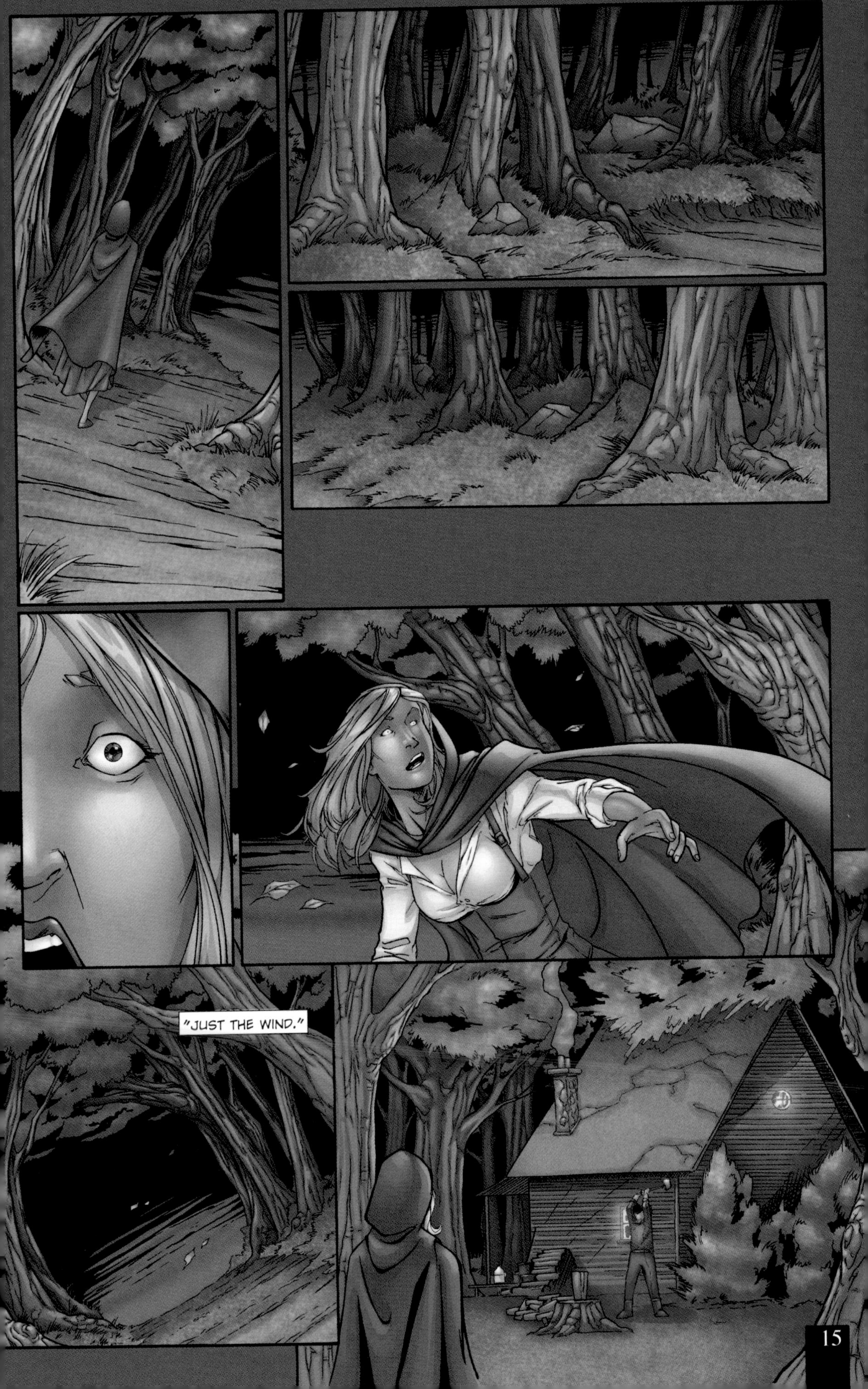
"JUST THE WIND."

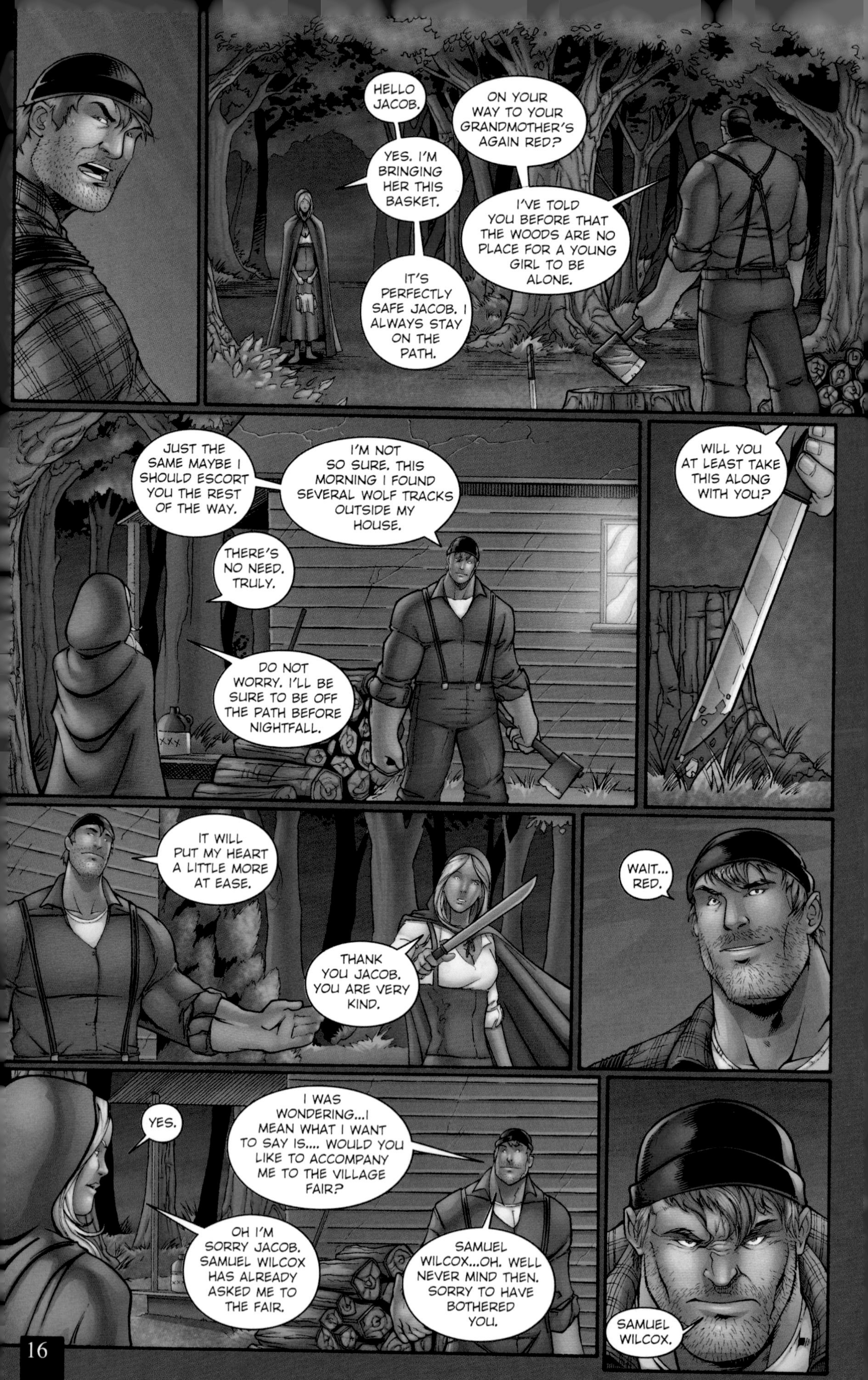
HELLO JACOB.
ON YOUR WAY TO YOUR GRANDMOTHER'S AGAIN RED?
YES. I'M BRINGING HER THIS BASKET.
I'VE TOLD YOU BEFORE THAT THE WOODS ARE NO PLACE FOR A YOUNG GIRL TO BE ALONE.
IT'S PERFECTLY SAFE JACOB. I ALWAYS STAY ON THE PATH.
JUST THE SAME MAYBE I SHOULD ESCORT YOU THE REST OF THE WAY.
I'M NOT SO SURE. THIS MORNING I FOUND SEVERAL WOLF TRACKS OUTSIDE MY HOUSE.
THERE'S NO NEED. TRULY.
DO NOT WORRY. I'LL BE SURE TO BE OFF THE PATH BEFORE NIGHTFALL.
WILL YOU AT LEAST TAKE THIS ALONG WITH YOU?
IT WILL PUT MY HEART A LITTLE MORE AT EASE.
THANK YOU JACOB. YOU ARE VERY KIND.
WAIT... RED.
YES.
I WAS WONDERING...I MEAN WHAT I WANT TO SAY IS.... WOULD YOU LIKE TO ACCOMPANY ME TO THE VILLAGE FAIR?
OH I'M SORRY JACOB. SAMUEL WILCOX HAS ALREADY ASKED ME TO THE FAIR.
SAMUEL WILCOX...OH. WELL NEVER MIND THEN. SORRY TO HAVE BOTHERED YOU.
SAMUEL WILCOX.

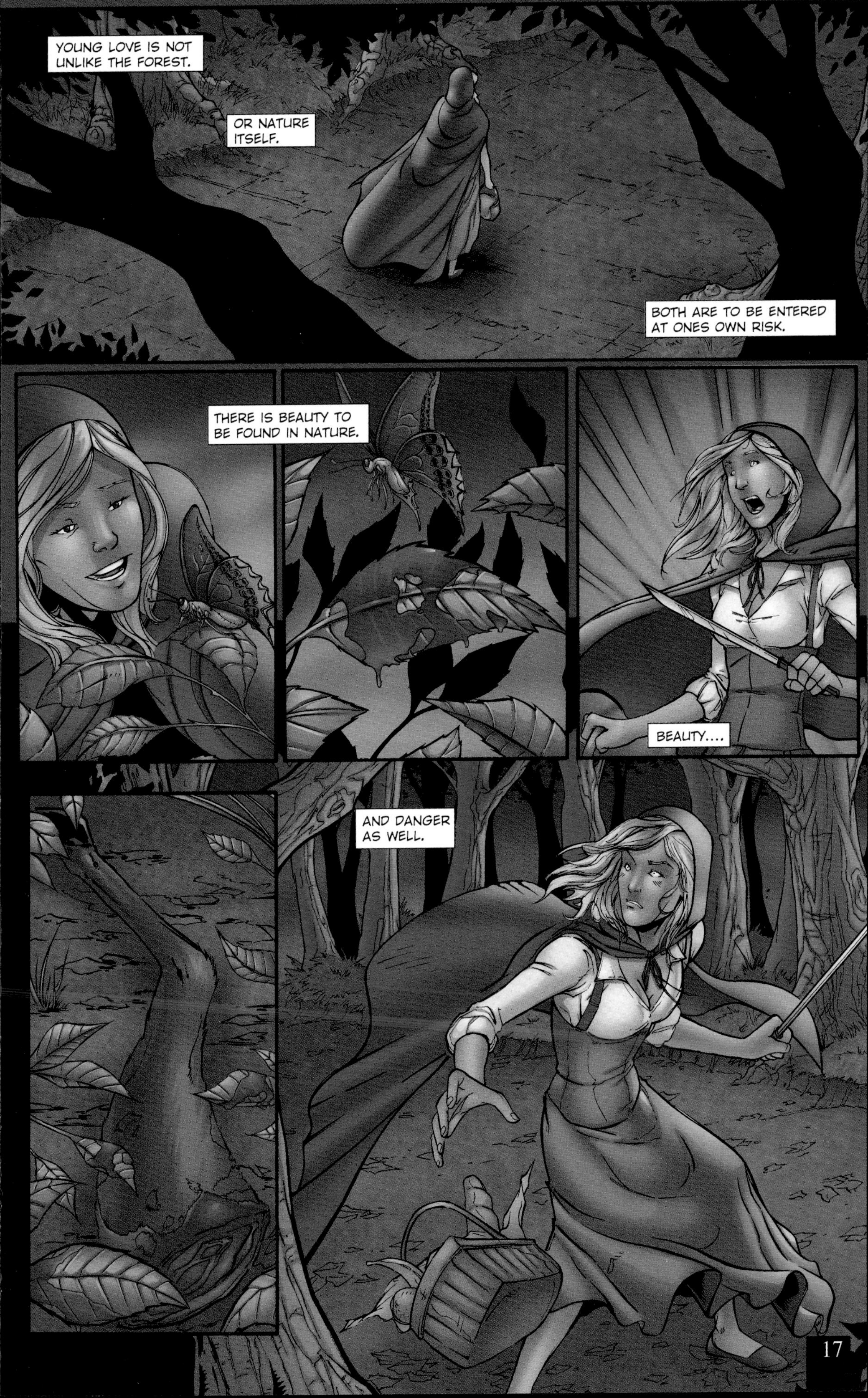
YOUNG LOVE IS NOT UNLIKE THE FOREST.
OR NATURE ITSELF.
BOTH ARE TO BE ENTERED AT ONES OWN RISK.
THERE IS BEAUTY TO BE FOUND IN NATURE.
BEAUTY....
AND DANGER AS WELL.

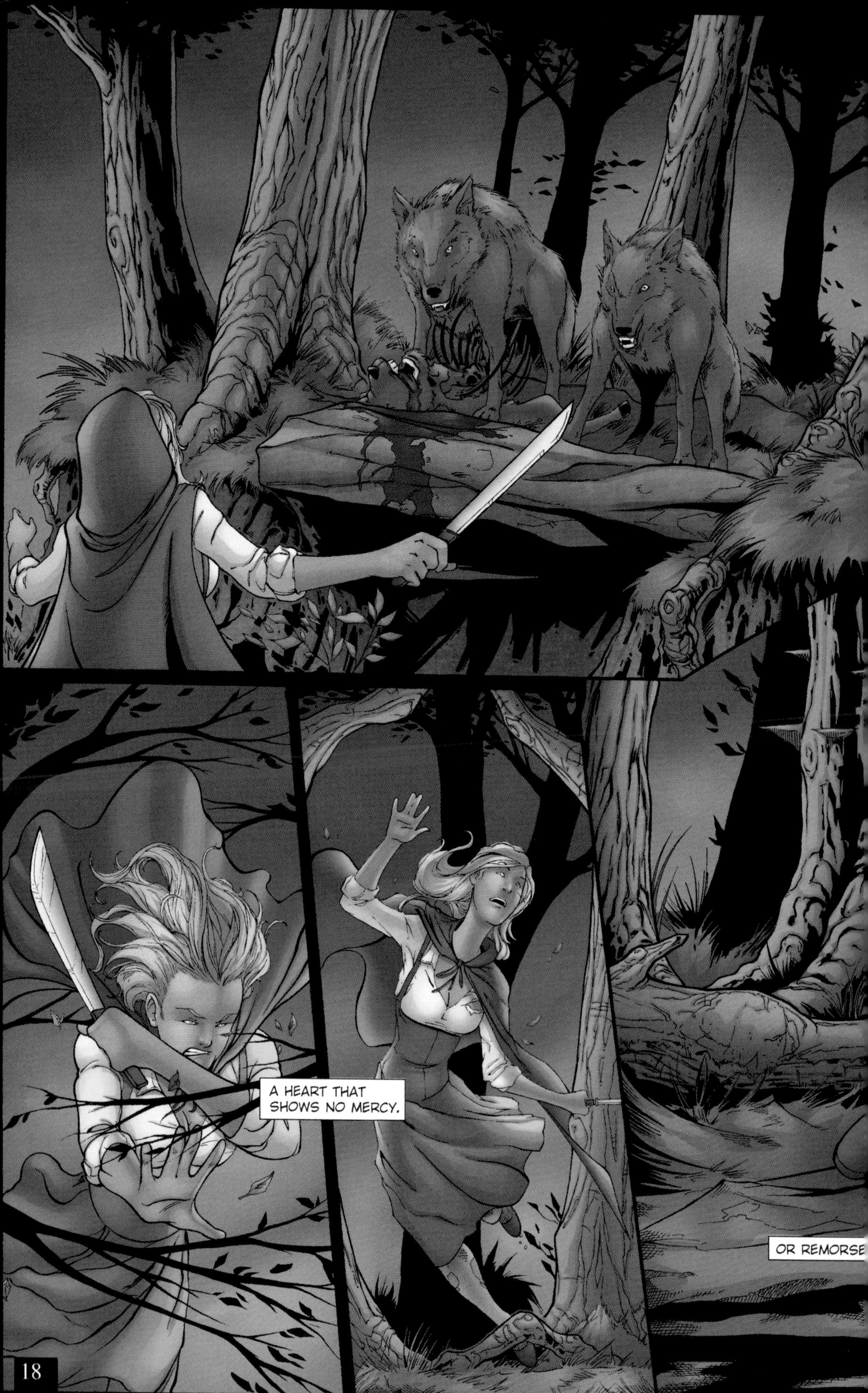
A HEART THAT
SHOWS NO MERCY.
OR REMORSE

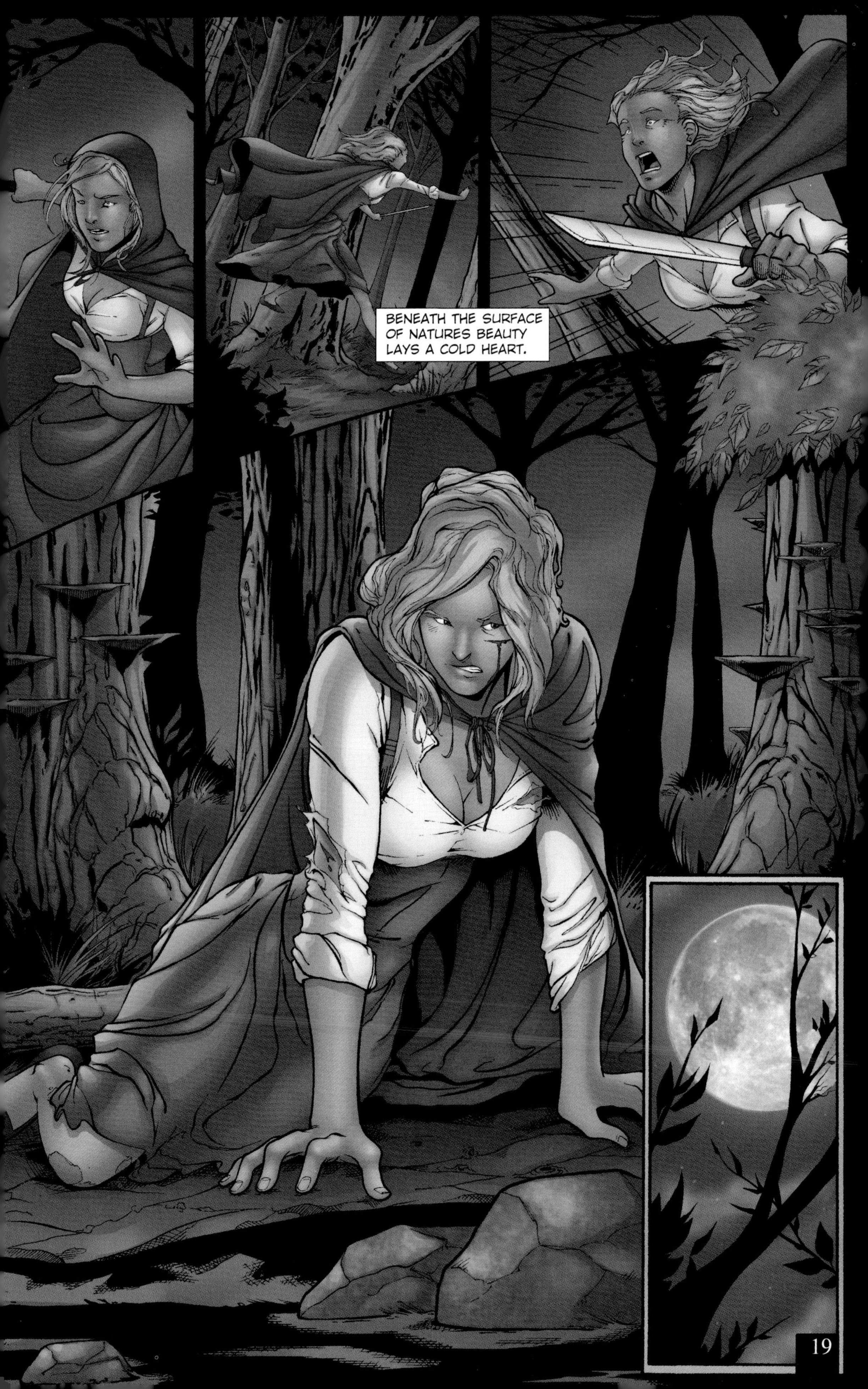
BENEATH THE SURFACE OF NATURES BEAUTY LAYS A COLD HEART.

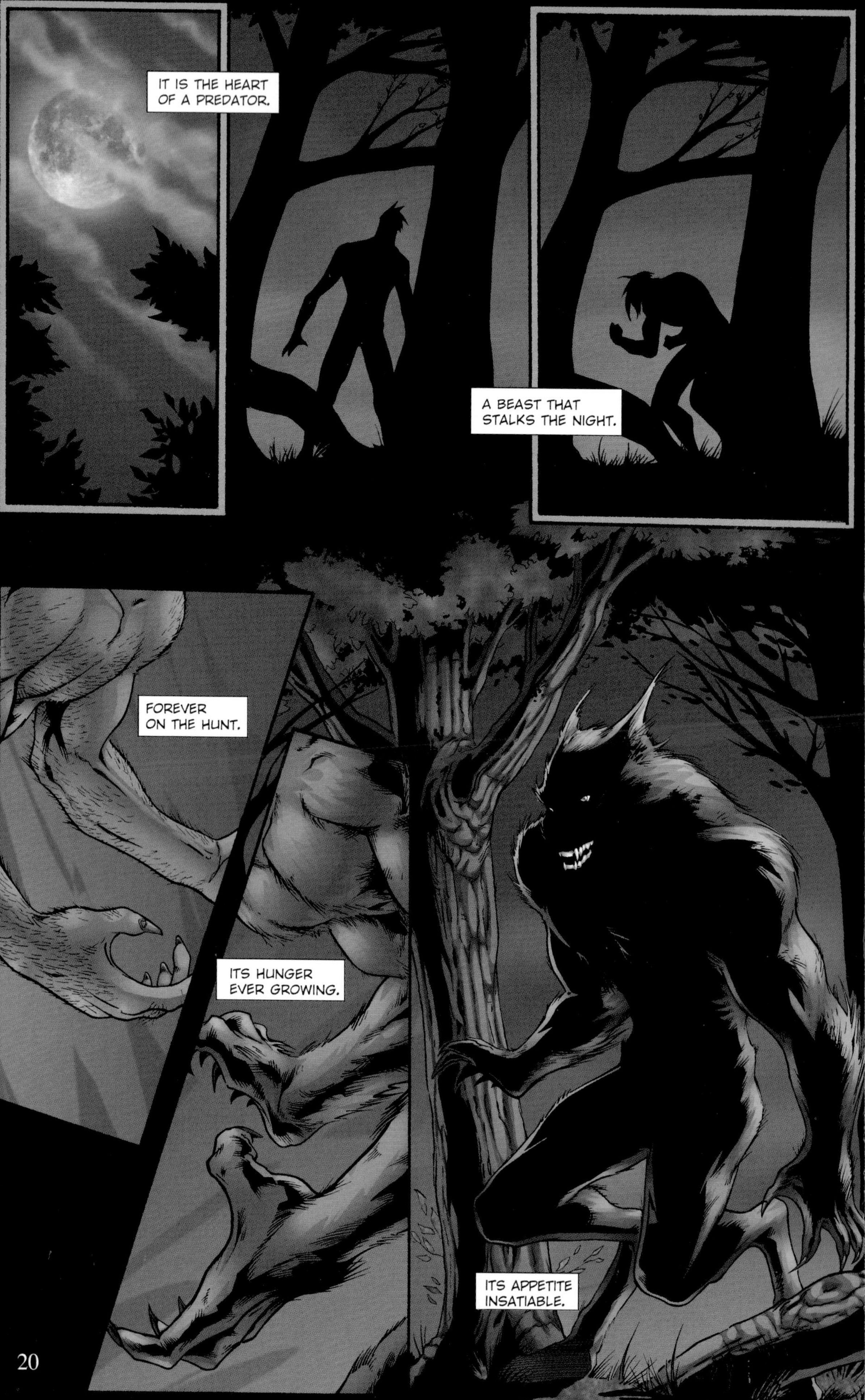
IT IS THE HEART OF A PREDATOR.
A BEAST THAT STALKS THE NIGHT.
FOREVER ON THE HUNT.
ITS HUNGER EVER GROWING.
ITS APPETITE INSATIABLE.

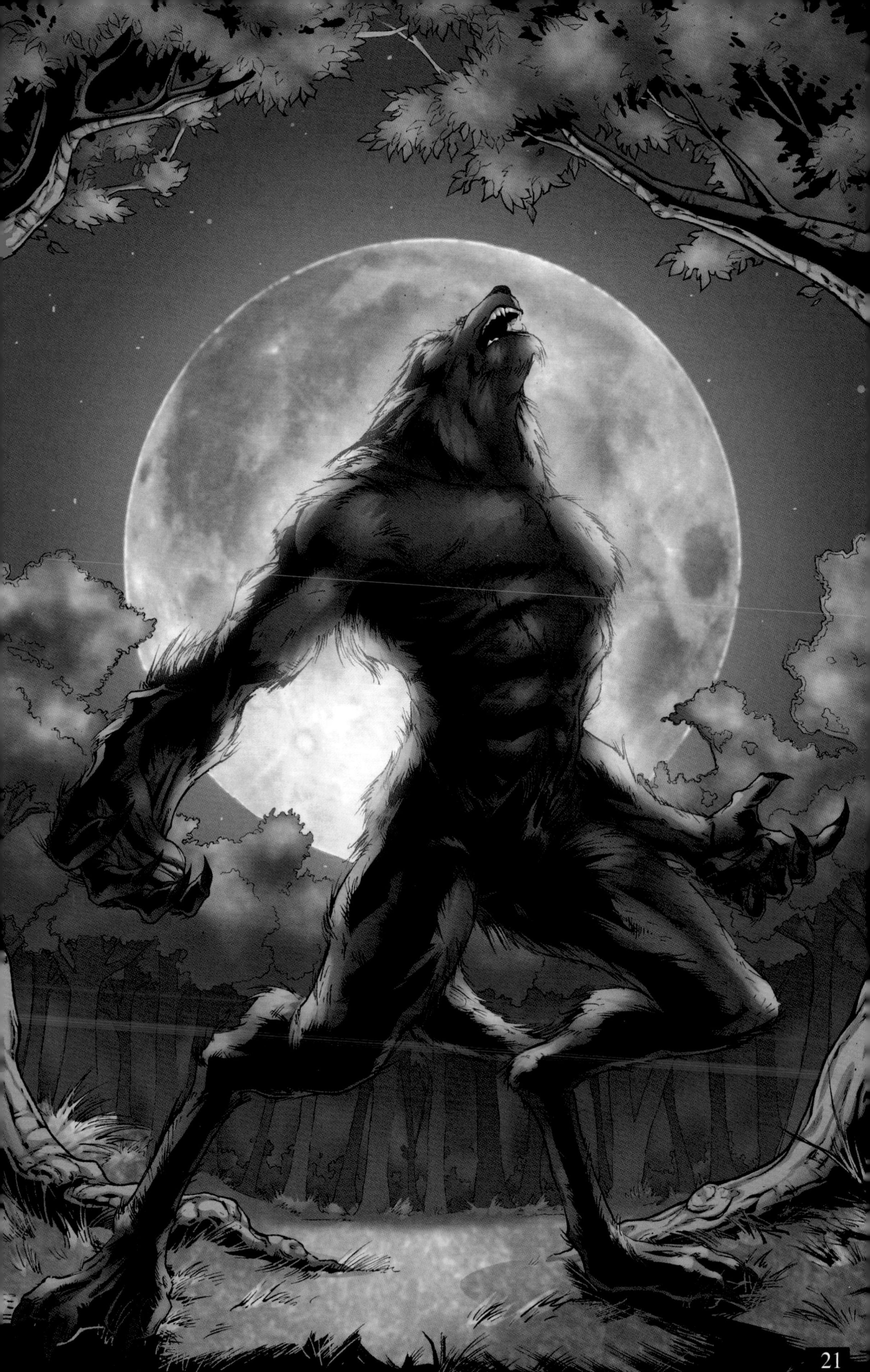

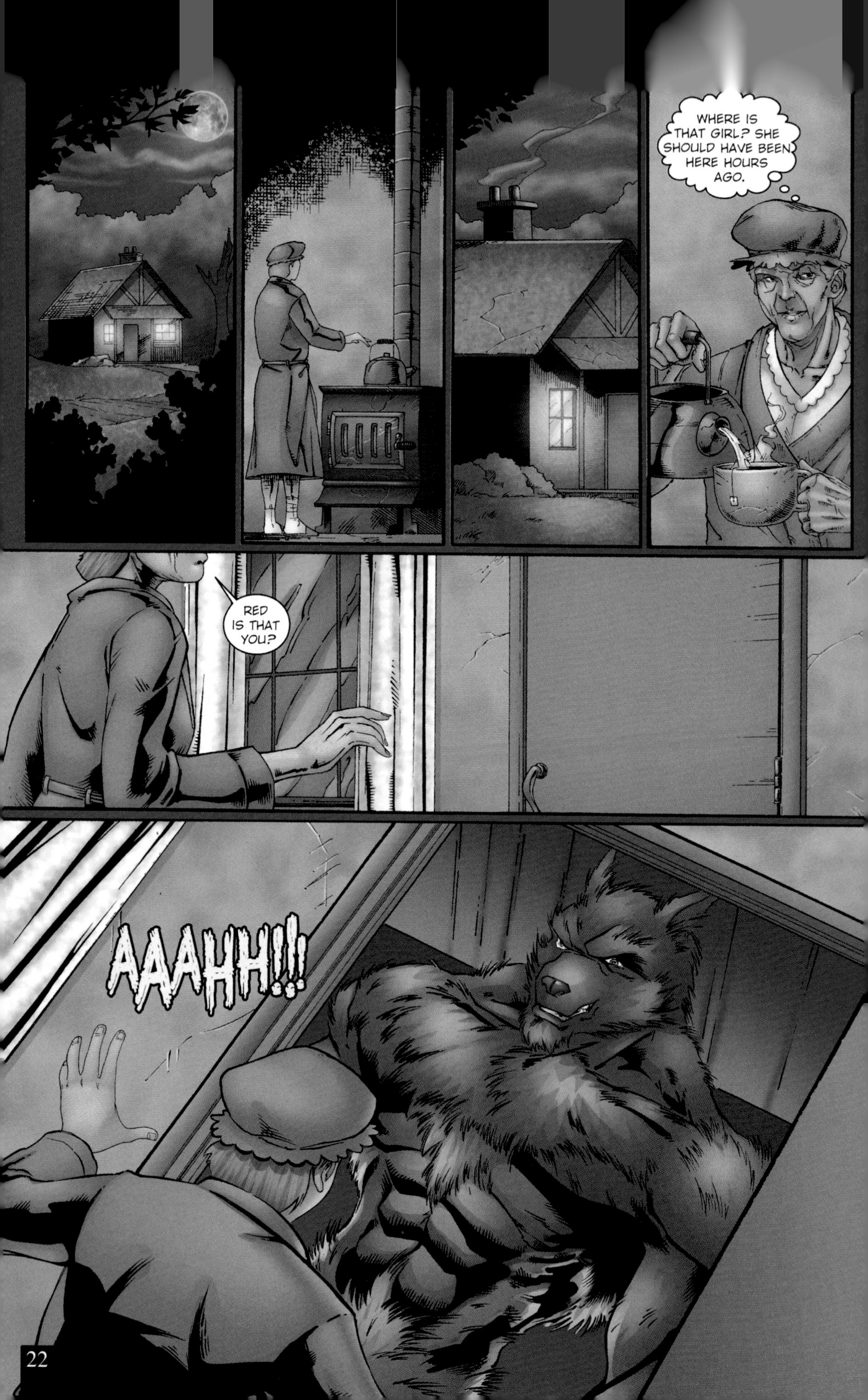
WHERE IS THAT GIRL? SHE SHOULD HAVE BEEN HERE HOURS AGO.
RED IS THAT YOU?
AAAHH!!!

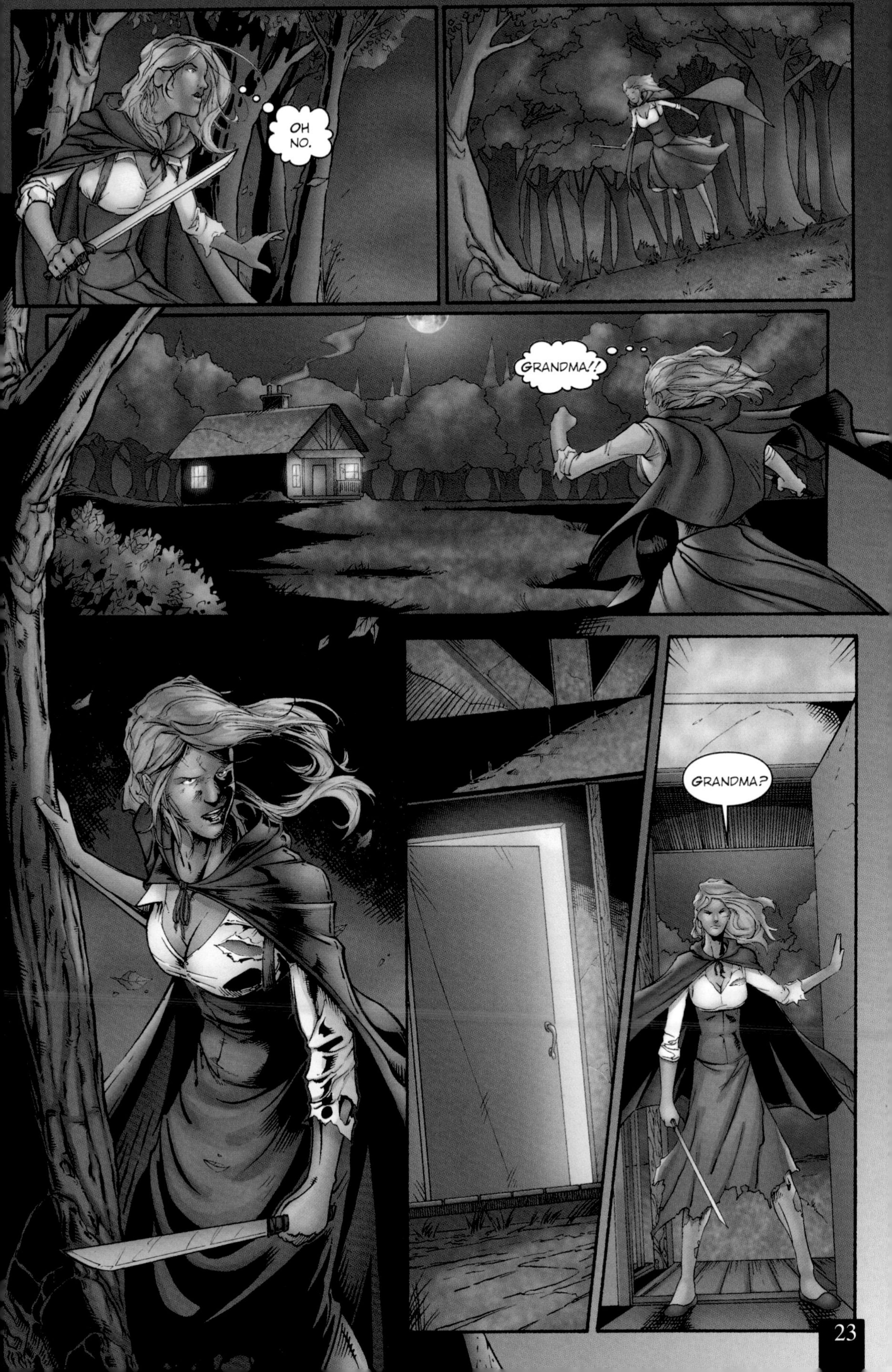
OH NO.
GRANDMA!!
GRANDMA?

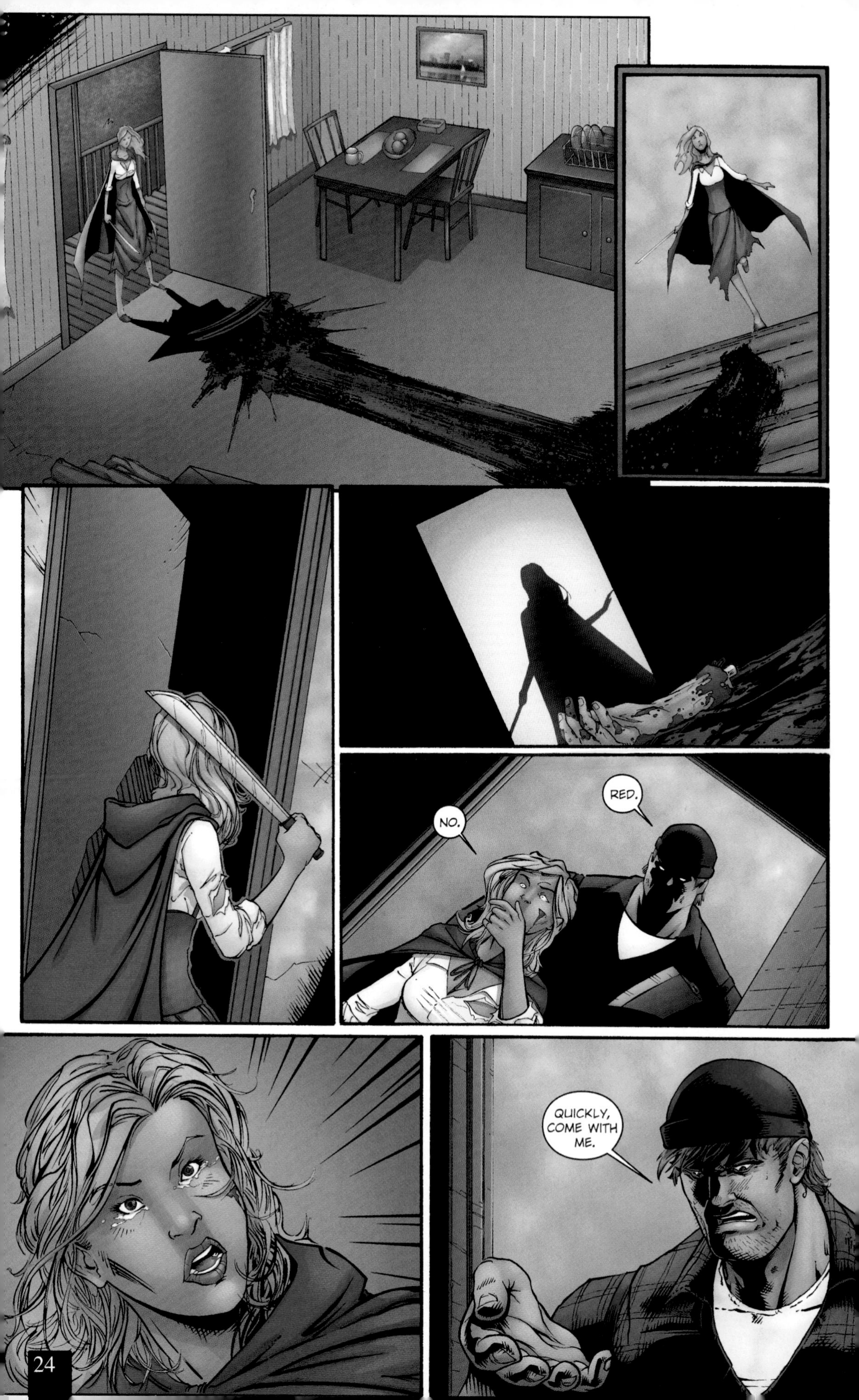
RED.
NO.
QUICKLY, COME WITH ME.

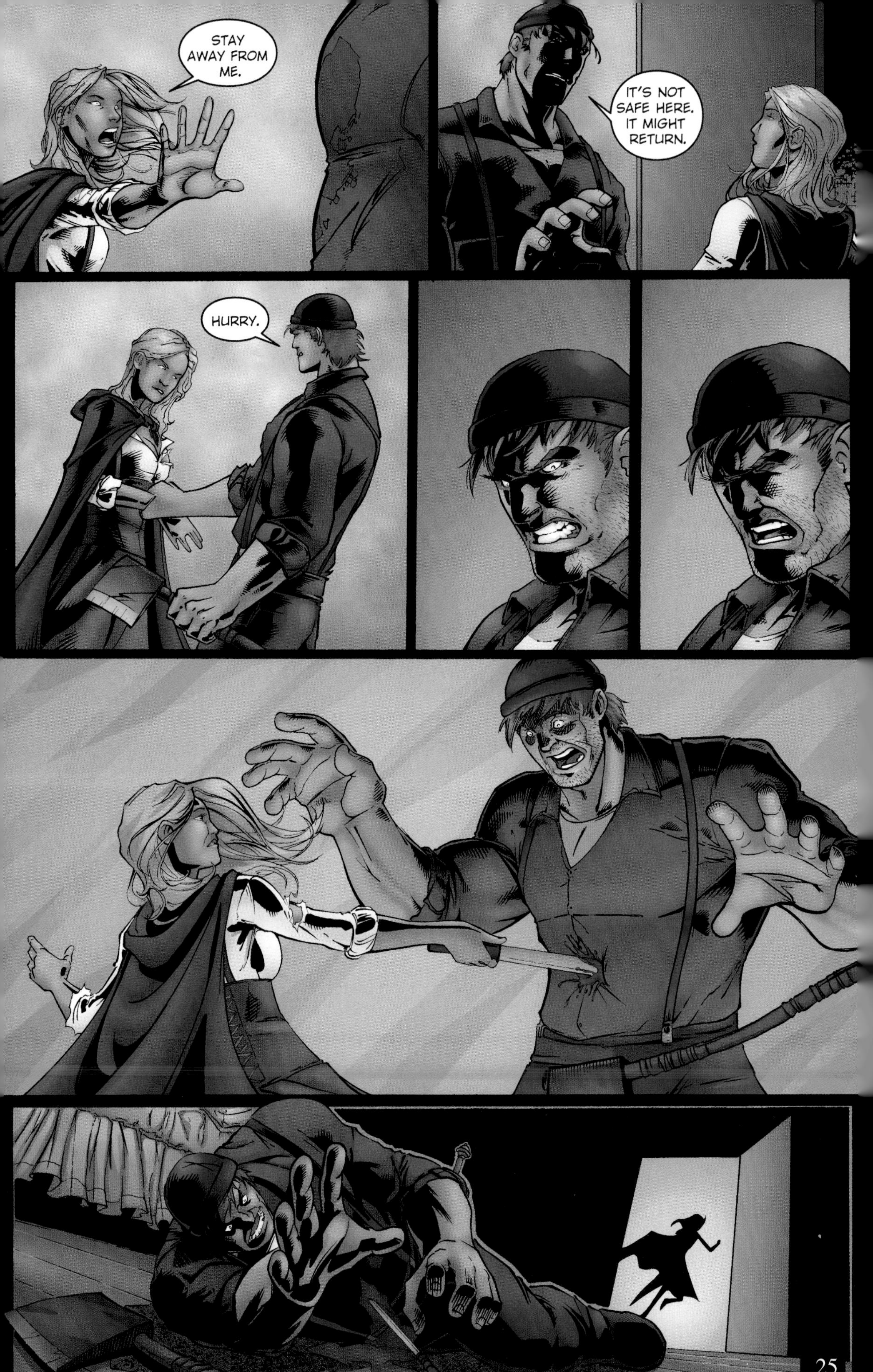
STAY AWAY FROM ME.
IT'S NOT SAFE HERE. IT MIGHT RETURN.
HURRY.

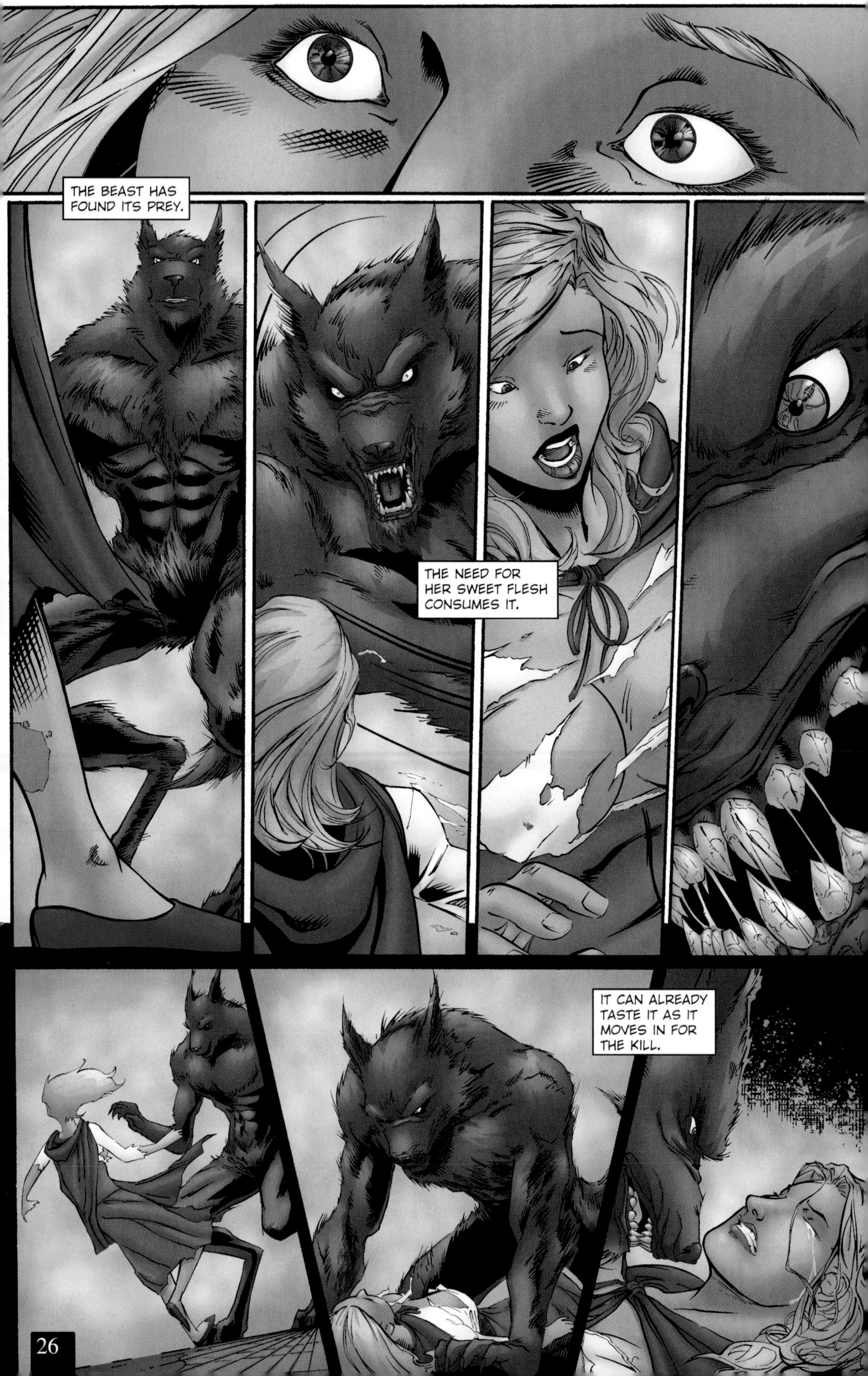
THE BEAST HAS FOUND ITS PREY.
THE NEED FOR HER SWEET FLESH CONSUMES IT.
IT CAN ALREADY TASTE IT AS IT MOVES IN FOR THE KILL.

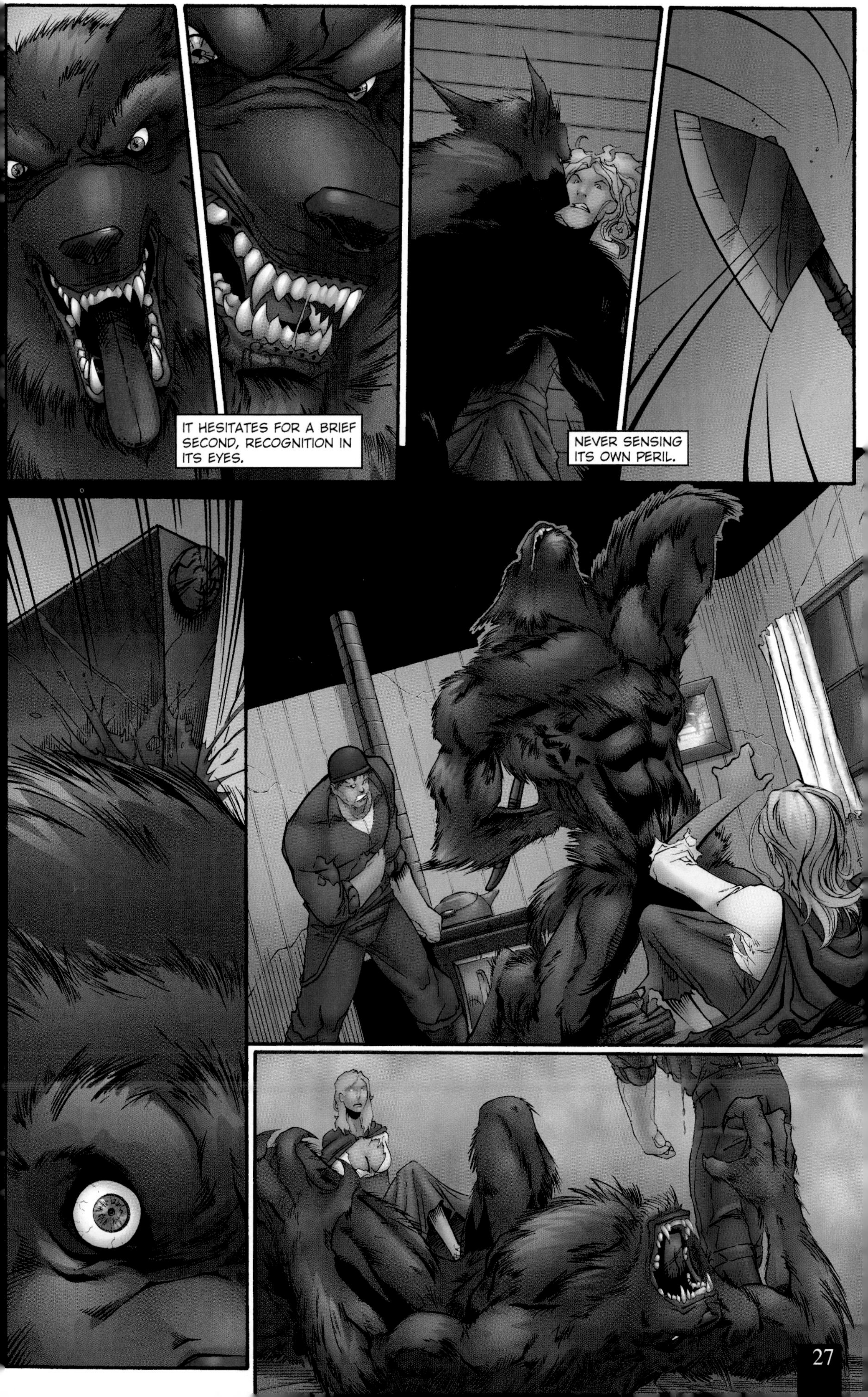
IT HESITATES FOR A BRIEF SECOND, RECOGNITION IN ITS EYES.
NEVER SENSING ITS OWN PERIL.

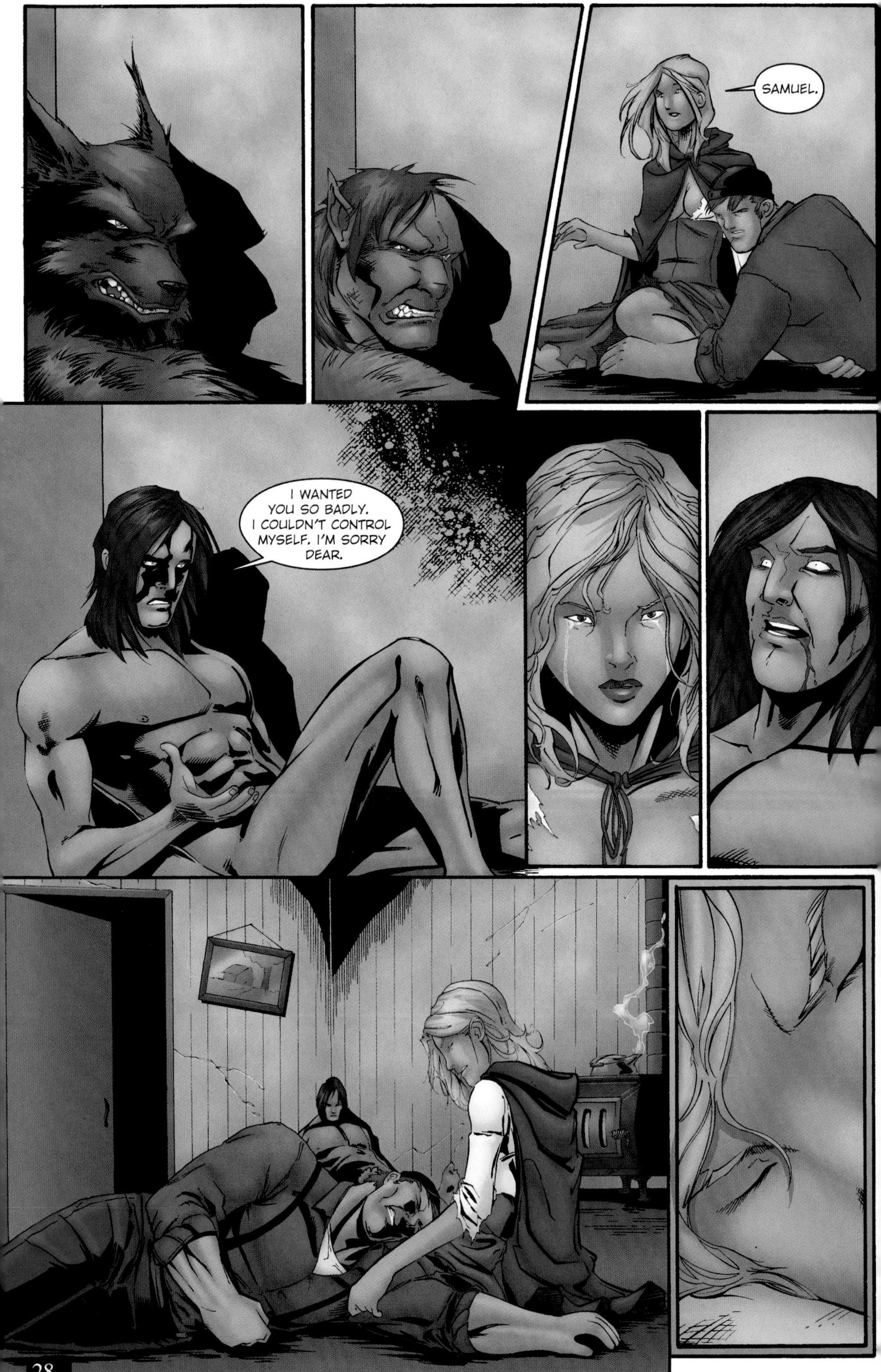
SAMUEL.
I WANTED YOU SO BADLY. I COULDN'T CONTROL MYSELF. I'M SORRY DEAR.

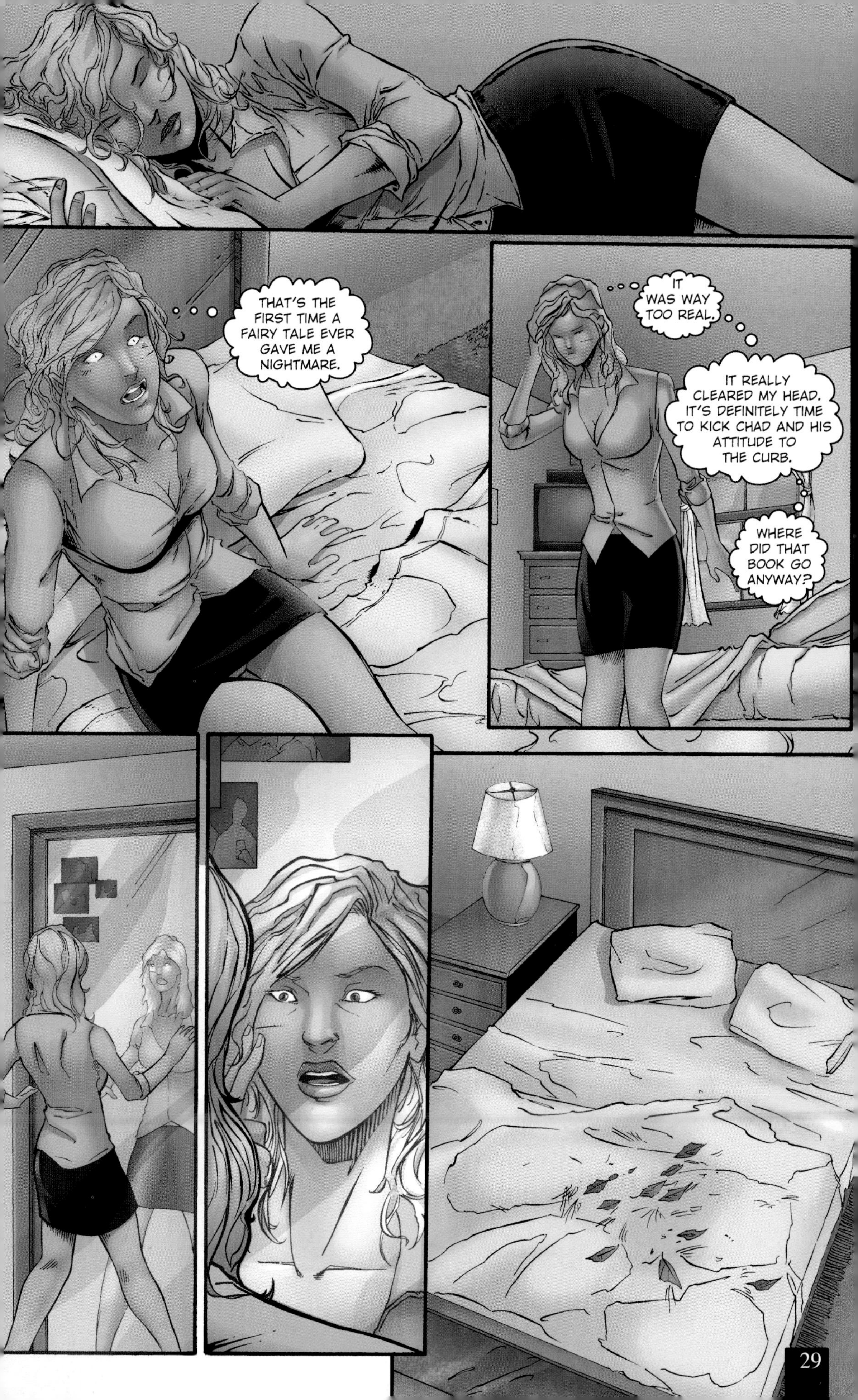
THAT'S THE FIRST TIME A FAIRY TALE EVER GAVE ME A NIGHTMARE.
IT WAS WAY TOO REAL.
IT REALLY CLEARED MY HEAD. IT'S DEFINITELY TIME TO KICK CHAD AND HIS ATTITUDE TO THE CURB.
WHERE DID THAT BOOK GO ANYWAY?

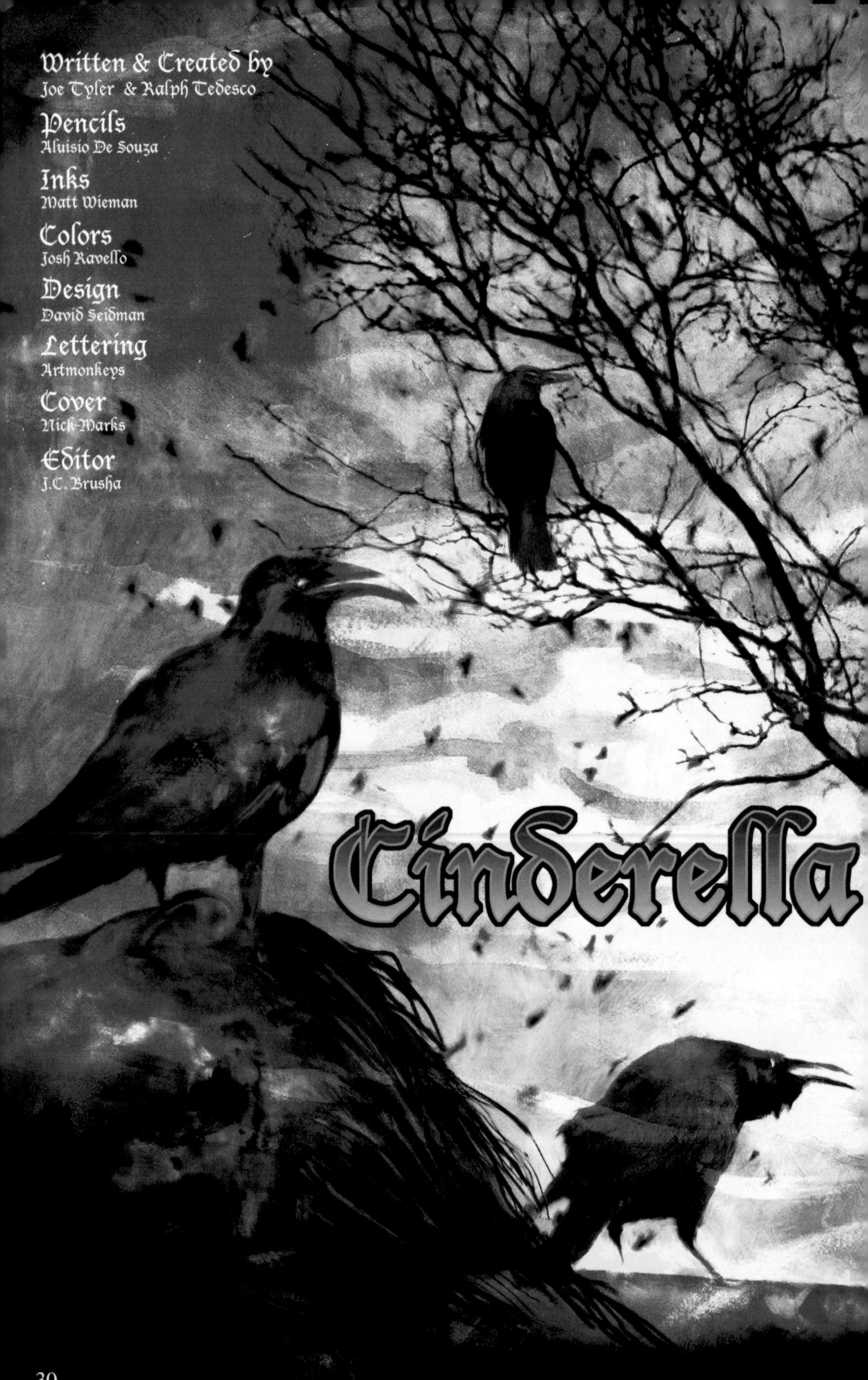
Written & Created by
Joe Tyler & Ralph Tedesco
Pencils
Aluisio De Souza
Inks
Matt Wieman
Colors
Josh Ravello
Design
David Seidman
Lettering
Artmonkeys
Cover
Nick Marks
Editor
J.C. Brusha
Cinderella

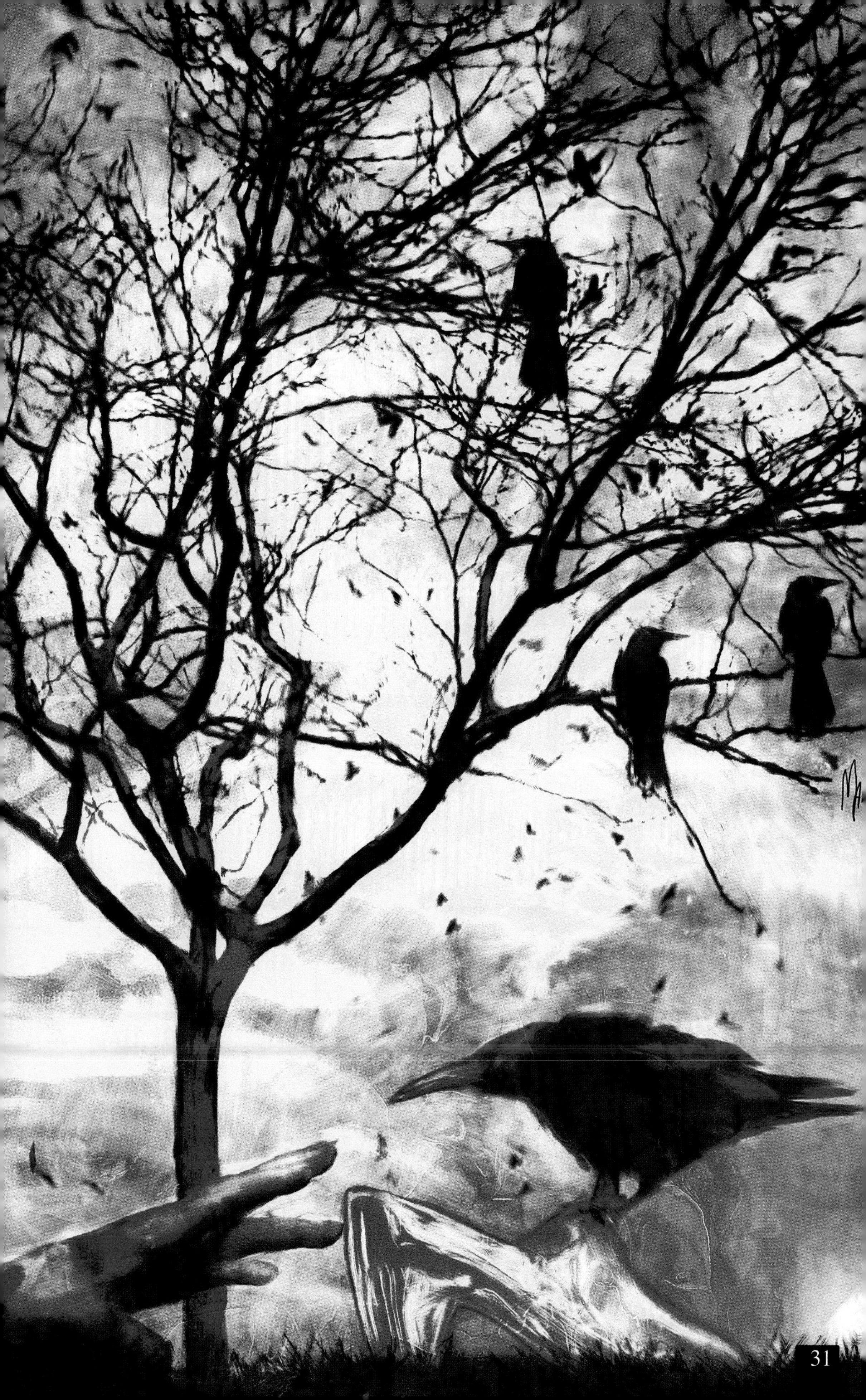

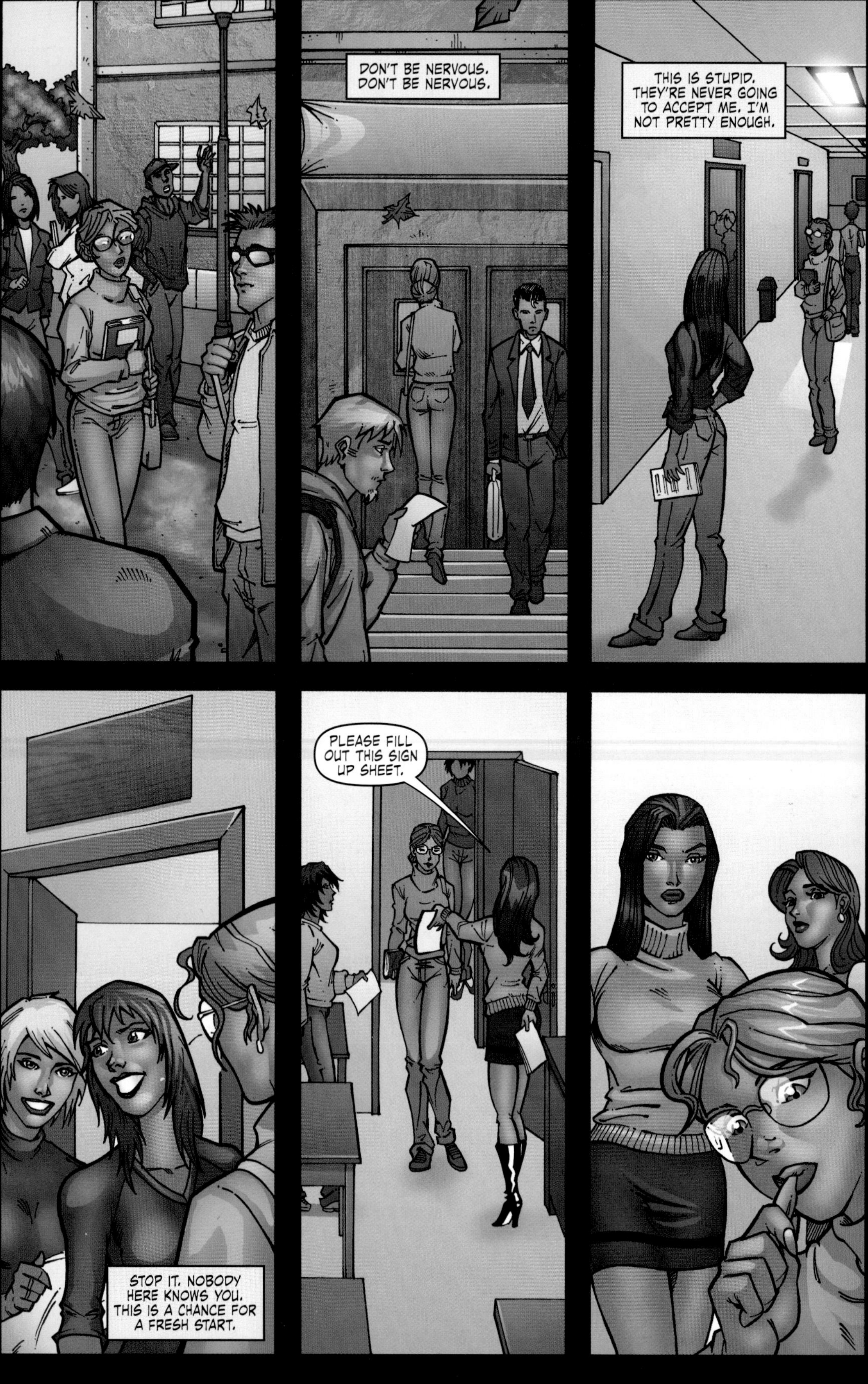
DON'T BE NERVOUS. DON'T BE NERVOUS.
THIS IS STUPID. THEY'RE NEVER GOING TO ACCEPT ME. I'M NOT PRETTY ENOUGH.
STOP IT. NOBODY HERE KNOWS YOU. THIS IS A CHANCE FOR A FRESH START.
PLEASE FILL OUT THIS SIGN UP SHEET.

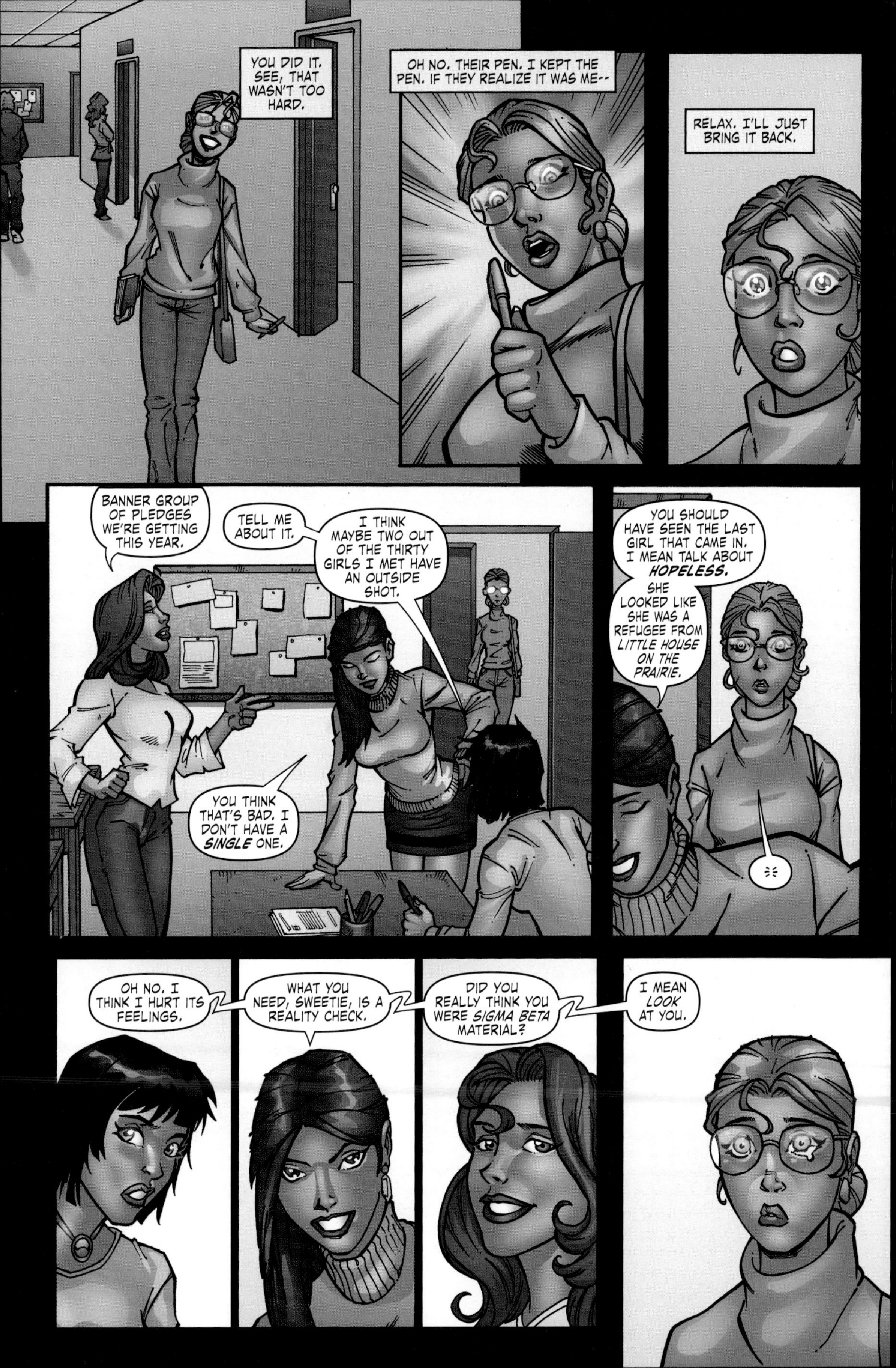

YOU DID IT. SEE, THAT WASN'T TOO HARD.
OH NO. THEIR PEN. I KEPT THE PEN. IF THEY REALIZE IT WAS ME--
RELAX. I'LL JUST BRING IT BACK.
BANNER GROUP OF PLEDGES WE'RE GETTING THIS YEAR.
TELL ME ABOUT IT.
I THINK MAYBE TWO OUT OF THE THIRTY GIRLS I MET HAVE AN OUTSIDE SHOT.
YOU THINK THAT'S BAD. I DON'T HAVE A SINGLE ONE.
YOU SHOULD HAVE SEEN THE LAST GIRL THAT CAME IN. I MEAN TALK ABOUT HOPELESS.
SHE LOOKED LIKE SHE WAS A REFUGEE FROM LITTLE HOUSE ON THE PRAIRIE.
OH NO. I THINK I HURT ITS FEELINGS.
WHAT YOU NEED, SWEETIE, IS A REALITY CHECK.
DID YOU REALLY THINK YOU WERE SIGMA BETA MATERIAL?
I MEAN LOOK AT YOU.

STUPID. STUPID. *STUPID.* YOU *KNEW* IT WOULD HAPPEN. IT ALWAYS DOES. WHY WOULD IT BE *ANY* DIFFERENT THIS TIME.

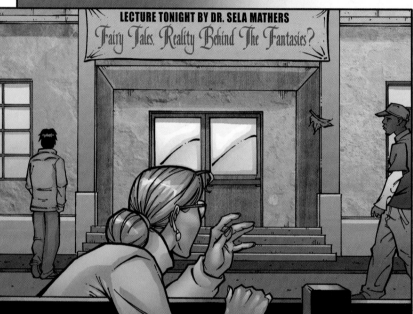

LECTURE TONIGHT BY DR. SELA MATHERS

Fairy Tales, Reality Behind The Fantasies?

I COULD USE AN ESCAPE FROM REALITY.

THE ORIGINS OF MOST MODERN FAIRY TALES CAN BE TRACED BACK TO THE LATE 1700'S.

TWO BROTHERS, JACOB AND WILHELM GRIMM, TRAVELED AROUND THEIR NATIVE GERMANY COLLECTING THE TALES OF FOLKLORE THAT HAD BEEN PASSED DOWN FROM GENERATION TO GENERATION.

MANY OF THE ORIGINAL STORIES WERE MUCH DARKER AND OMINOUS THAN THE ONES WE KNOW TODAY. TO GIVE YOU AN *EXAMPLE,* I'D LIKE TO READ TO YOU THE ORIGINAL VERSION OF *CINDERELLA.*

ONCE UPON A TIME...

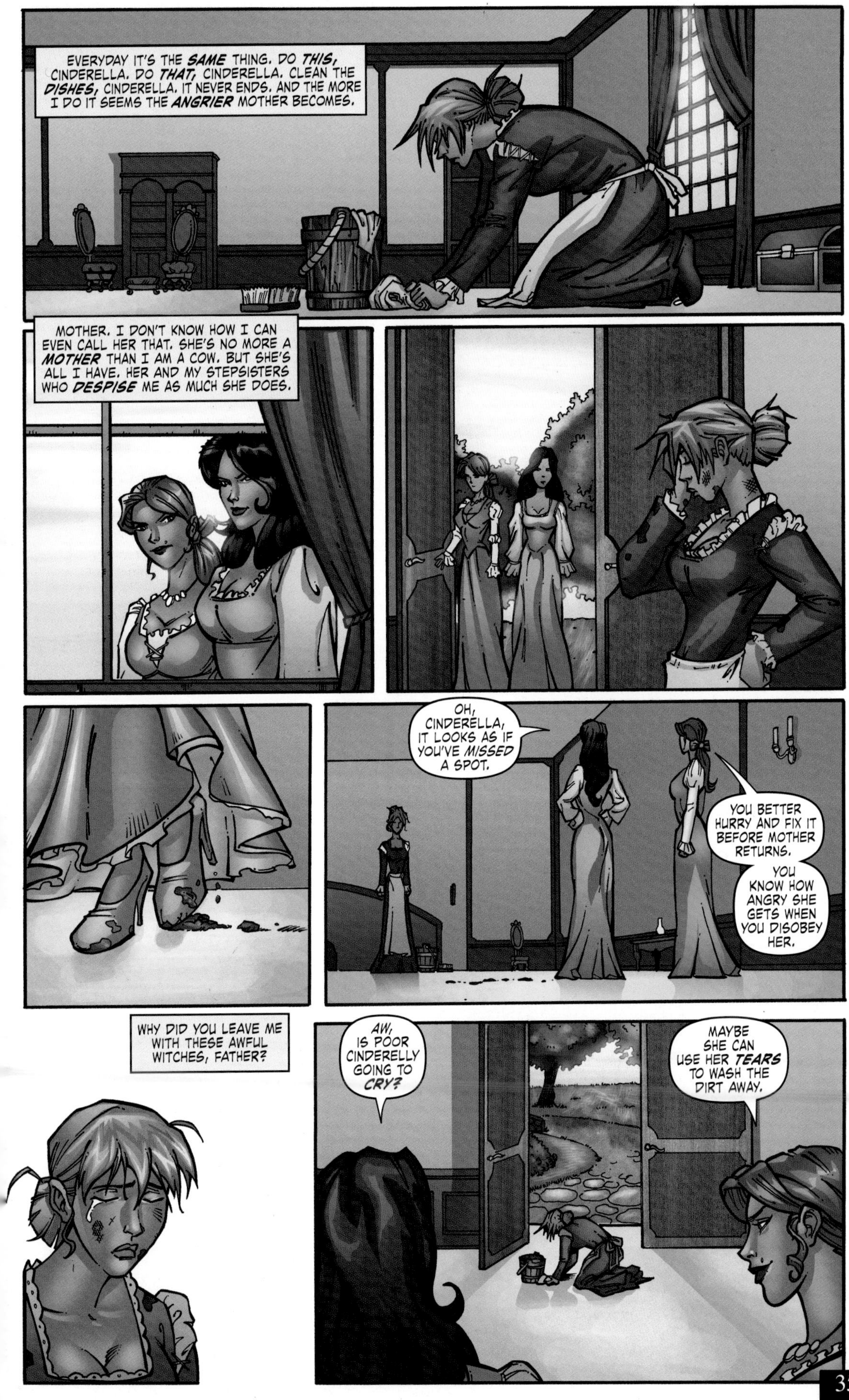
EVERYDAY IT'S THE SAME THING. DO THIS, CINDERELLA. DO THAT, CINDERELLA. CLEAN THE DISHES, CINDERELLA. IT NEVER ENDS. AND THE MORE I DO IT SEEMS THE ANGRIER MOTHER BECOMES.
MOTHER. I DON'T KNOW HOW I CAN EVEN CALL HER THAT. SHE'S NO MORE A MOTHER THAN I AM A COW. BUT SHE'S ALL I HAVE. HER AND MY STEPSISTERS WHO DESPISE ME AS MUCH SHE DOES.
OH, CINDERELLA, IT LOOKS AS IF YOU'VE MISSED A SPOT.
YOU BETTER HURRY AND FIX IT BEFORE MOTHER RETURNS.
YOU KNOW HOW ANGRY SHE GETS WHEN YOU DISOBEY HER.
WHY DID YOU LEAVE ME WITH THESE AWFUL WITCHES, FATHER?
AW, IS POOR CINDERELLY GOING TO CRY?
MAYBE SHE CAN USE HER TEARS TO WASH THE DIRT AWAY.

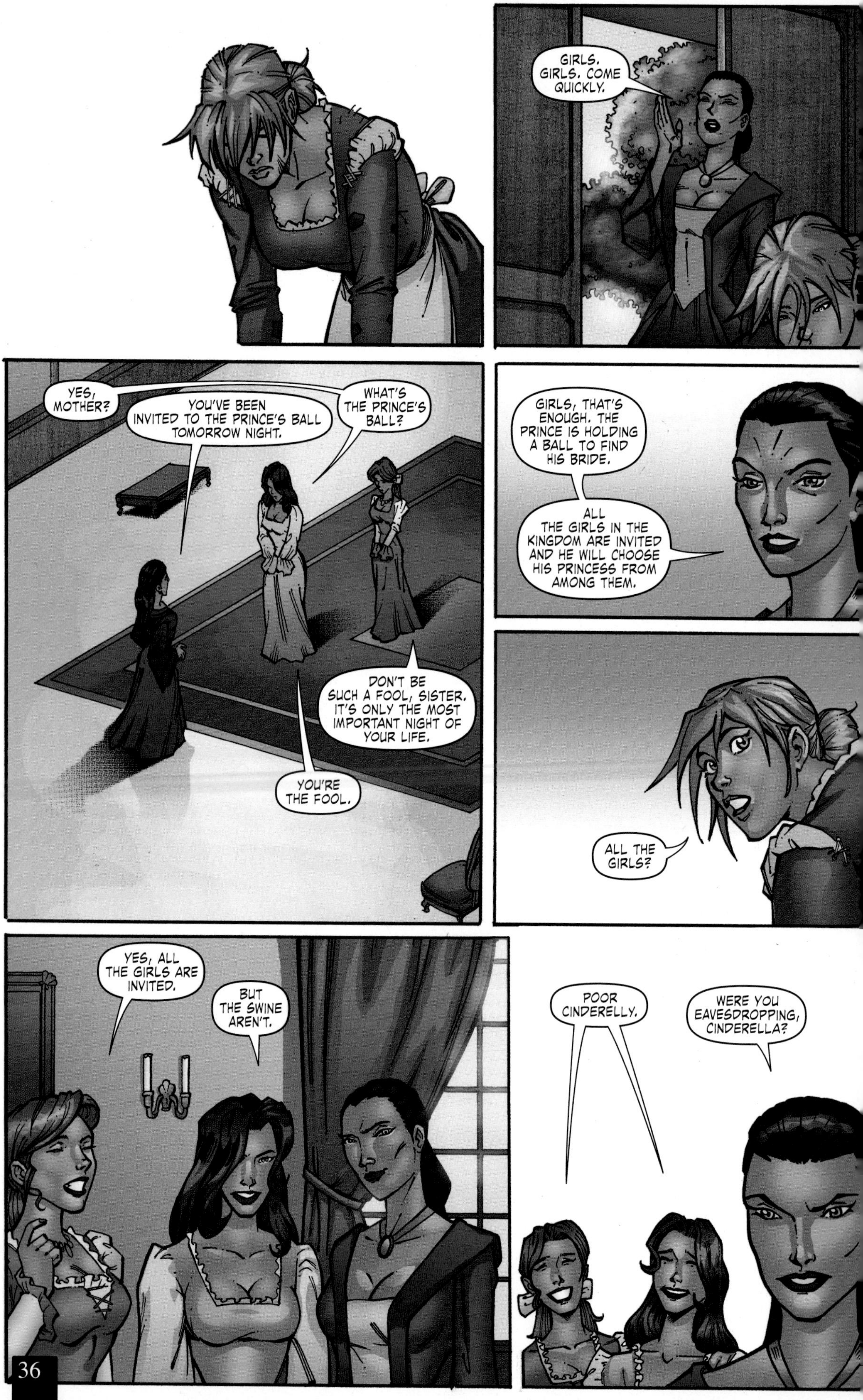
GIRLS. GIRLS. COME QUICKLY.
YES, MOTHER?
YOU'VE BEEN INVITED TO THE PRINCE'S BALL TOMORROW NIGHT.
WHAT'S THE PRINCE'S BALL?
DON'T BE SUCH A FOOL, SISTER. IT'S ONLY THE MOST IMPORTANT NIGHT OF YOUR LIFE.
YOU'RE THE FOOL.
GIRLS, THAT'S ENOUGH. THE PRINCE IS HOLDING A BALL TO FIND HIS BRIDE.
ALL THE GIRLS IN THE KINGDOM ARE INVITED AND HE WILL CHOOSE HIS PRINCESS FROM AMONG THEM.
ALL THE GIRLS?
YES, ALL THE GIRLS ARE INVITED.
BUT THE SWINE AREN'T.
POOR CINDERELLY.
WERE YOU EAVESDROPPING, CINDERELLA?

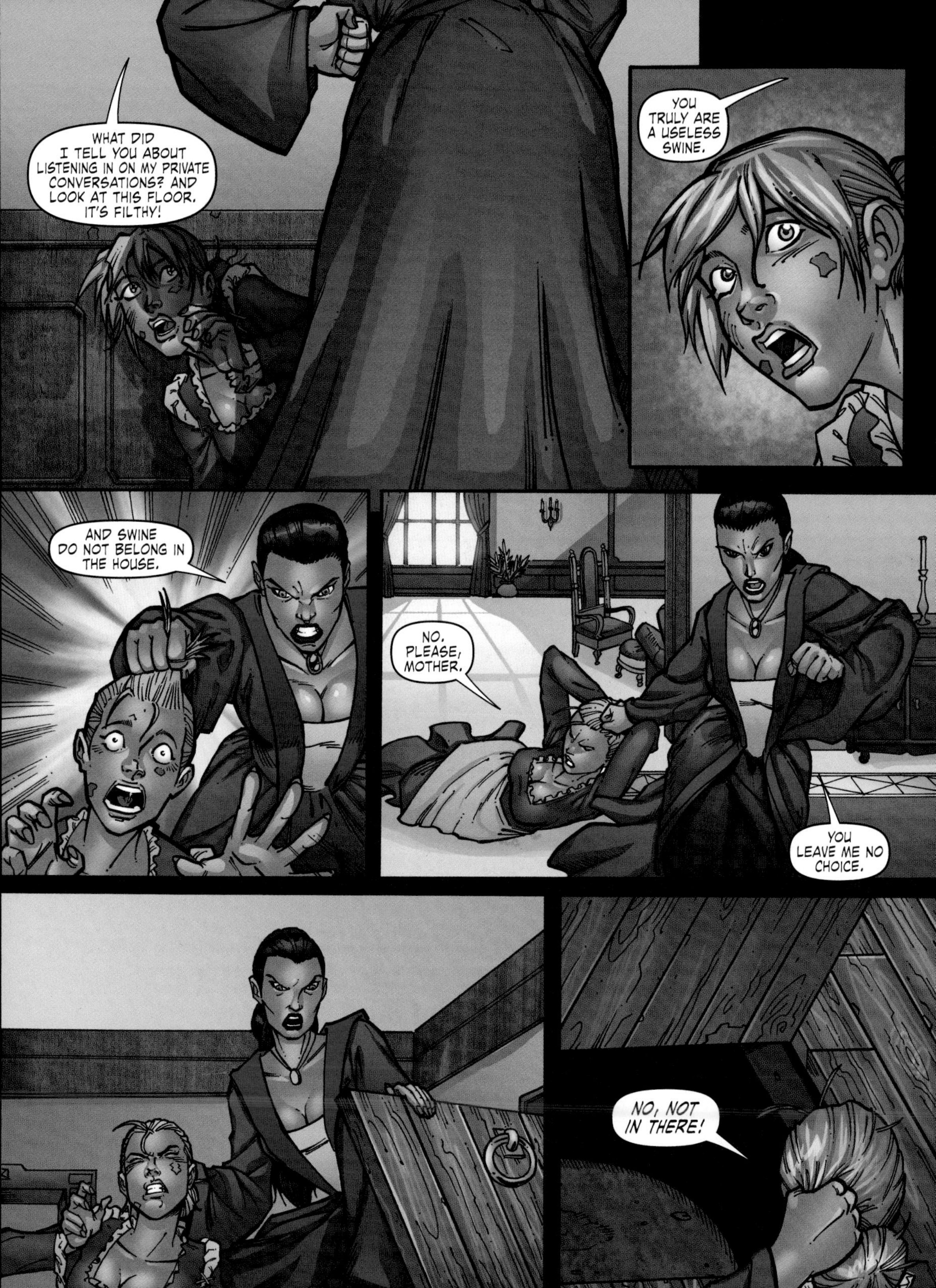
WHAT DID I TELL YOU ABOUT LISTENING IN ON MY PRIVATE CONVERSATIONS? AND LOOK AT THIS FLOOR. IT'S FILTHY!
YOU TRULY ARE A USELESS SWINE.
AND SWINE DO NOT BELONG IN THE HOUSE.
NO. PLEASE, MOTHER.
YOU LEAVE ME NO CHOICE.
NO, NOT IN THERE!

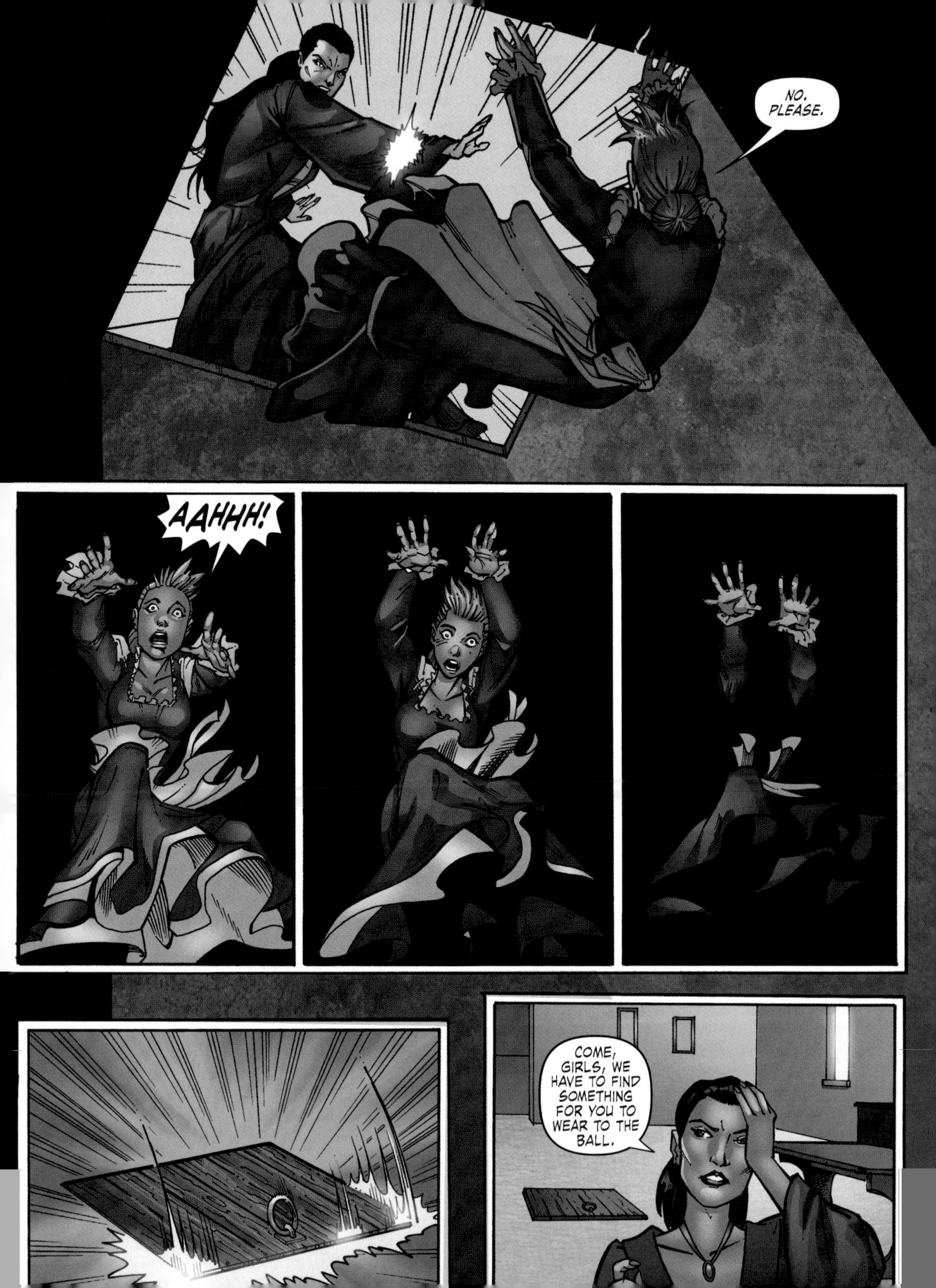
NO. PLEASE.
AAHHH!
COME, GIRLS, WE HAVE TO FIND SOMETHING FOR YOU TO WEAR TO THE BALL.

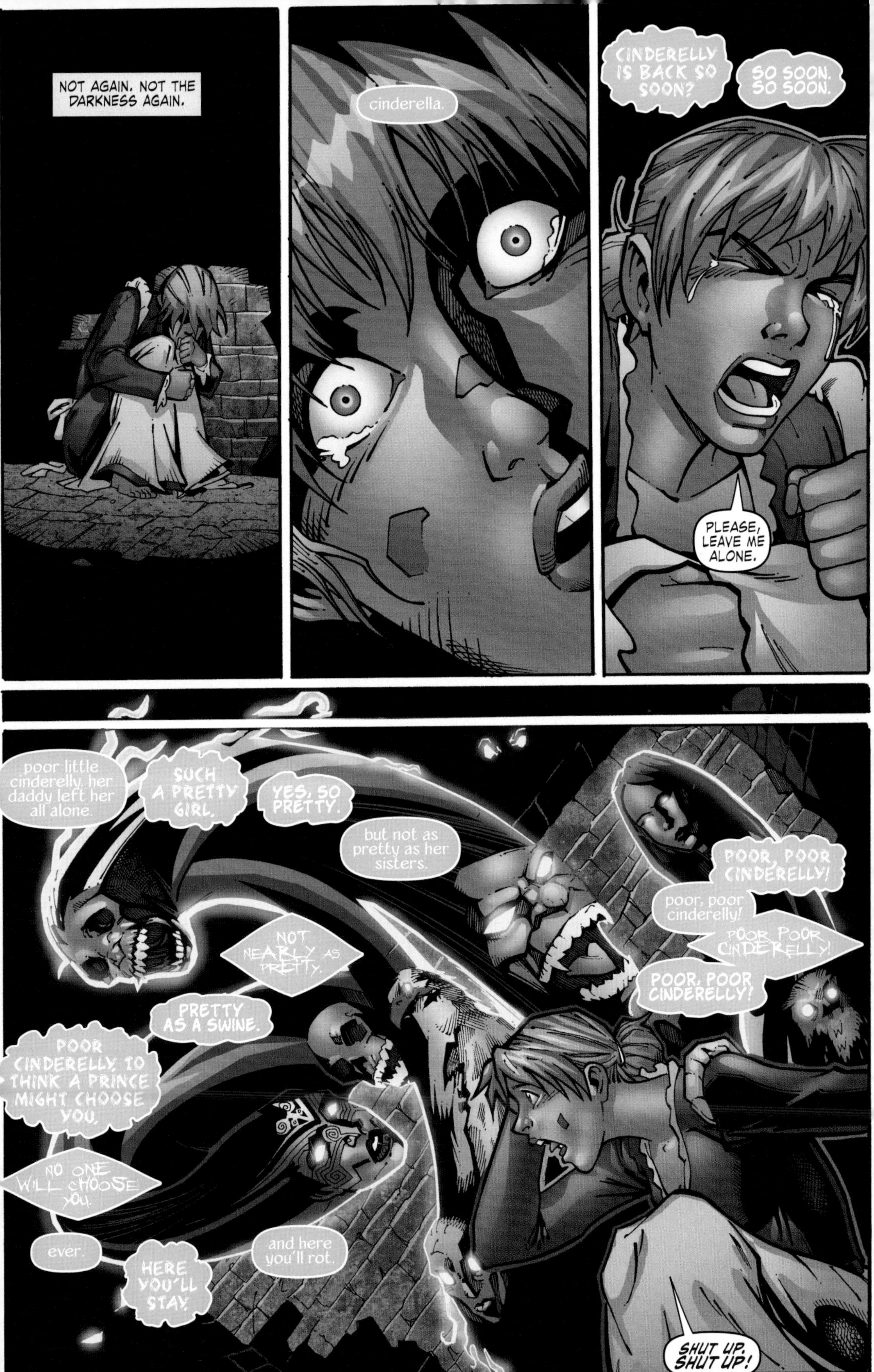
NOT AGAIN. NOT THE DARKNESS AGAIN.
cinderella.
CINDERELLY IS BACK SO SOON?
SO SOON. SO SOON.
PLEASE, LEAVE ME ALONE.
poor little cinderelly, her daddy left her all alone.
SUCH A PRETTY GIRL.
YES, SO PRETTY.
but not as pretty as her sisters.
NOT NEARLY AS PRETTY.
PRETTY AS A SWINE.
POOR CINDERELLY, TO THINK A PRINCE MIGHT CHOOSE YOU.
NO ONE WILL CHOOSE YOU.
ever.
HERE YOU'LL STAY.
and here you'll rot.
POOR, POOR CINDERELLY!
poor, poor cinderelly!
POOR POOR CINDERELLY!
POOR, POOR CINDERELLY!
SHUT UP. SHUT UP!

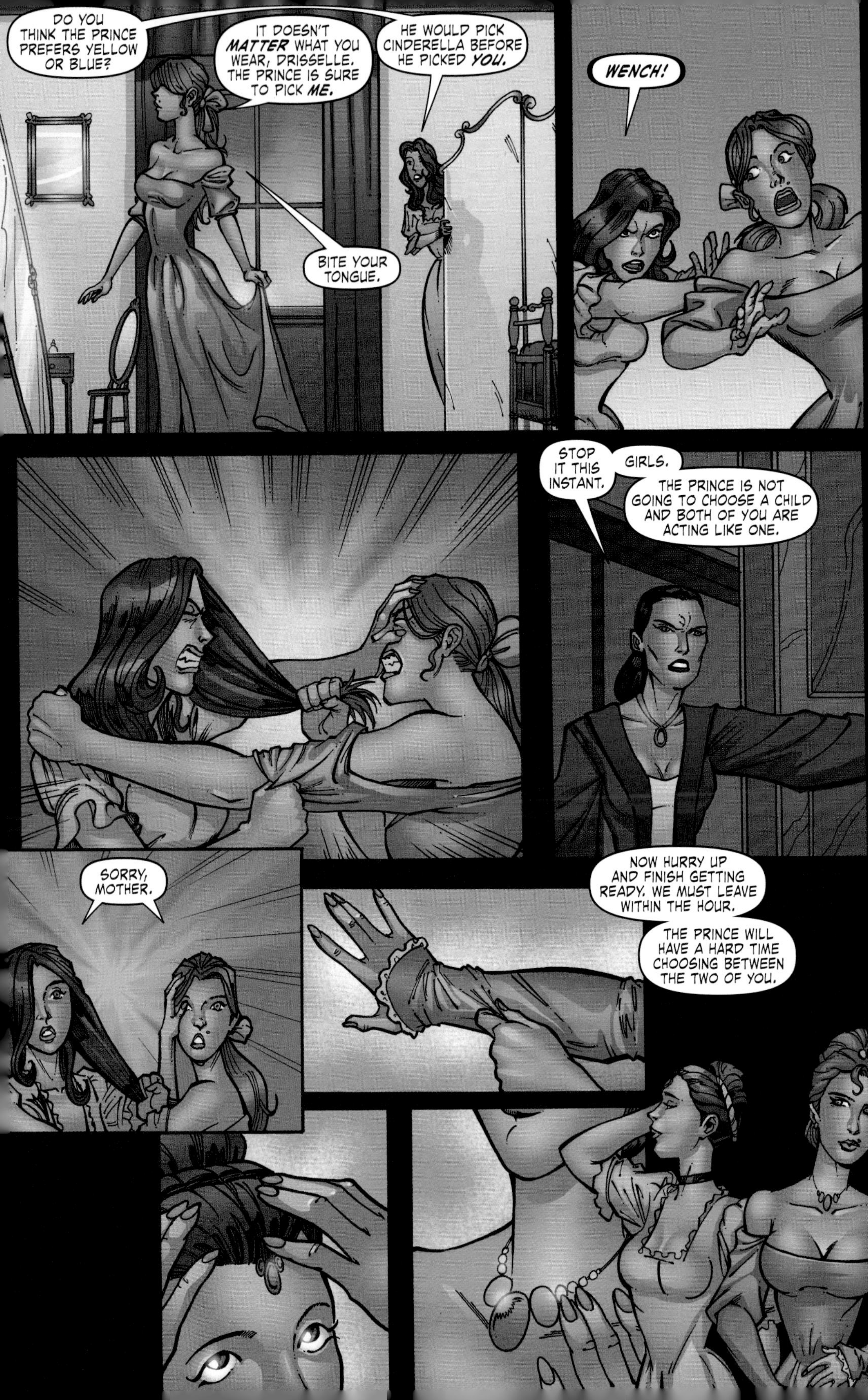

DO YOU THINK THE PRINCE PREFERS YELLOW OR BLUE?
IT DOESN'T MATTER WHAT YOU WEAR, DRISSELLE. THE PRINCE IS SURE TO PICK ME.
HE WOULD PICK CINDERELLA BEFORE HE PICKED YOU.
BITE YOUR TONGUE.
WENCH!
STOP IT THIS INSTANT.
GIRLS.
THE PRINCE IS NOT GOING TO CHOOSE A CHILD AND BOTH OF YOU ARE ACTING LIKE ONE.
SORRY, MOTHER.
NOW HURRY UP AND FINISH GETTING READY. WE MUST LEAVE WITHIN THE HOUR.
THE PRINCE WILL HAVE A HARD TIME CHOOSING BETWEEN THE TWO OF YOU.

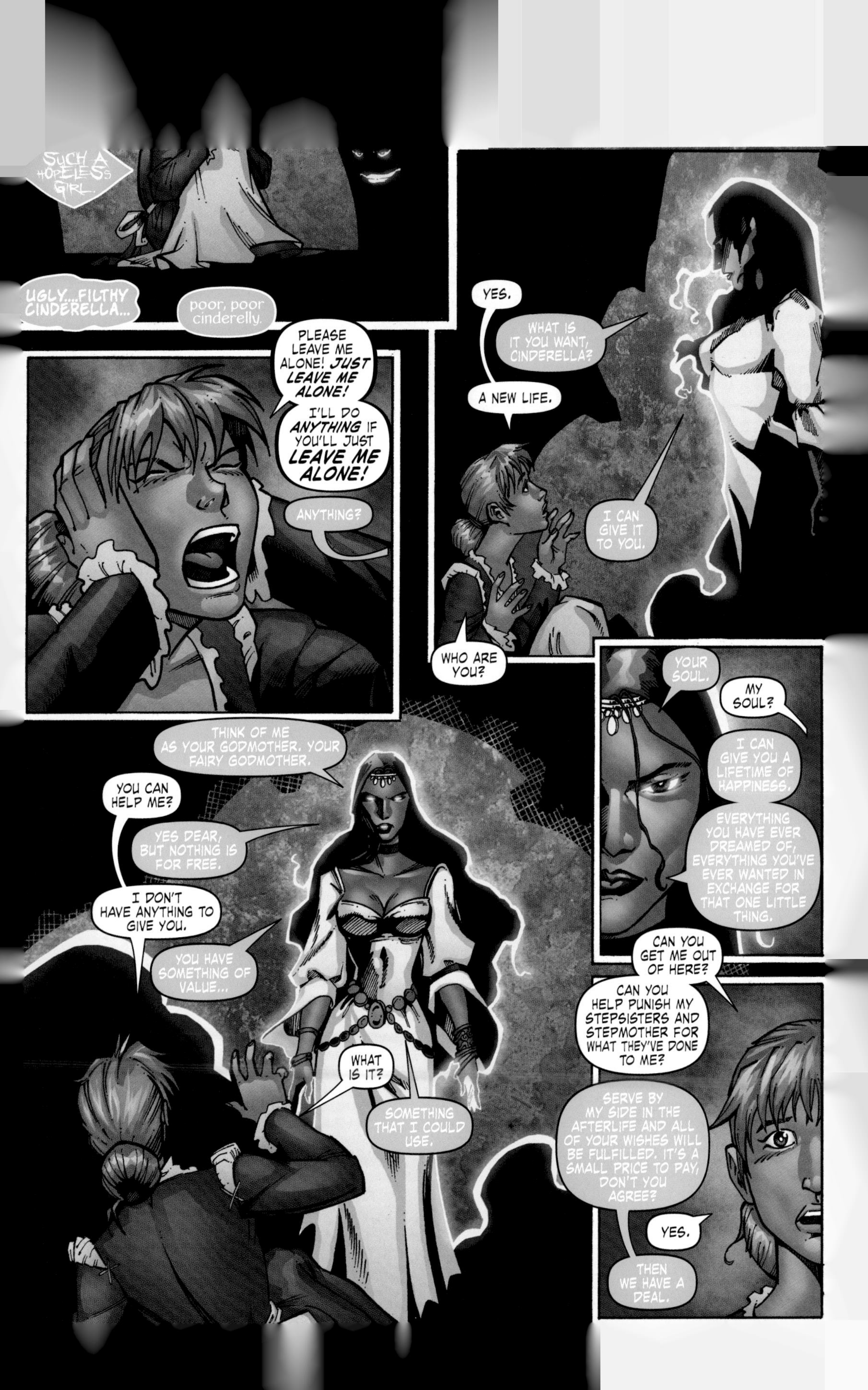
SUCH A HOPELESS GIRL.
UGLY...FILTHY CINDERELLA...
poor, poor cinderelly.
PLEASE LEAVE ME ALONE! JUST LEAVE ME ALONE!
I'LL DO ANYTHING IF YOU'LL JUST LEAVE ME ALONE!
ANYTHING?
YES.
WHAT IS IT YOU WANT, CINDERELLA?
A NEW LIFE.
I CAN GIVE IT TO YOU.
WHO ARE YOU?
THINK OF ME AS YOUR GODMOTHER. YOUR FAIRY GODMOTHER.
YOU CAN HELP ME?
YES DEAR, BUT NOTHING IS FOR FREE.
I DON'T HAVE ANYTHING TO GIVE YOU.
YOU HAVE SOMETHING OF VALUE...
WHAT IS IT?
SOMETHING THAT I COULD USE.
YOUR SOUL.
MY SOUL?
I CAN GIVE YOU A LIFETIME OF HAPPINESS.
EVERYTHING YOU HAVE EVER DREAMED OF, EVERYTHING YOU'VE EVER WANTED IN EXCHANGE FOR THAT ONE LITTLE THING.
CAN YOU GET ME OUT OF HERE?
CAN YOU HELP PUNISH MY STEPSISTERS AND STEPMOTHER FOR WHAT THEY'VE DONE TO ME?
SERVE BY MY SIDE IN THE AFTERLIFE AND ALL OF YOUR WISHES WILL BE FULFILLED. IT'S A SMALL PRICE TO PAY, DON'T YOU AGREE?
YES.
THEN WE HAVE A DEAL.

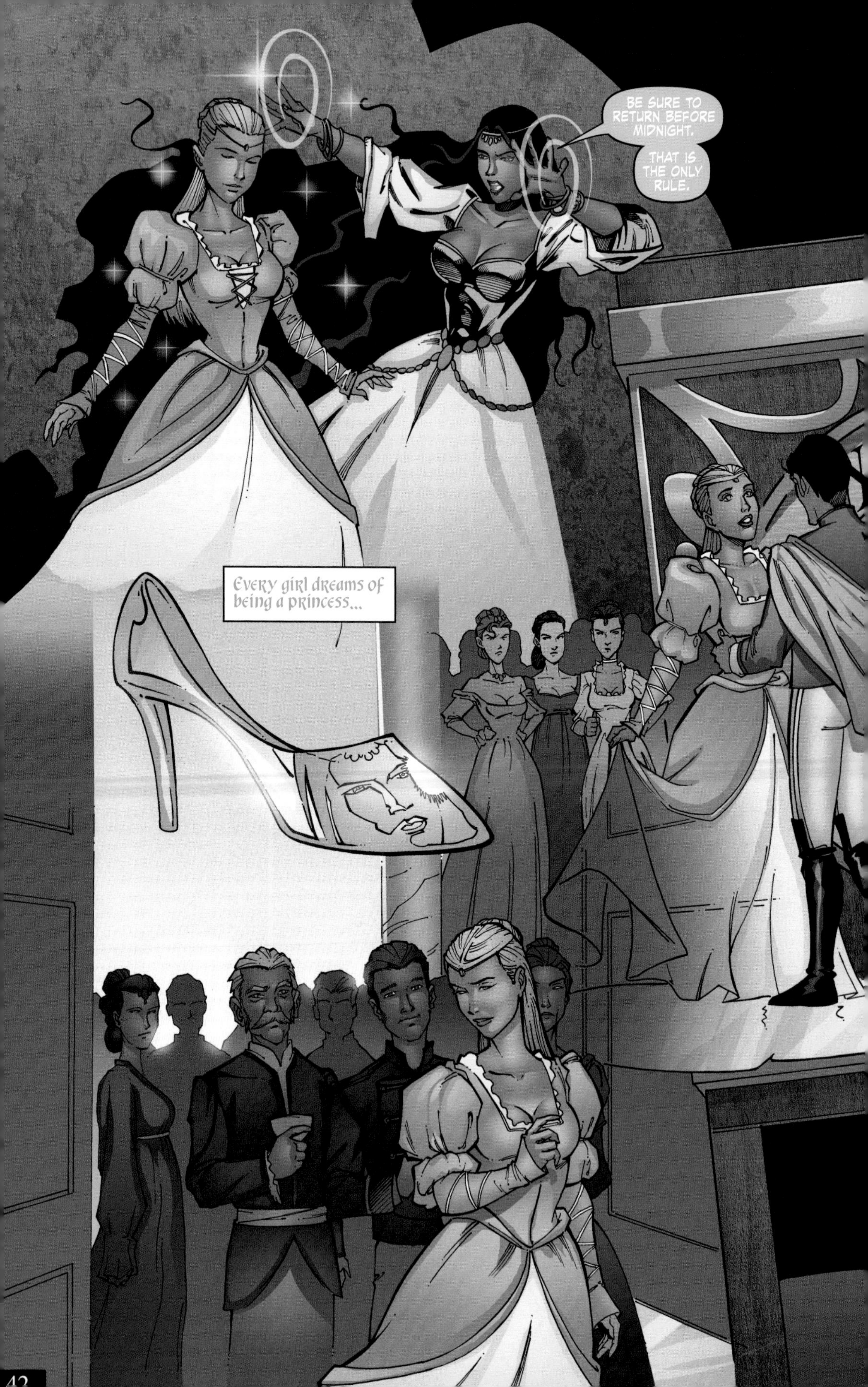
BE SURE TO RETURN BEFORE MIDNIGHT.
THAT IS THE ONLY RULE.
Every girl dreams of being a princess...

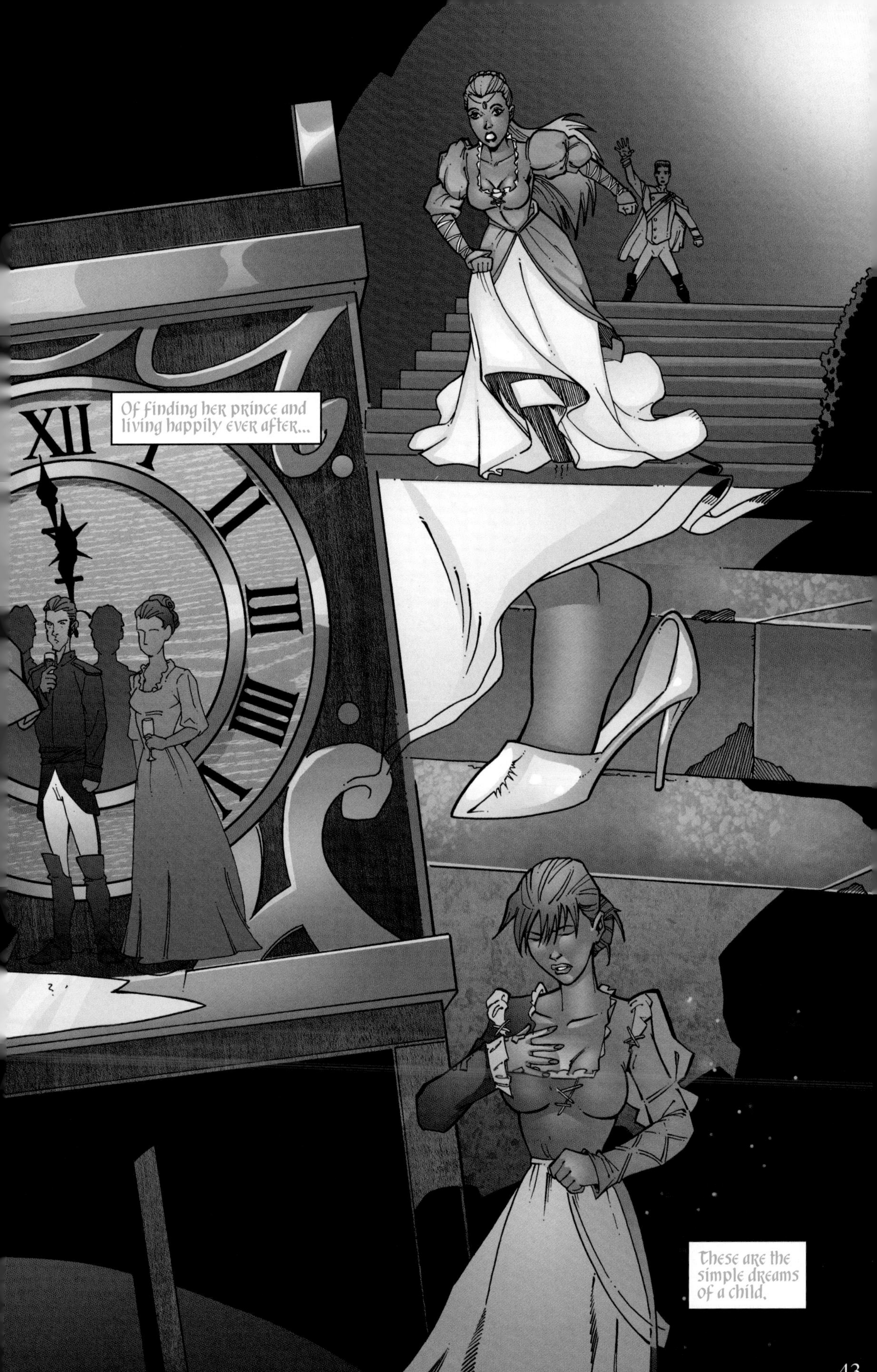
Of finding her prince and living happily ever after...
These are the simple dreams of a child.

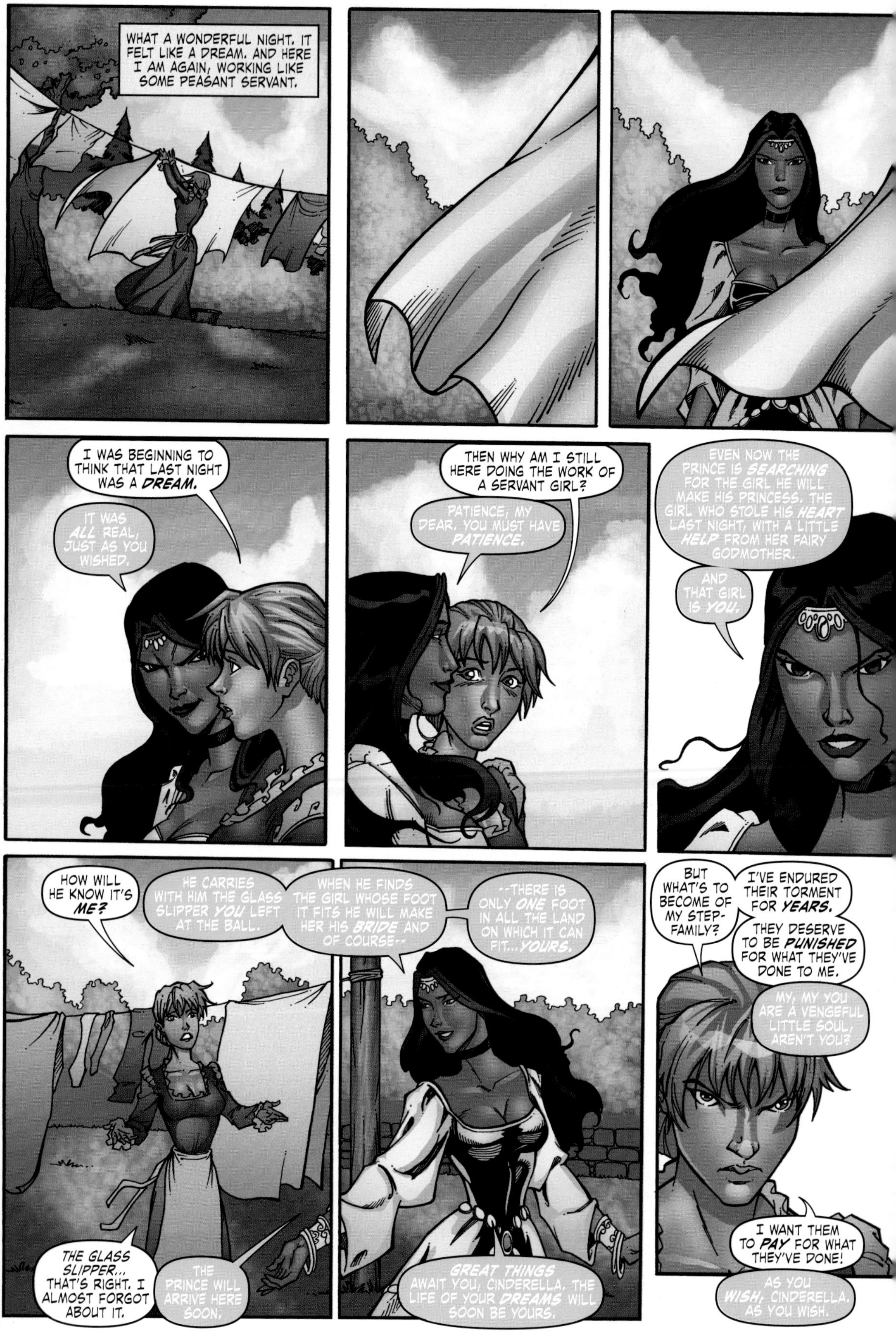
WHAT A WONDERFUL NIGHT. IT FELT LIKE A DREAM. AND HERE I AM AGAIN, WORKING LIKE SOME PEASANT SERVANT.
I WAS BEGINNING TO THINK THAT LAST NIGHT WAS A DREAM.
IT WAS ALL REAL, JUST AS YOU WISHED.
THEN WHY AM I STILL HERE DOING THE WORK OF A SERVANT GIRL?
PATIENCE, MY DEAR. YOU MUST HAVE PATIENCE.
EVEN NOW THE PRINCE IS SEARCHING FOR THE GIRL HE WILL MAKE HIS PRINCESS. THE GIRL WHO STOLE HIS HEART LAST NIGHT, WITH A LITTLE HELP FROM HER FAIRY GODMOTHER.
AND THAT GIRL IS YOU.
HOW WILL HE KNOW IT'S ME?
HE CARRIES WITH HIM THE GLASS SLIPPER YOU LEFT AT THE BALL.
THE GLASS SLIPPER... THAT'S RIGHT. I ALMOST FORGOT ABOUT IT.
THE PRINCE WILL ARRIVE HERE SOON.
WHEN HE FINDS THE GIRL WHOSE FOOT IT FITS HE WILL MAKE HER HIS BRIDE AND OF COURSE--
--THERE IS ONLY ONE FOOT IN ALL THE LAND ON WHICH IT CAN FIT...YOURS.
GREAT THINGS AWAIT YOU, CINDERELLA. THE LIFE OF YOUR DREAMS WILL SOON BE YOURS.
BUT WHAT'S TO BECOME OF MY STEP-FAMILY?
I'VE ENDURED THEIR TORMENT FOR YEARS.
THEY DESERVE TO BE PUNISHED FOR WHAT THEY'VE DONE TO ME.
MY, MY YOU ARE A VENGEFUL LITTLE SOUL, AREN'T YOU?
I WANT THEM TO PAY FOR WHAT THEY'VE DONE!
AS YOU WISH, CINDERELLA. AS YOU WISH.

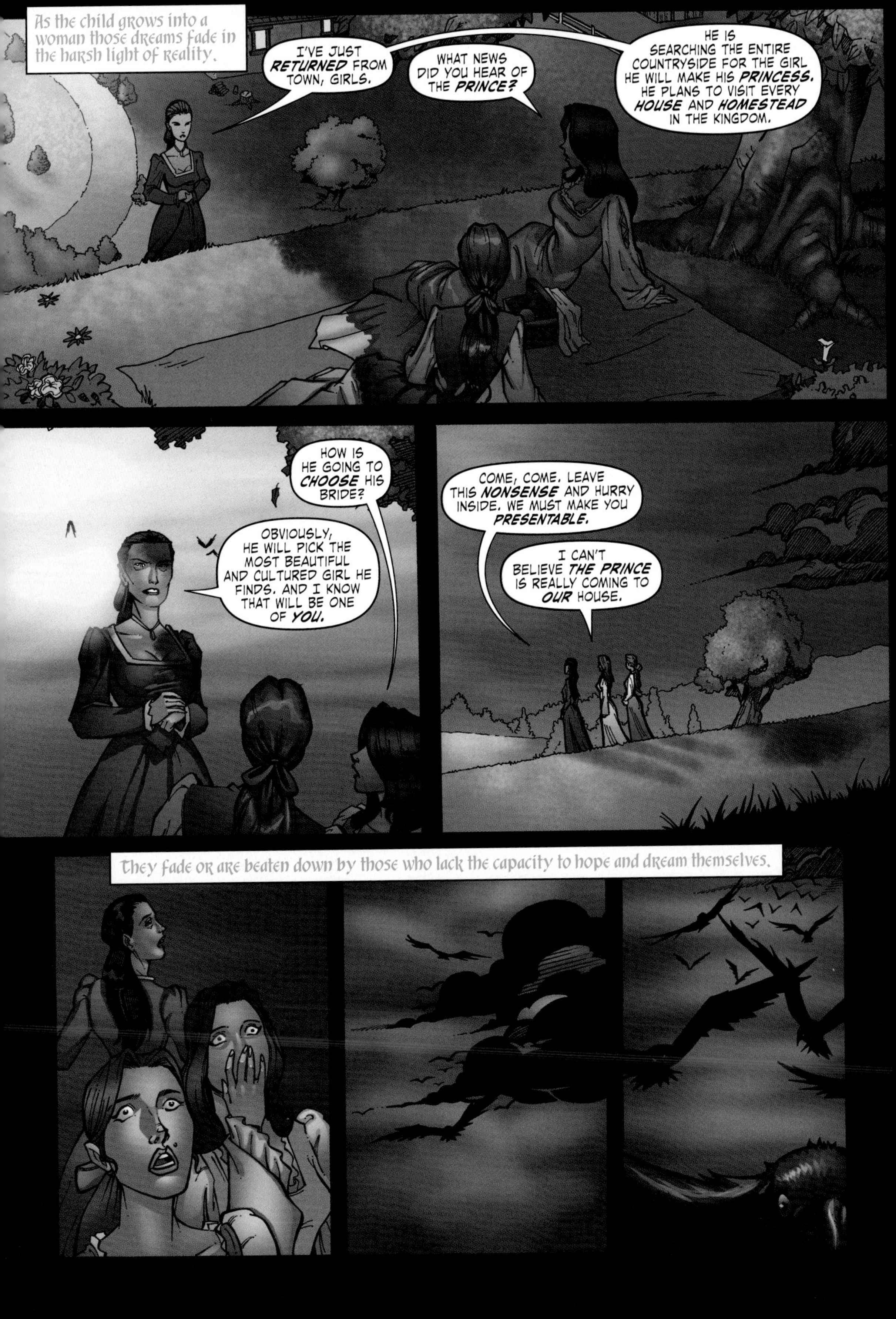

As the child grows into a woman those dreams fade in the harsh light of reality.
I'VE JUST RETURNED FROM TOWN, GIRLS.
WHAT NEWS DID YOU HEAR OF THE PRINCE?
HE IS SEARCHING THE ENTIRE COUNTRYSIDE FOR THE GIRL HE WILL MAKE HIS PRINCESS. HE PLANS TO VISIT EVERY HOUSE AND HOMESTEAD IN THE KINGDOM.
HOW IS HE GOING TO CHOOSE HIS BRIDE?
OBVIOUSLY, HE WILL PICK THE MOST BEAUTIFUL AND CULTURED GIRL HE FINDS. AND I KNOW THAT WILL BE ONE OF YOU.
COME, COME. LEAVE THIS NONSENSE AND HURRY INSIDE. WE MUST MAKE YOU PRESENTABLE.
I CAN'T BELIEVE THE PRINCE IS REALLY COMING TO OUR HOUSE.
They fade or are beaten down by those who lack the capacity to hope and dream themselves.

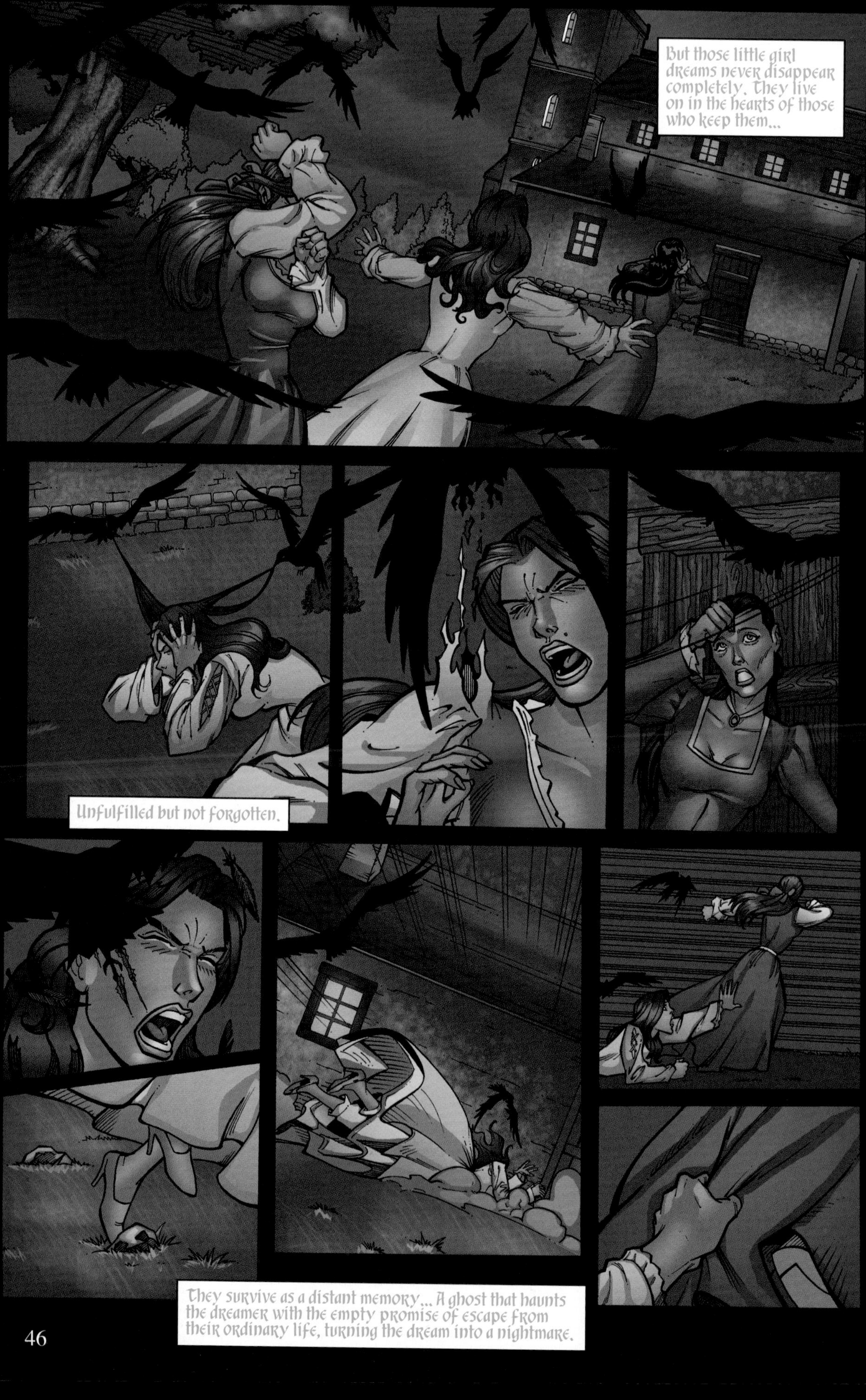

But those little girl dreams never disappear completely. They live on in the hearts of those who keep them...
Unfulfilled but not forgotten.
They survive as a distant memory... A ghost that haunts the dreamer with the empty promise of escape from their ordinary life, turning the dream into a nightmare.

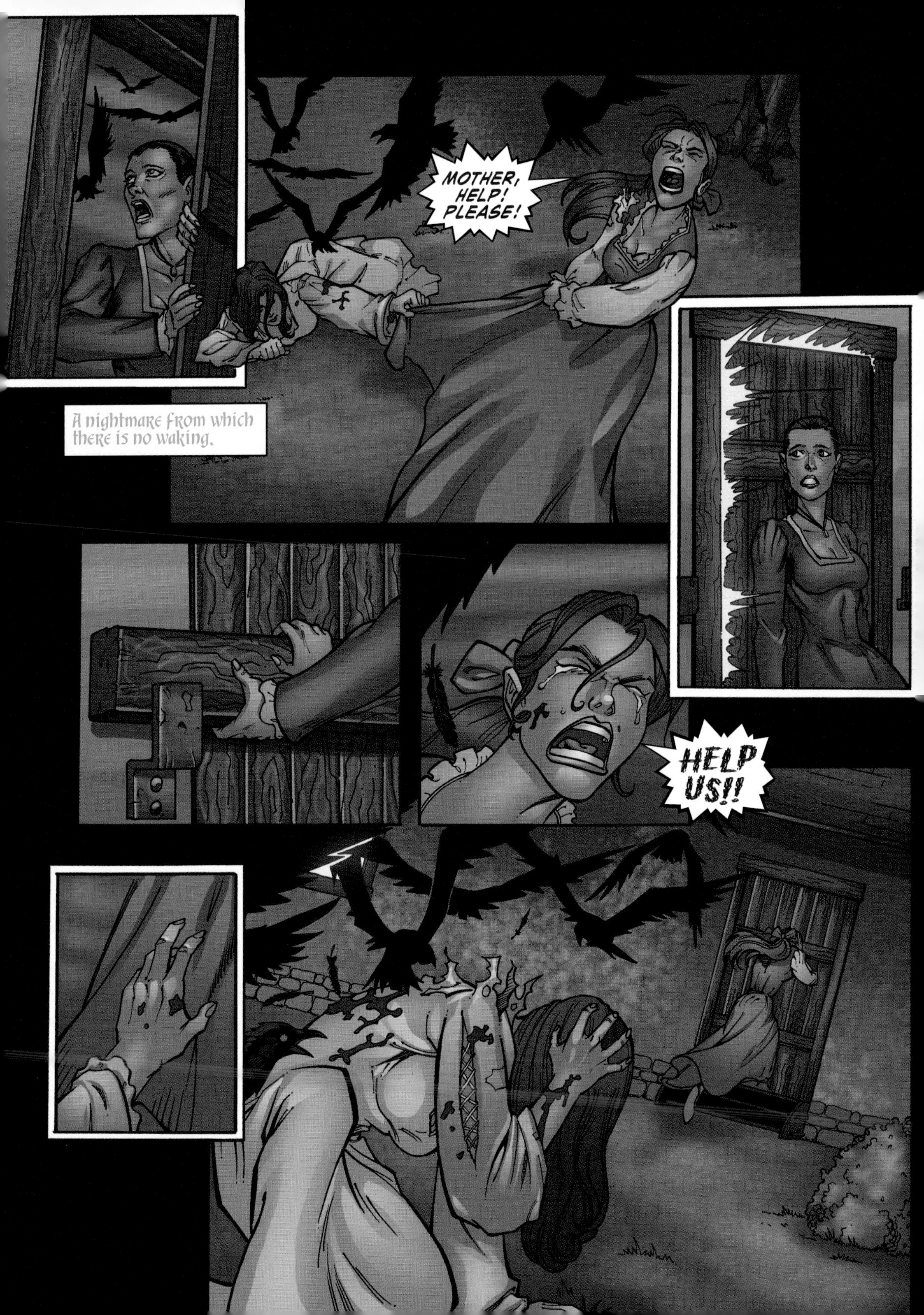
MOTHER, HELP! PLEASE!
A nightmare from which there is no waking.
HELP US!!

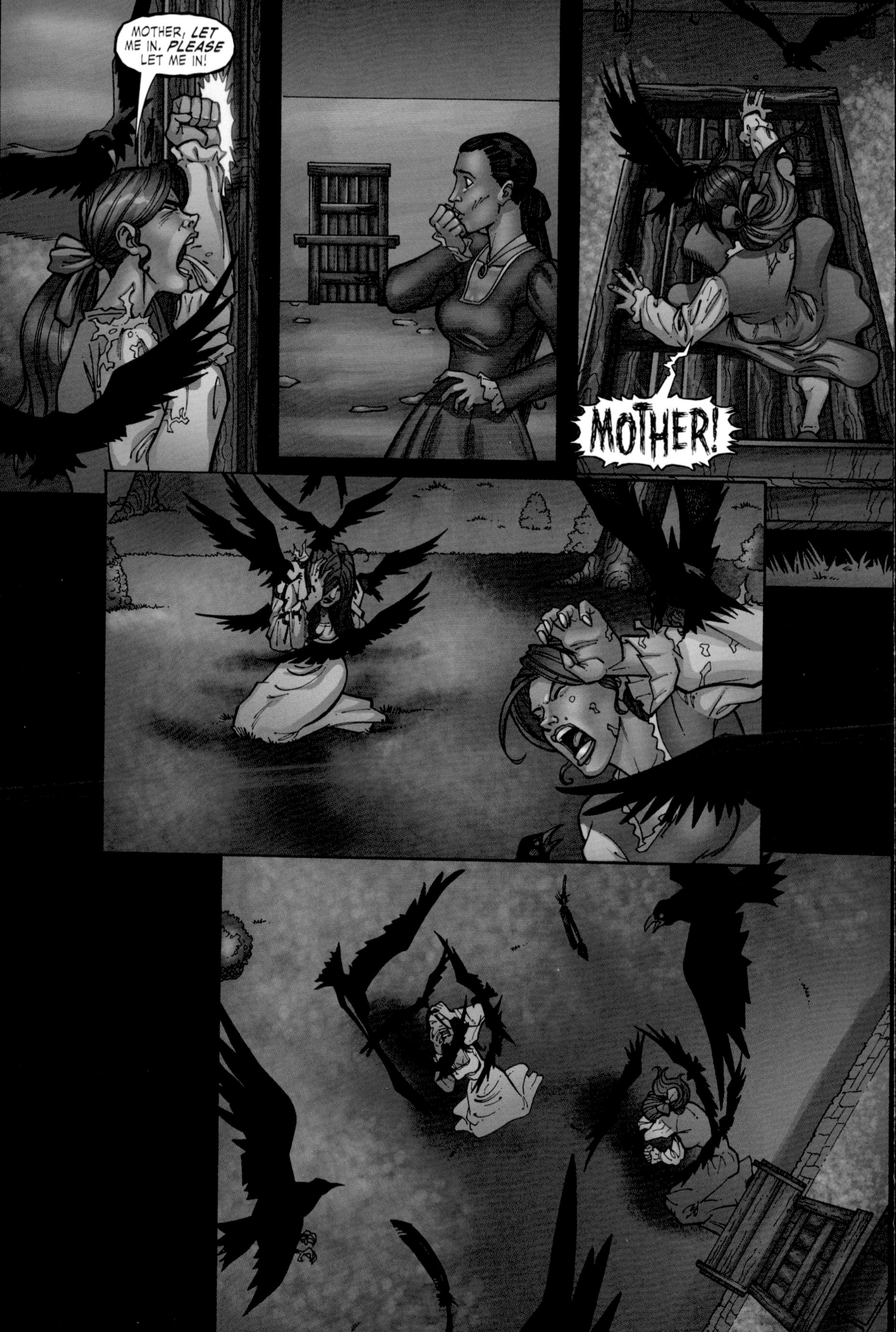
MOTHER, LET ME IN. PLEASE LET ME IN!
MOTHER!

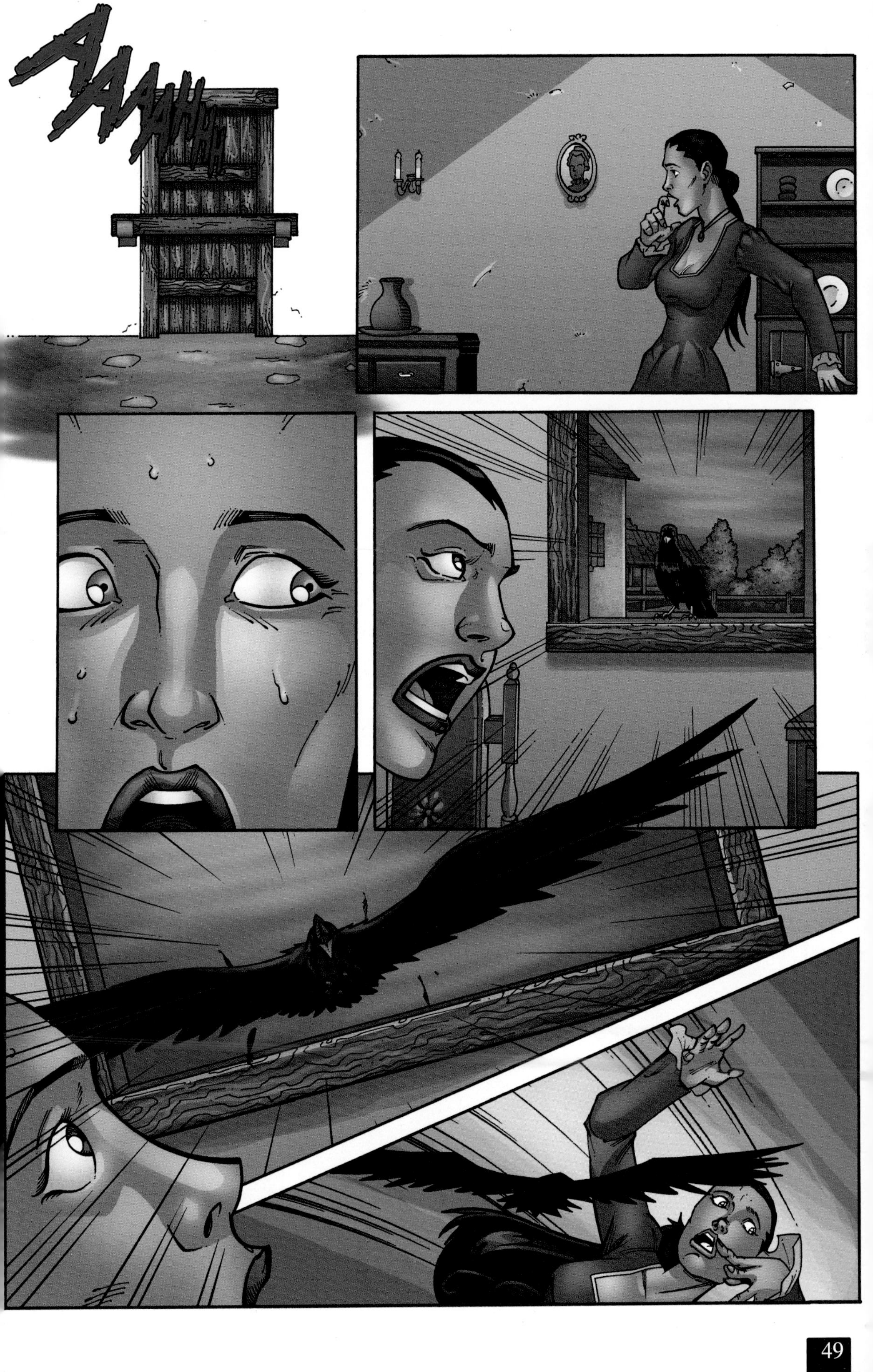
AAAAHHH!

UMPH

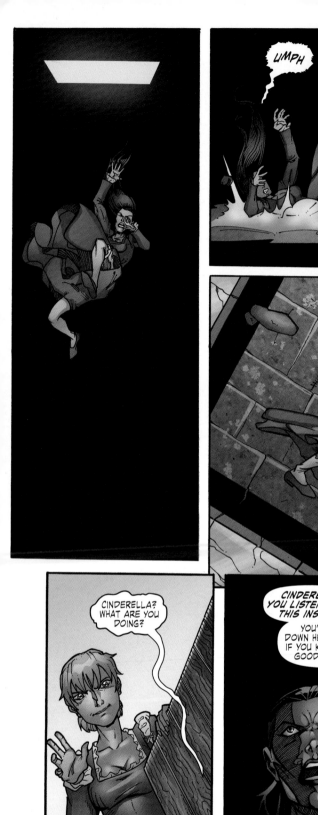

CINDERELLA,
OH THANK HEAVENS.
PLEASE... I NEED
YOUR HELP. MOTHER'S
BEEN HURT.

CINDERELLA?
WHAT ARE YOU
DOING?

CINDERELLA,
YOU LISTEN TO ME
THIS INSTANT!

YOU'LL COME
DOWN HERE AT ONCE
IF YOU KNOW WHAT'S
GOOD FOR YOU.

CINDERELLA.

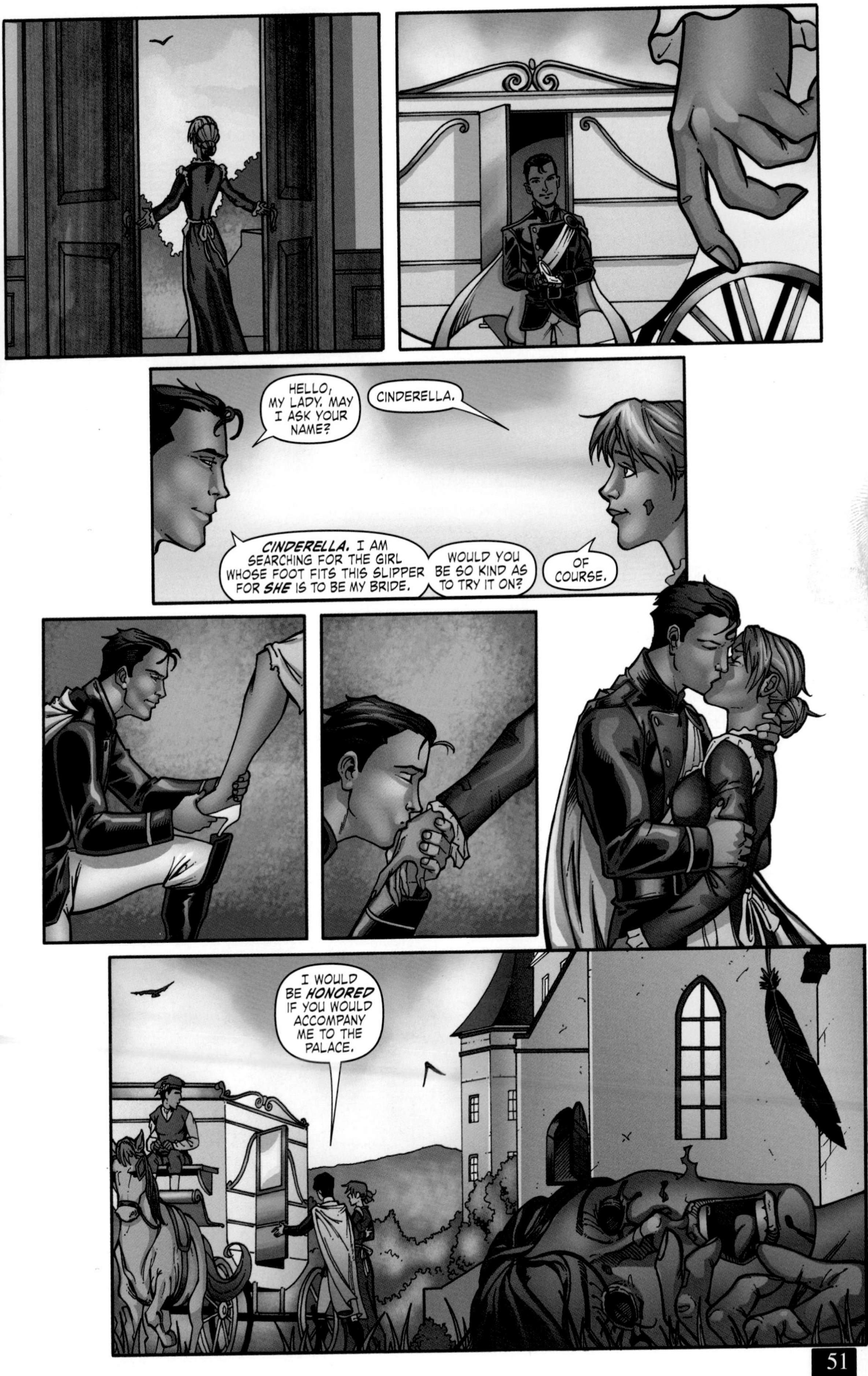
HELLO, MY LADY. MAY I ASK YOUR NAME?
CINDERELLA.
CINDERELLA. I AM SEARCHING FOR THE GIRL WHOSE FOOT FITS THIS SLIPPER FOR SHE IS TO BE MY BRIDE.
WOULD YOU BE SO KIND AS TO TRY IT ON?
OF COURSE.
I WOULD BE HONORED IF YOU WOULD ACCOMPANY ME TO THE PALACE.

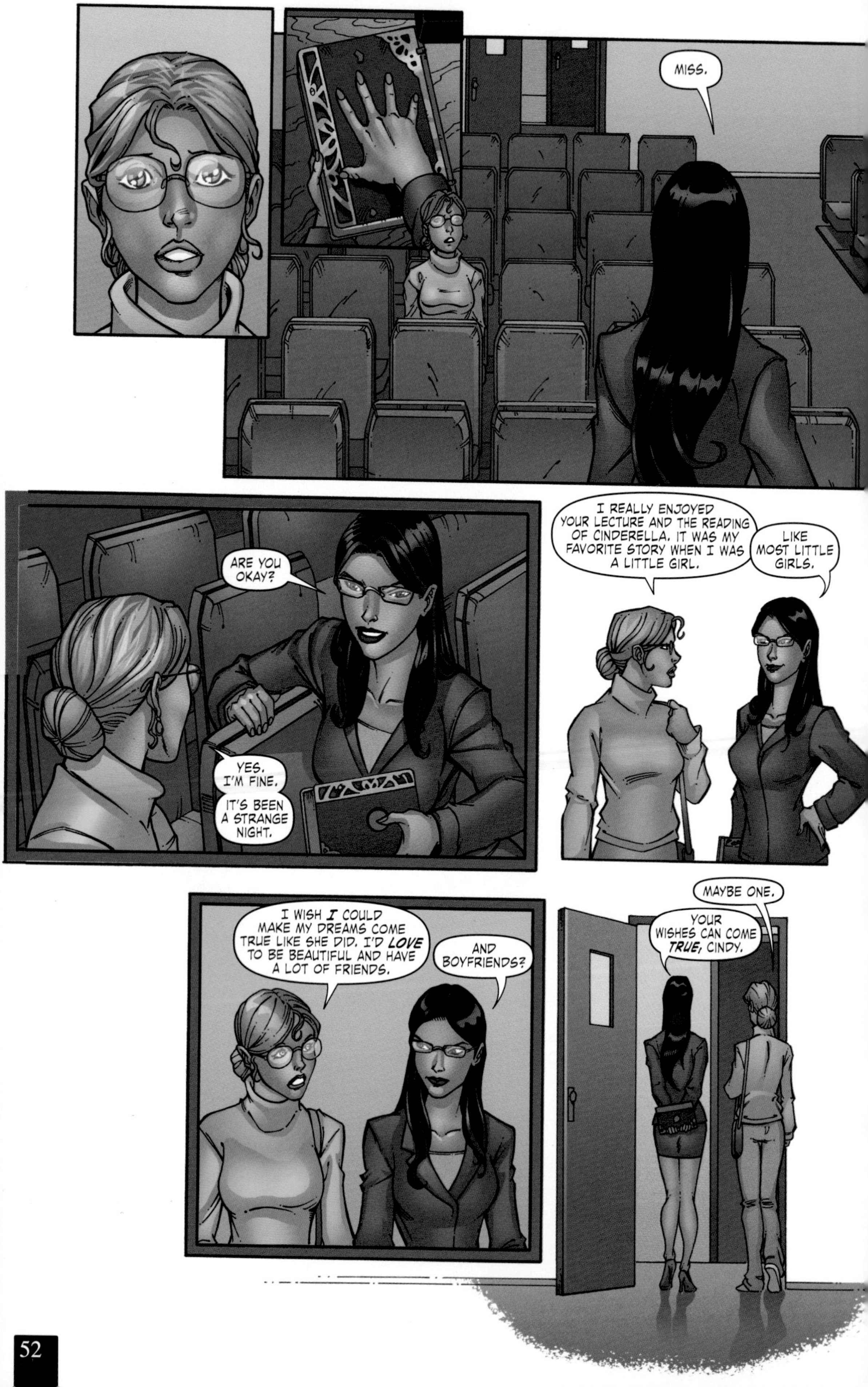
MISS.
ARE YOU OKAY?
YES. I'M FINE.
IT'S BEEN A STRANGE NIGHT.
I REALLY ENJOYED YOUR LECTURE AND THE READING OF CINDERELLA. IT WAS MY FAVORITE STORY WHEN I WAS A LITTLE GIRL.
LIKE MOST LITTLE GIRLS.
I WISH I COULD MAKE MY DREAMS COME TRUE LIKE SHE DID. I'D LOVE TO BE BEAUTIFUL AND HAVE A LOT OF FRIENDS.
AND BOYFRIENDS?
MAYBE ONE.
YOUR WISHES CAN COME TRUE, CINDY.

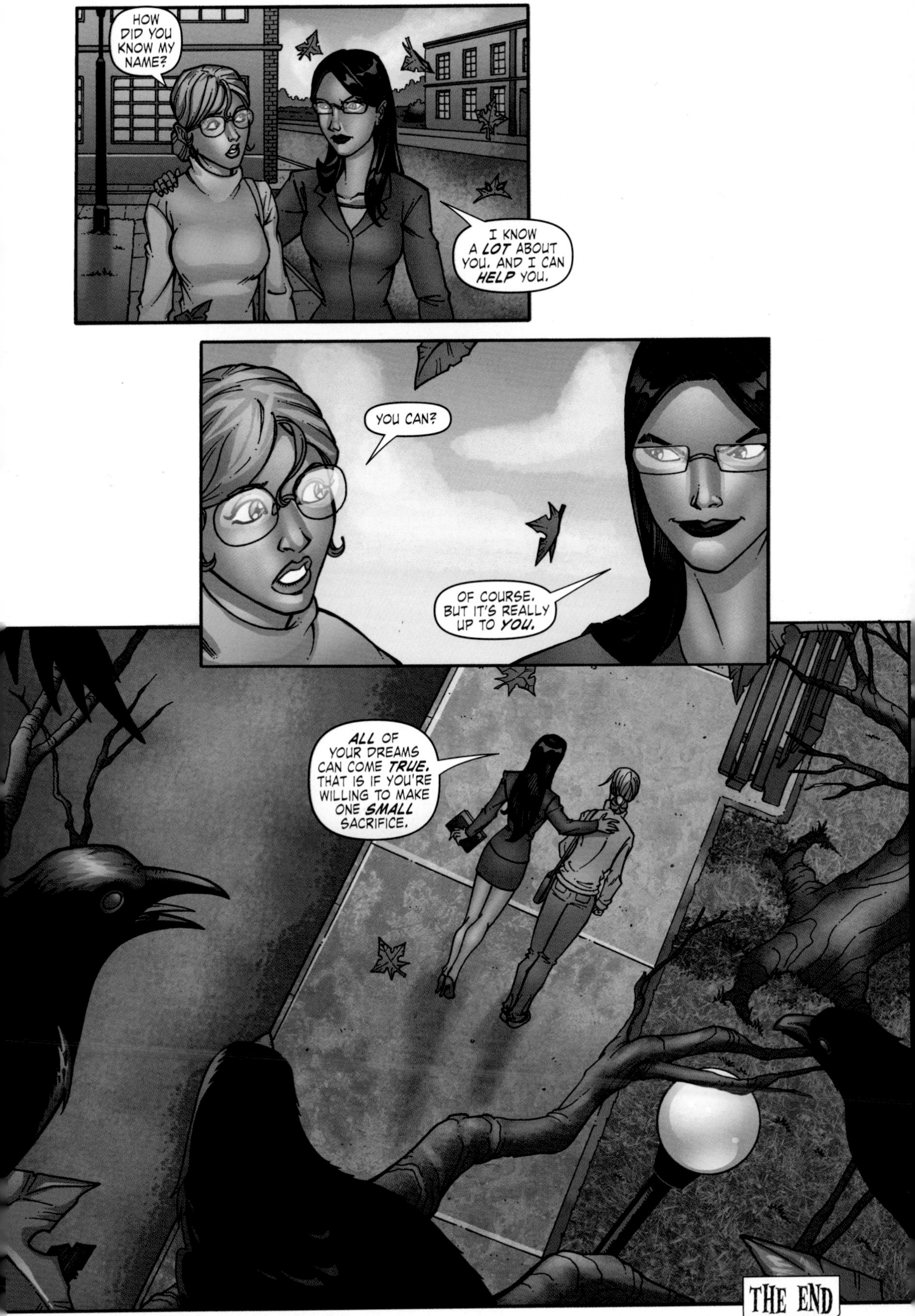
HOW DID YOU KNOW MY NAME?
I KNOW A LOT ABOUT YOU. AND I CAN HELP YOU.
YOU CAN?
OF COURSE. BUT IT'S REALLY UP TO YOU.
ALL OF YOUR DREAMS CAN COME TRUE. THAT IS IF YOU'RE WILLING TO MAKE ONE SMALL SACRIFICE.
THE END

Hansel & Gretel

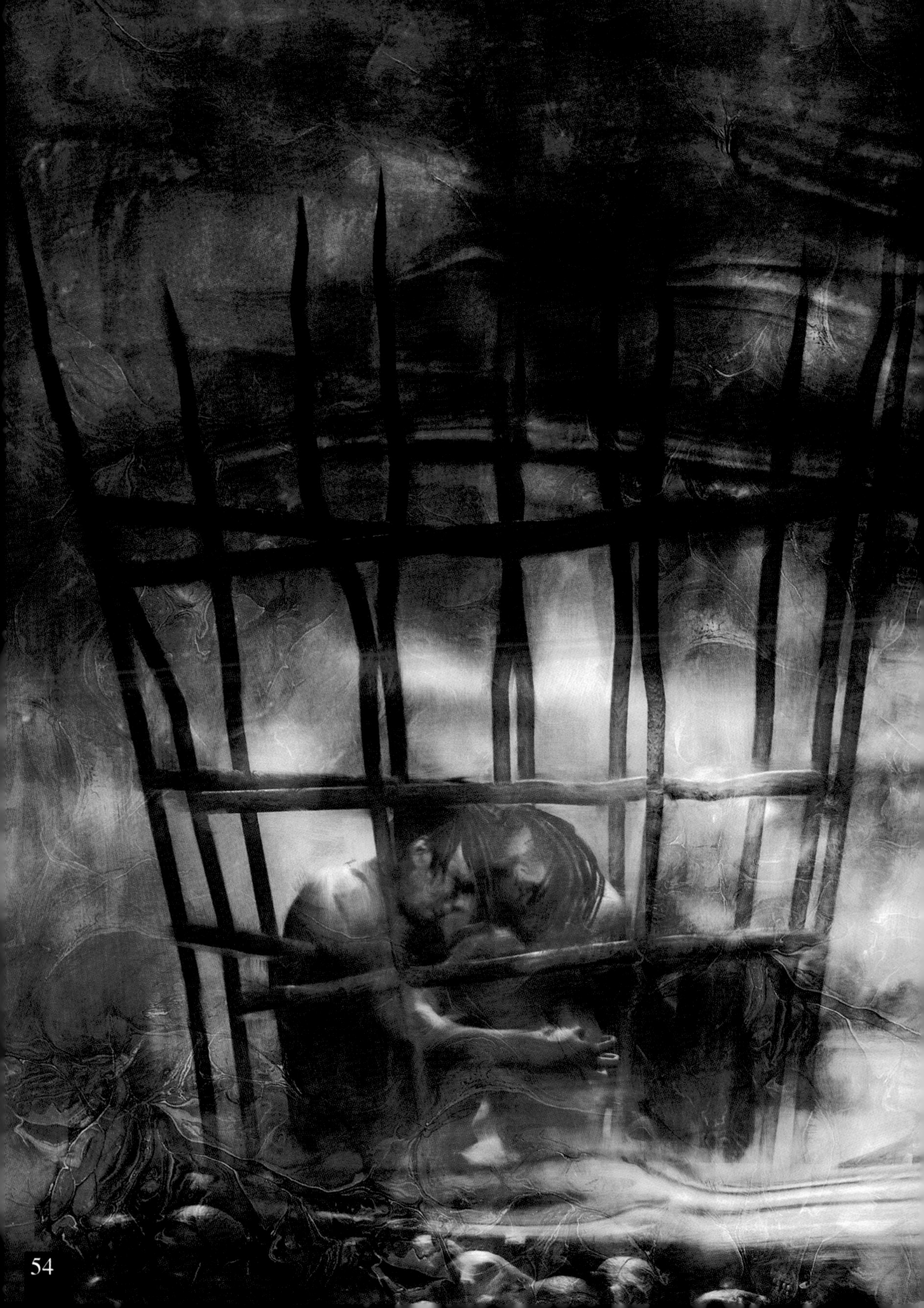

Written & Created by
Joe Tyler & Ralph Tedesco

Pencils
Alexandre Benhossi

Inks
Blake Wilke

Colors
Eric Rodriguez

Design
David Seidman

Lettering
Artmonkeys

Cover
Nick Marks

Editor
Ralph Tedesco

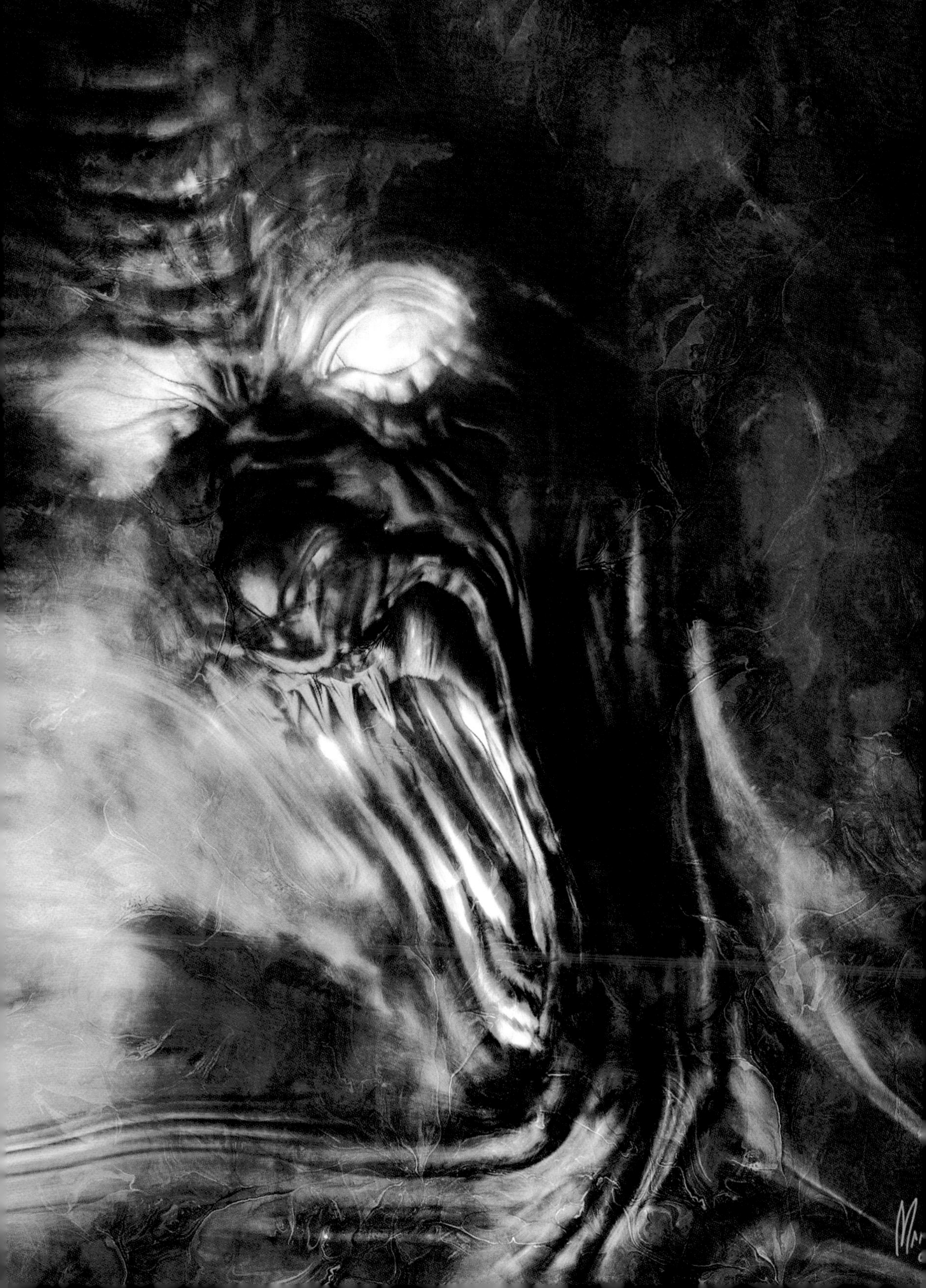

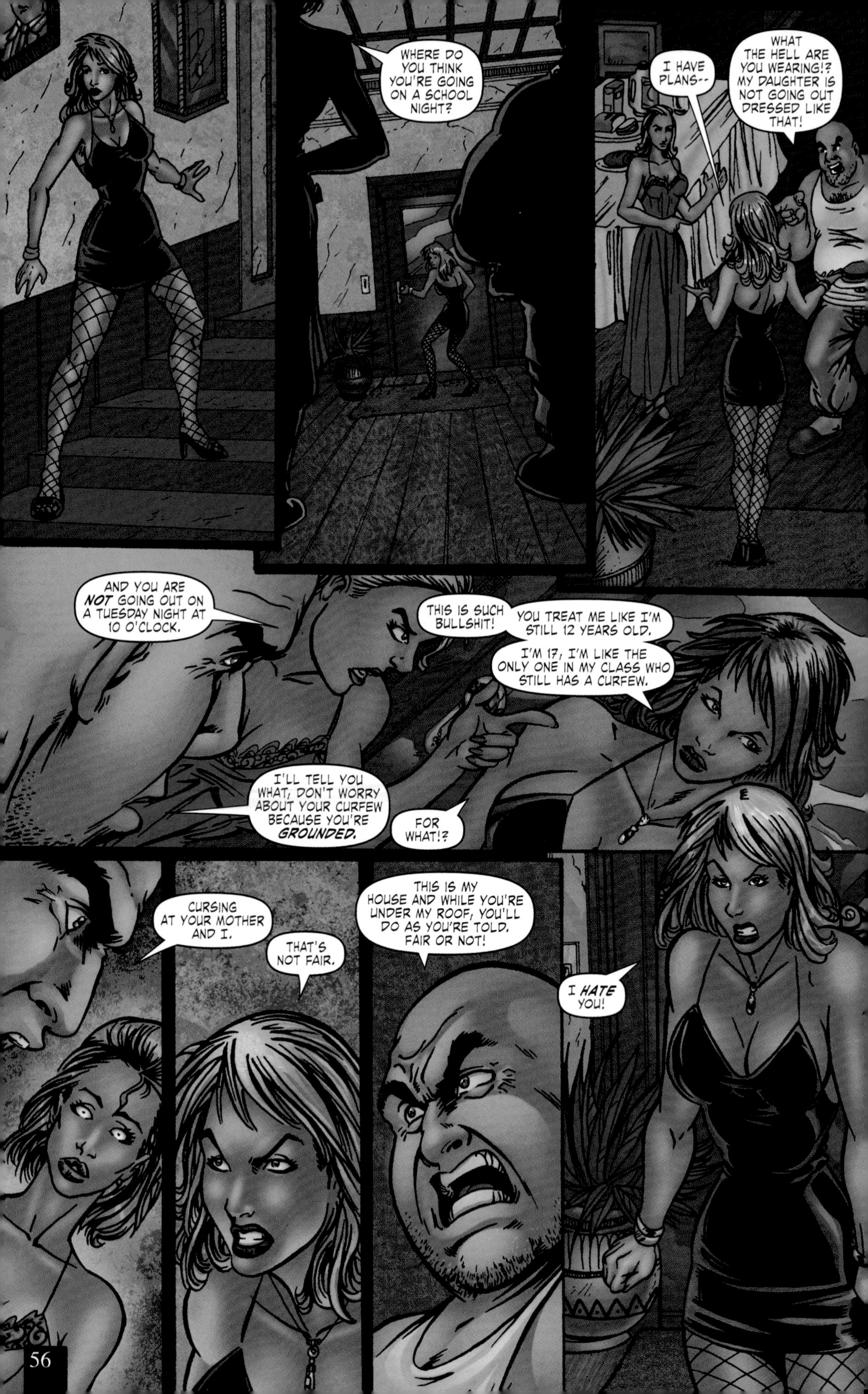
WHERE DO YOU THINK YOU'RE GOING ON A SCHOOL NIGHT?
I HAVE PLANS--
WHAT THE HELL ARE YOU WEARING!? MY DAUGHTER IS NOT GOING OUT DRESSED LIKE THAT!
AND YOU ARE NOT GOING OUT ON A TUESDAY NIGHT AT 10 O'CLOCK.
THIS IS SUCH BULLSHIT!
YOU TREAT ME LIKE I'M STILL 12 YEARS OLD.
I'M 17, I'M LIKE THE ONLY ONE IN MY CLASS WHO STILL HAS A CURFEW.
I'LL TELL YOU WHAT, DON'T WORRY ABOUT YOUR CURFEW BECAUSE YOU'RE GROUNDED.
FOR WHAT!?
CURSING AT YOUR MOTHER AND I.
THAT'S NOT FAIR.
THIS IS MY HOUSE AND WHILE YOU'RE UNDER MY ROOF, YOU'LL DO AS YOU'RE TOLD. FAIR OR NOT!
I HATE YOU!

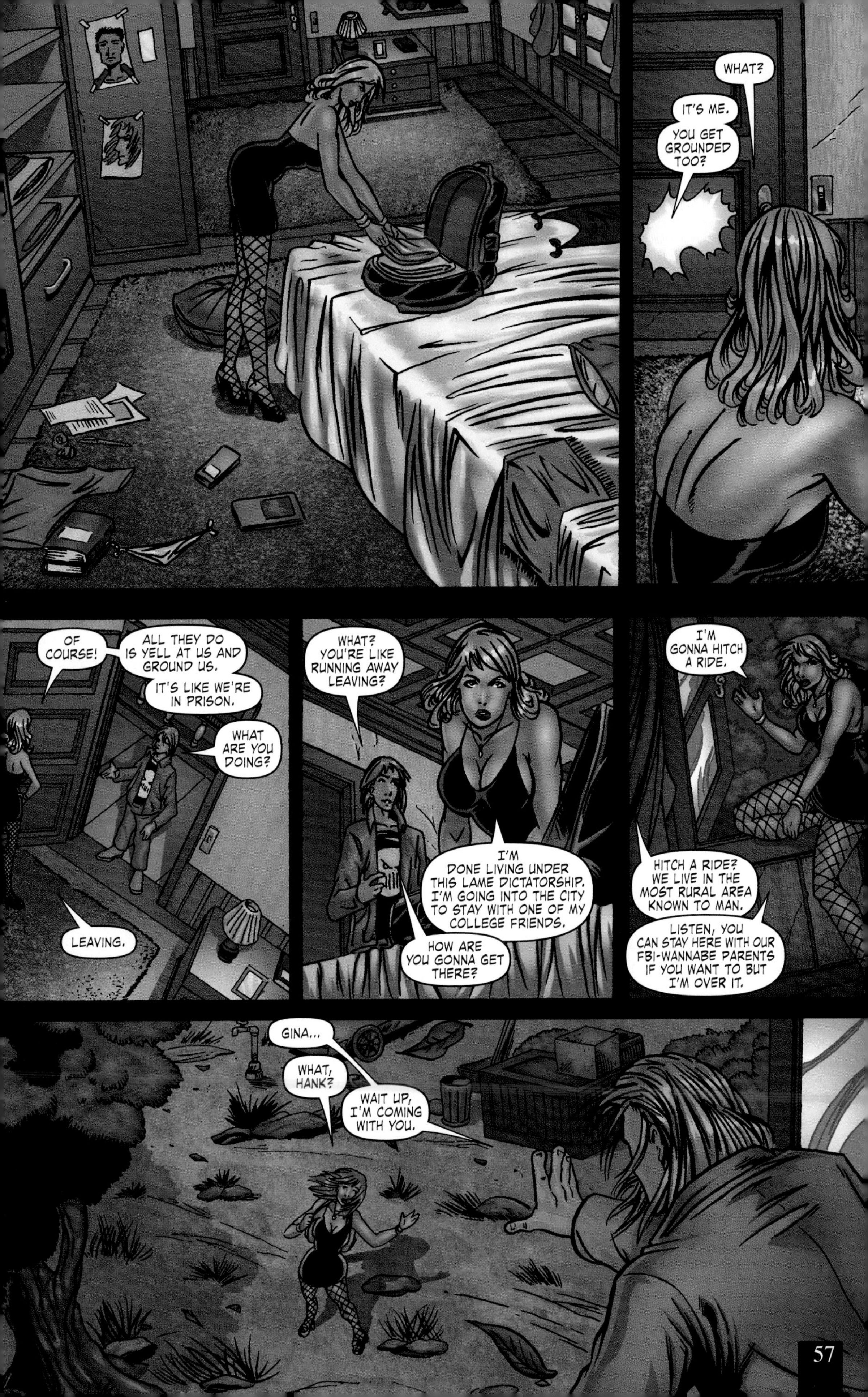
WHAT?
IT'S ME.
YOU GET GROUNDED TOO?
OF COURSE!
ALL THEY DO IS YELL AT US AND GROUND US.
IT'S LIKE WE'RE IN PRISON.
WHAT ARE YOU DOING?
LEAVING.
WHAT? YOU'RE LIKE RUNNING AWAY LEAVING?
I'M DONE LIVING UNDER THIS LAME DICTATORSHIP. I'M GOING INTO THE CITY TO STAY WITH ONE OF MY COLLEGE FRIENDS.
HOW ARE YOU GONNA GET THERE?
I'M GONNA HITCH A RIDE.
HITCH A RIDE? WE LIVE IN THE MOST RURAL AREA KNOWN TO MAN.
LISTEN, YOU CAN STAY HERE WITH OUR FBI-WANNABE PARENTS IF YOU WANT TO BUT I'M OVER IT.
GINA...
WHAT, HANK?
WAIT UP, I'M COMING WITH YOU.

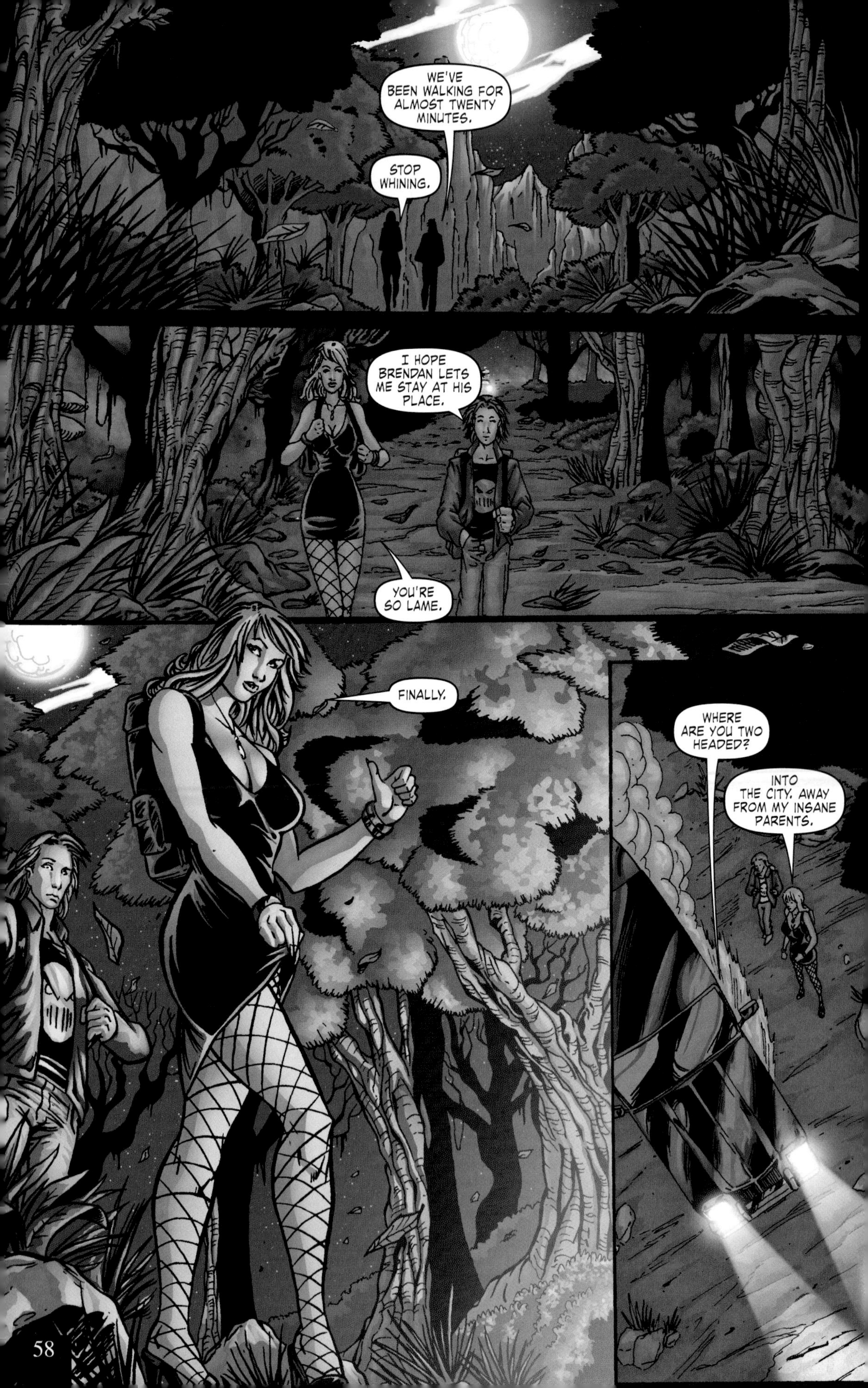
WE'VE BEEN WALKING FOR ALMOST TWENTY MINUTES.
STOP WHINING.
I HOPE BRENDAN LETS ME STAY AT HIS PLACE.
YOU'RE SO LAME.
FINALLY.
WHERE ARE YOU TWO HEADED?
INTO THE CITY. AWAY FROM MY INSANE PARENTS.

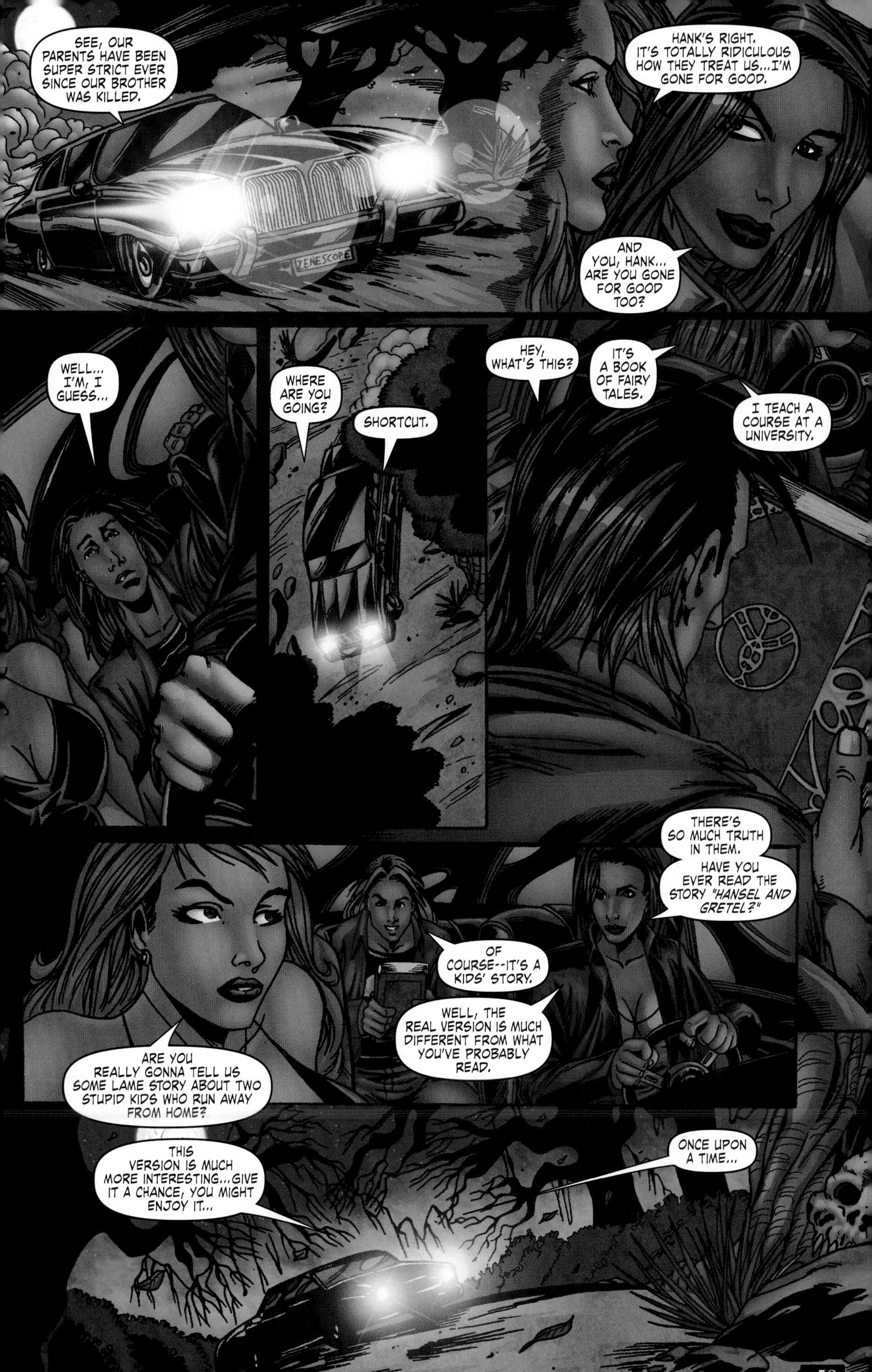
SEE, OUR PARENTS HAVE BEEN SUPER STRICT EVER SINCE OUR BROTHER WAS KILLED.
ZENESCOPE
HANK'S RIGHT. IT'S TOTALLY RIDICULOUS HOW THEY TREAT US...I'M GONE FOR GOOD.
AND YOU, HANK... ARE YOU GONE FOR GOOD TOO?
WELL... I'M, I GUESS...
WHERE ARE YOU GOING?
SHORTCUT.
HEY, WHAT'S THIS?
IT'S A BOOK OF FAIRY TALES.
I TEACH A COURSE AT A UNIVERSITY.
THERE'S SO MUCH TRUTH IN THEM.
HAVE YOU EVER READ THE STORY "HANSEL AND GRETEL?"
OF COURSE--IT'S A KIDS' STORY.
WELL, THE REAL VERSION IS MUCH DIFFERENT FROM WHAT YOU'VE PROBABLY READ.
ARE YOU REALLY GONNA TELL US SOME LAME STORY ABOUT TWO STUPID KIDS WHO RUN AWAY FROM HOME?
THIS VERSION IS MUCH MORE INTERESTING...GIVE IT A CHANCE, YOU MIGHT ENJOY IT...
ONCE UPON A TIME...

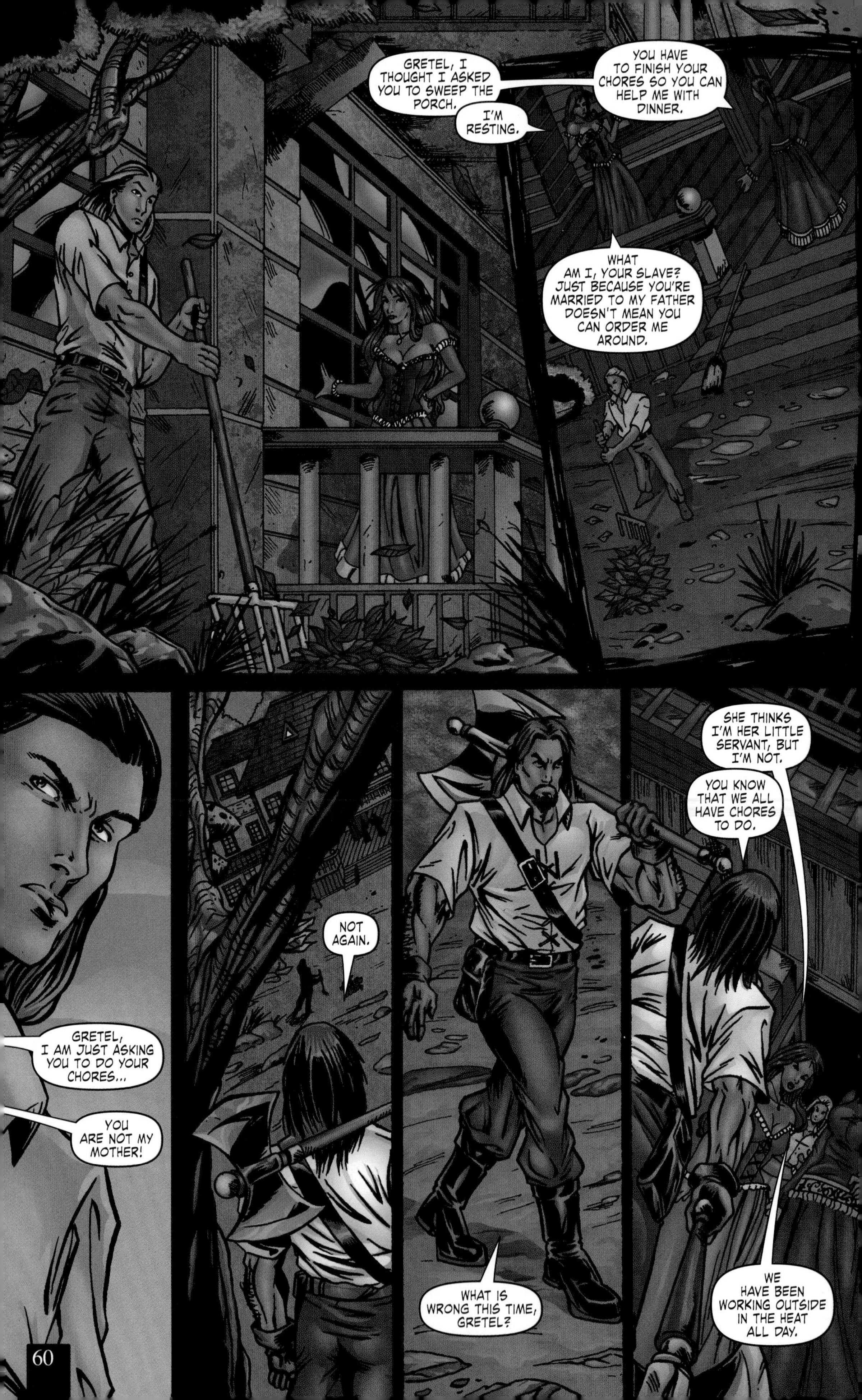
GRETEL, I THOUGHT I ASKED YOU TO SWEEP THE PORCH.
I'M RESTING.
YOU HAVE TO FINISH YOUR CHORES SO YOU CAN HELP ME WITH DINNER.
WHAT AM I, YOUR SLAVE? JUST BECAUSE YOU'RE MARRIED TO MY FATHER DOESN'T MEAN YOU CAN ORDER ME AROUND.
GRETEL, I AM JUST ASKING YOU TO DO YOUR CHORES...
YOU ARE NOT MY MOTHER!
NOT AGAIN.
WHAT IS WRONG THIS TIME, GRETEL?
SHE THINKS I'M HER LITTLE SERVANT, BUT I'M NOT.
YOU KNOW THAT WE ALL HAVE CHORES TO DO.
WE HAVE BEEN WORKING OUTSIDE IN THE HEAT ALL DAY.

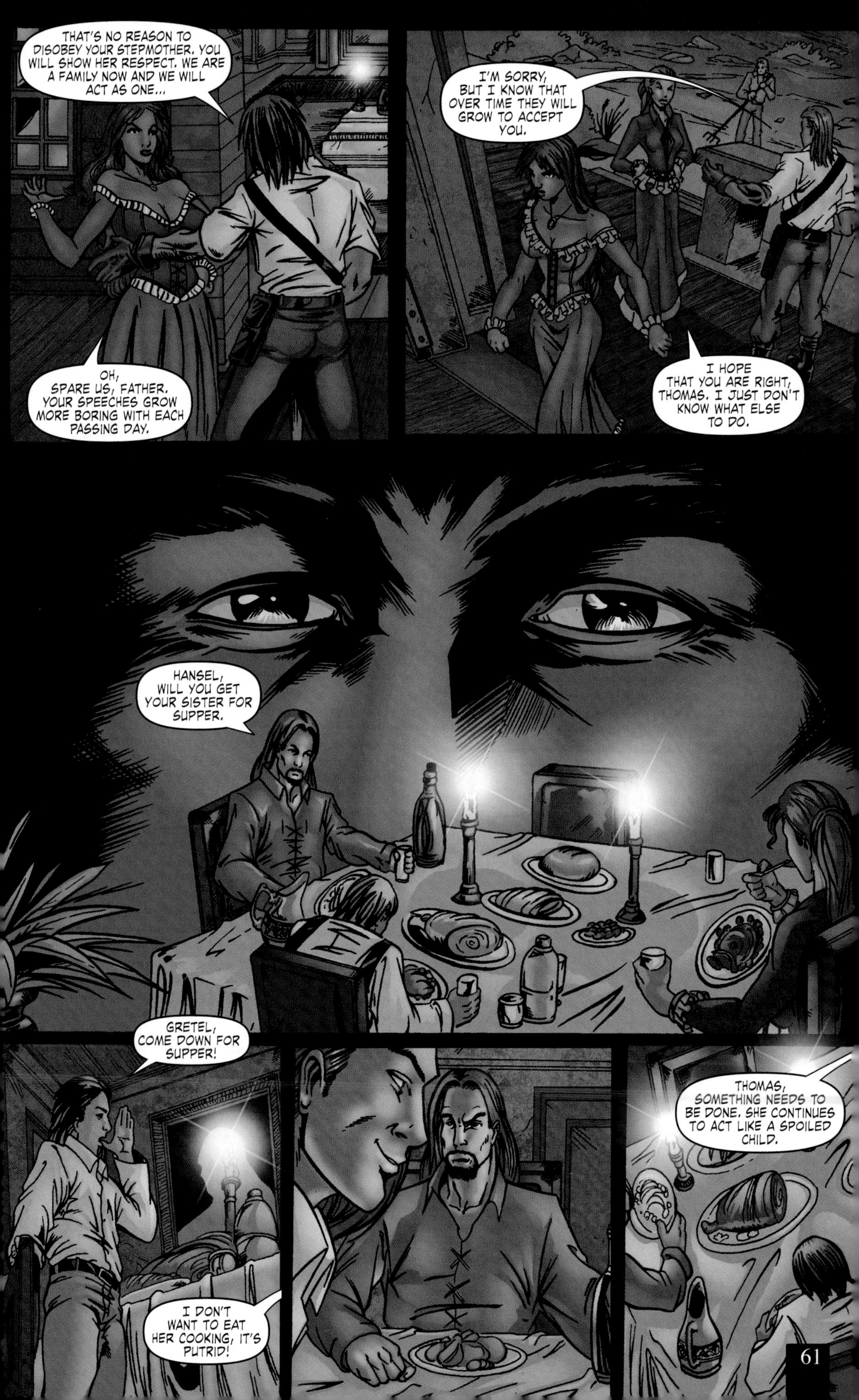
THAT'S NO REASON TO DISOBEY YOUR STEPMOTHER. YOU WILL SHOW HER RESPECT. WE ARE A FAMILY NOW AND WE WILL ACT AS ONE...
OH, SPARE US, FATHER. YOUR SPEECHES GROW MORE BORING WITH EACH PASSING DAY.
I'M SORRY, BUT I KNOW THAT OVER TIME THEY WILL GROW TO ACCEPT YOU.
I HOPE THAT YOU ARE RIGHT, THOMAS. I JUST DON'T KNOW WHAT ELSE TO DO.
HANSEL, WILL YOU GET YOUR SISTER FOR SUPPER.
GRETEL, COME DOWN FOR SUPPER!
I DON'T WANT TO EAT HER COOKING, IT'S PUTRID!
THOMAS, SOMETHING NEEDS TO BE DONE. SHE CONTINUES TO ACT LIKE A SPOILED CHILD.

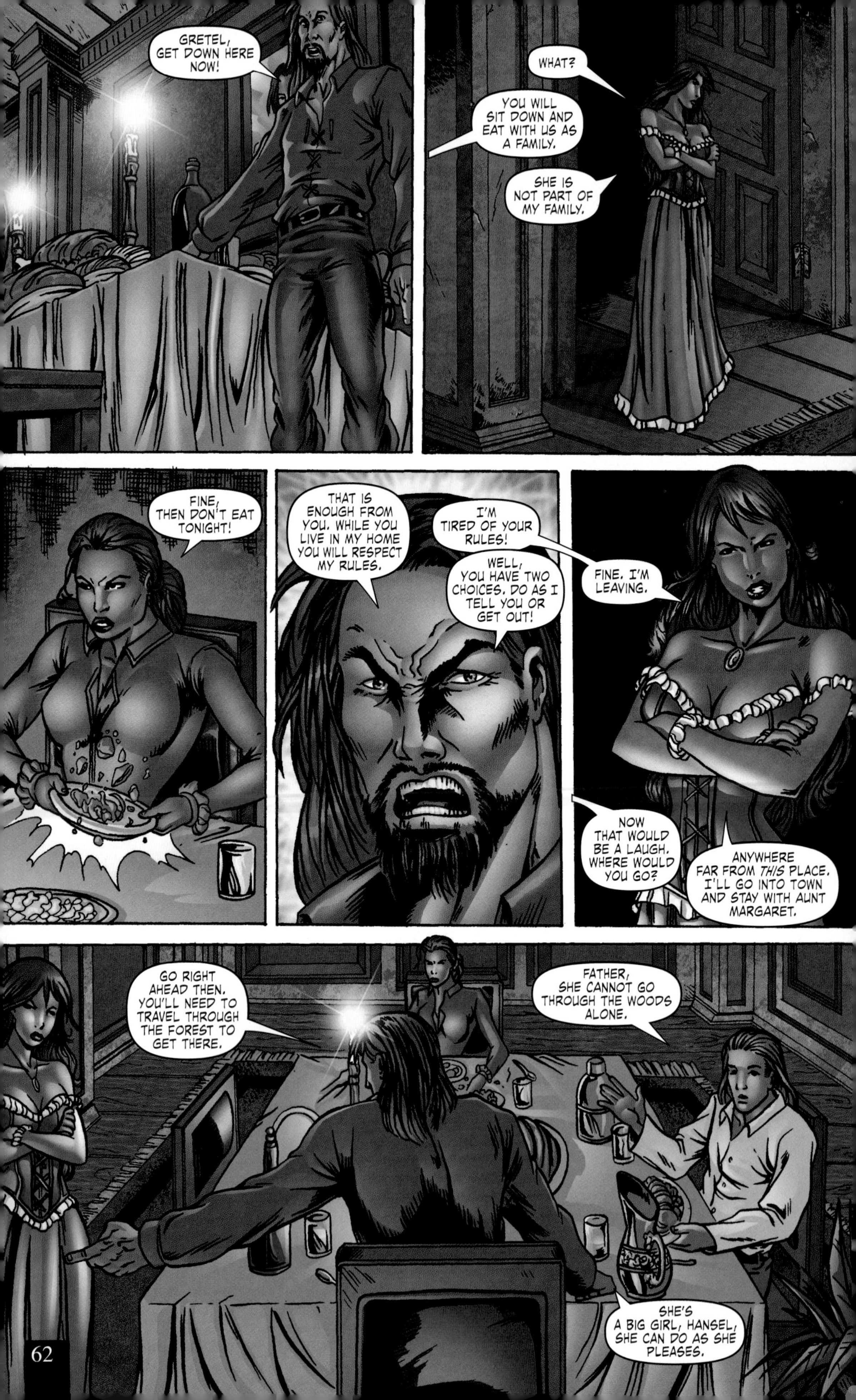
GRETEL, GET DOWN HERE NOW!
WHAT?
YOU WILL SIT DOWN AND EAT WITH US AS A FAMILY.
SHE IS NOT PART OF MY FAMILY.
FINE, THEN DON'T EAT TONIGHT!
THAT IS ENOUGH FROM YOU. WHILE YOU LIVE IN MY HOME YOU WILL RESPECT MY RULES.
I'M TIRED OF YOUR RULES!
WELL, YOU HAVE TWO CHOICES. DO AS I TELL YOU OR GET OUT!
FINE. I'M LEAVING.
NOW THAT WOULD BE A LAUGH. WHERE WOULD YOU GO?
ANYWHERE FAR FROM *THIS* PLACE. I'LL GO INTO TOWN AND STAY WITH AUNT MARGARET.
GO RIGHT AHEAD THEN. YOU'LL NEED TO TRAVEL THROUGH THE FOREST TO GET THERE.
FATHER, SHE CANNOT GO THROUGH THE WOODS ALONE.
SHE'S A BIG GIRL, HANSEL, SHE CAN DO AS SHE PLEASES.

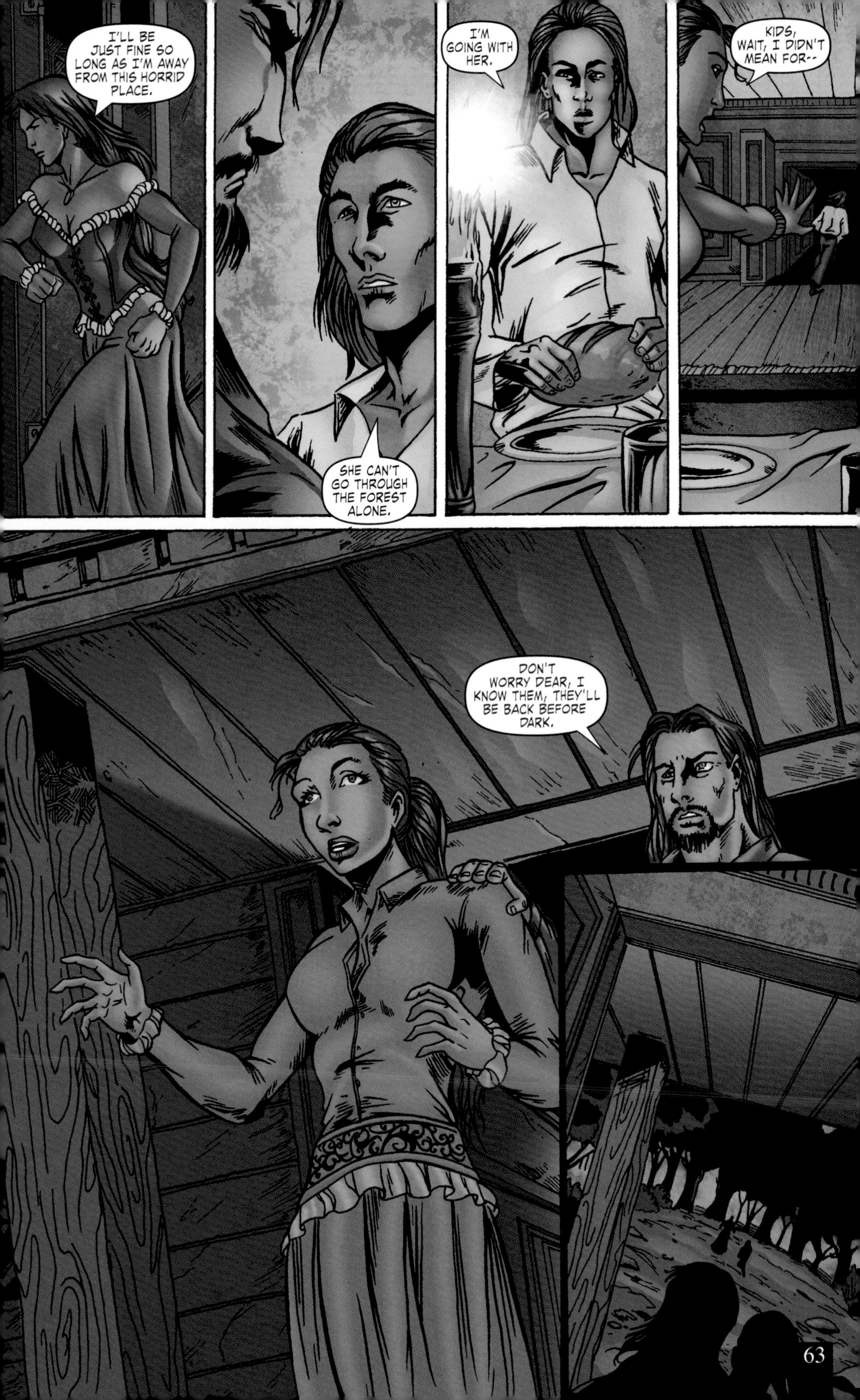
I'LL BE JUST FINE SO LONG AS I'M AWAY FROM THIS HORRID PLACE.
SHE CAN'T GO THROUGH THE FOREST ALONE.
I'M GOING WITH HER.
KIDS, WAIT, I DIDN'T MEAN FOR--
DON'T WORRY DEAR, I KNOW THEM, THEY'LL BE BACK BEFORE DARK.

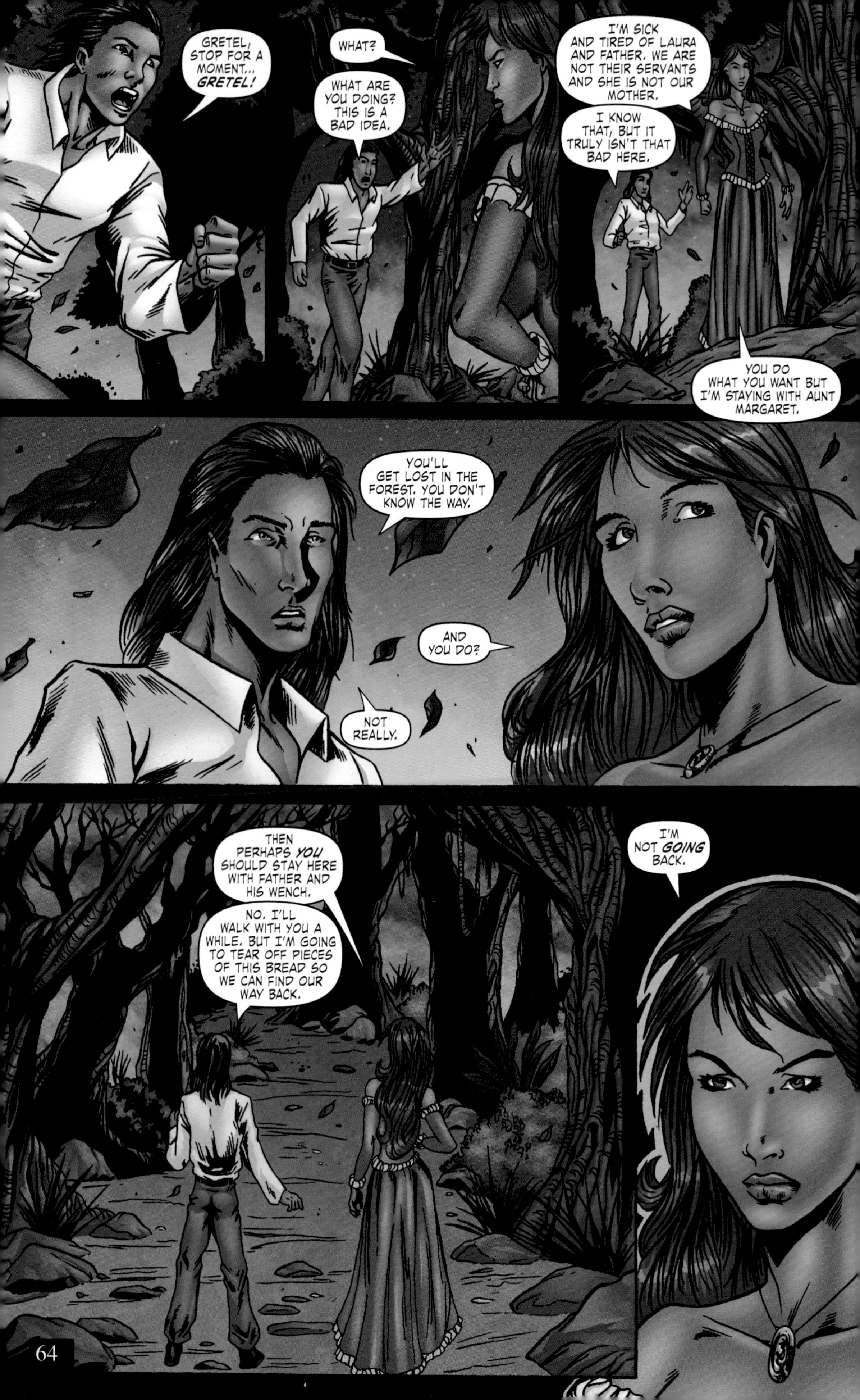
GRETEL, STOP FOR A MOMENT... GRETEL!
WHAT?
WHAT ARE YOU DOING? THIS IS A BAD IDEA.
I'M SICK AND TIRED OF LAURA AND FATHER. WE ARE NOT THEIR SERVANTS AND SHE IS NOT OUR MOTHER.
I KNOW THAT, BUT IT TRULY ISN'T THAT BAD HERE.
YOU DO WHAT YOU WANT BUT I'M STAYING WITH AUNT MARGARET.
YOU'LL GET LOST IN THE FOREST. YOU DON'T KNOW THE WAY.
AND YOU DO?
NOT REALLY.
THEN PERHAPS YOU SHOULD STAY HERE WITH FATHER AND HIS WENCH.
NO. I'LL WALK WITH YOU A WHILE. BUT I'M GOING TO TEAR OFF PIECES OF THIS BREAD SO WE CAN FIND OUR WAY BACK.
I'M NOT GOING BACK.

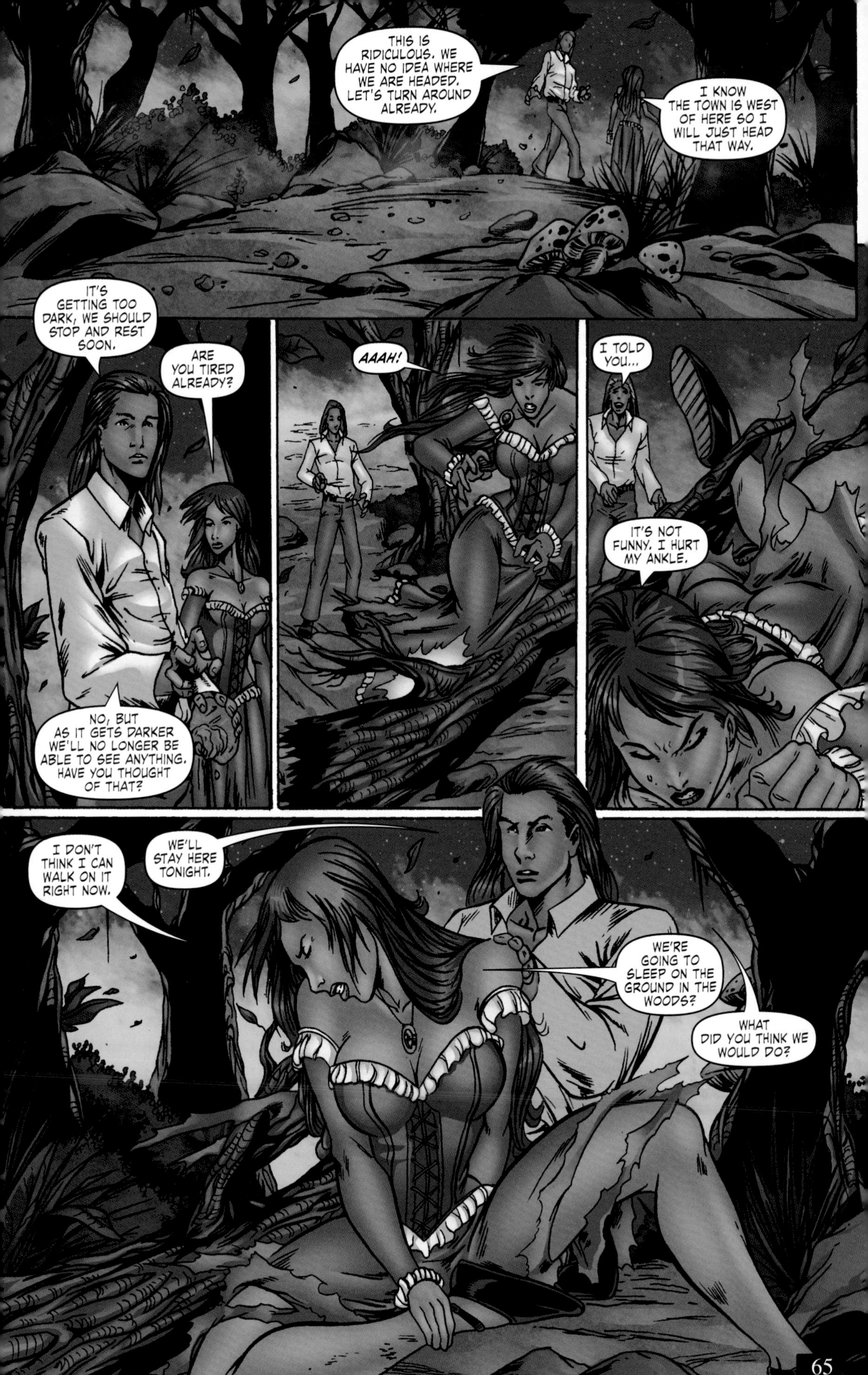
THIS IS RIDICULOUS. WE HAVE NO IDEA WHERE WE ARE HEADED. LET'S TURN AROUND ALREADY.
I KNOW THE TOWN IS WEST OF HERE SO I WILL JUST HEAD THAT WAY.
IT'S GETTING TOO DARK, WE SHOULD STOP AND REST SOON.
ARE YOU TIRED ALREADY?
NO, BUT AS IT GETS DARKER WE'LL NO LONGER BE ABLE TO SEE ANYTHING. HAVE YOU THOUGHT OF THAT?
AAAH!
I TOLD YOU...
IT'S NOT FUNNY. I HURT MY ANKLE.
I DON'T THINK I CAN WALK ON IT RIGHT NOW.
WE'LL STAY HERE TONIGHT.
WE'RE GOING TO SLEEP ON THE GROUND IN THE WOODS?
WHAT DID YOU THINK WE WOULD DO?

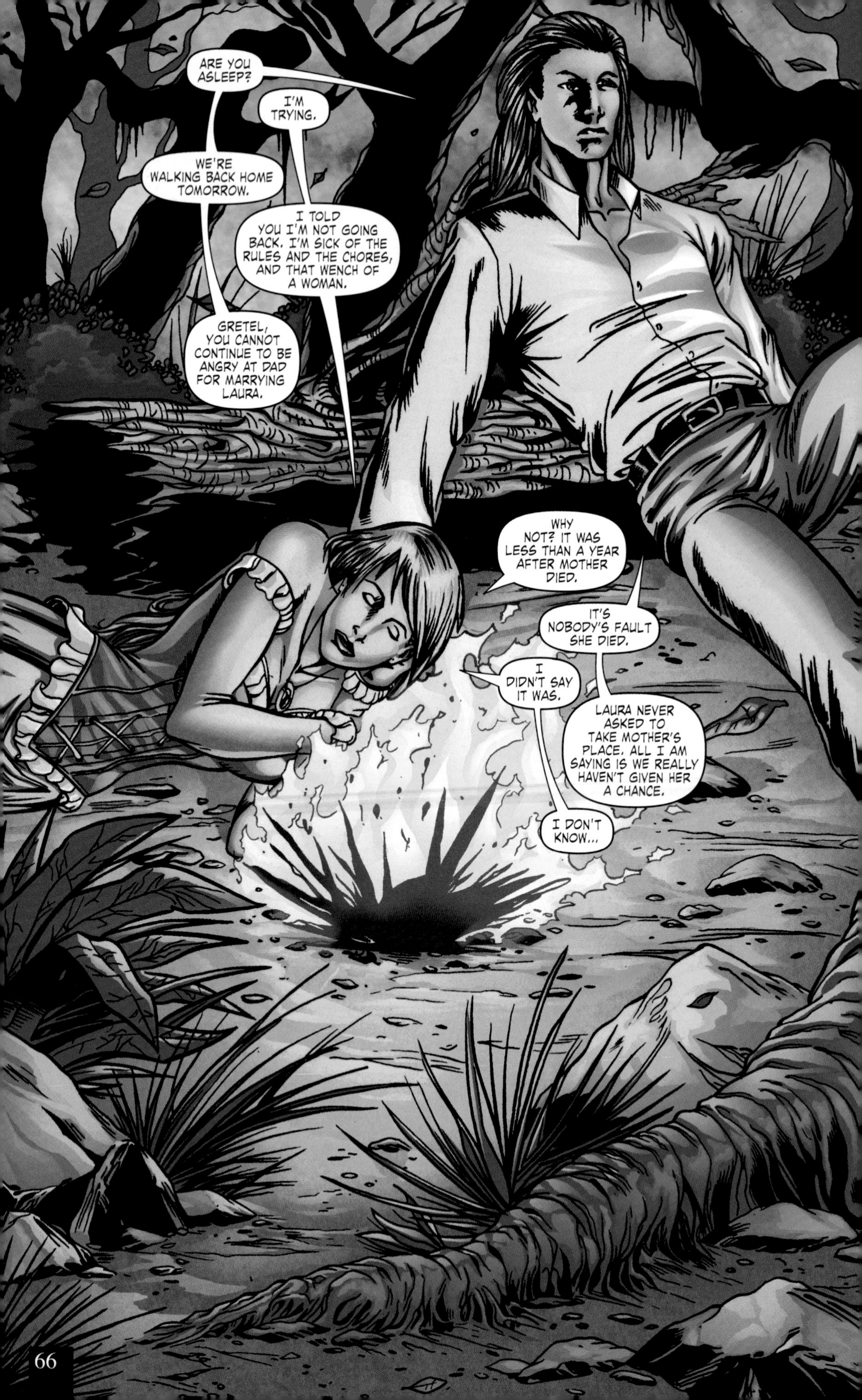
ARE YOU ASLEEP?
I'M TRYING.
WE'RE WALKING BACK HOME TOMORROW.
I TOLD YOU I'M NOT GOING BACK. I'M SICK OF THE RULES AND THE CHORES, AND THAT WENCH OF A WOMAN.
GRETEL, YOU CANNOT CONTINUE TO BE ANGRY AT DAD FOR MARRYING LAURA.
WHY NOT? IT WAS LESS THAN A YEAR AFTER MOTHER DIED.
IT'S NOBODY'S FAULT SHE DIED.
I DIDN'T SAY IT WAS.
LAURA NEVER ASKED TO TAKE MOTHER'S PLACE. ALL I AM SAYING IS WE REALLY HAVEN'T GIVEN HER A CHANCE.
I DON'T KNOW...

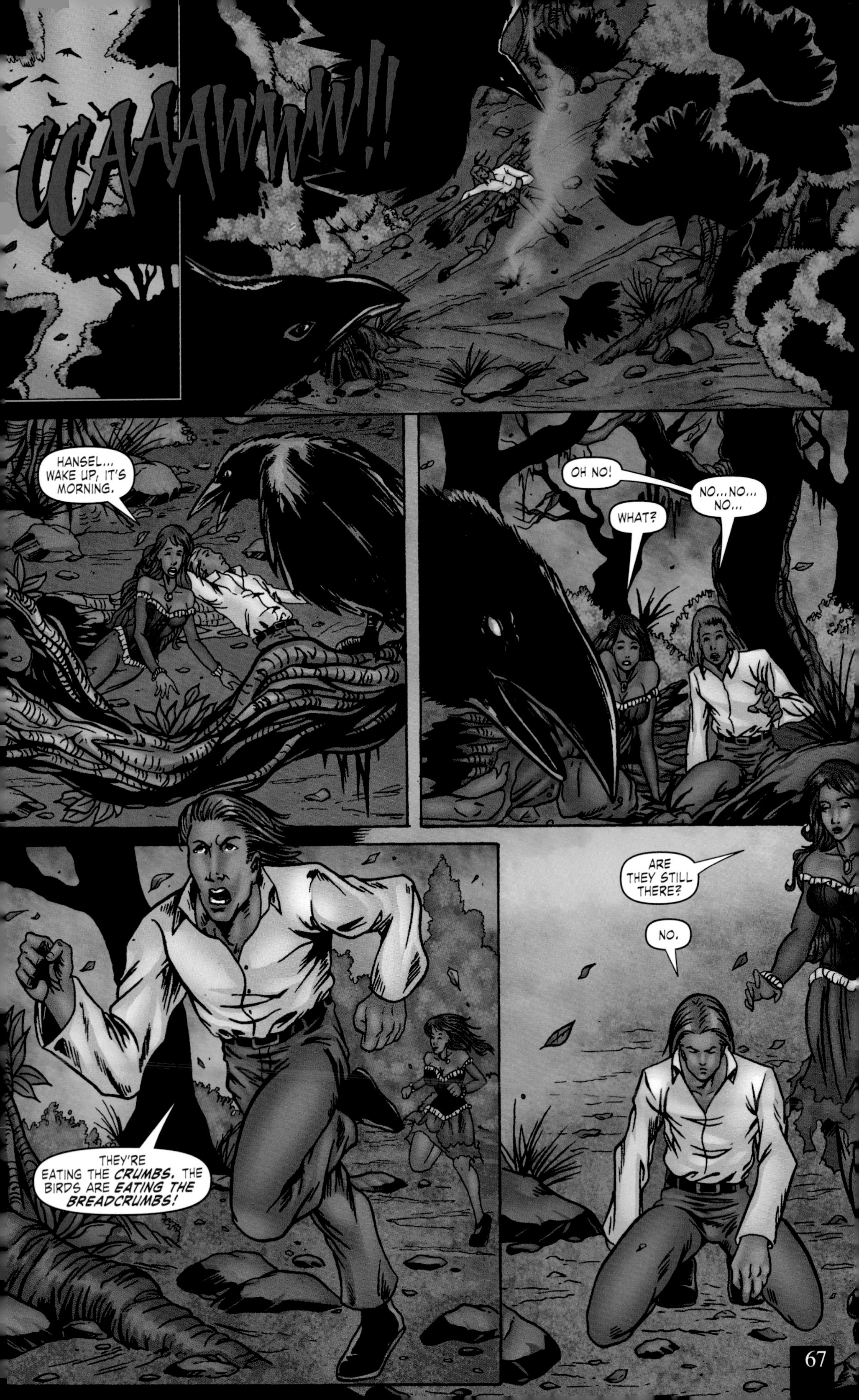
CCAAAWWW!!
HANSEL... WAKE UP, IT'S MORNING.
OH NO!
WHAT?
NO...NO... NO...
THEY'RE EATING THE CRUMBS. THE BIRDS ARE EATING THE BREADCRUMBS!
ARE THEY STILL THERE?
NO.

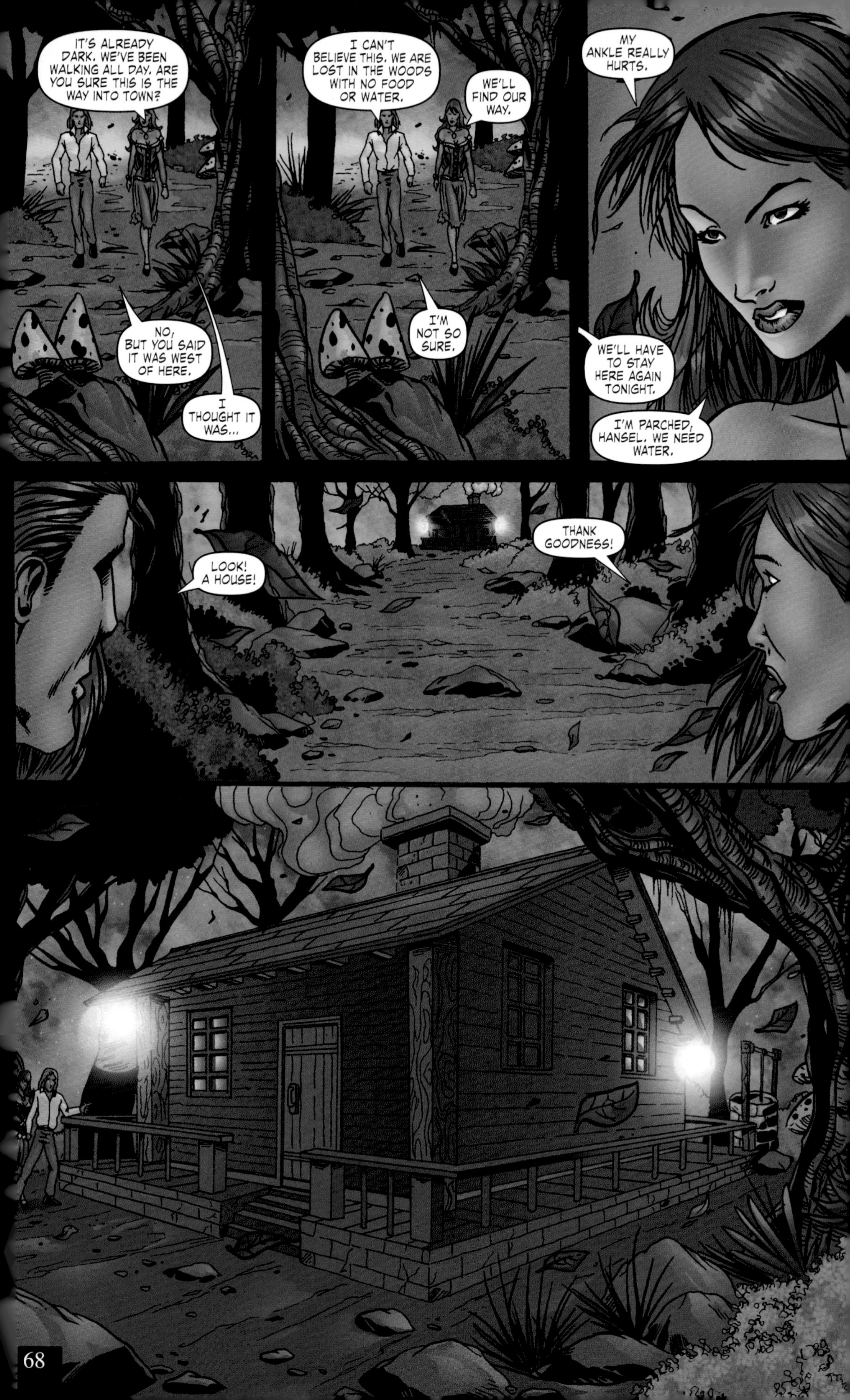
IT'S ALREADY DARK. WE'VE BEEN WALKING ALL DAY. ARE YOU SURE THIS IS THE WAY INTO TOWN?
NO, BUT YOU SAID IT WAS WEST OF HERE.
I THOUGHT IT WAS...
I CAN'T BELIEVE THIS. WE ARE LOST IN THE WOODS WITH NO FOOD OR WATER.
WE'LL FIND OUR WAY.
I'M NOT SO SURE.
MY ANKLE REALLY HURTS.
WE'LL HAVE TO STAY HERE AGAIN TONIGHT.
I'M PARCHED, HANSEL. WE NEED WATER.
LOOK! A HOUSE!
THANK GOODNESS!

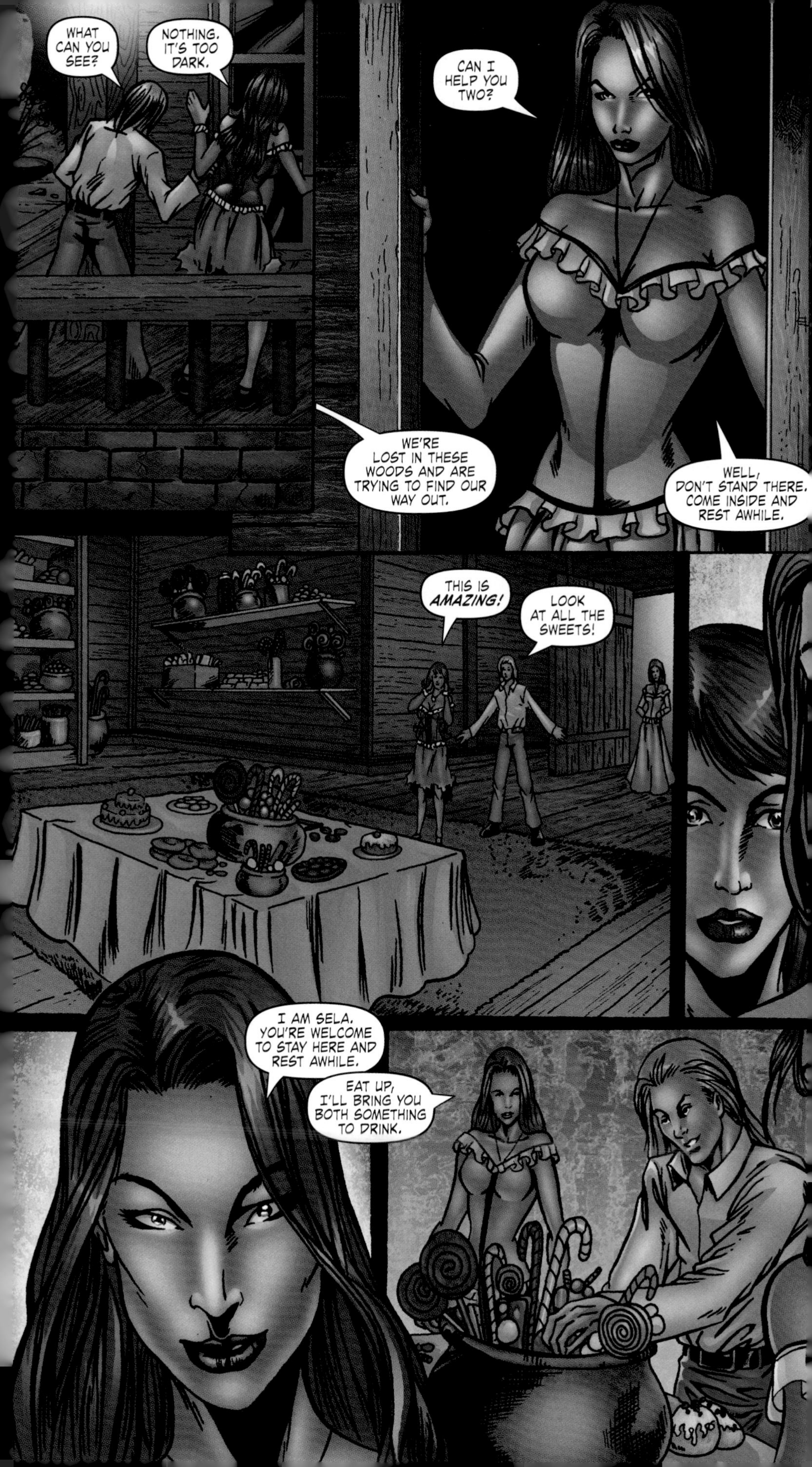
WHAT CAN YOU SEE?
NOTHING. IT'S TOO DARK.
CAN I HELP YOU TWO?
WE'RE LOST IN THESE WOODS AND ARE TRYING TO FIND OUR WAY OUT.
WELL, DON'T STAND THERE. COME INSIDE AND REST AWHILE.
THIS IS AMAZING!
LOOK AT ALL THE SWEETS!
I AM SELA. YOU'RE WELCOME TO STAY HERE AND REST AWHILE.
EAT UP, I'LL BRING YOU BOTH SOMETHING TO DRINK.

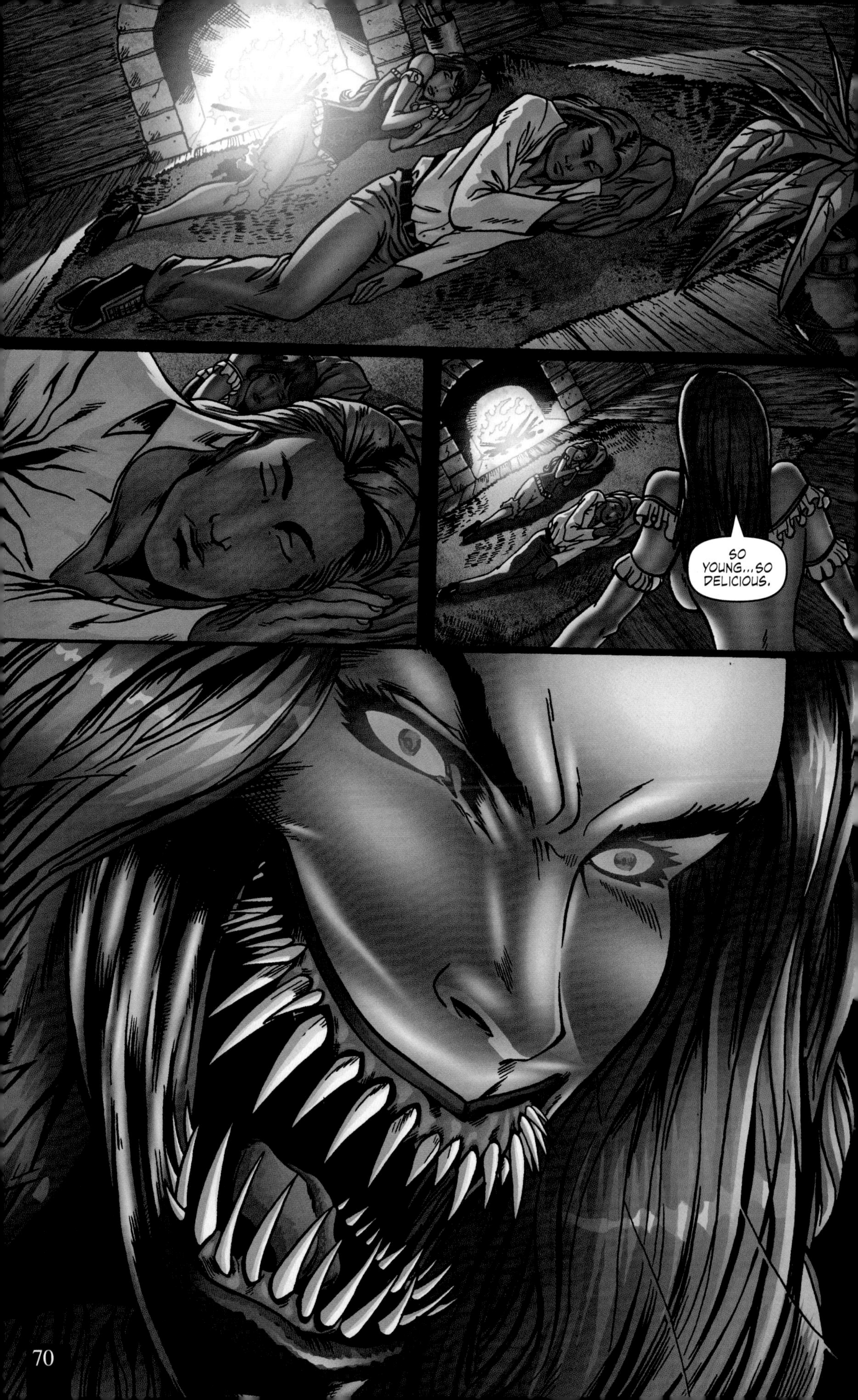
SO YOUNG...SO DELICIOUS.

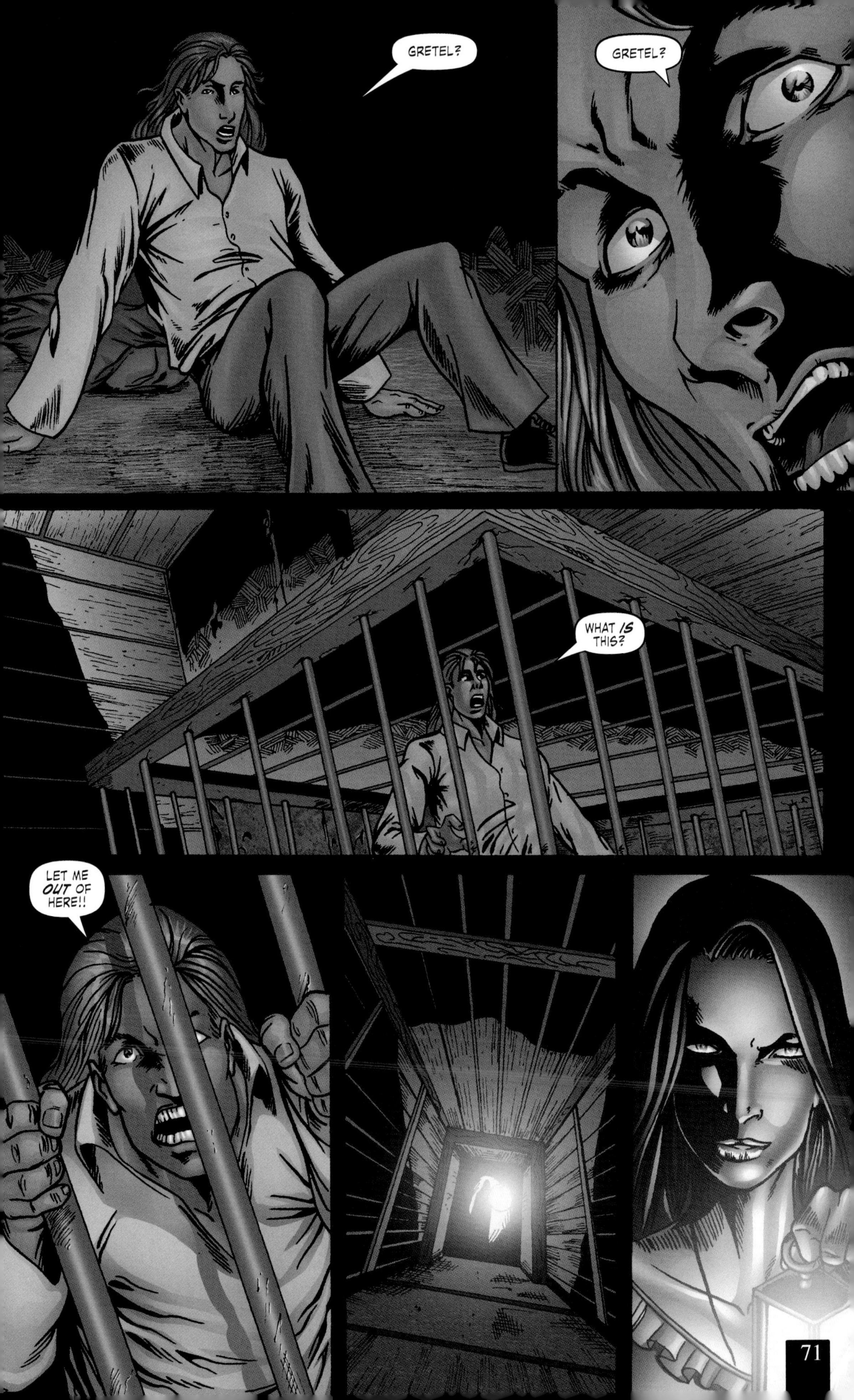
GRETEL?
GRETEL?
WHAT *IS* THIS?
LET ME *OUT* OF HERE!!

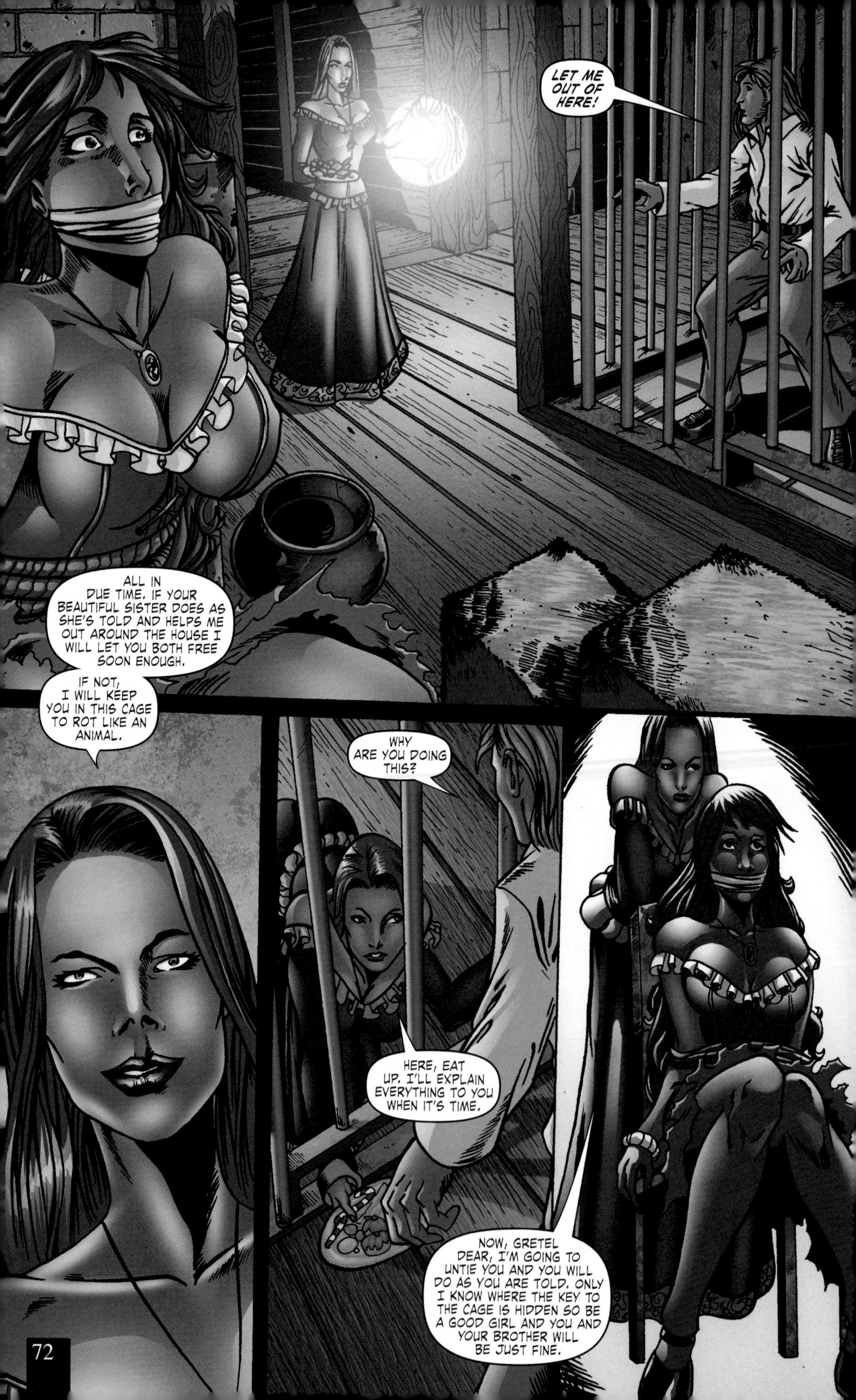
LET ME OUT OF HERE!
ALL IN DUE TIME. IF YOUR BEAUTIFUL SISTER DOES AS SHE'S TOLD AND HELPS ME OUT AROUND THE HOUSE I WILL LET YOU BOTH FREE SOON ENOUGH.
IF NOT, I WILL KEEP YOU IN THIS CAGE TO ROT LIKE AN ANIMAL.
WHY ARE YOU DOING THIS?
HERE, EAT UP. I'LL EXPLAIN EVERYTHING TO YOU WHEN IT'S TIME.
NOW, GRETEL DEAR, I'M GOING TO UNTIE YOU AND YOU WILL DO AS YOU ARE TOLD. ONLY I KNOW WHERE THE KEY TO THE CAGE IS HIDDEN SO BE A GOOD GIRL AND YOU AND YOUR BROTHER WILL BE JUST FINE.

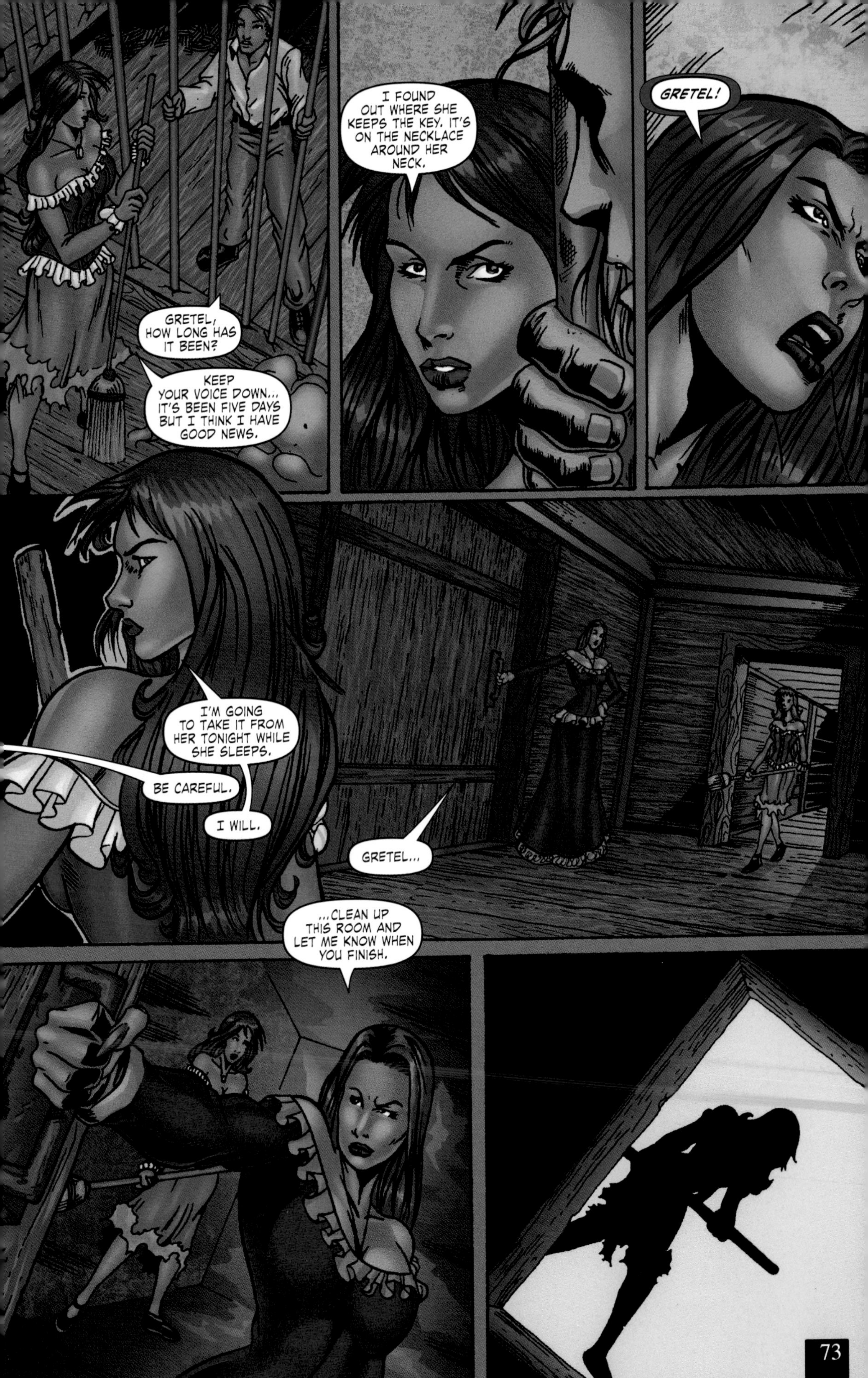
GRETEL, HOW LONG HAS IT BEEN?
KEEP YOUR VOICE DOWN... IT'S BEEN FIVE DAYS BUT I THINK I HAVE GOOD NEWS.
I FOUND OUT WHERE SHE KEEPS THE KEY. IT'S ON THE NECKLACE AROUND HER NECK.
GRETEL!
I'M GOING TO TAKE IT FROM HER TONIGHT WHILE SHE SLEEPS.
BE CAREFUL.
I WILL.
GRETEL...
...CLEAN UP THIS ROOM AND LET ME KNOW WHEN YOU FINISH.

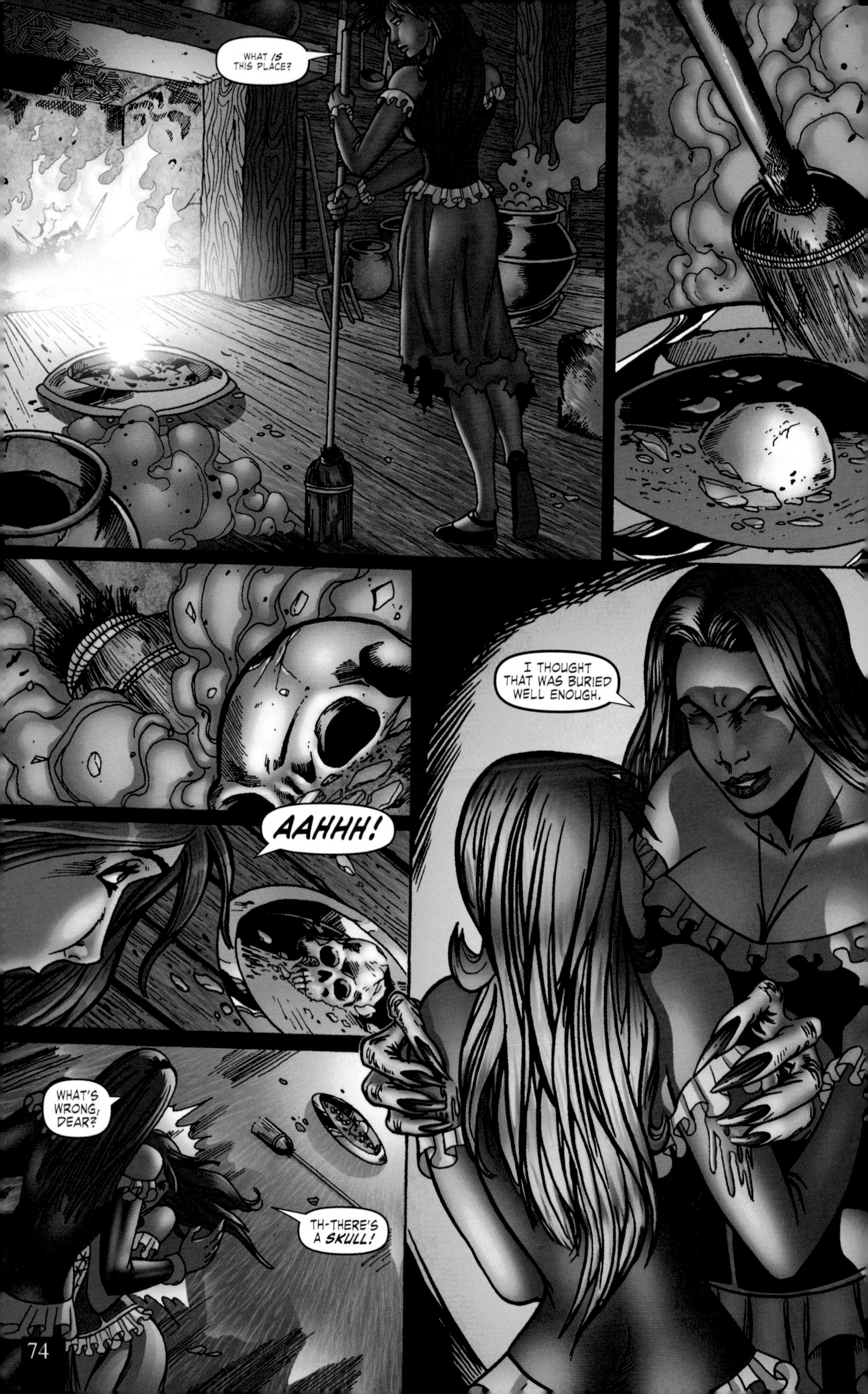
WHAT *IS* THIS PLACE?
I THOUGHT THAT WAS BURIED WELL ENOUGH.
AAHHH!
WHAT'S WRONG, DEAR?
TH-THERE'S A *SKULL*!

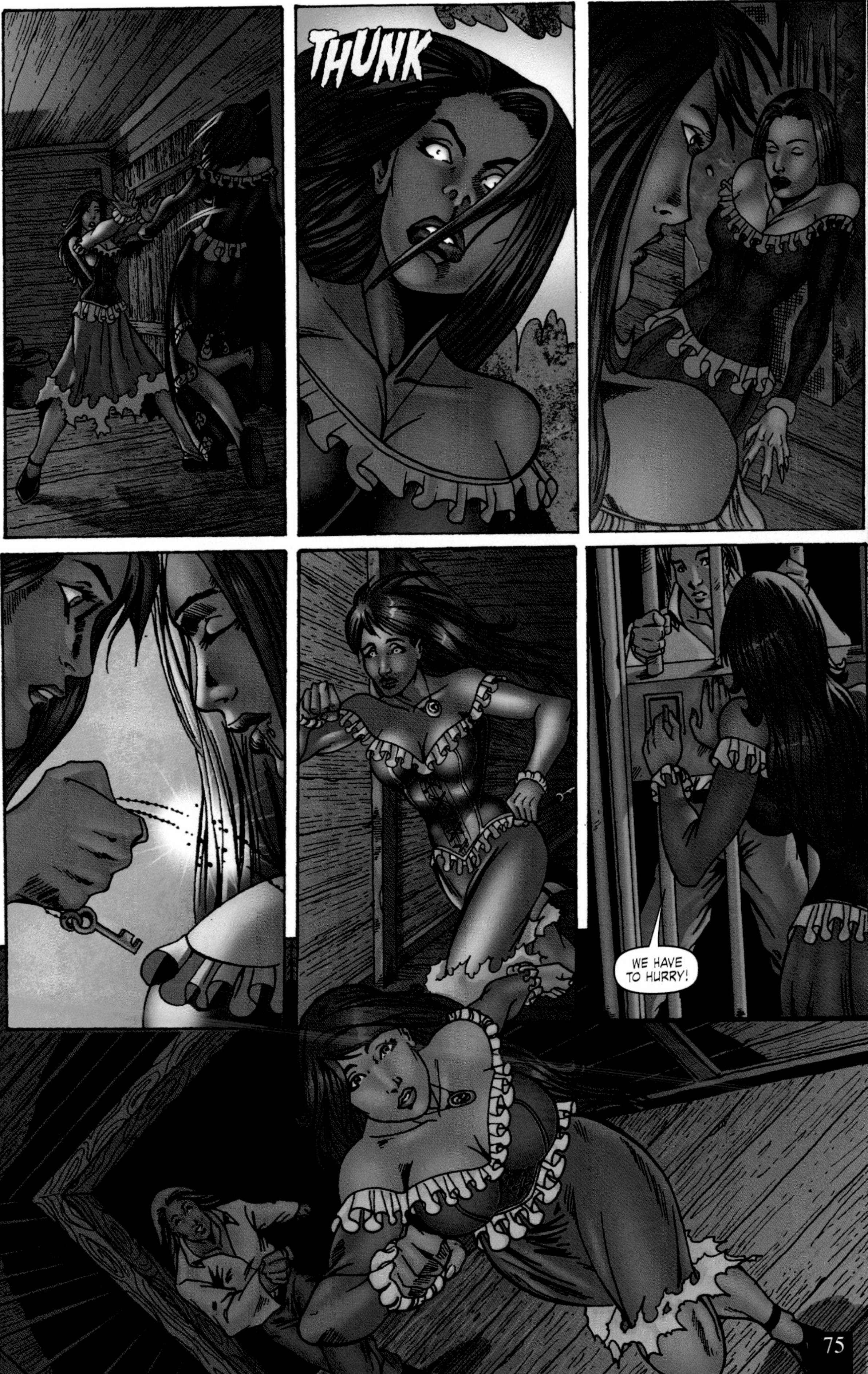
THUNK
WE HAVE TO HURRY!

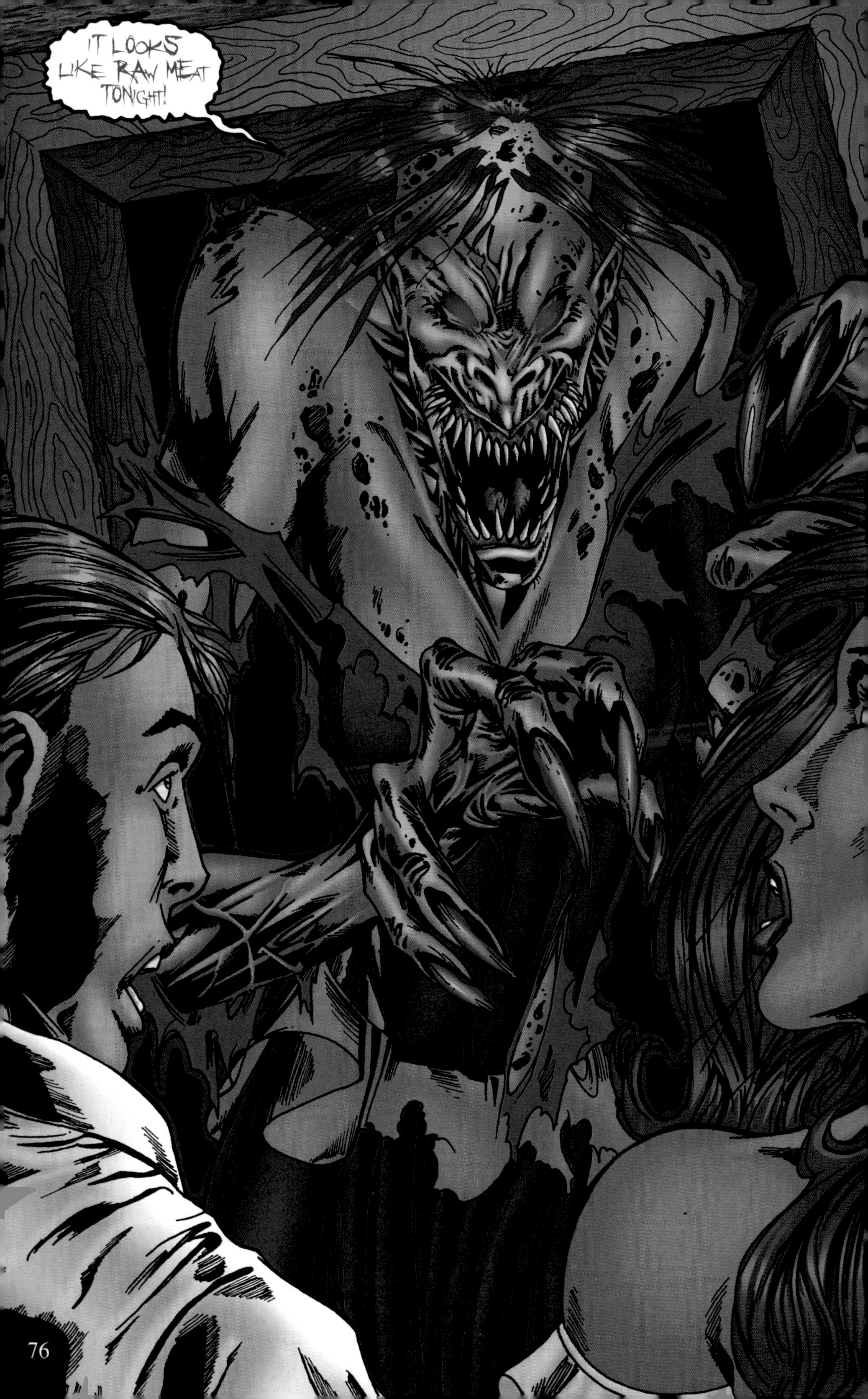
IT LOOKS LIKE RAW MEAT TONIGHT!

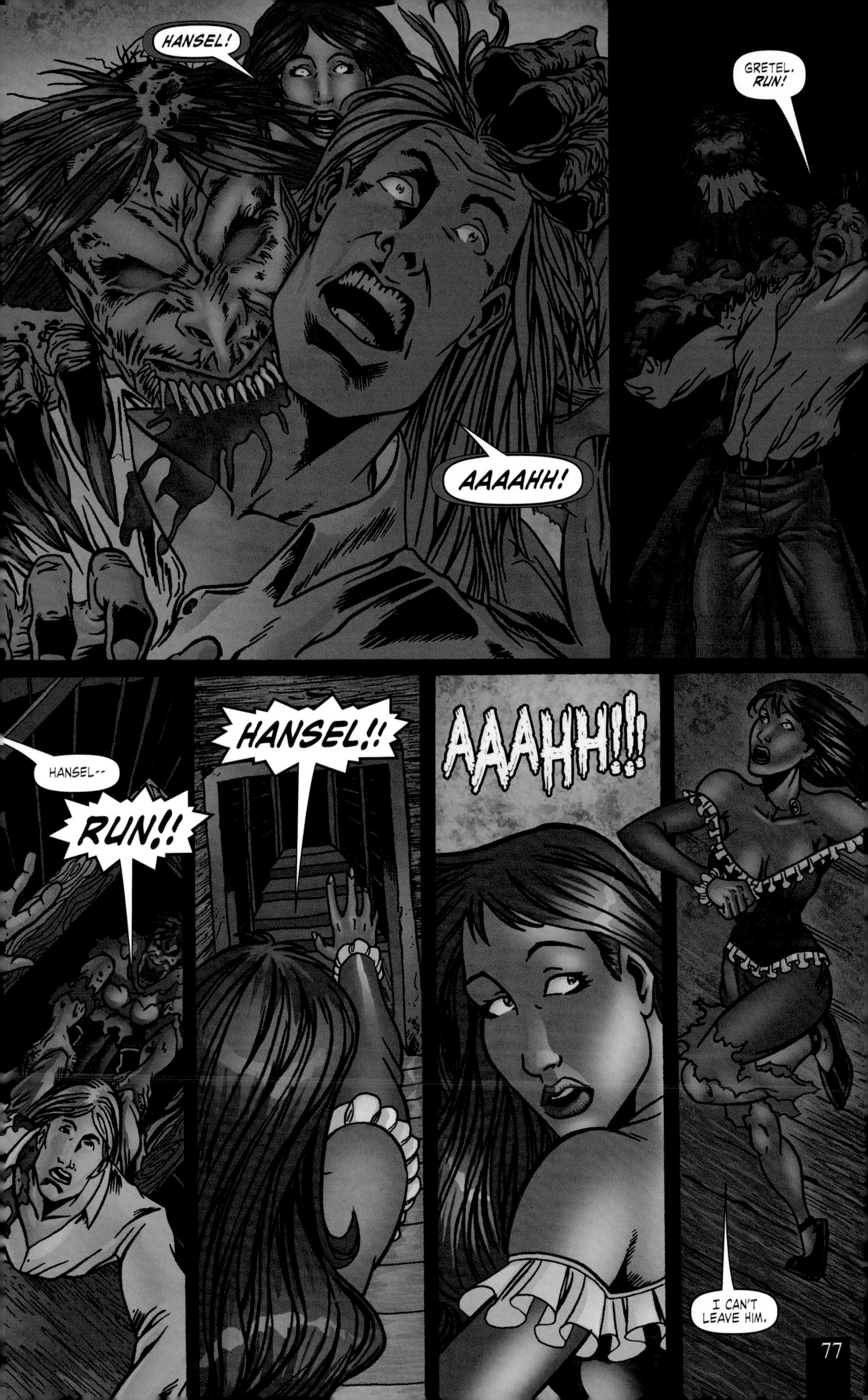
HANSEL!
AAAAHH!
GRETEL. RUN!
HANSEL--
RUN!!
HANSEL!!
AAAHH!!!
I CAN'T LEAVE HIM.

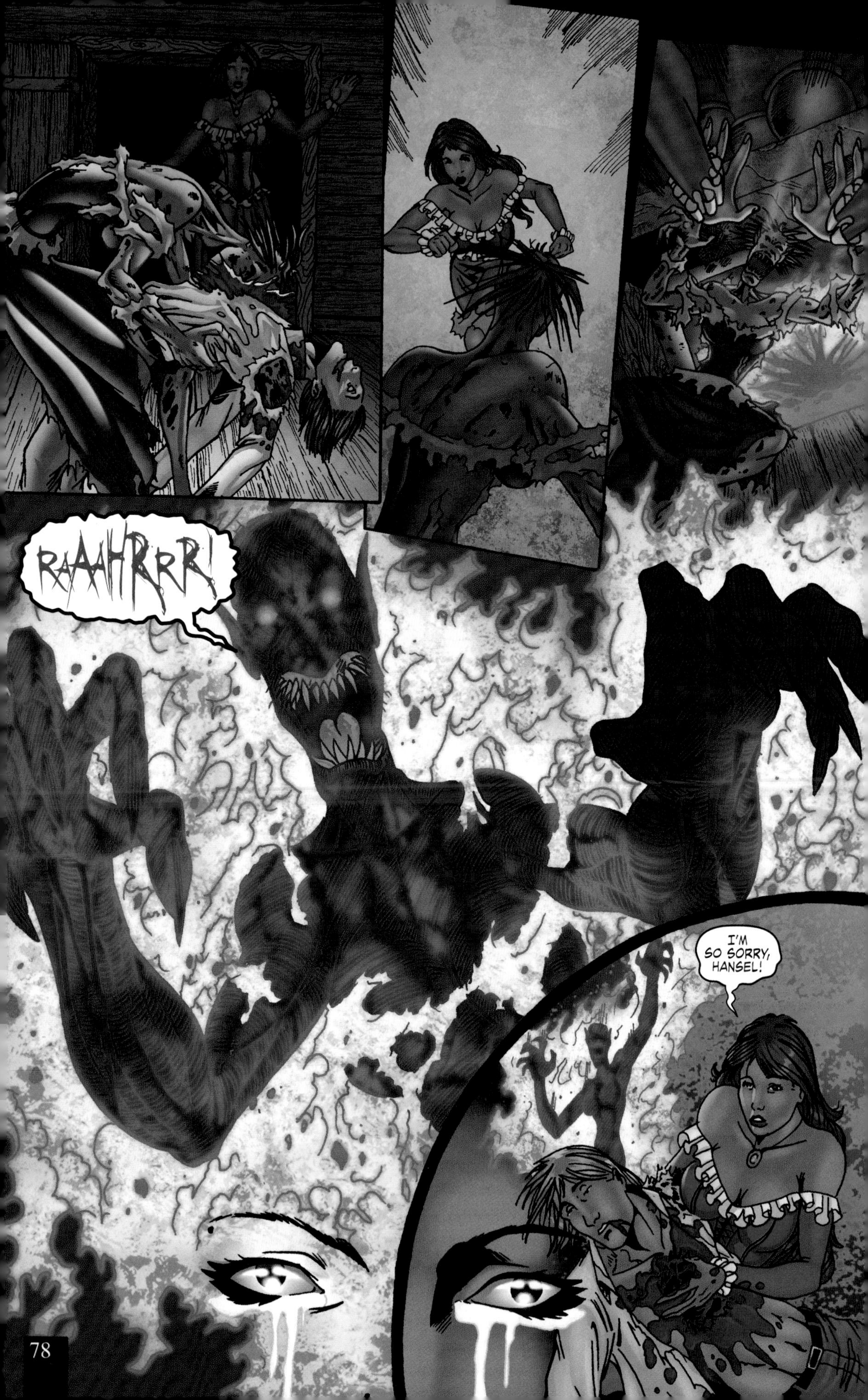
RAAAHRRR!
I'M SO SORRY, HANSEL!

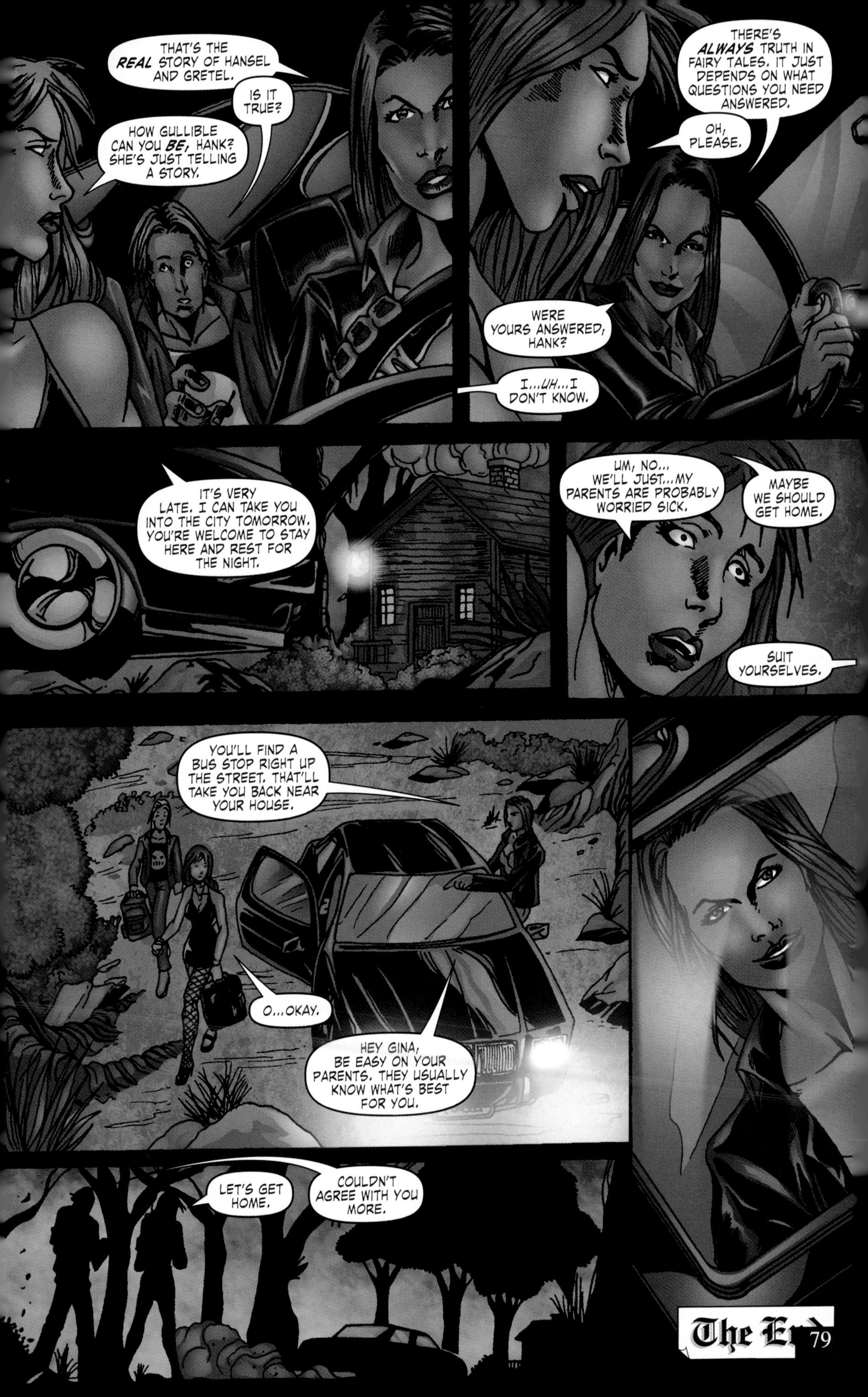
THAT'S THE REAL STORY OF HANSEL AND GRETEL.
IS IT TRUE?
HOW GULLIBLE CAN YOU BE, HANK? SHE'S JUST TELLING A STORY.
THERE'S ALWAYS TRUTH IN FAIRY TALES. IT JUST DEPENDS ON WHAT QUESTIONS YOU NEED ANSWERED.
OH, PLEASE.
WERE YOURS ANSWERED, HANK?
I...UH...I DON'T KNOW.
IT'S VERY LATE. I CAN TAKE YOU INTO THE CITY TOMORROW. YOU'RE WELCOME TO STAY HERE AND REST FOR THE NIGHT.
UM, NO... WE'LL JUST...MY PARENTS ARE PROBABLY WORRIED SICK.
MAYBE WE SHOULD GET HOME.
SUIT YOURSELVES.
YOU'LL FIND A BUS STOP RIGHT UP THE STREET. THAT'LL TAKE YOU BACK NEAR YOUR HOUSE.
O...OKAY.
HEY GINA, BE EASY ON YOUR PARENTS. THEY USUALLY KNOW WHAT'S BEST FOR YOU.
LET'S GET HOME.
COULDN'T AGREE WITH YOU MORE.
The End

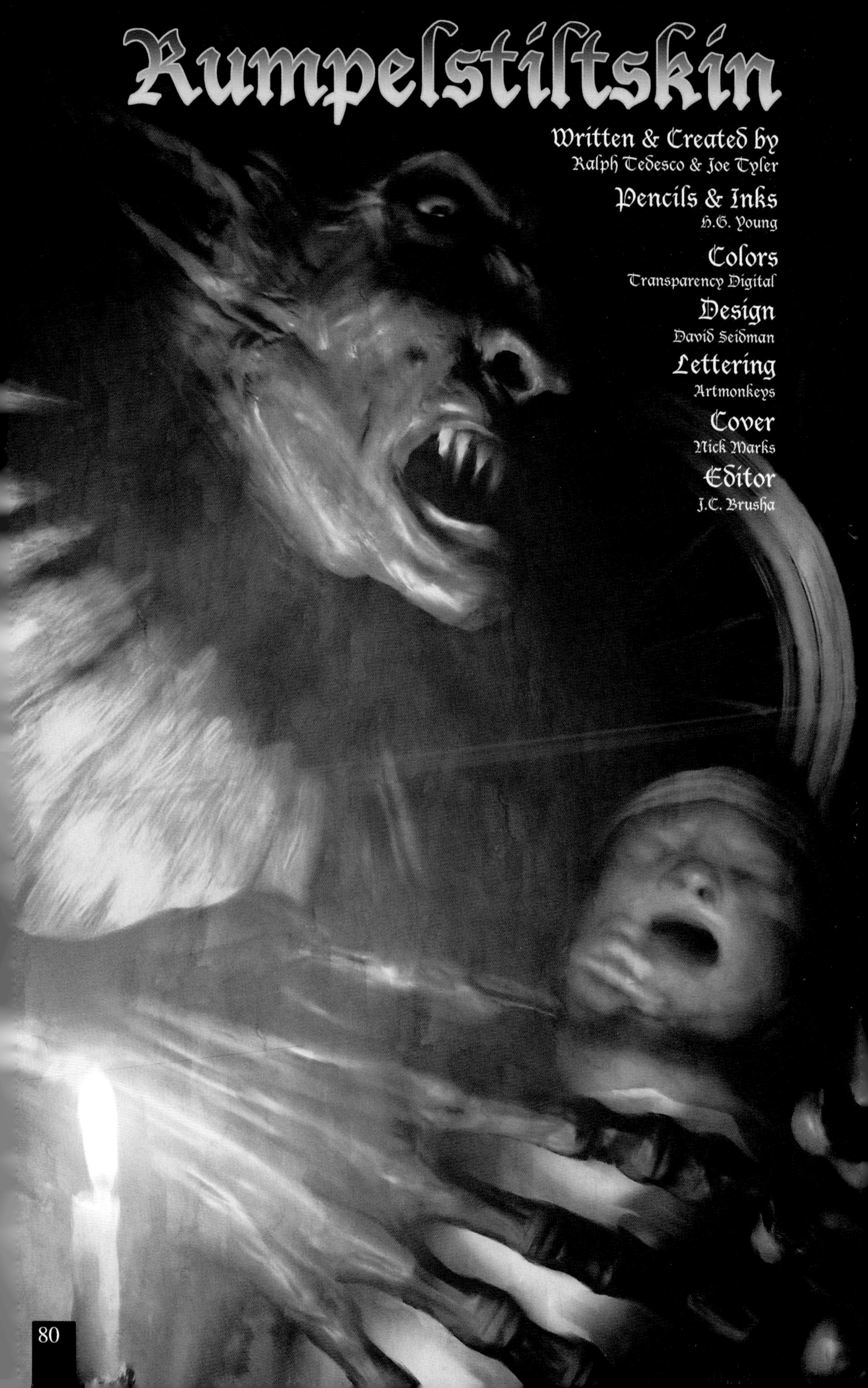
Rumpelstiltskin
Written & Created by
Ralph Tedesco & Joe Tyler
Pencils & Inks
H.G. Young
Colors
Transparency Digital
Design
David Seidman
Lettering
Artmonkeys
Cover
Nick Marks
Editor
J.C. Brusha

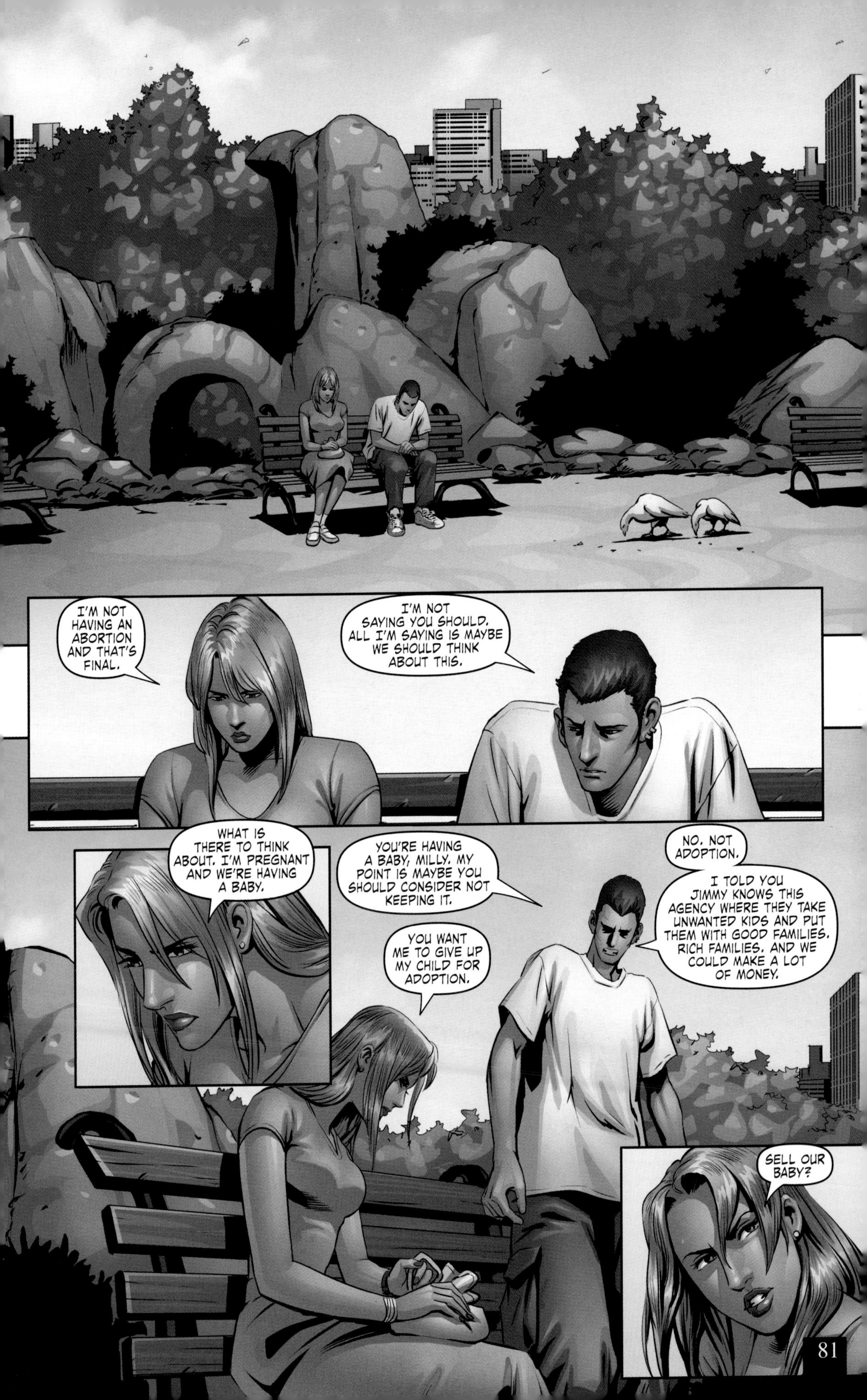
I'M NOT HAVING AN ABORTION AND THAT'S FINAL.
I'M NOT SAYING YOU SHOULD. ALL I'M SAYING IS MAYBE WE SHOULD THINK ABOUT THIS.
WHAT IS THERE TO THINK ABOUT. I'M PREGNANT AND WE'RE HAVING A BABY.
YOU'RE HAVING A BABY, MILLY. MY POINT IS MAYBE YOU SHOULD CONSIDER NOT KEEPING IT.
YOU WANT ME TO GIVE UP MY CHILD FOR ADOPTION.
NO. NOT ADOPTION.
I TOLD YOU JIMMY KNOWS THIS AGENCY WHERE THEY TAKE UNWANTED KIDS AND PUT THEM WITH GOOD FAMILIES. RICH FAMILIES. AND WE COULD MAKE A LOT OF MONEY.
SELL OUR BABY?

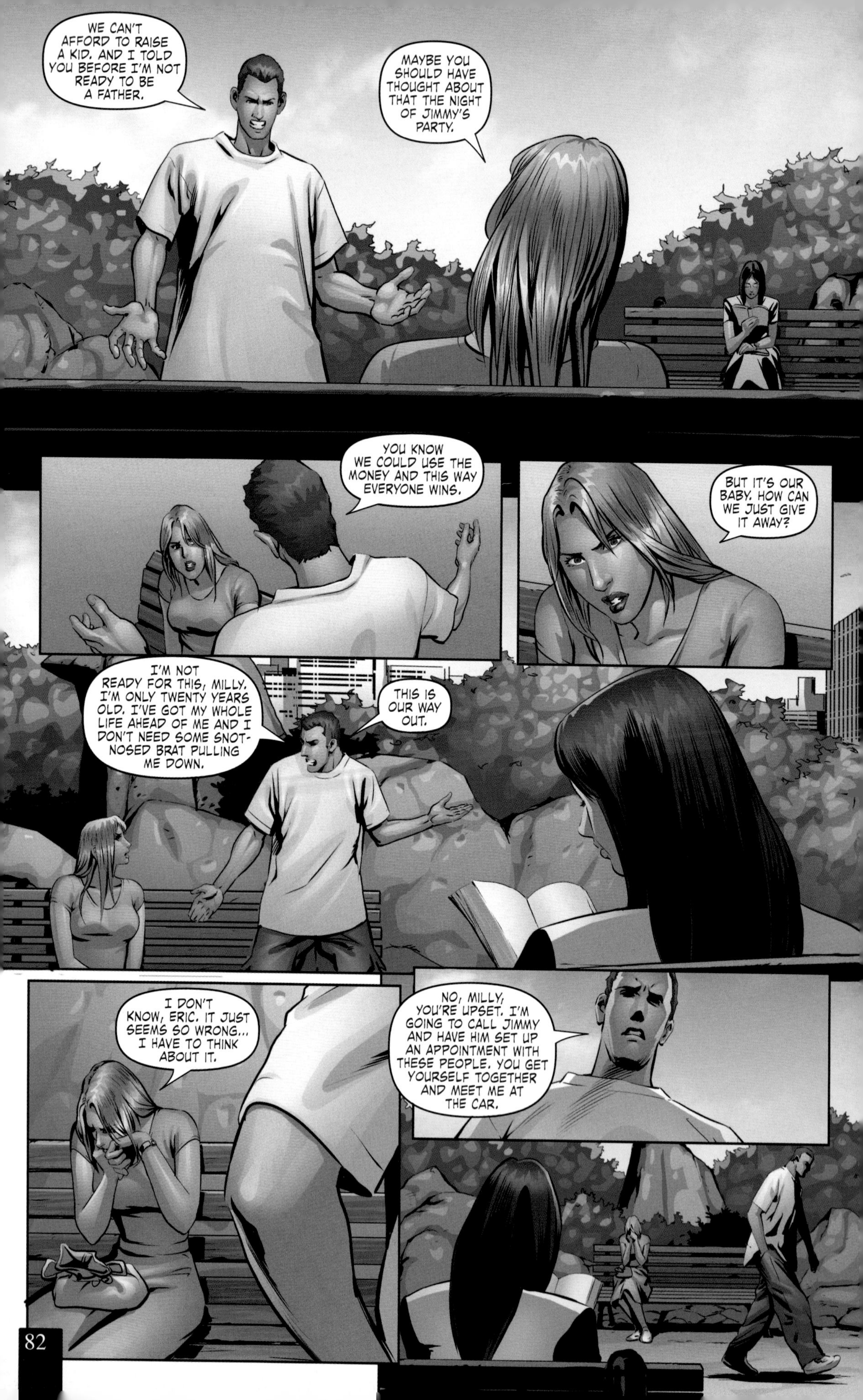

WE CAN'T AFFORD TO RAISE A KID. AND I TOLD YOU BEFORE I'M NOT READY TO BE A FATHER.
MAYBE YOU SHOULD HAVE THOUGHT ABOUT THAT THE NIGHT OF JIMMY'S PARTY.
YOU KNOW WE COULD USE THE MONEY AND THIS WAY EVERYONE WINS.
BUT IT'S OUR BABY. HOW CAN WE JUST GIVE IT AWAY?
I'M NOT READY FOR THIS, MILLY. I'M ONLY TWENTY YEARS OLD. I'VE GOT MY WHOLE LIFE AHEAD OF ME AND I DON'T NEED SOME SNOT-NOSED BRAT PULLING ME DOWN.
THIS IS OUR WAY OUT.
I DON'T KNOW, ERIC. IT JUST SEEMS SO WRONG... I HAVE TO THINK ABOUT IT.
NO, MILLY, YOU'RE UPSET. I'M GOING TO CALL JIMMY AND HAVE HIM SET UP AN APPOINTMENT WITH THESE PEOPLE. YOU GET YOURSELF TOGETHER AND MEET ME AT THE CAR.

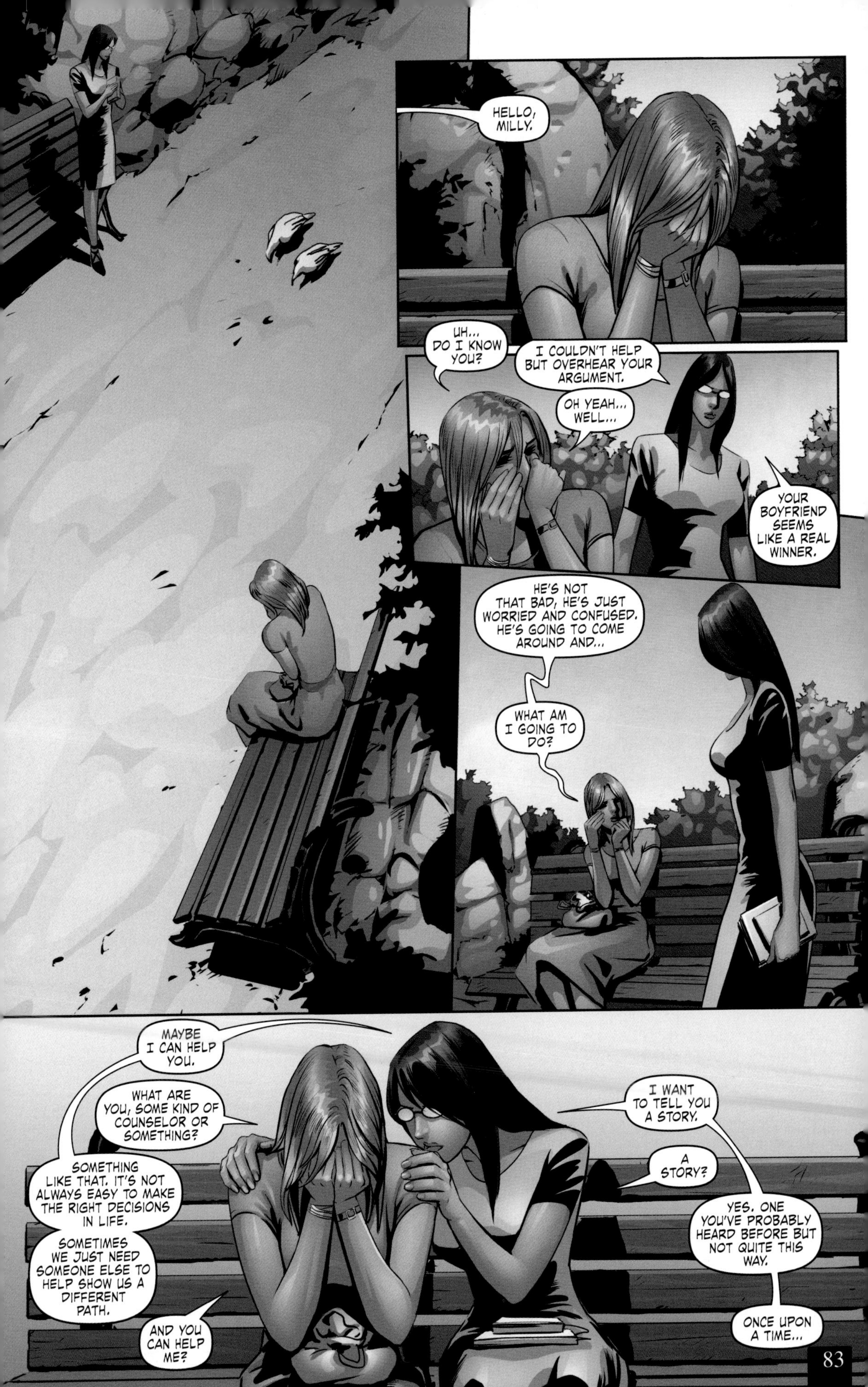
HELLO, MILLY.
UH... DO I KNOW YOU?
I COULDN'T HELP BUT OVERHEAR YOUR ARGUMENT.
OH YEAH... WELL...
YOUR BOYFRIEND SEEMS LIKE A REAL WINNER.
HE'S NOT THAT BAD, HE'S JUST WORRIED AND CONFUSED. HE'S GOING TO COME AROUND AND...
WHAT AM I GOING TO DO?
MAYBE I CAN HELP YOU.
WHAT ARE YOU, SOME KIND OF COUNSELOR OR SOMETHING?
SOMETHING LIKE THAT. IT'S NOT ALWAYS EASY TO MAKE THE RIGHT DECISIONS IN LIFE.
SOMETIMES WE JUST NEED SOMEONE ELSE TO HELP SHOW US A DIFFERENT PATH.
AND YOU CAN HELP ME?
I WANT TO TELL YOU A STORY.
A STORY?
YES. ONE YOU'VE PROBABLY HEARD BEFORE BUT NOT QUITE THIS WAY.
ONCE UPON A TIME...

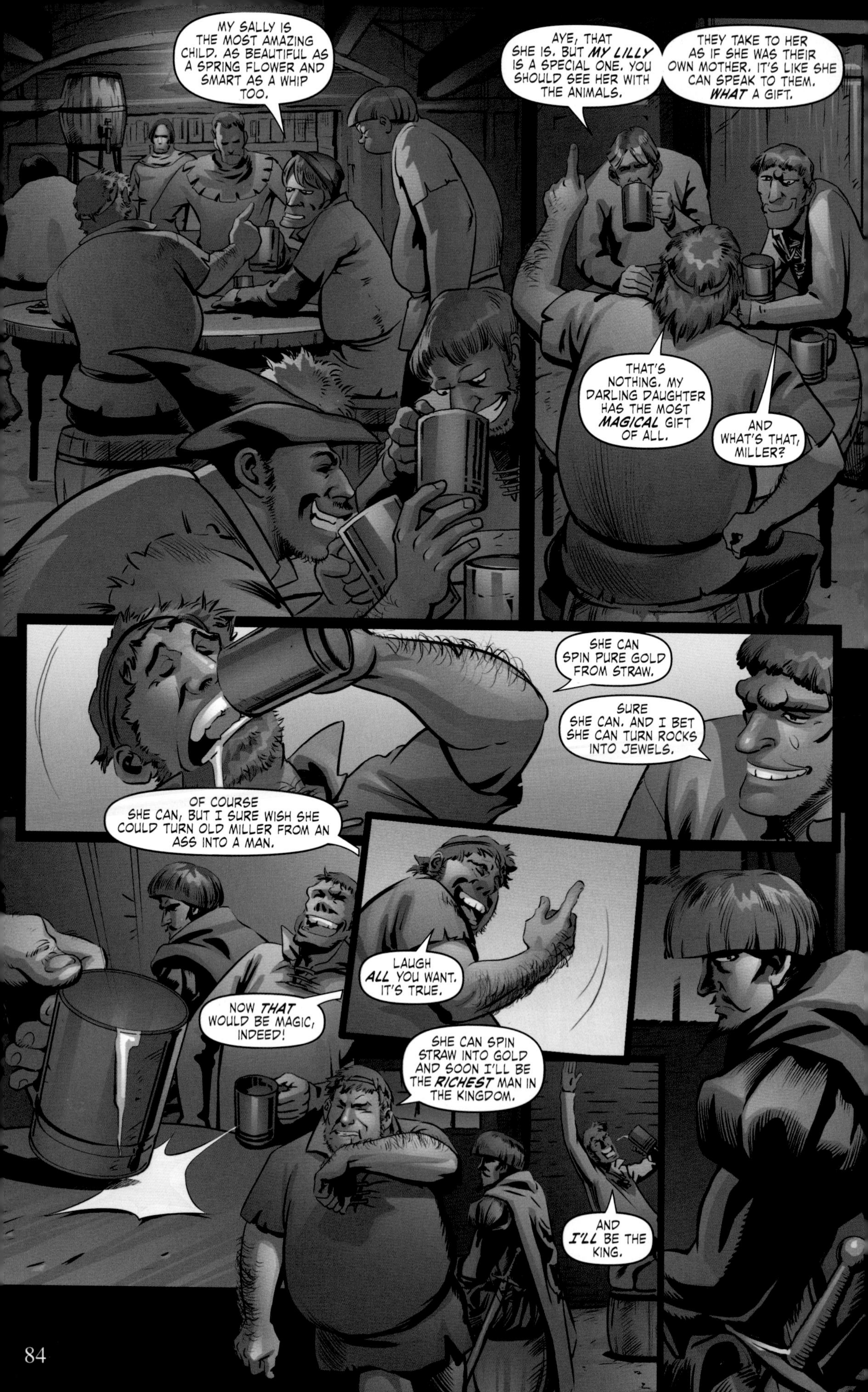
MY SALLY IS THE MOST AMAZING CHILD. AS BEAUTIFUL AS A SPRING FLOWER AND SMART AS A WHIP TOO.
AYE, THAT SHE IS. BUT MY LILLY IS A SPECIAL ONE. YOU SHOULD SEE HER WITH THE ANIMALS.
THEY TAKE TO HER AS IF SHE WAS THEIR OWN MOTHER. IT'S LIKE SHE CAN SPEAK TO THEM. WHAT A GIFT.
THAT'S NOTHING. MY DARLING DAUGHTER HAS THE MOST MAGICAL GIFT OF ALL.
AND WHAT'S THAT, MILLER?
SHE CAN SPIN PURE GOLD FROM STRAW.
SURE SHE CAN. AND I BET SHE CAN TURN ROCKS INTO JEWELS.
OF COURSE SHE CAN, BUT I SURE WISH SHE COULD TURN OLD MILLER FROM AN ASS INTO A MAN.
LAUGH ALL YOU WANT. IT'S TRUE.
NOW THAT WOULD BE MAGIC, INDEED!
SHE CAN SPIN STRAW INTO GOLD AND SOON I'LL BE THE RICHEST MAN IN THE KINGDOM.
AND I'LL BE THE KING.

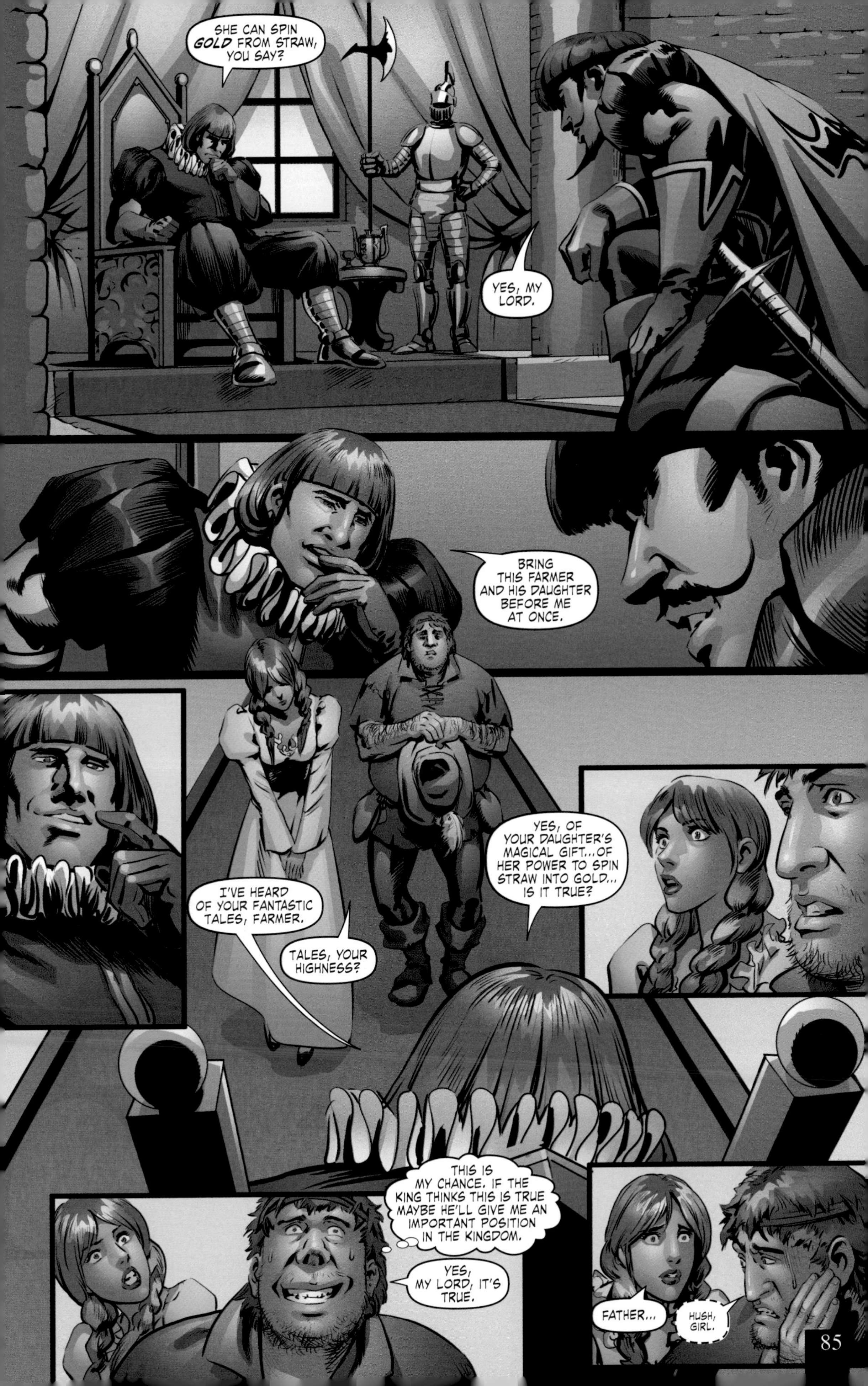
SHE CAN SPIN GOLD FROM STRAW, YOU SAY?
YES, MY LORD.
BRING THIS FARMER AND HIS DAUGHTER BEFORE ME AT ONCE.
I'VE HEARD OF YOUR FANTASTIC TALES, FARMER.
TALES, YOUR HIGHNESS?
YES, OF YOUR DAUGHTER'S MAGICAL GIFT...OF HER POWER TO SPIN STRAW INTO GOLD... IS IT TRUE?
THIS IS MY CHANCE. IF THE KING THINKS THIS IS TRUE MAYBE HE'LL GIVE ME AN IMPORTANT POSITION IN THE KINGDOM.
YES, MY LORD, IT'S TRUE.
FATHER...
HUSH, GIRL.

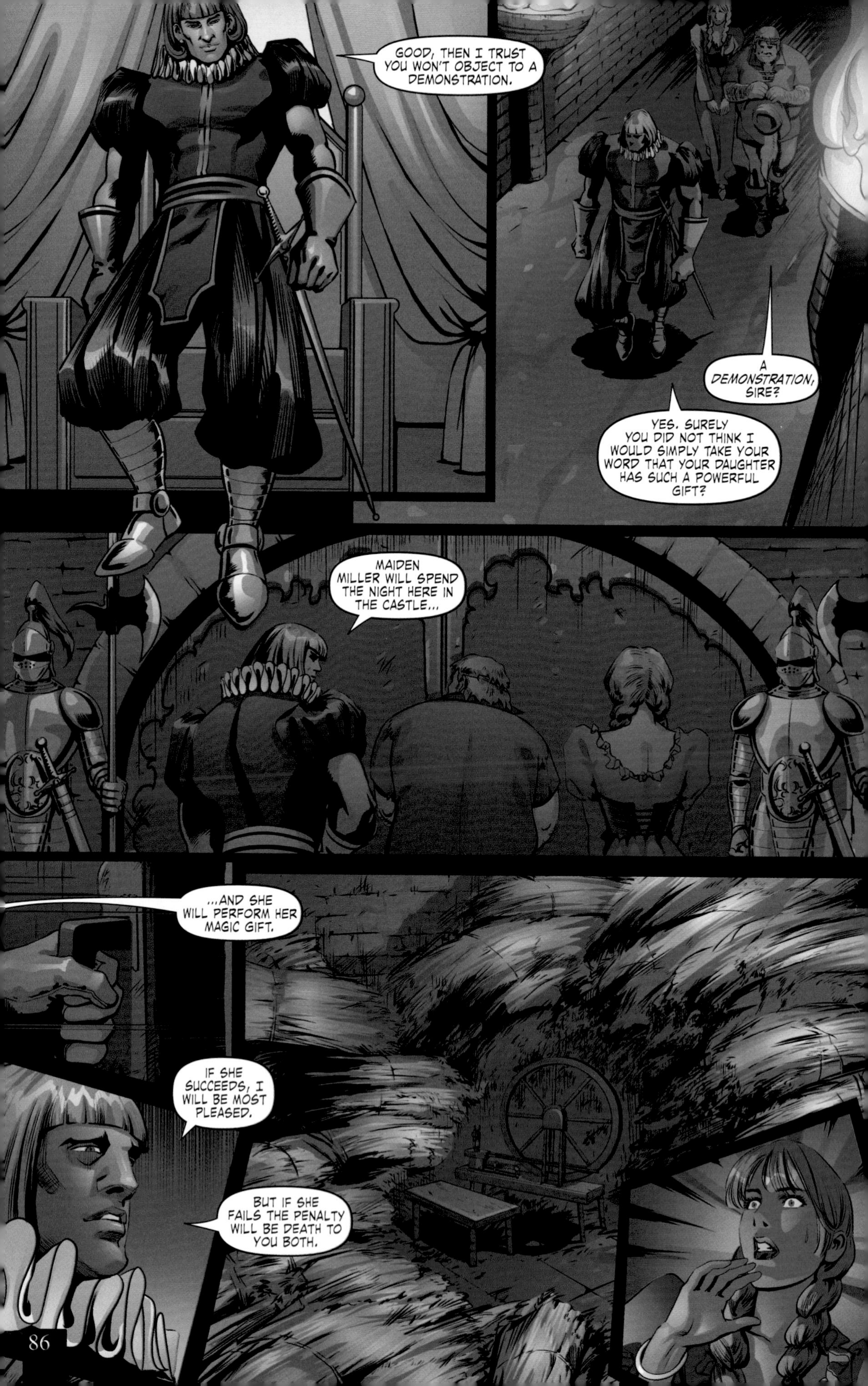
GOOD, THEN I TRUST YOU WON'T OBJECT TO A DEMONSTRATION.
A *DEMONSTRATION,* SIRE?
YES. SURELY YOU DID NOT THINK I WOULD SIMPLY TAKE YOUR WORD THAT YOUR DAUGHTER HAS SUCH A POWERFUL GIFT?
MAIDEN MILLER WILL SPEND THE NIGHT HERE IN THE CASTLE...
...AND SHE WILL PERFORM HER MAGIC GIFT.
IF SHE SUCCEEDS, I WILL BE MOST PLEASED.
BUT IF SHE FAILS THE PENALTY WILL BE DEATH TO YOU BOTH.

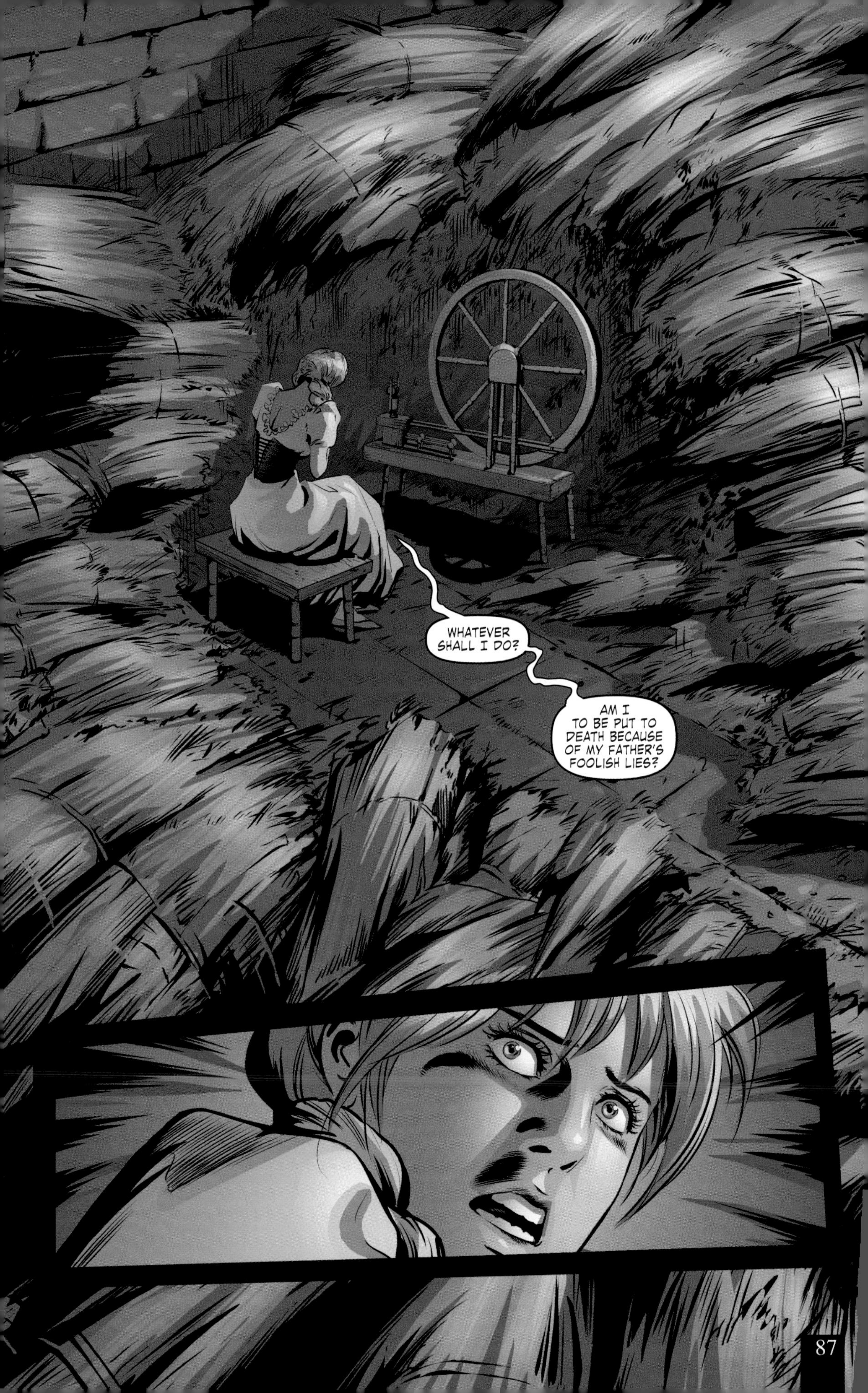
WHATEVER SHALL I DO?
AM I TO BE PUT TO DEATH BECAUSE OF MY FATHER'S FOOLISH LIES?

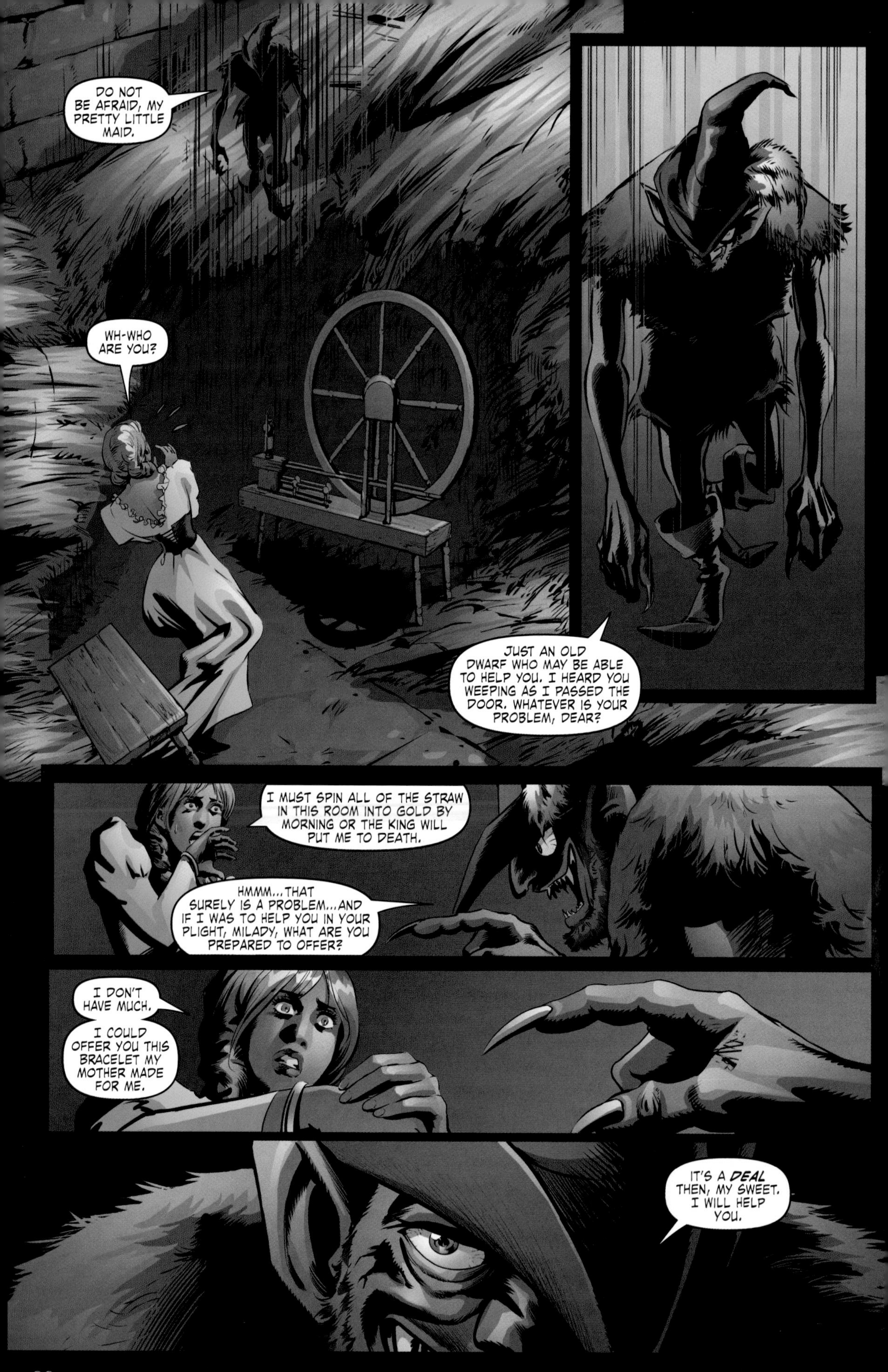
DO NOT BE AFRAID, MY PRETTY LITTLE MAID.
WH-WHO ARE YOU?
JUST AN OLD DWARF WHO MAY BE ABLE TO HELP YOU. I HEARD YOU WEEPING AS I PASSED THE DOOR. WHATEVER IS YOUR PROBLEM, DEAR?
I MUST SPIN ALL OF THE STRAW IN THIS ROOM INTO GOLD BY MORNING OR THE KING WILL PUT ME TO DEATH.
HMMM...THAT SURELY IS A PROBLEM...AND IF I WAS TO HELP YOU IN YOUR PLIGHT, MILADY, WHAT ARE YOU PREPARED TO OFFER?
I DON'T HAVE MUCH.
I COULD OFFER YOU THIS BRACELET MY MOTHER MADE FOR ME.
IT'S A DEAL THEN, MY SWEET. I WILL HELP YOU.

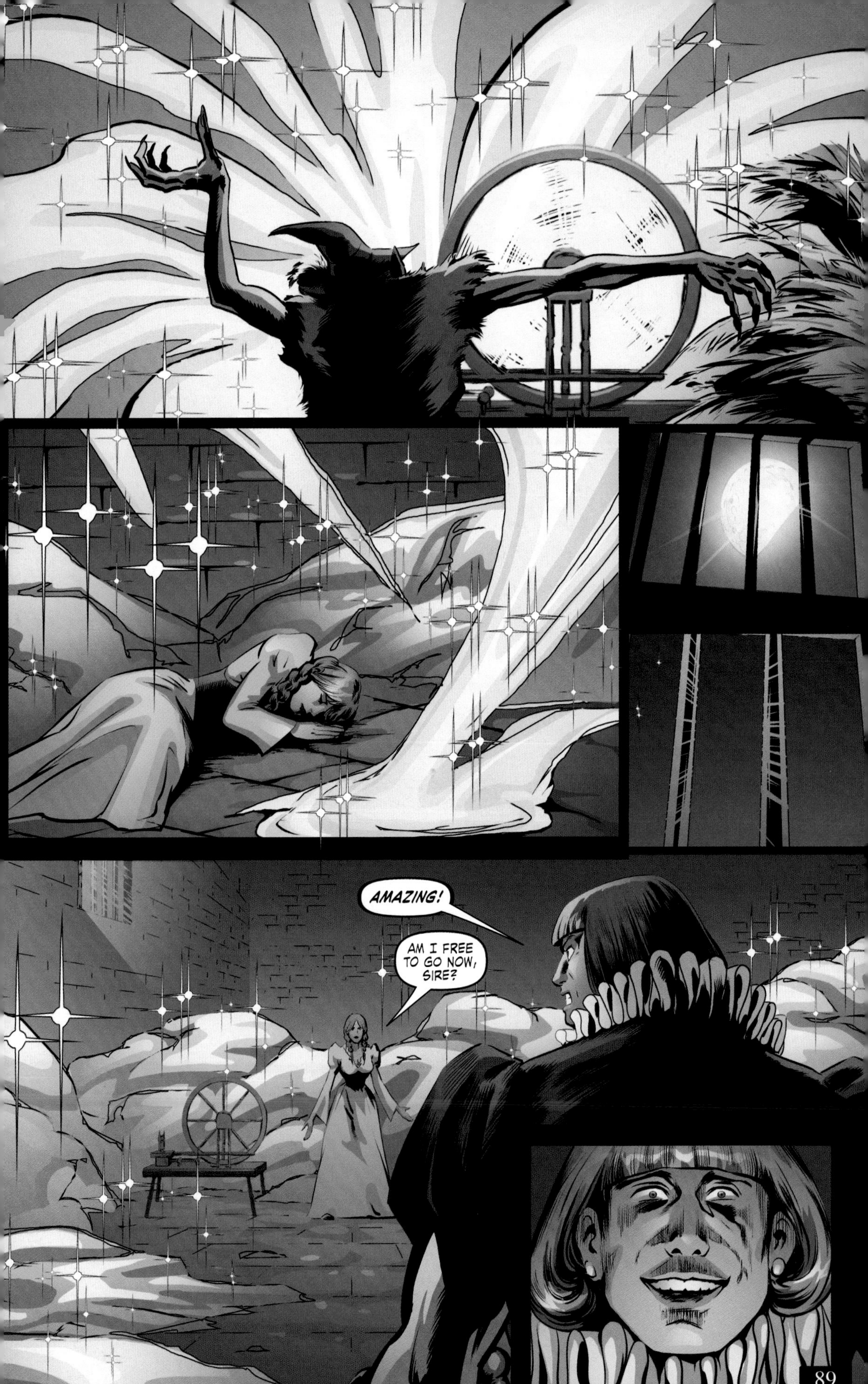
AMAZING!
AM I FREE TO GO NOW, SIRE?

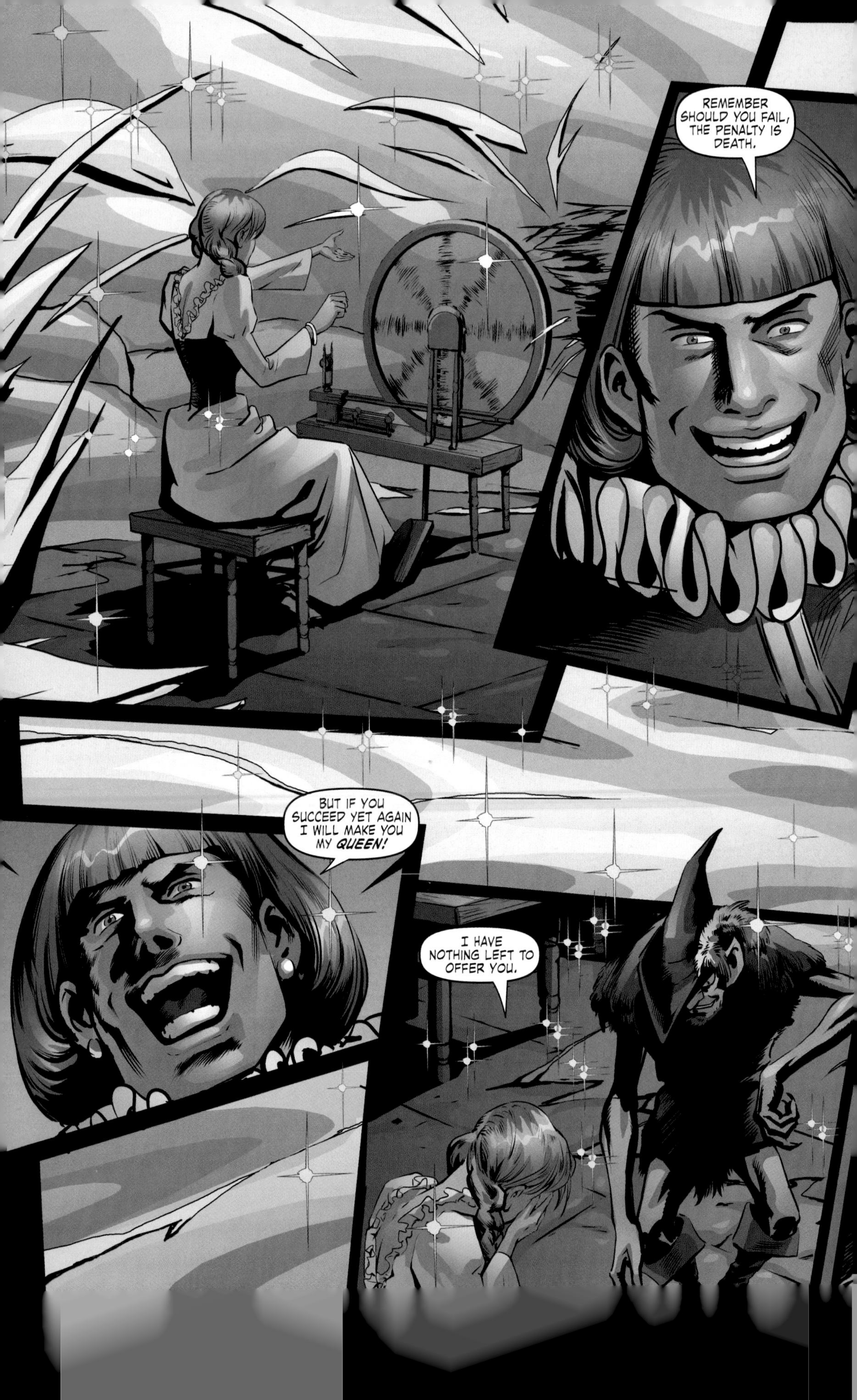
REMEMBER SHOULD YOU FAIL, THE PENALTY IS DEATH.
BUT IF YOU SUCCEED YET AGAIN I WILL MAKE YOU MY *QUEEN!*
I HAVE NOTHING LEFT TO OFFER YOU.

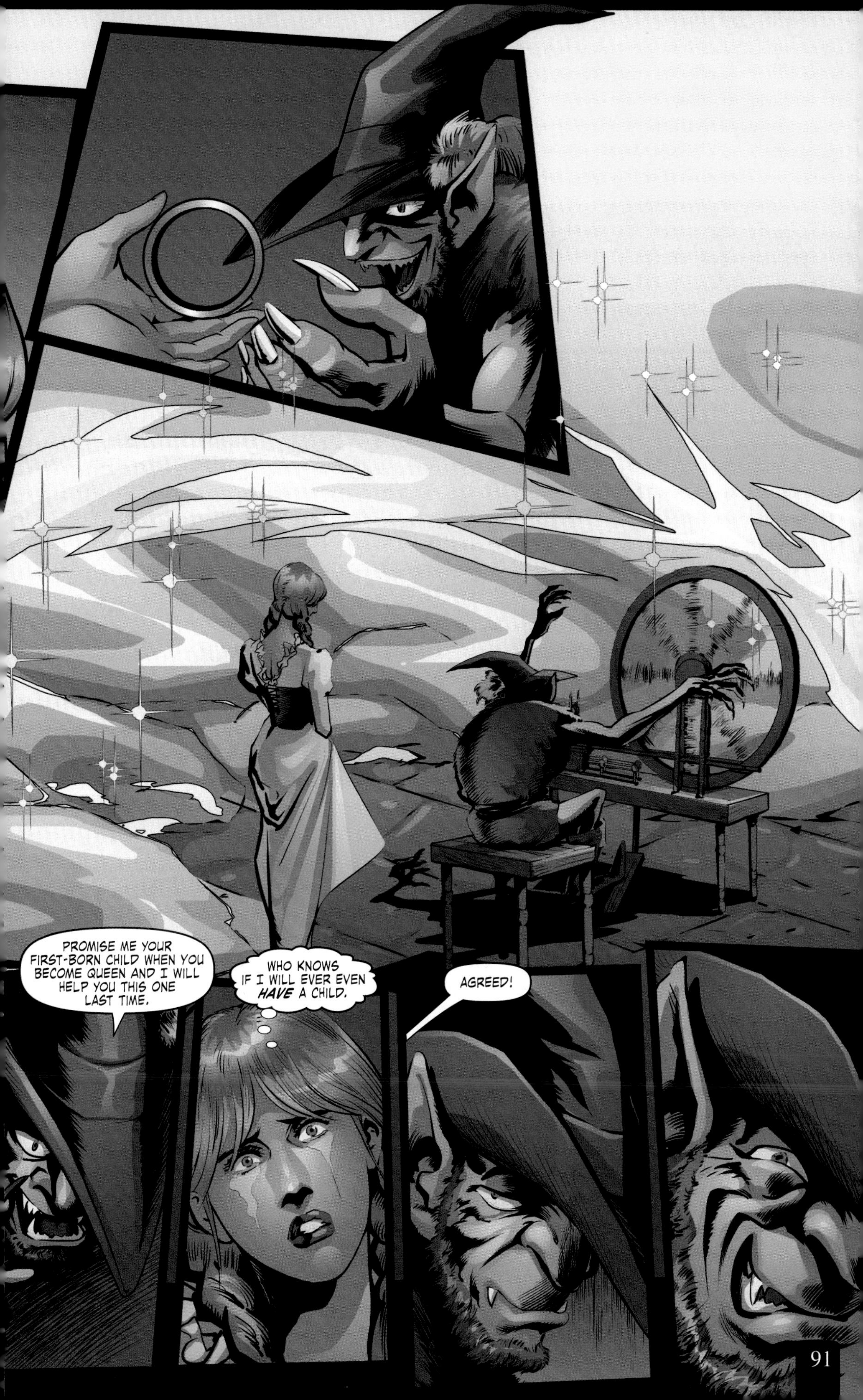
PROMISE ME YOUR FIRST-BORN CHILD WHEN YOU BECOME QUEEN AND I WILL HELP YOU THIS ONE LAST TIME.
WHO KNOWS IF I WILL EVER EVEN HAVE A CHILD.
AGREED!

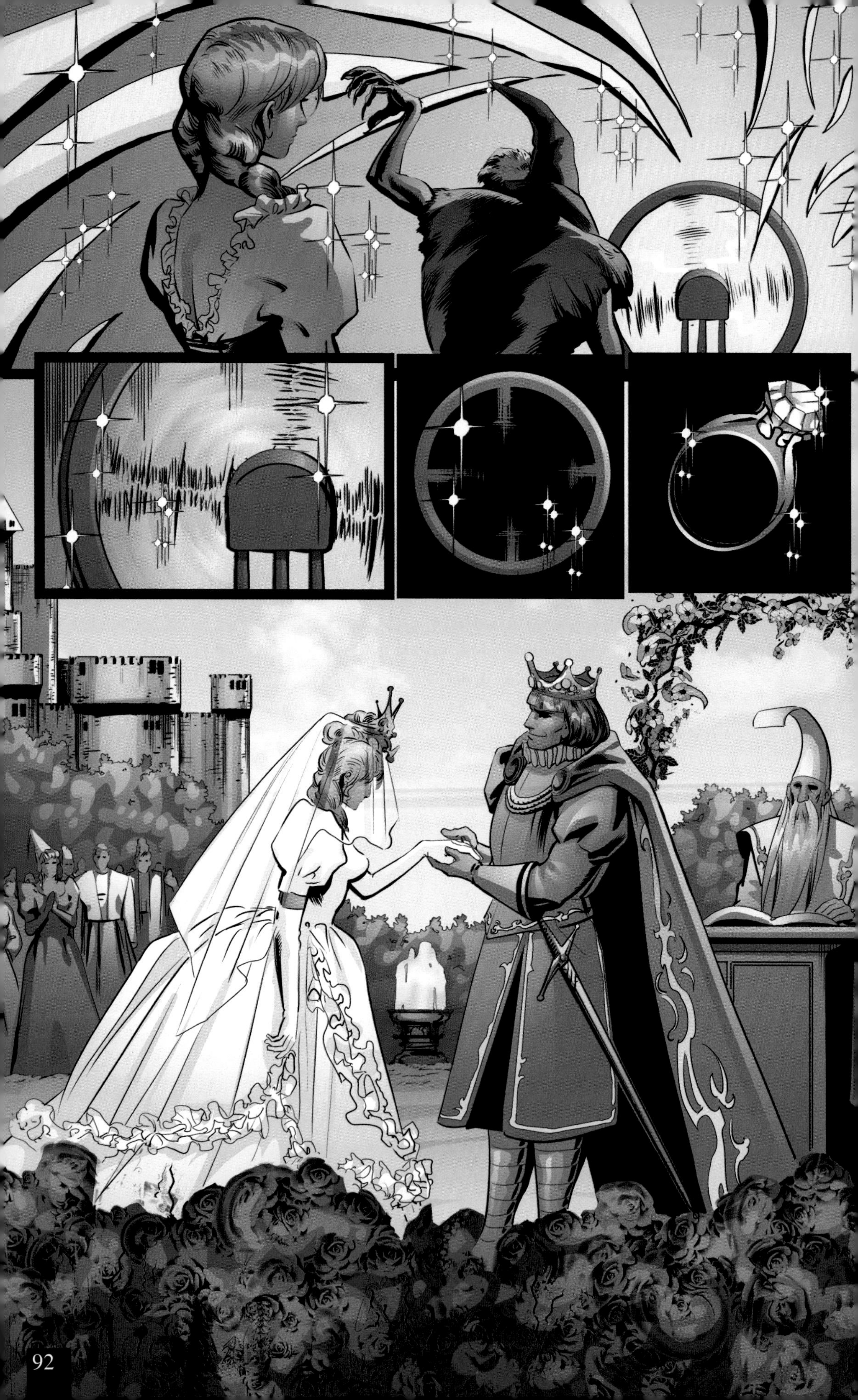

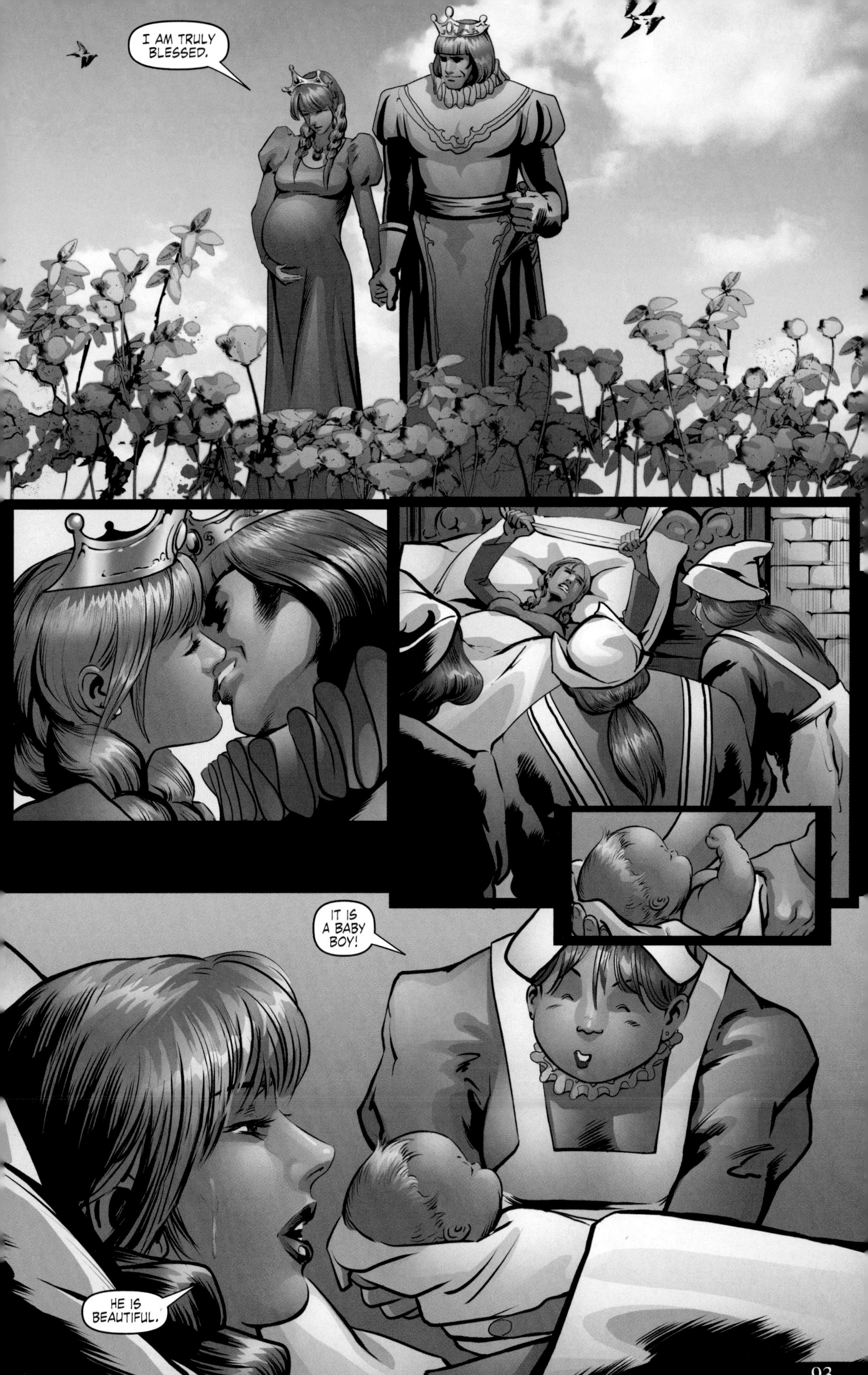
I AM TRULY BLESSED.
IT IS A BABY BOY!
HE IS BEAUTIFUL.

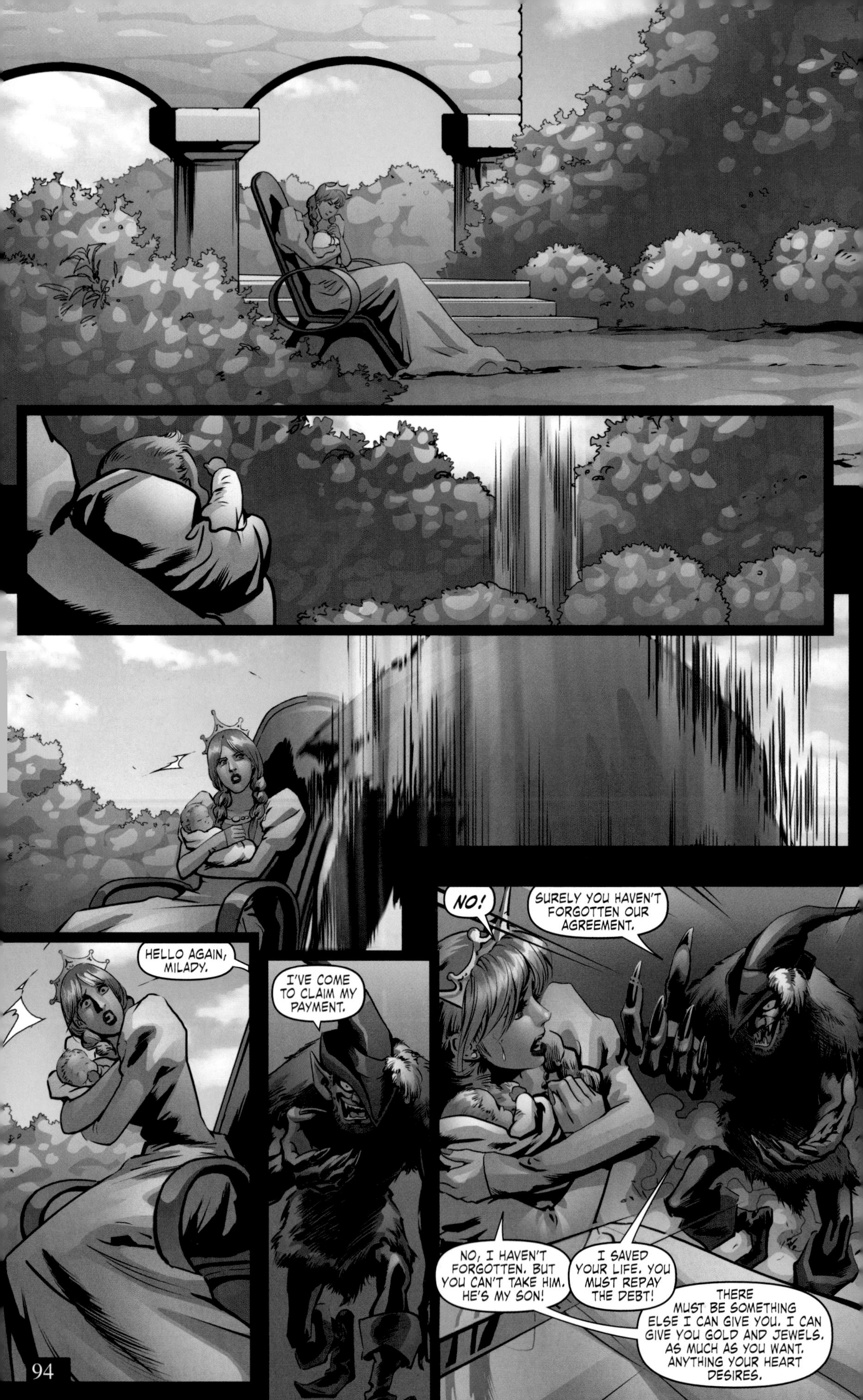

HELLO AGAIN, MILADY.
I'VE COME TO CLAIM MY PAYMENT.
NO!
SURELY YOU HAVEN'T FORGOTTEN OUR AGREEMENT.
NO, I HAVEN'T FORGOTTEN. BUT YOU CAN'T TAKE HIM. HE'S MY SON!
I SAVED YOUR LIFE. YOU MUST REPAY THE DEBT!
THERE MUST BE SOMETHING ELSE I CAN GIVE YOU. I CAN GIVE YOU GOLD AND JEWELS. AS MUCH AS YOU WANT. ANYTHING YOUR HEART DESIRES.

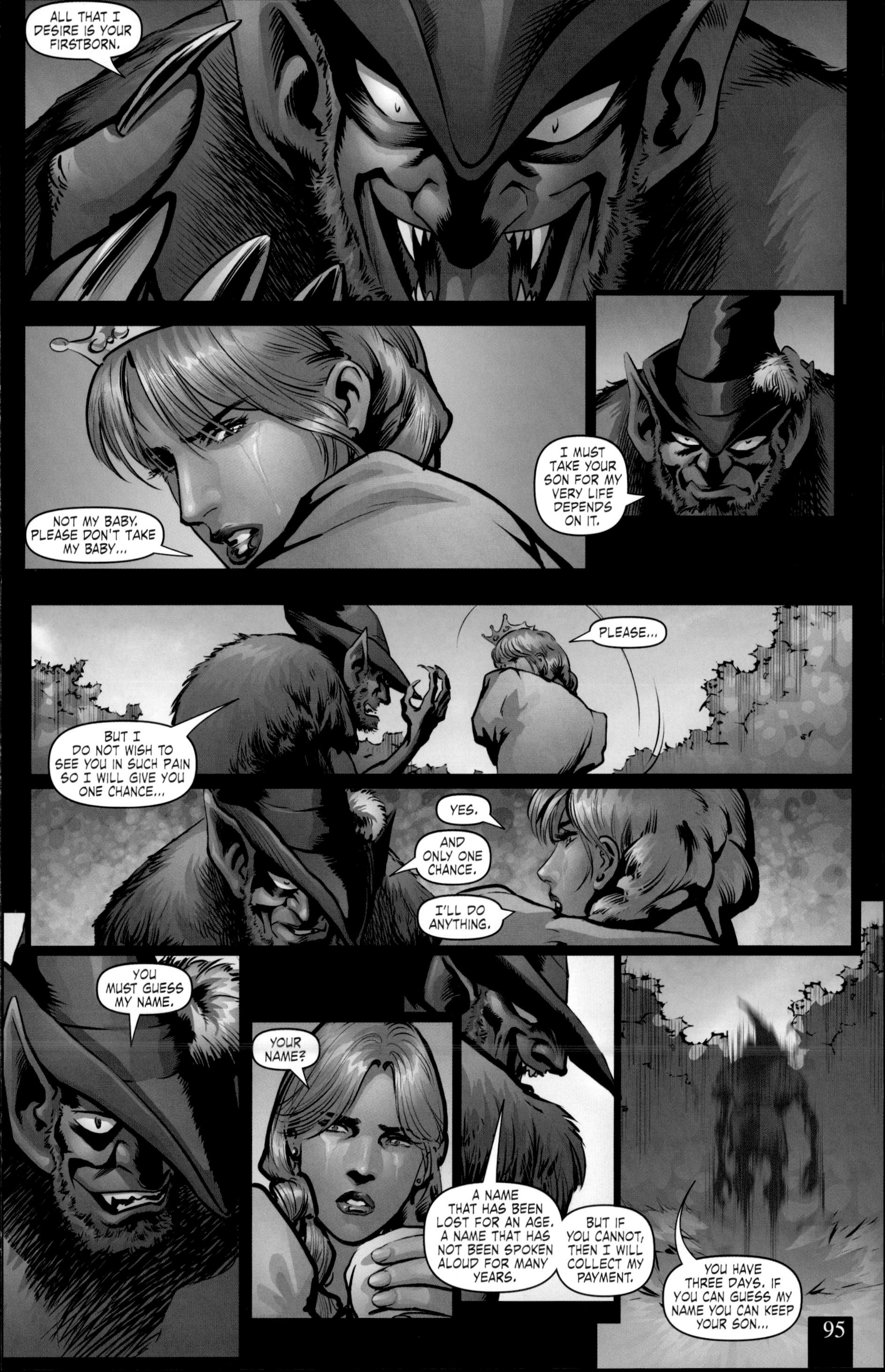
ALL THAT I DESIRE IS YOUR FIRSTBORN.
NOT MY BABY. PLEASE DON'T TAKE MY BABY...
I MUST TAKE YOUR SON FOR MY VERY LIFE DEPENDS ON IT.
PLEASE...
BUT I DO NOT WISH TO SEE YOU IN SUCH PAIN SO I WILL GIVE YOU ONE CHANCE...
YES.
AND ONLY ONE CHANCE.
I'LL DO ANYTHING.
YOU MUST GUESS MY NAME.
YOUR NAME?
A NAME THAT HAS BEEN LOST FOR AN AGE. A NAME THAT HAS NOT BEEN SPOKEN ALOUD FOR MANY YEARS.
BUT IF YOU CANNOT, THEN I WILL COLLECT MY PAYMENT.
YOU HAVE THREE DAYS. IF YOU CAN GUESS MY NAME YOU CAN KEEP YOUR SON...

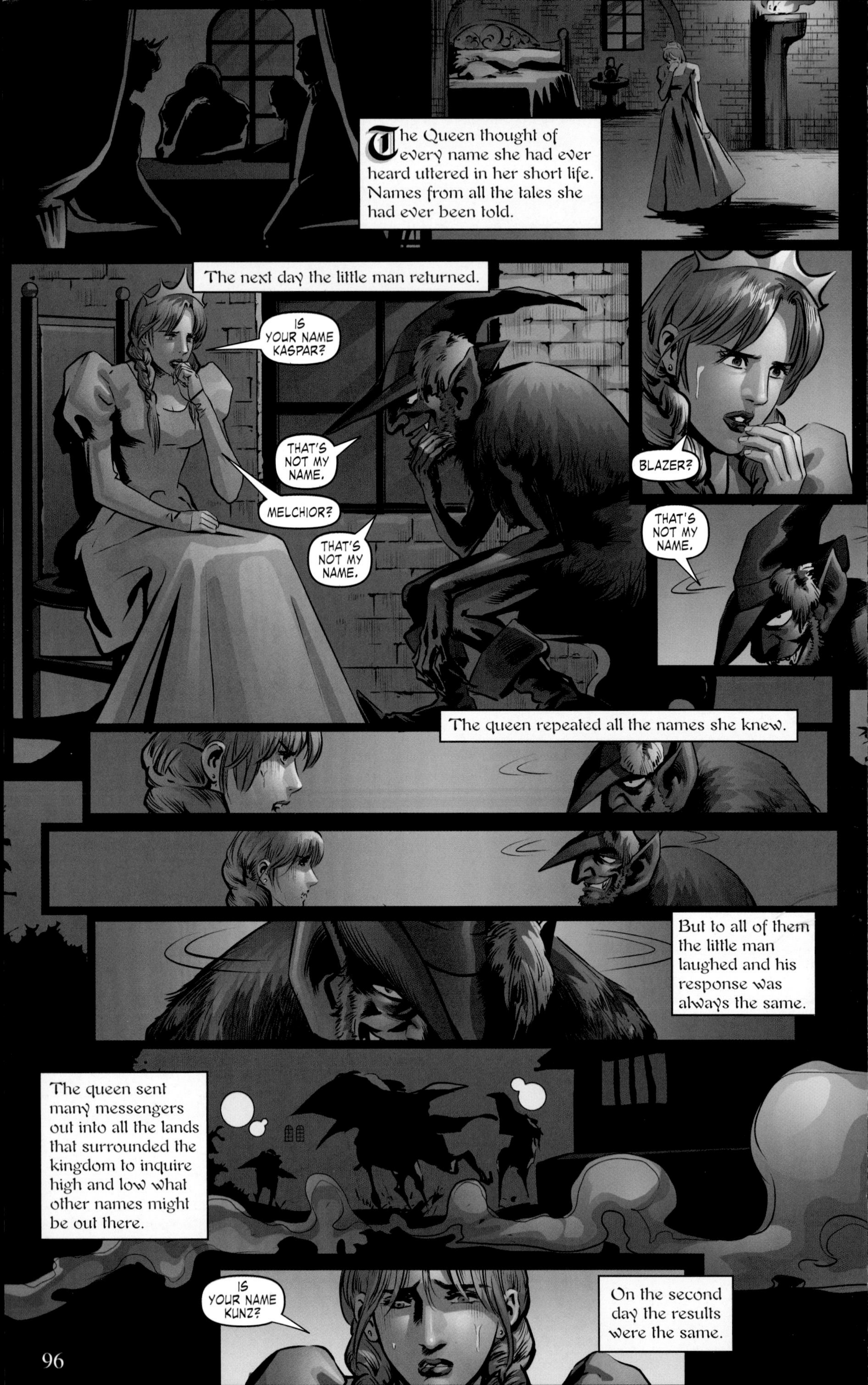
The Queen thought of every name she had ever heard uttered in her short life. Names from all the tales she had ever been told.
The next day the little man returned.
IS YOUR NAME KASPAR?
THAT'S NOT MY NAME.
MELCHIOR?
THAT'S NOT MY NAME.
BLAZER?
THAT'S NOT MY NAME.
The queen repeated all the names she knew.
But to all of them the little man laughed and his response was always the same.
The queen sent many messengers out into all the lands that surrounded the kingdom to inquire high and low what other names might be out there.
IS YOUR NAME KUNZ?
On the second day the results were the same.

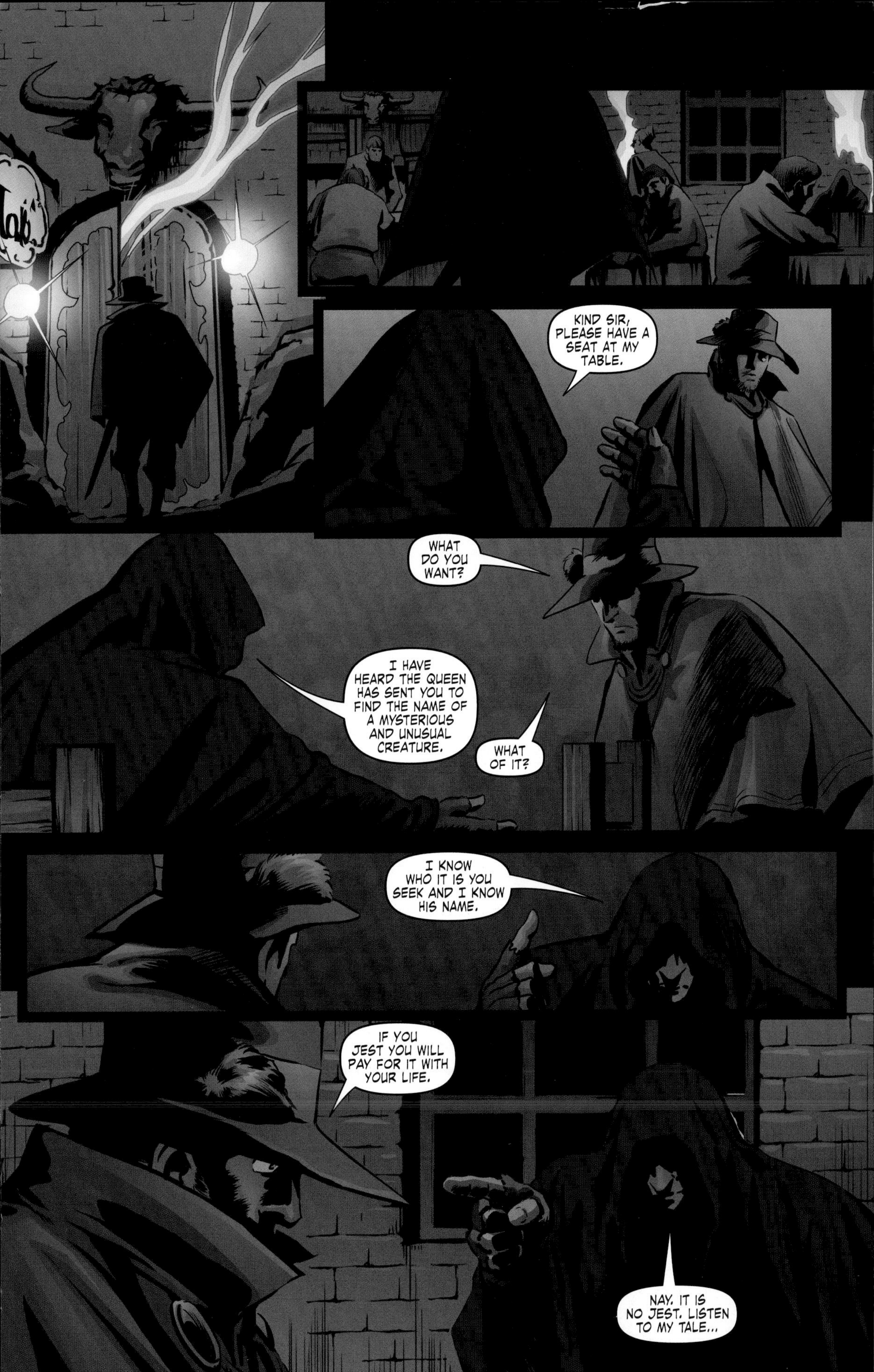
KIND SIR, PLEASE HAVE A SEAT AT MY TABLE.
WHAT DO YOU WANT?
I HAVE HEARD THE QUEEN HAS SENT YOU TO FIND THE NAME OF A MYSTERIOUS AND UNUSUAL CREATURE.
WHAT OF IT?
I KNOW WHO IT IS YOU SEEK AND I KNOW HIS NAME.
IF YOU JEST YOU WILL PAY FOR IT WITH YOUR LIFE.
NAY. IT IS NO JEST. LISTEN TO MY TALE...

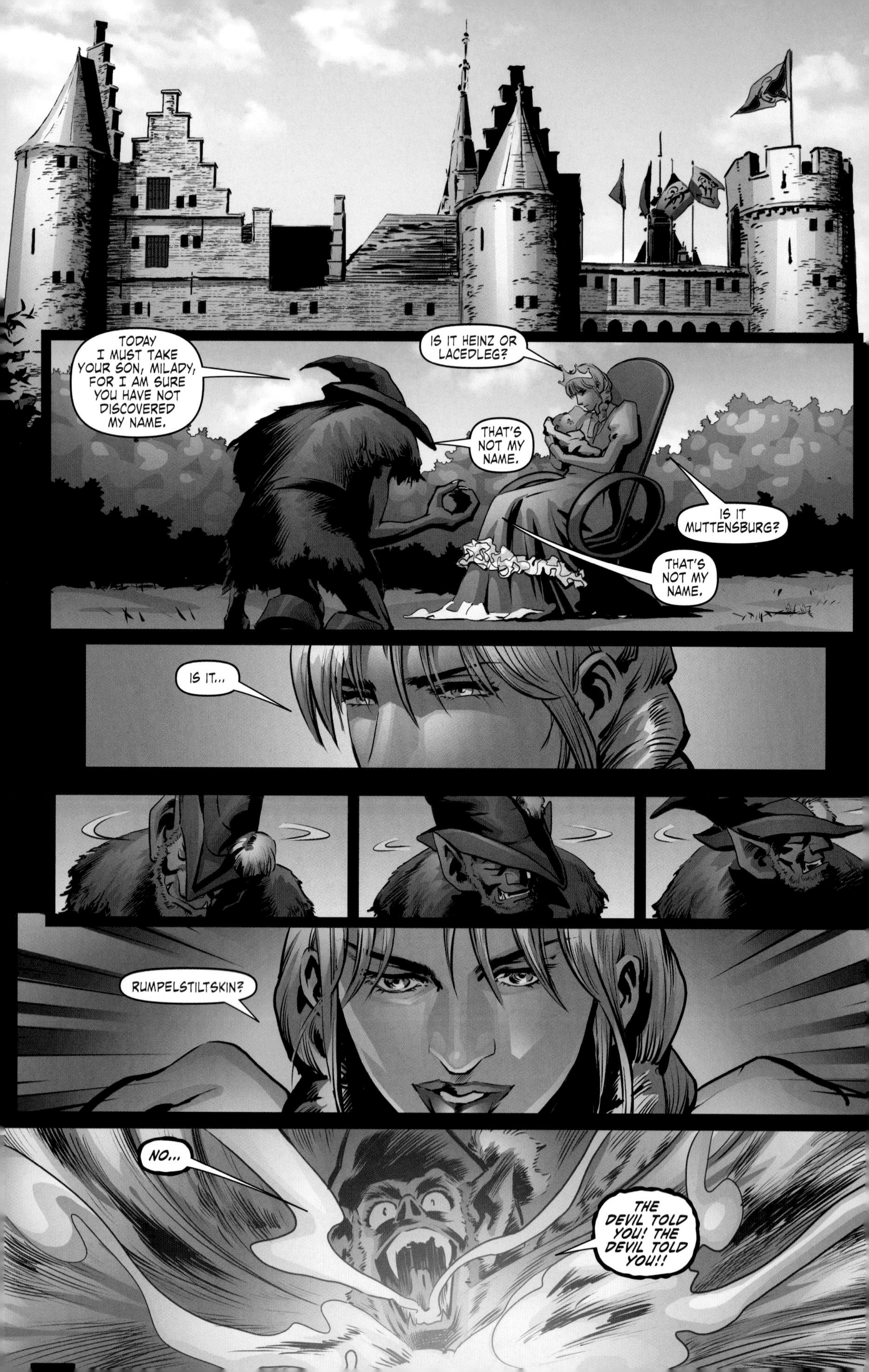
TODAY I MUST TAKE YOUR SON, MILADY, FOR I AM SURE YOU HAVE NOT DISCOVERED MY NAME.
IS IT HEINZ OR LACEDLEG?
THAT'S NOT MY NAME.
IS IT MUTTENSBURG?
THAT'S NOT MY NAME.
IS IT...
RUMPELSTILTSKIN?
NO...
THE DEVIL TOLD YOU! THE DEVIL TOLD YOU!!

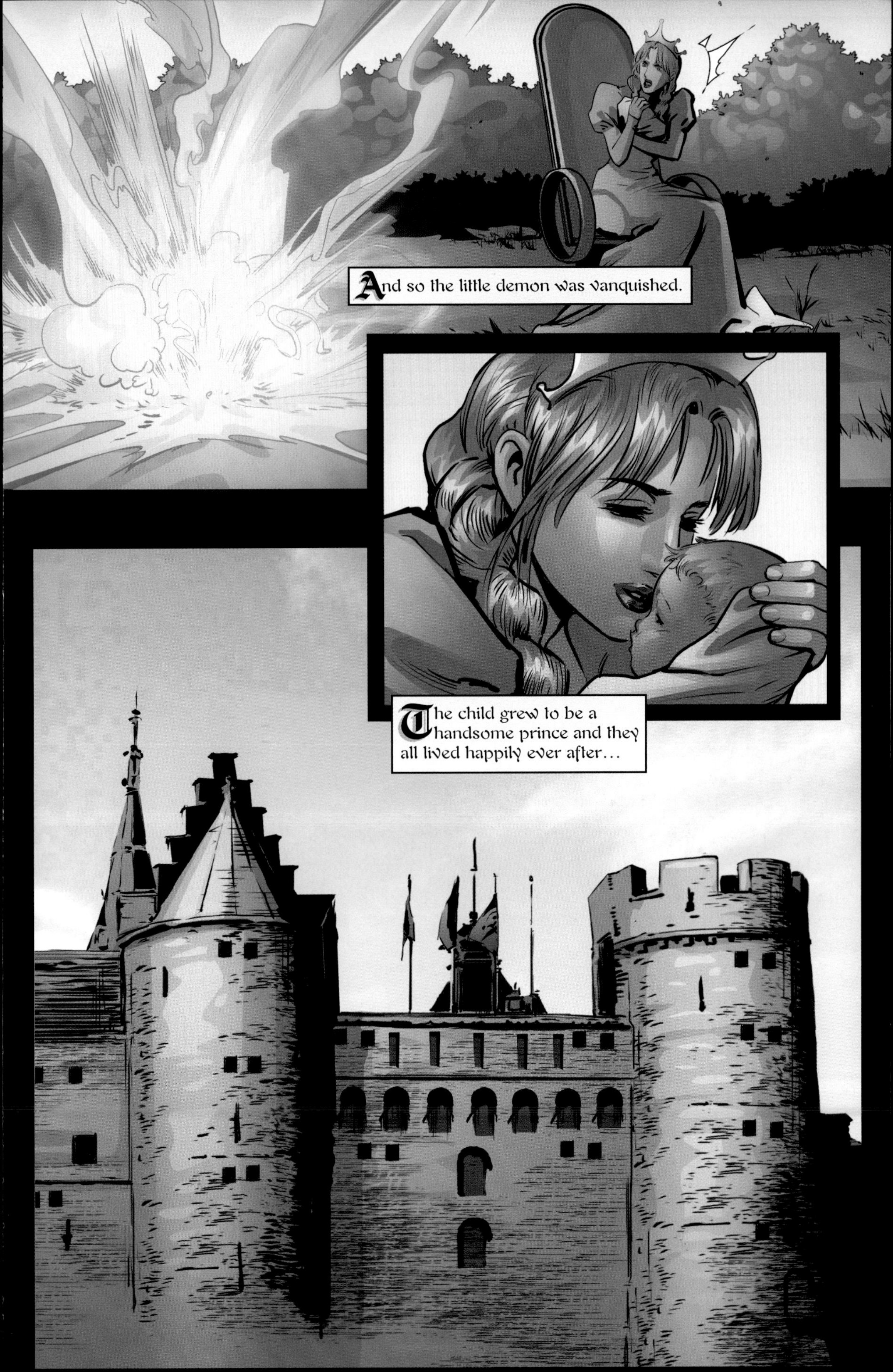
And so the little demon was vanquished.
The child grew to be a handsome prince and they all lived happily ever after...

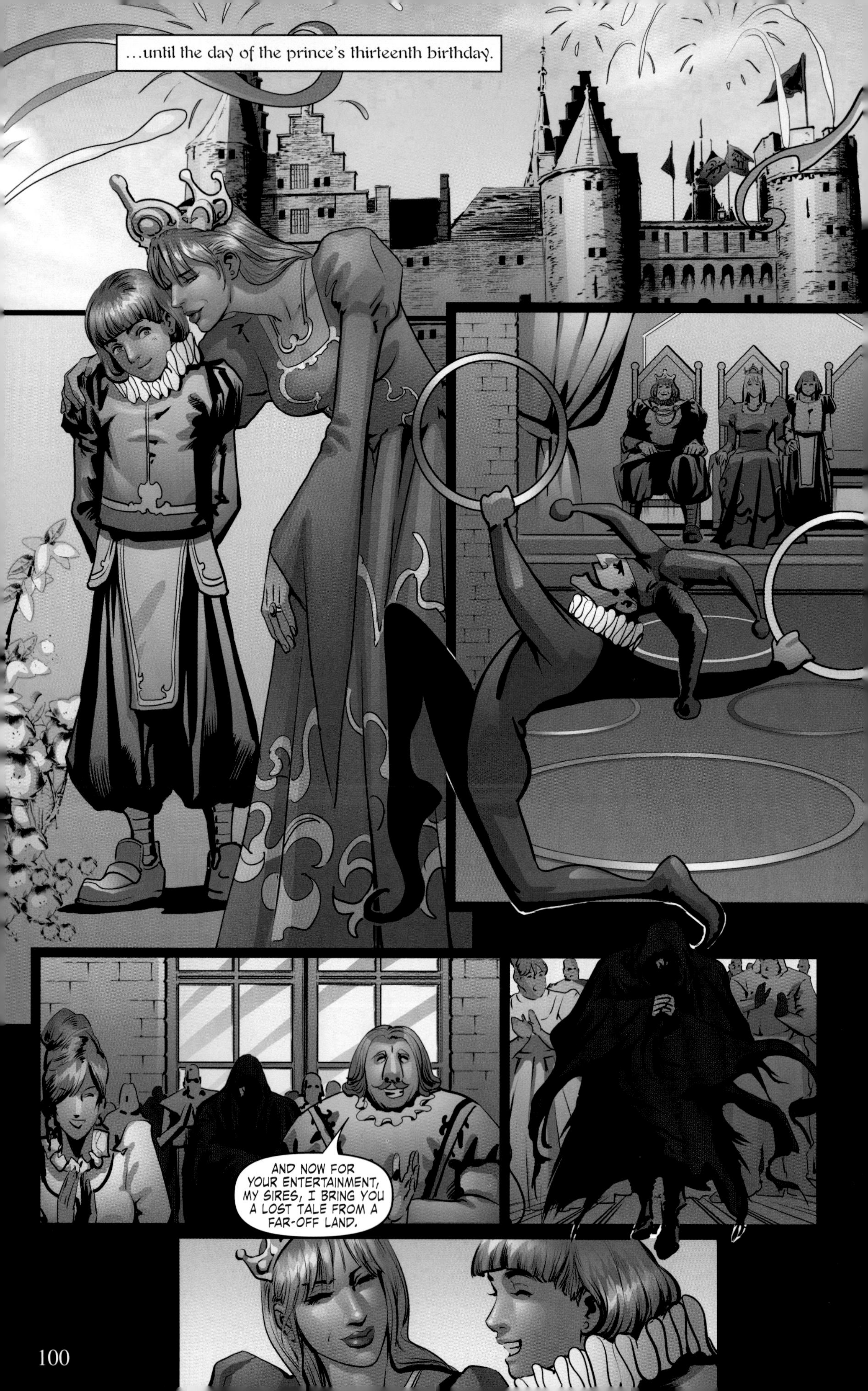
...until the day of the prince's thirteenth birthday.
AND NOW FOR YOUR ENTERTAINMENT, MY SIRES, I BRING YOU A LOST TALE FROM A FAR-OFF LAND.

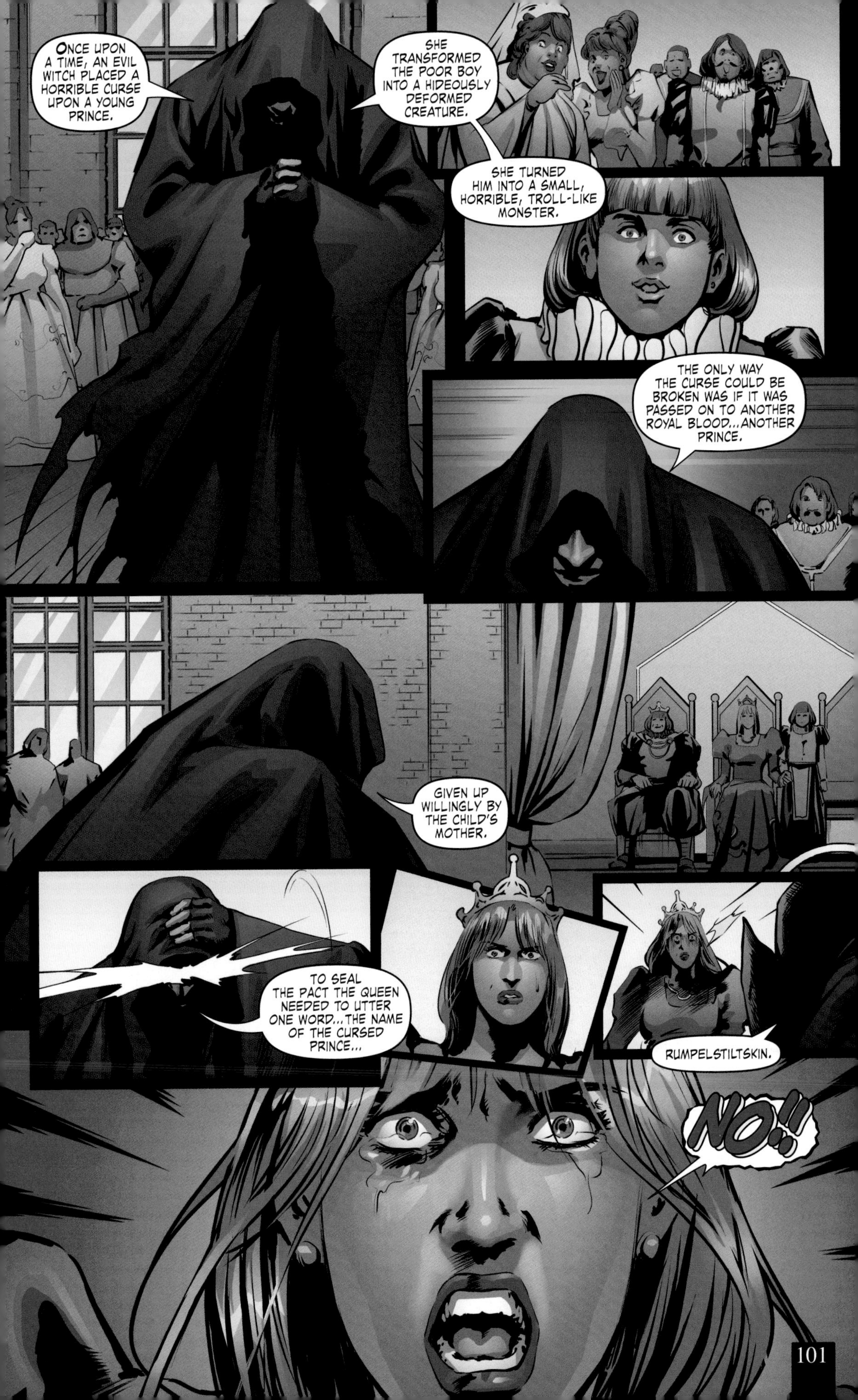
ONCE UPON A TIME, AN EVIL WITCH PLACED A HORRIBLE CURSE UPON A YOUNG PRINCE.
SHE TRANSFORMED THE POOR BOY INTO A HIDEOUSLY DEFORMED CREATURE.
SHE TURNED HIM INTO A SMALL, HORRIBLE, TROLL-LIKE MONSTER.
THE ONLY WAY THE CURSE COULD BE BROKEN WAS IF IT WAS PASSED ON TO ANOTHER ROYAL BLOOD...ANOTHER PRINCE.
GIVEN UP WILLINGLY BY THE CHILD'S MOTHER.
TO SEAL THE PACT THE QUEEN NEEDED TO UTTER ONE WORD...THE NAME OF THE CURSED PRINCE...
RUMPELSTILTSKIN.
NO!!

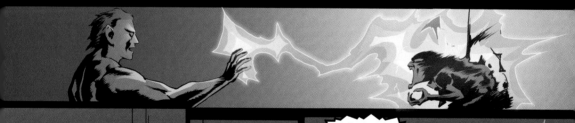

NO! PLEASE!!

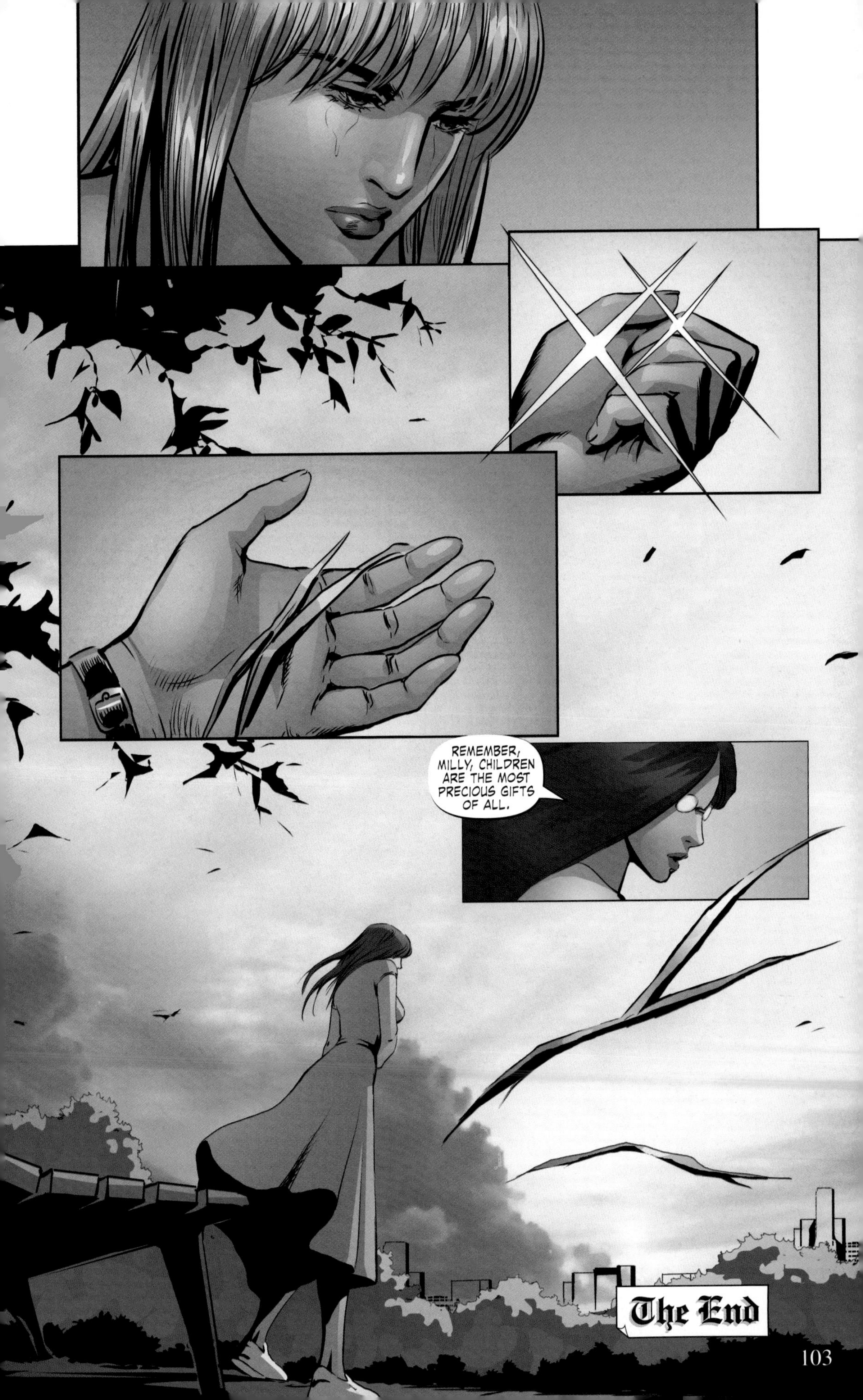
REMEMBER, MILLY, CHILDREN ARE THE MOST PRECIOUS GIFTS OF ALL.
The End

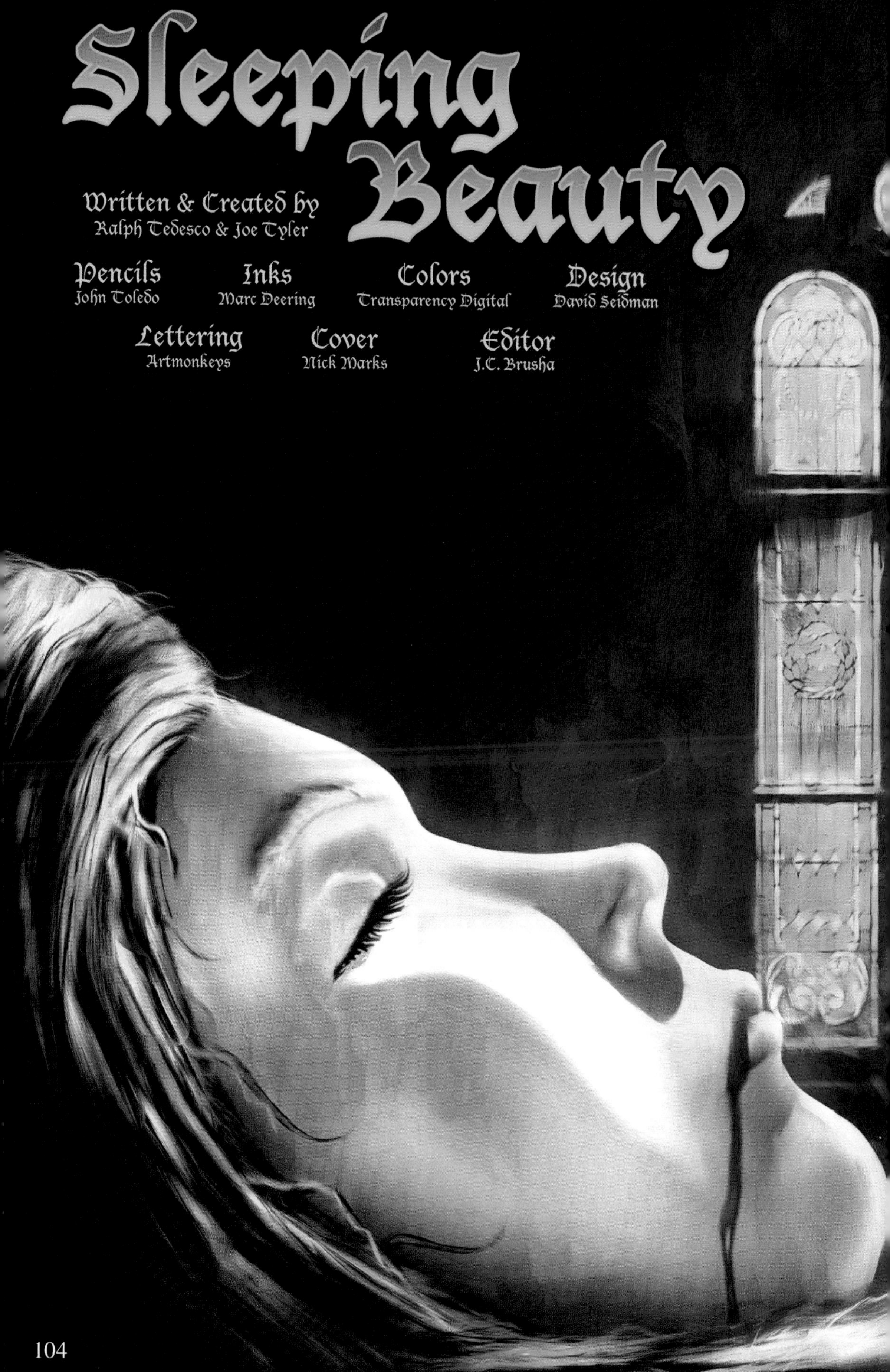
Sleeping Beauty
Written & Created by
Ralph Tedesco & Joe Tyler
Pencils
John Toledo
Inks
Marc Deering
Colors
Transparency Digital
Design
David Seidman
Lettering
Artmonkeys
Cover
Nick Marks
Editor
J.C. Brusha

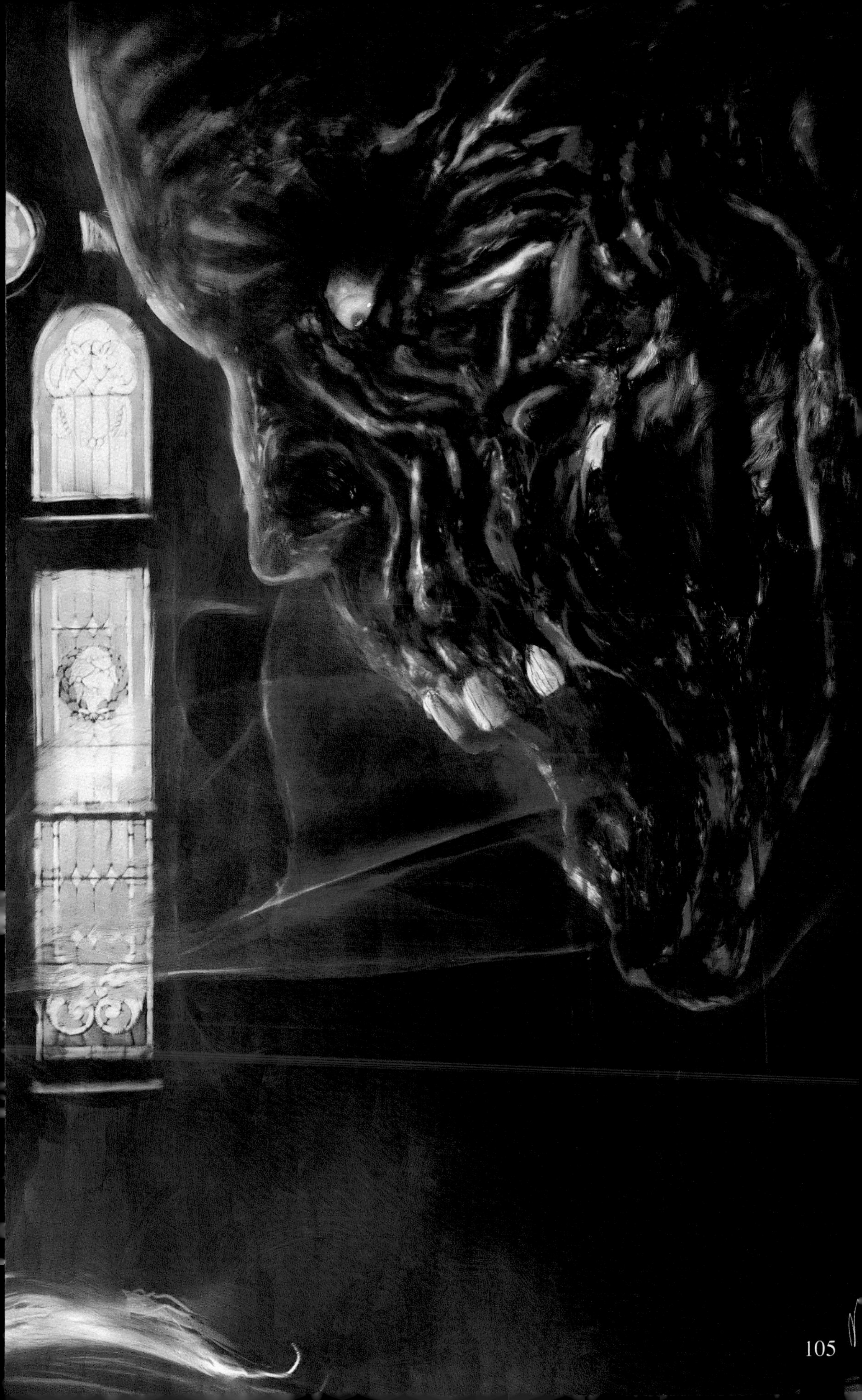

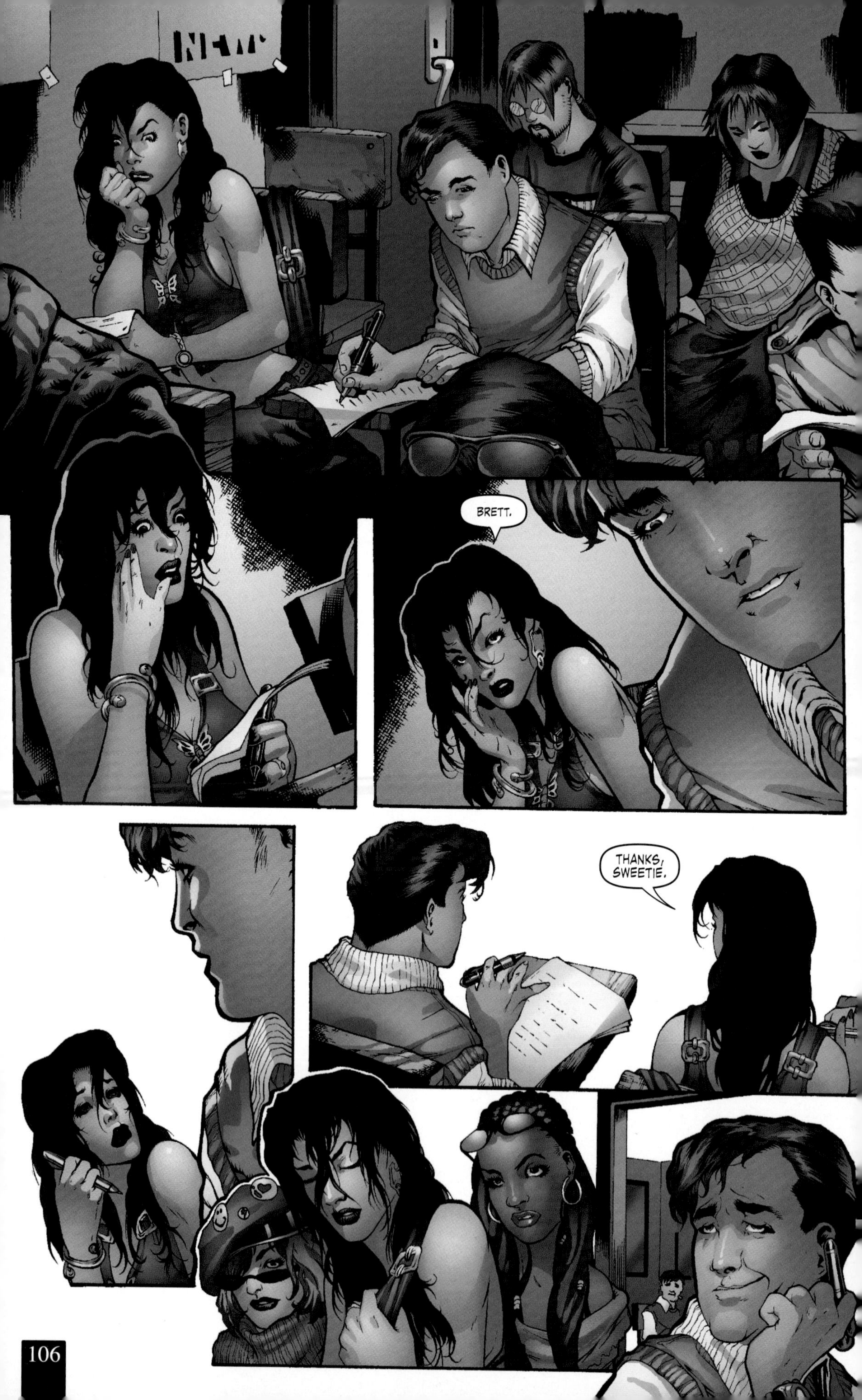
BRETT.
THANKS, SWEETIE.

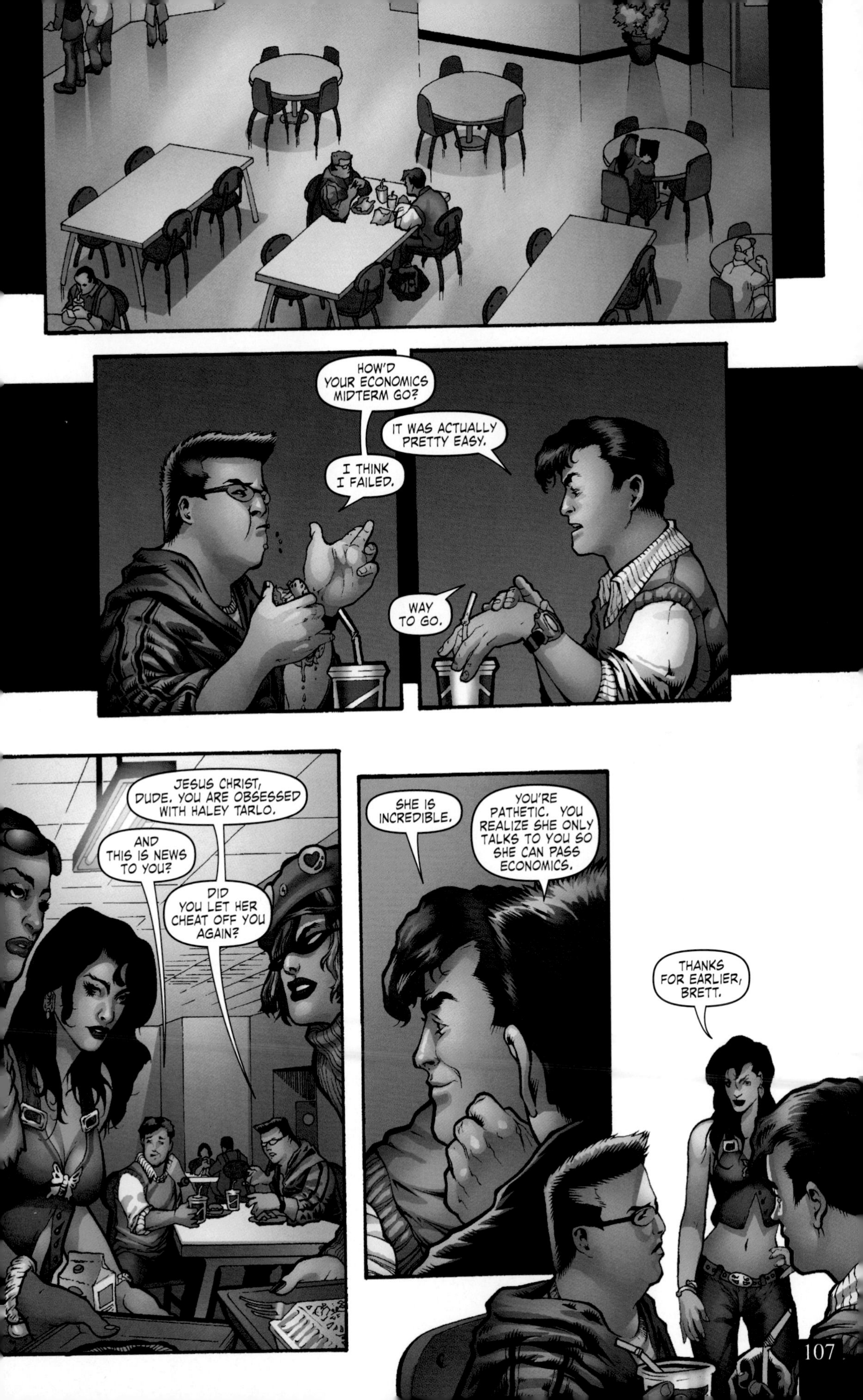
HOW'D YOUR ECONOMICS MIDTERM GO?
IT WAS ACTUALLY PRETTY EASY.
I THINK I FAILED.
WAY TO GO.
JESUS CHRIST, DUDE. YOU ARE OBSESSED WITH HALEY TARLO.
AND THIS IS NEWS TO YOU?
DID YOU LET HER CHEAT OFF YOU AGAIN?
SHE IS INCREDIBLE.
YOU'RE PATHETIC. YOU REALIZE SHE ONLY TALKS TO YOU SO SHE CAN PASS ECONOMICS.
THANKS FOR EARLIER, BRETT.

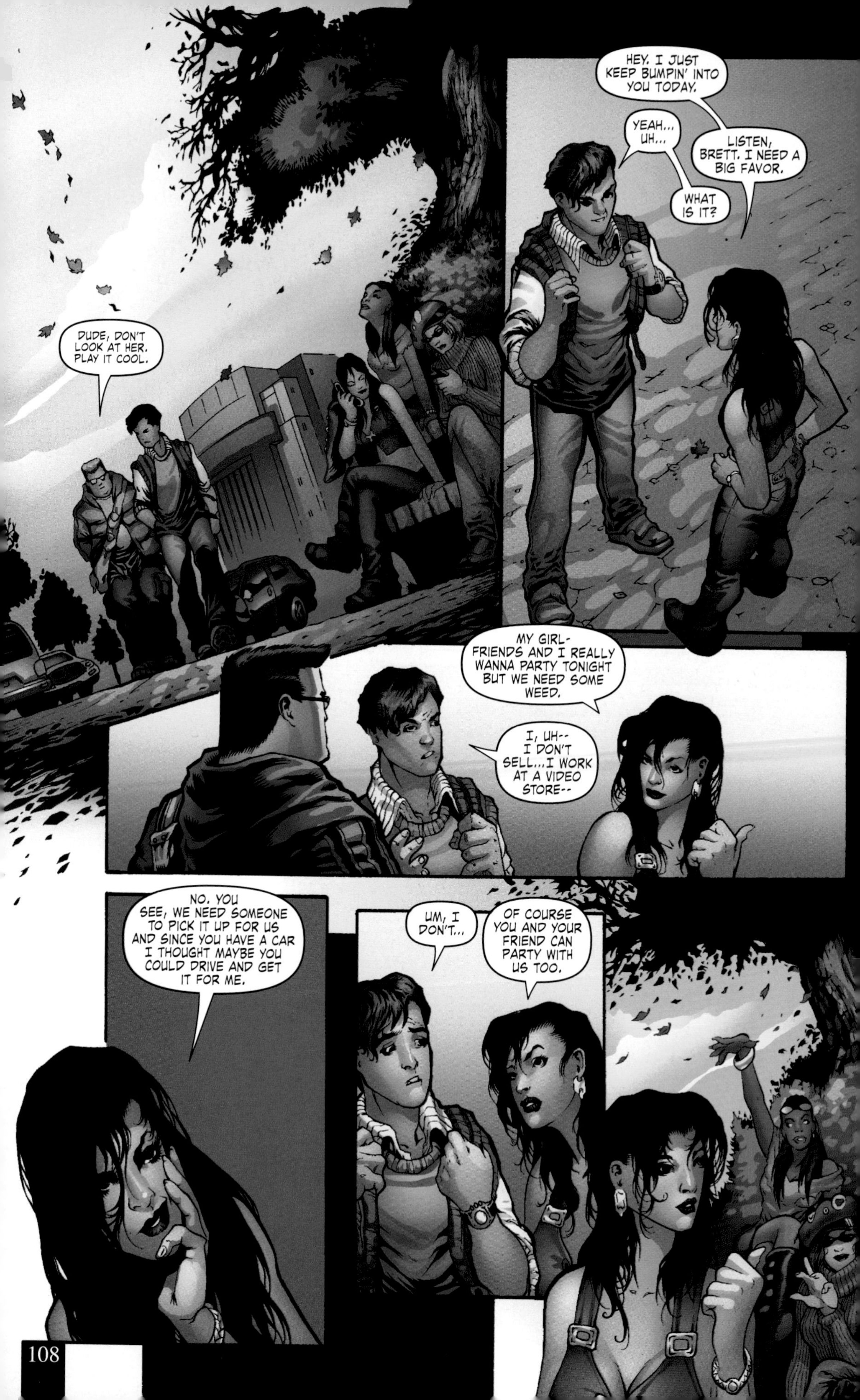
DUDE, DON'T LOOK AT HER. PLAY IT COOL.
HEY. I JUST KEEP BUMPIN' INTO YOU TODAY.
YEAH... UH...
LISTEN, BRETT. I NEED A BIG FAVOR.
WHAT IS IT?
MY GIRL-FRIENDS AND I REALLY WANNA PARTY TONIGHT BUT WE NEED SOME WEED.
I, UH-- I DON'T SELL...I WORK AT A VIDEO STORE--
NO. YOU SEE, WE NEED SOMEONE TO PICK IT UP FOR US AND SINCE YOU HAVE A CAR I THOUGHT MAYBE YOU COULD DRIVE AND GET IT FOR ME.
UM, I DON'T...
OF COURSE YOU AND YOUR FRIEND CAN PARTY WITH US TOO.

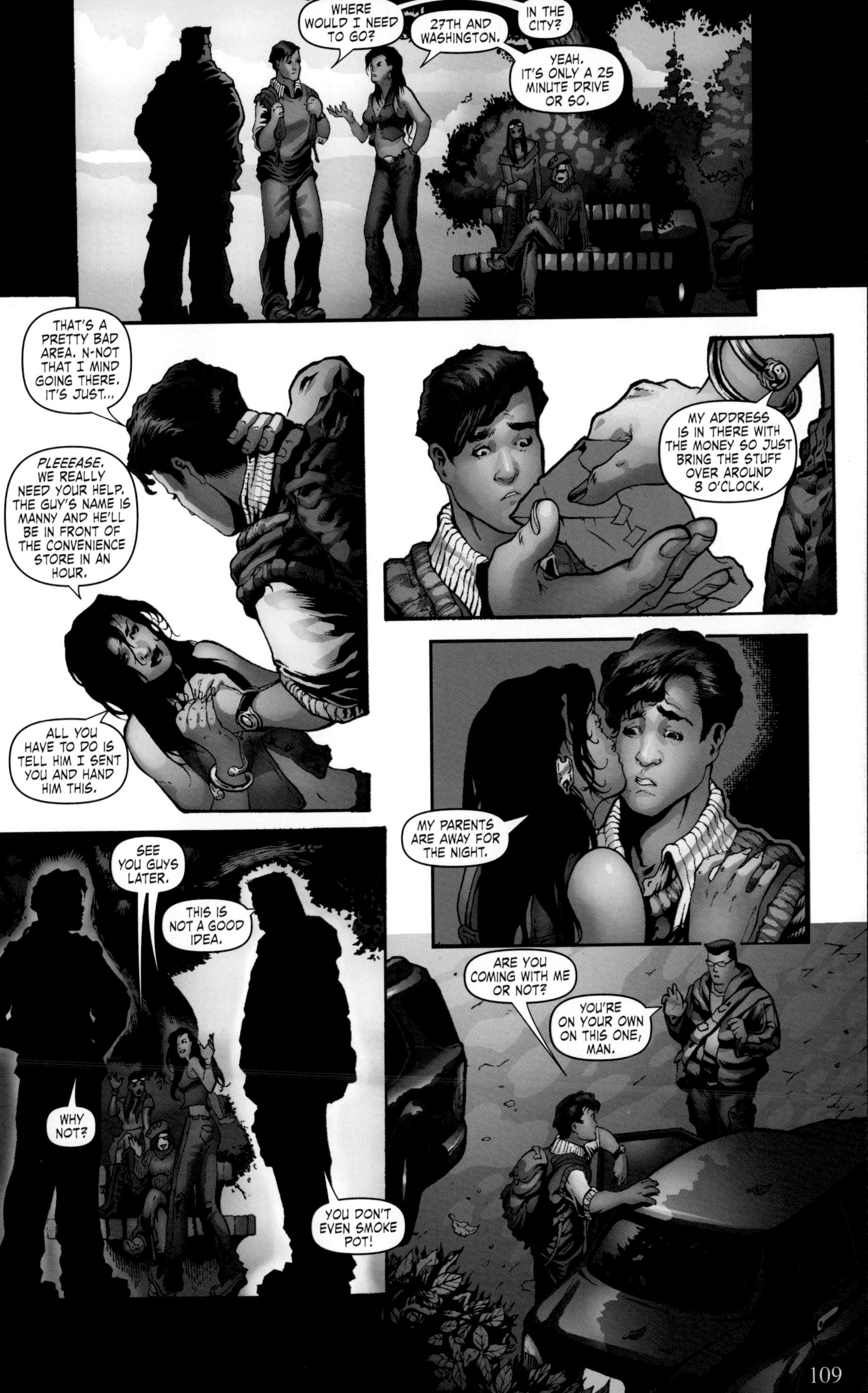
WHERE WOULD I NEED TO GO?
IN THE CITY?
27TH AND WASHINGTON.
YEAH. IT'S ONLY A 25 MINUTE DRIVE OR SO.
THAT'S A PRETTY BAD AREA. N-NOT THAT I MIND GOING THERE. IT'S JUST...
PLEEEASE. WE REALLY NEED YOUR HELP. THE GUY'S NAME IS MANNY AND HE'LL BE IN FRONT OF THE CONVENIENCE STORE IN AN HOUR.
ALL YOU HAVE TO DO IS TELL HIM I SENT YOU AND HAND HIM THIS.
MY ADDRESS IS IN THERE WITH THE MONEY SO JUST BRING THE STUFF OVER AROUND 8 O'CLOCK.
MY PARENTS ARE AWAY FOR THE NIGHT.
SEE YOU GUYS LATER.
THIS IS NOT A GOOD IDEA.
WHY NOT?
YOU DON'T EVEN SMOKE POT!
ARE YOU COMING WITH ME OR NOT?
YOU'RE ON YOUR OWN ON THIS ONE, MAN.

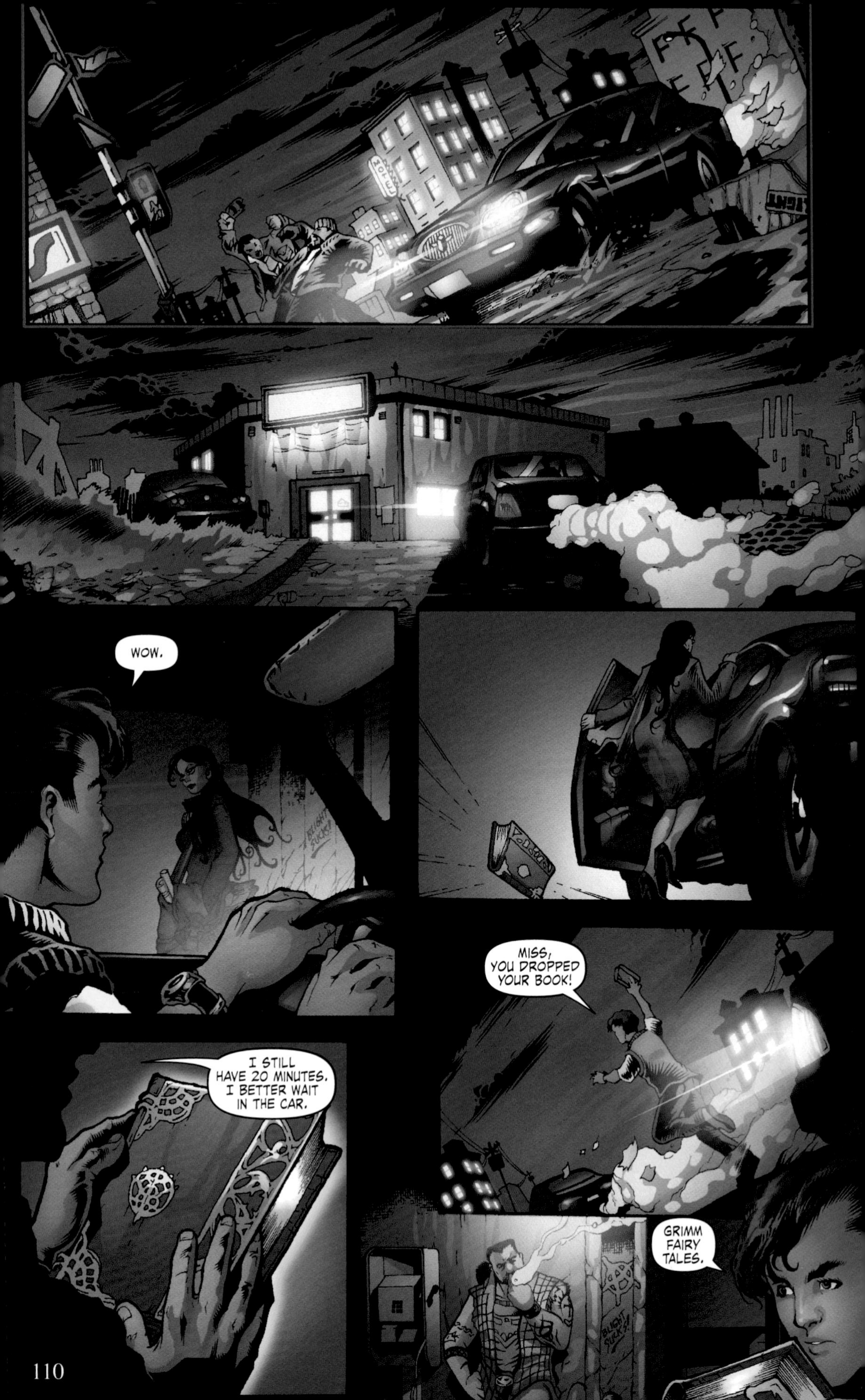
MOTEL
WOW.
MISS, YOU DROPPED YOUR BOOK!
I STILL HAVE 20 MINUTES. I BETTER WAIT IN THE CAR.
GRIMM FAIRY TALES.

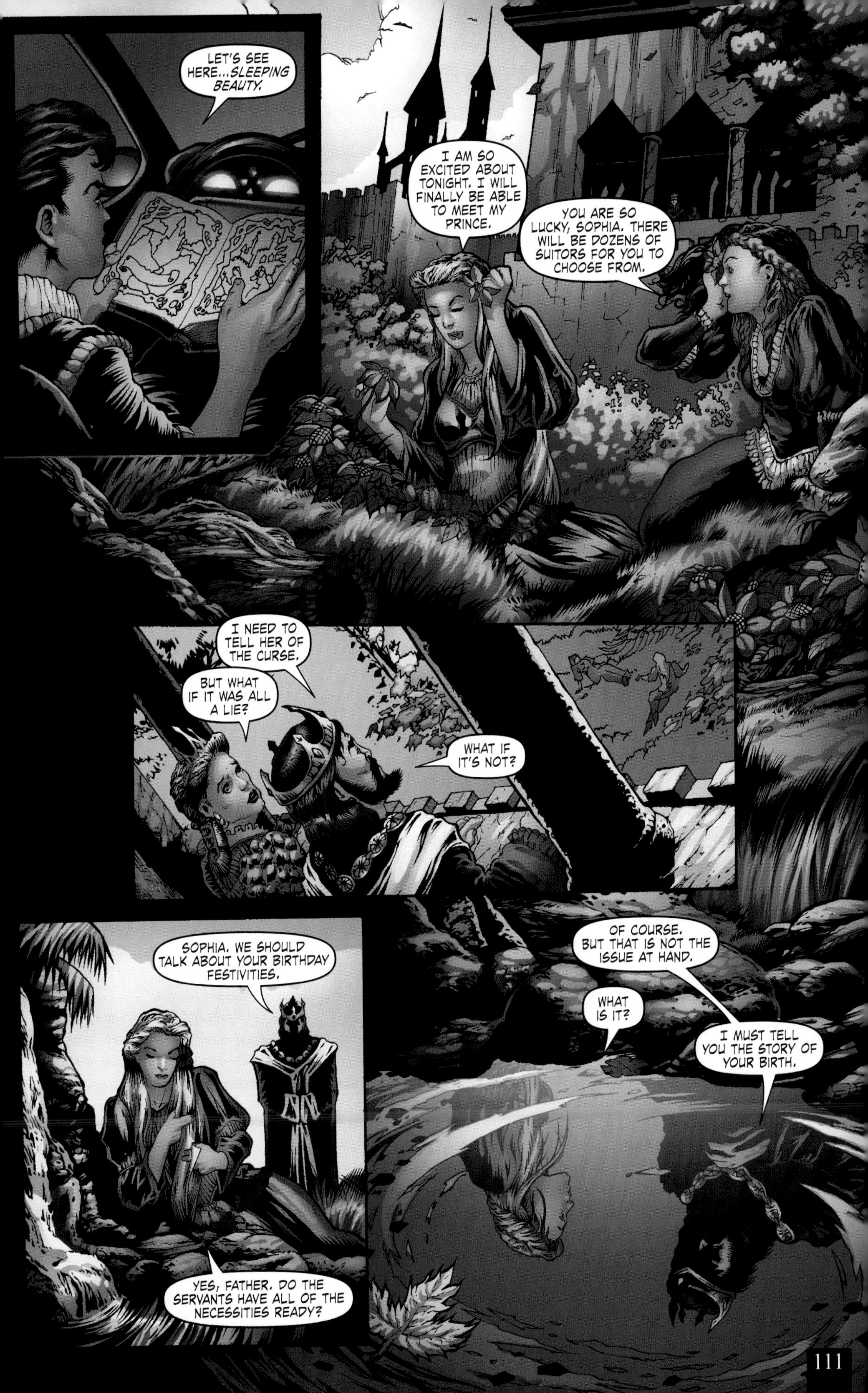
LET'S SEE HERE...SLEEPING BEAUTY.
I AM SO EXCITED ABOUT TONIGHT. I WILL FINALLY BE ABLE TO MEET MY PRINCE.
YOU ARE SO LUCKY, SOPHIA. THERE WILL BE DOZENS OF SUITORS FOR YOU TO CHOOSE FROM.
I NEED TO TELL HER OF THE CURSE.
BUT WHAT IF IT WAS ALL A LIE?
WHAT IF IT'S NOT?
SOPHIA. WE SHOULD TALK ABOUT YOUR BIRTHDAY FESTIVITIES.
YES, FATHER. DO THE SERVANTS HAVE ALL OF THE NECESSITIES READY?
OF COURSE. BUT THAT IS NOT THE ISSUE AT HAND.
WHAT IS IT?
I MUST TELL YOU THE STORY OF YOUR BIRTH.

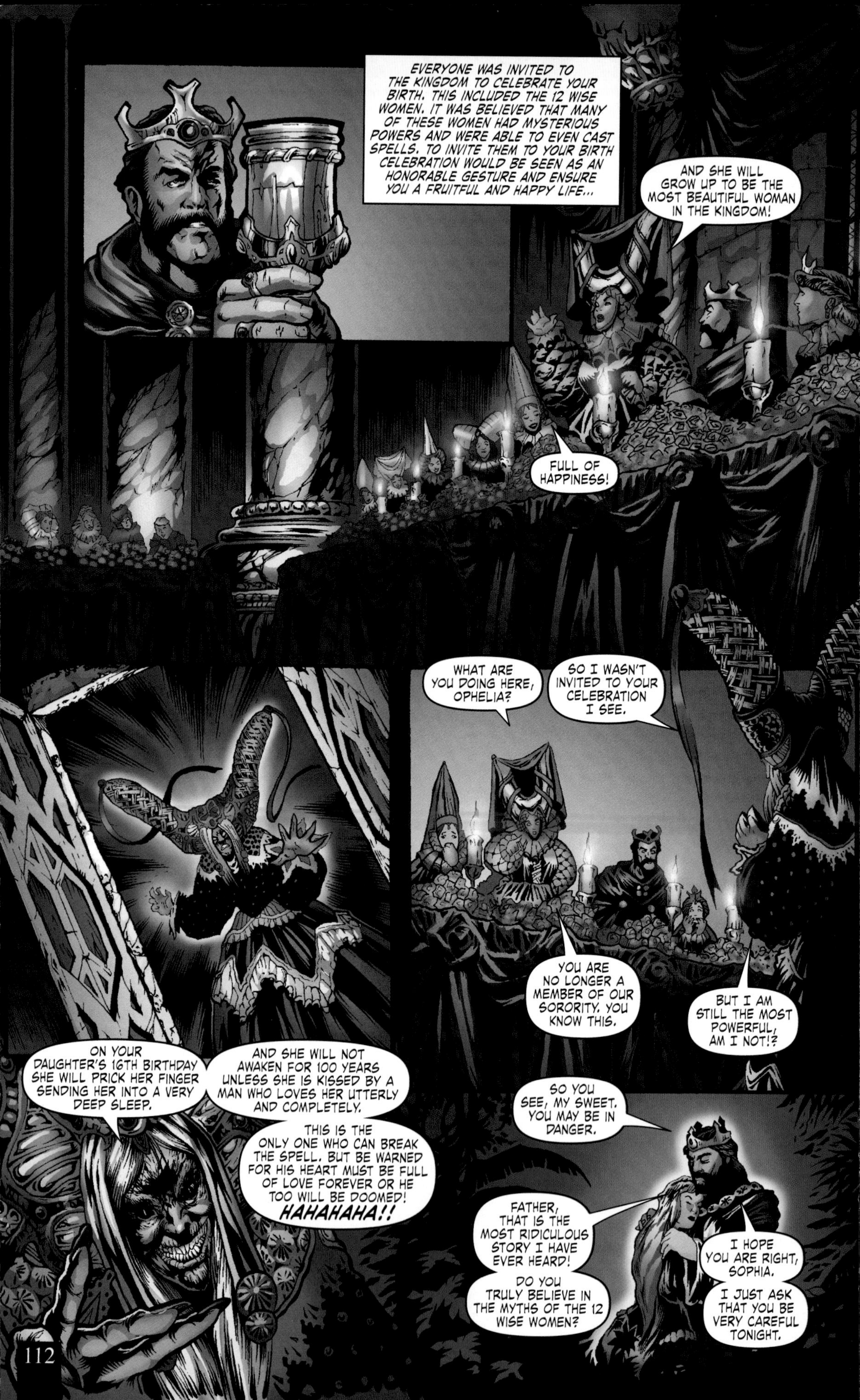
EVERYONE WAS INVITED TO THE KINGDOM TO CELEBRATE YOUR BIRTH. THIS INCLUDED THE 12 WISE WOMEN. IT WAS BELIEVED THAT MANY OF THESE WOMEN HAD MYSTERIOUS POWERS AND WERE ABLE TO EVEN CAST SPELLS. TO INVITE THEM TO YOUR BIRTH CELEBRATION WOULD BE SEEN AS AN HONORABLE GESTURE AND ENSURE YOU A FRUITFUL AND HAPPY LIFE...
AND SHE WILL GROW UP TO BE THE MOST BEAUTIFUL WOMAN IN THE KINGDOM!
FULL OF HAPPINESS!
WHAT ARE YOU DOING HERE, OPHELIA?
SO I WASN'T INVITED TO YOUR CELEBRATION I SEE.
YOU ARE NO LONGER A MEMBER OF OUR SORORITY. YOU KNOW THIS.
BUT I AM STILL THE MOST POWERFUL, AM I NOT!?
ON YOUR DAUGHTER'S 16TH BIRTHDAY SHE WILL PRICK HER FINGER SENDING HER INTO A VERY DEEP SLEEP.
AND SHE WILL NOT AWAKEN FOR 100 YEARS UNLESS SHE IS KISSED BY A MAN WHO LOVES HER UTTERLY AND COMPLETELY.
THIS IS THE ONLY ONE WHO CAN BREAK THE SPELL. BUT BE WARNED FOR HIS HEART MUST BE FULL OF LOVE FOREVER OR HE TOO WILL BE DOOMED! HAHAHAHA!!
SO YOU SEE, MY SWEET. YOU MAY BE IN DANGER.
FATHER, THAT IS THE MOST RIDICULOUS STORY I HAVE EVER HEARD!
DO YOU TRULY BELIEVE IN THE MYTHS OF THE 12 WISE WOMEN?
I HOPE YOU ARE RIGHT, SOPHIA.
I JUST ASK THAT YOU BE VERY CAREFUL TONIGHT.

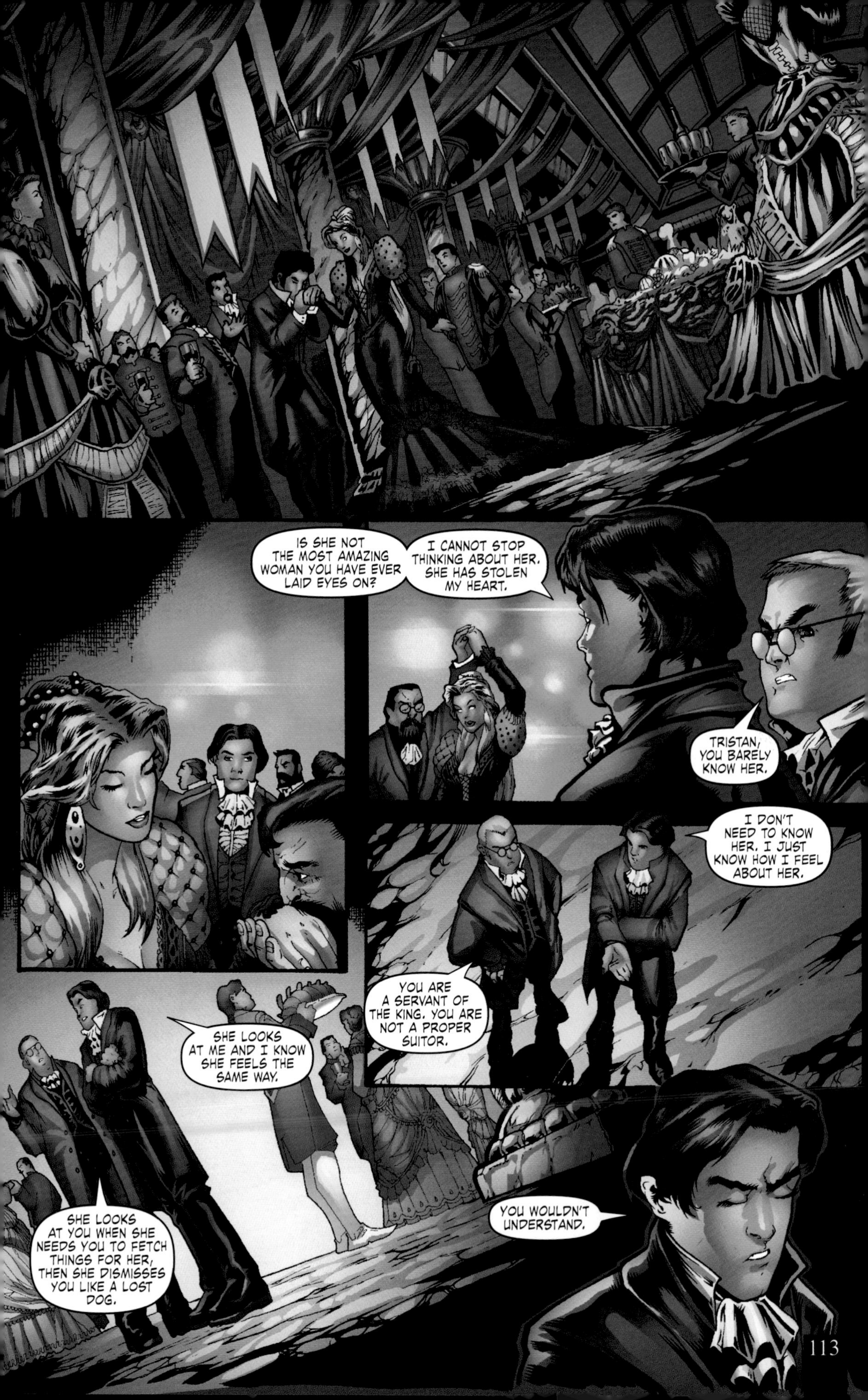

IS SHE NOT THE MOST AMAZING WOMAN YOU HAVE EVER LAID EYES ON?
I CANNOT STOP THINKING ABOUT HER. SHE HAS STOLEN MY HEART.
TRISTAN, YOU BARELY KNOW HER.
I DON'T NEED TO KNOW HER. I JUST KNOW HOW I FEEL ABOUT HER.
YOU ARE A SERVANT OF THE KING. YOU ARE NOT A PROPER SUITOR.
SHE LOOKS AT ME AND I KNOW SHE FEELS THE SAME WAY.
SHE LOOKS AT YOU WHEN SHE NEEDS YOU TO FETCH THINGS FOR HER, THEN SHE DISMISSES YOU LIKE A LOST DOG.
YOU WOULDN'T UNDERSTAND.

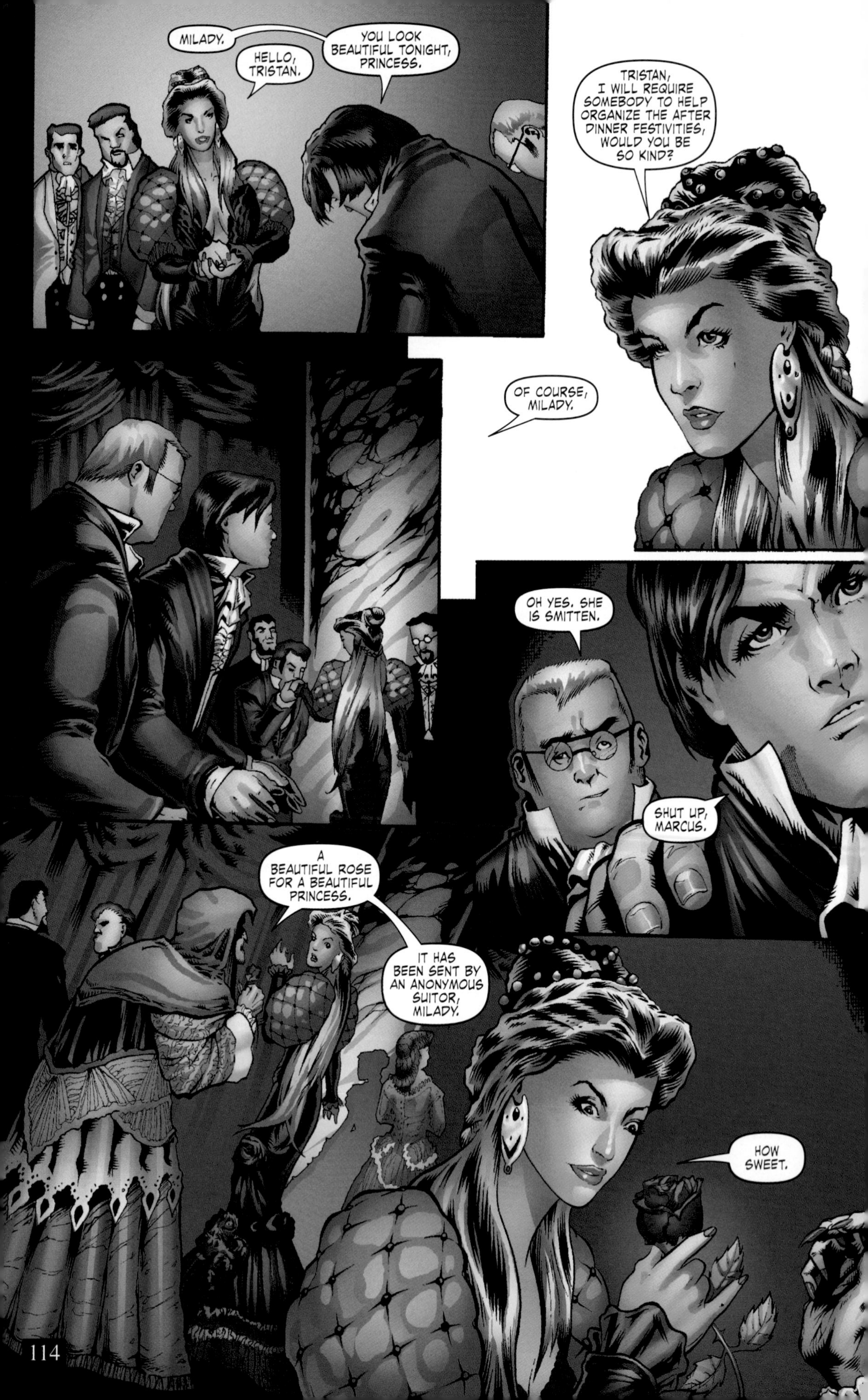

MILADY.
HELLO, TRISTAN.
YOU LOOK BEAUTIFUL TONIGHT, PRINCESS.
TRISTAN, I WILL REQUIRE SOMEBODY TO HELP ORGANIZE THE AFTER DINNER FESTIVITIES, WOULD YOU BE SO KIND?
OF COURSE, MILADY.
OH YES. SHE IS SMITTEN.
SHUT UP, MARCUS.
A BEAUTIFUL ROSE FOR A BEAUTIFUL PRINCESS.
IT HAS BEEN SENT BY AN ANONYMOUS SUITOR, MILADY.
HOW SWEET.

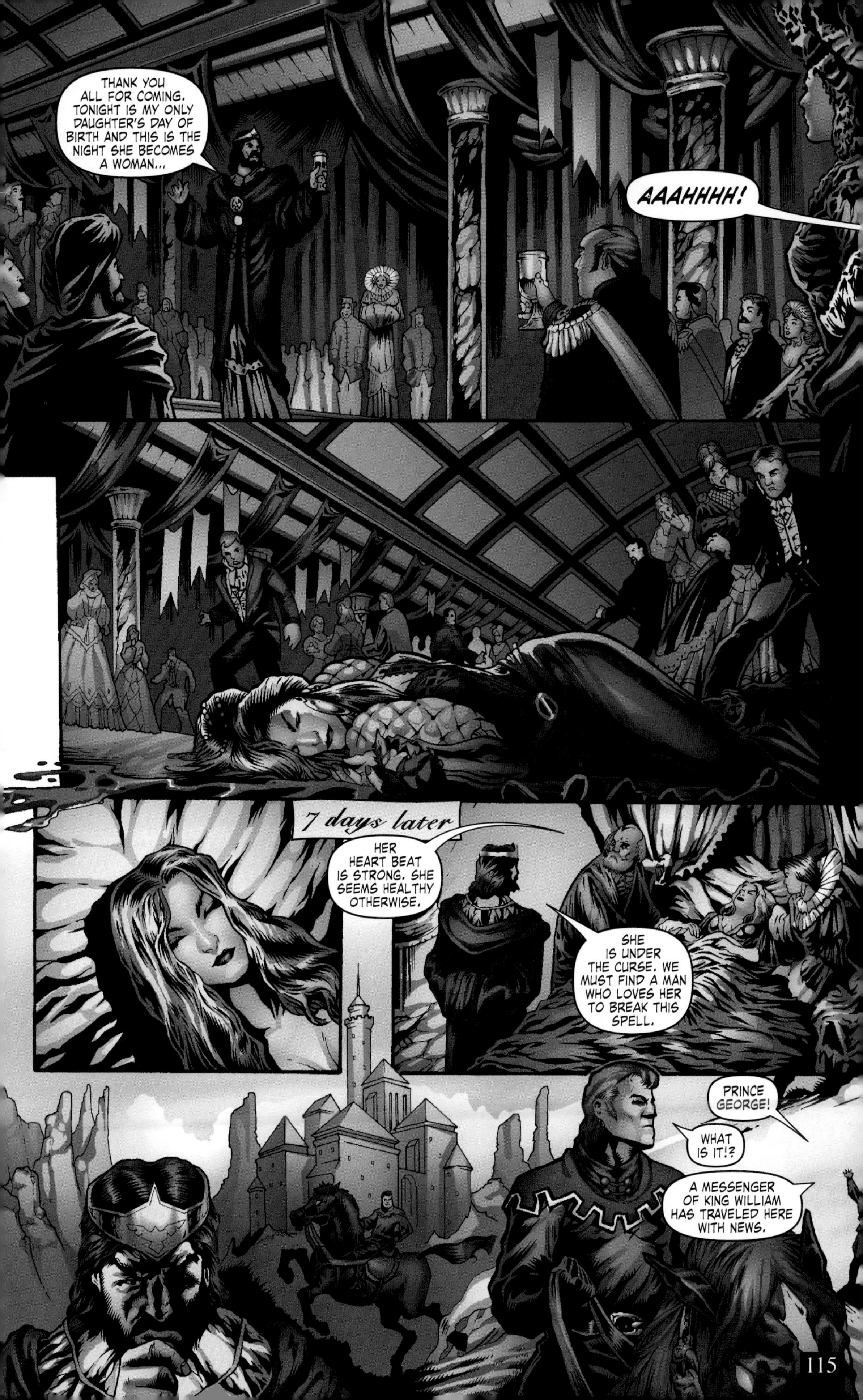
THANK YOU ALL FOR COMING. TONIGHT IS MY ONLY DAUGHTER'S DAY OF BIRTH AND THIS IS THE NIGHT SHE BECOMES A WOMAN...
AAAHHHH!
7 days later
HER HEART BEAT IS STRONG. SHE SEEMS HEALTHY OTHERWISE.
SHE IS UNDER THE CURSE. WE MUST FIND A MAN WHO LOVES HER TO BREAK THIS SPELL.
PRINCE GEORGE!
WHAT IS IT!?
A MESSENGER OF KING WILLIAM HAS TRAVELED HERE WITH NEWS.

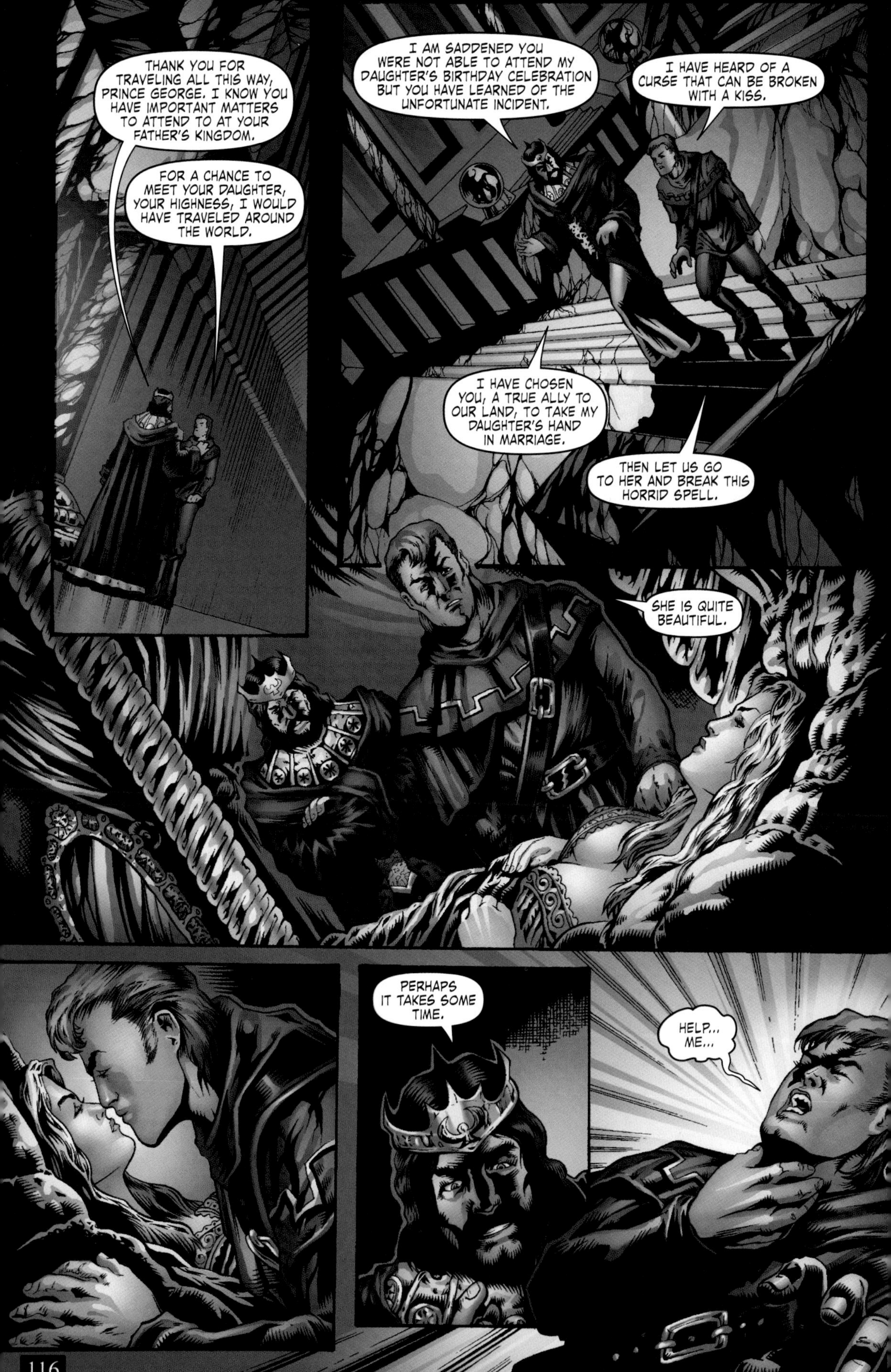
THANK YOU FOR TRAVELING ALL THIS WAY, PRINCE GEORGE. I KNOW YOU HAVE IMPORTANT MATTERS TO ATTEND TO AT YOUR FATHER'S KINGDOM.
FOR A CHANCE TO MEET YOUR DAUGHTER, YOUR HIGHNESS, I WOULD HAVE TRAVELED AROUND THE WORLD.
I AM SADDENED YOU WERE NOT ABLE TO ATTEND MY DAUGHTER'S BIRTHDAY CELEBRATION BUT YOU HAVE LEARNED OF THE UNFORTUNATE INCIDENT.
I HAVE HEARD OF A CURSE THAT CAN BE BROKEN WITH A KISS.
I HAVE CHOSEN YOU, A TRUE ALLY TO OUR LAND, TO TAKE MY DAUGHTER'S HAND IN MARRIAGE.
THEN LET US GO TO HER AND BREAK THIS HORRID SPELL.
SHE IS QUITE BEAUTIFUL.
PERHAPS IT TAKES SOME TIME.
HELP... ME...

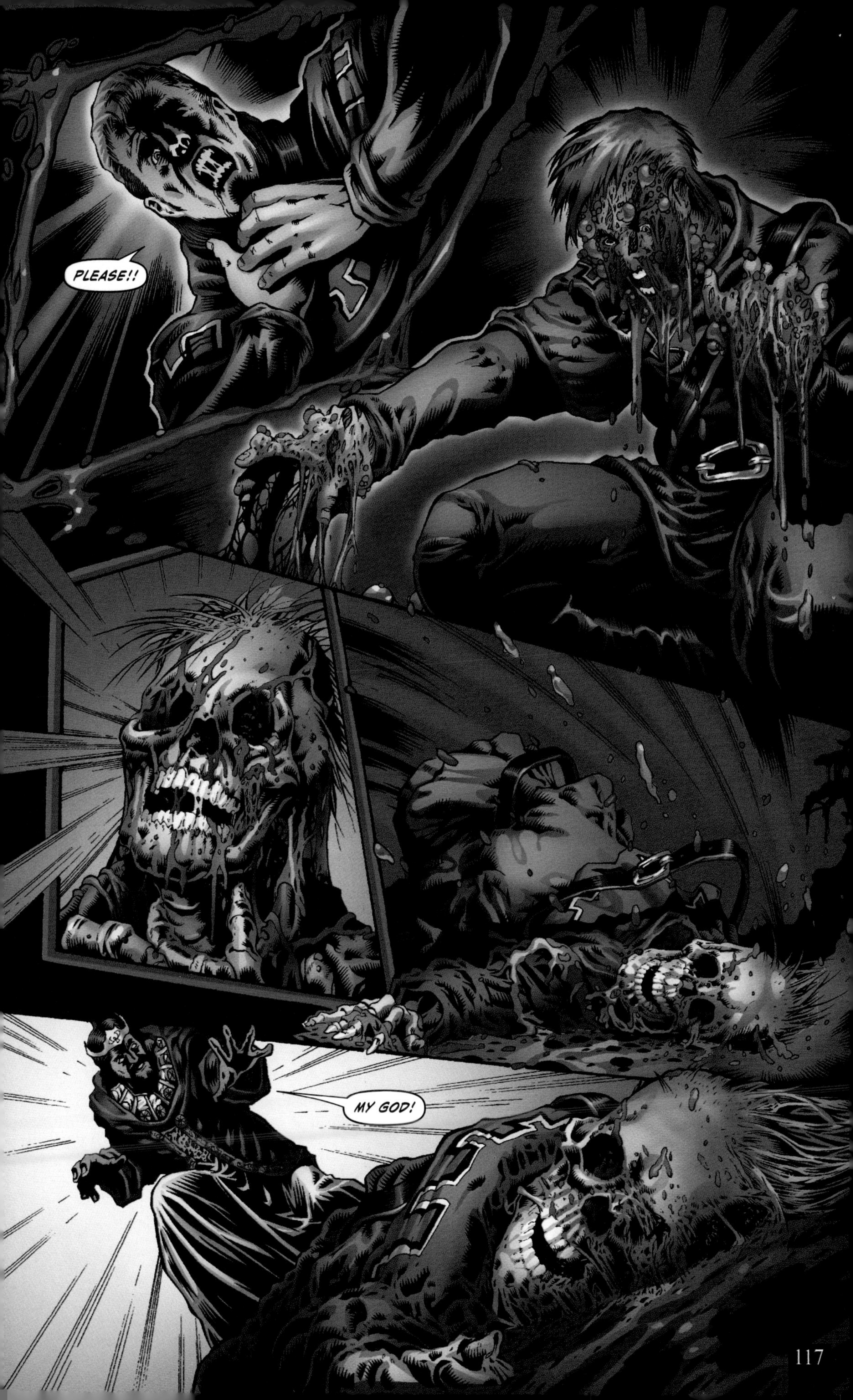
PLEASE!!
MY GOD!

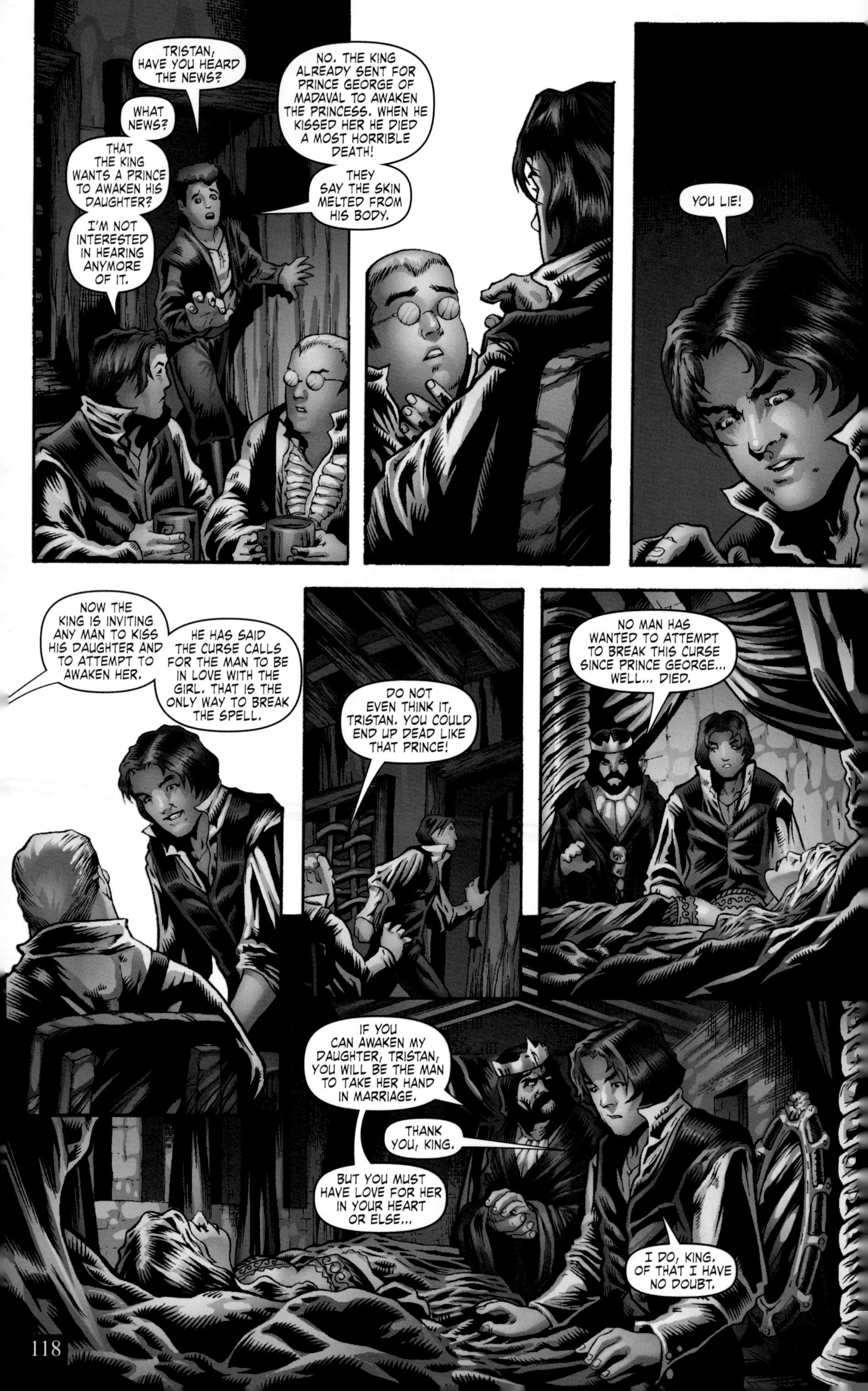
TRISTAN, HAVE YOU HEARD THE NEWS?
WHAT NEWS?
THAT THE KING WANTS A PRINCE TO AWAKEN HIS DAUGHTER?
I'M NOT INTERESTED IN HEARING ANYMORE OF IT.
NO. THE KING ALREADY SENT FOR PRINCE GEORGE OF MADAVAL TO AWAKEN THE PRINCESS. WHEN HE KISSED HER HE DIED A MOST HORRIBLE DEATH!
THEY SAY THE SKIN MELTED FROM HIS BODY.
YOU LIE!
NOW THE KING IS INVITING ANY MAN TO KISS HIS DAUGHTER AND TO ATTEMPT TO AWAKEN HER.
HE HAS SAID THE CURSE CALLS FOR THE MAN TO BE IN LOVE WITH THE GIRL. THAT IS THE ONLY WAY TO BREAK THE SPELL.
DO NOT EVEN THINK IT, TRISTAN. YOU COULD END UP DEAD LIKE THAT PRINCE!
NO MAN HAS WANTED TO ATTEMPT TO BREAK THIS CURSE SINCE PRINCE GEORGE... WELL... DIED.
IF YOU CAN AWAKEN MY DAUGHTER, TRISTAN, YOU WILL BE THE MAN TO TAKE HER HAND IN MARRIAGE.
THANK YOU, KING.
BUT YOU MUST HAVE LOVE FOR HER IN YOUR HEART OR ELSE...
I DO, KING. OF THAT I HAVE NO DOUBT.

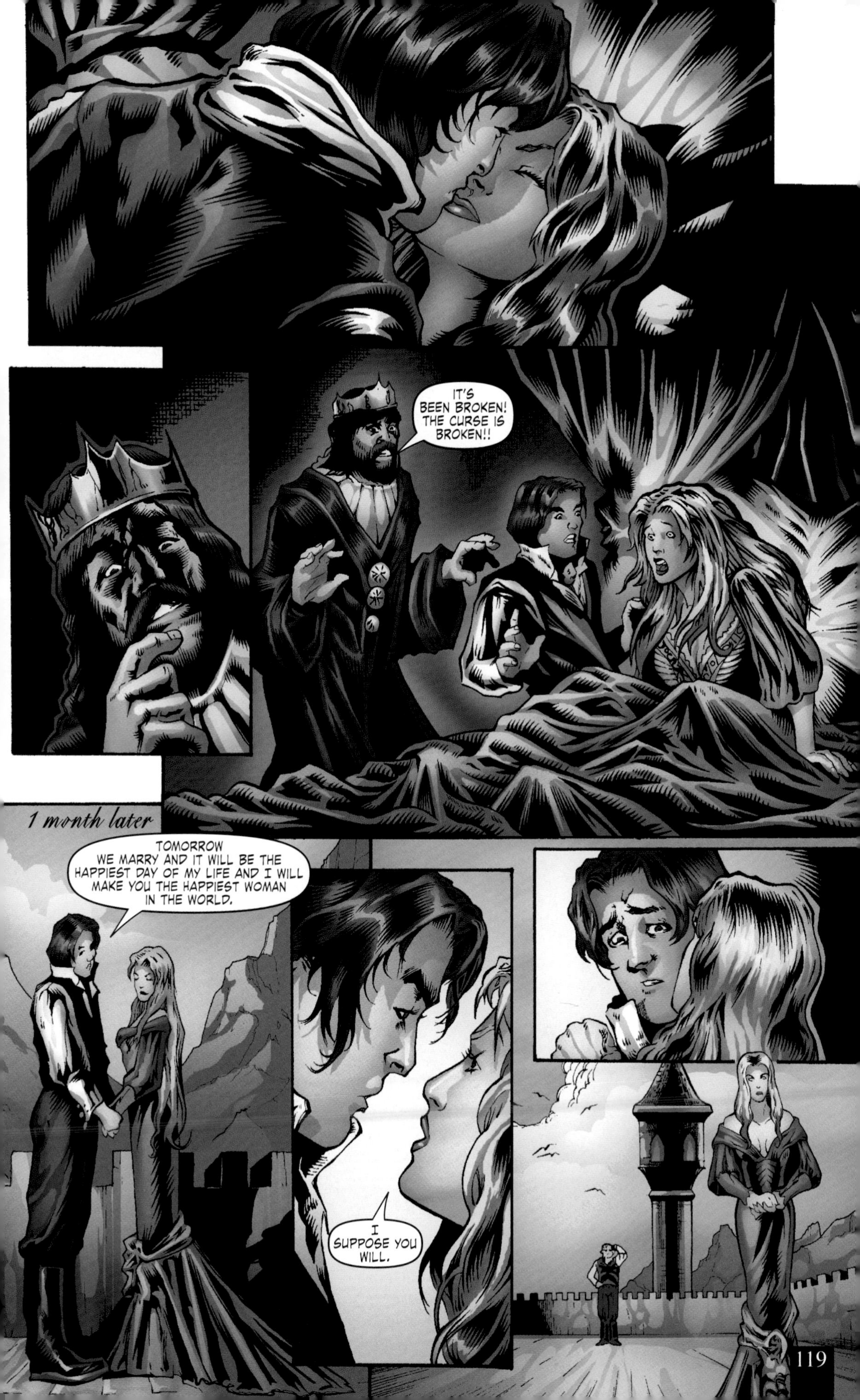
IT'S BEEN BROKEN! THE CURSE IS BROKEN!!
1 month later
TOMORROW WE MARRY AND IT WILL BE THE HAPPIEST DAY OF MY LIFE AND I WILL MAKE YOU THE HAPPIEST WOMAN IN THE WORLD.
I SUPPOSE YOU WILL.

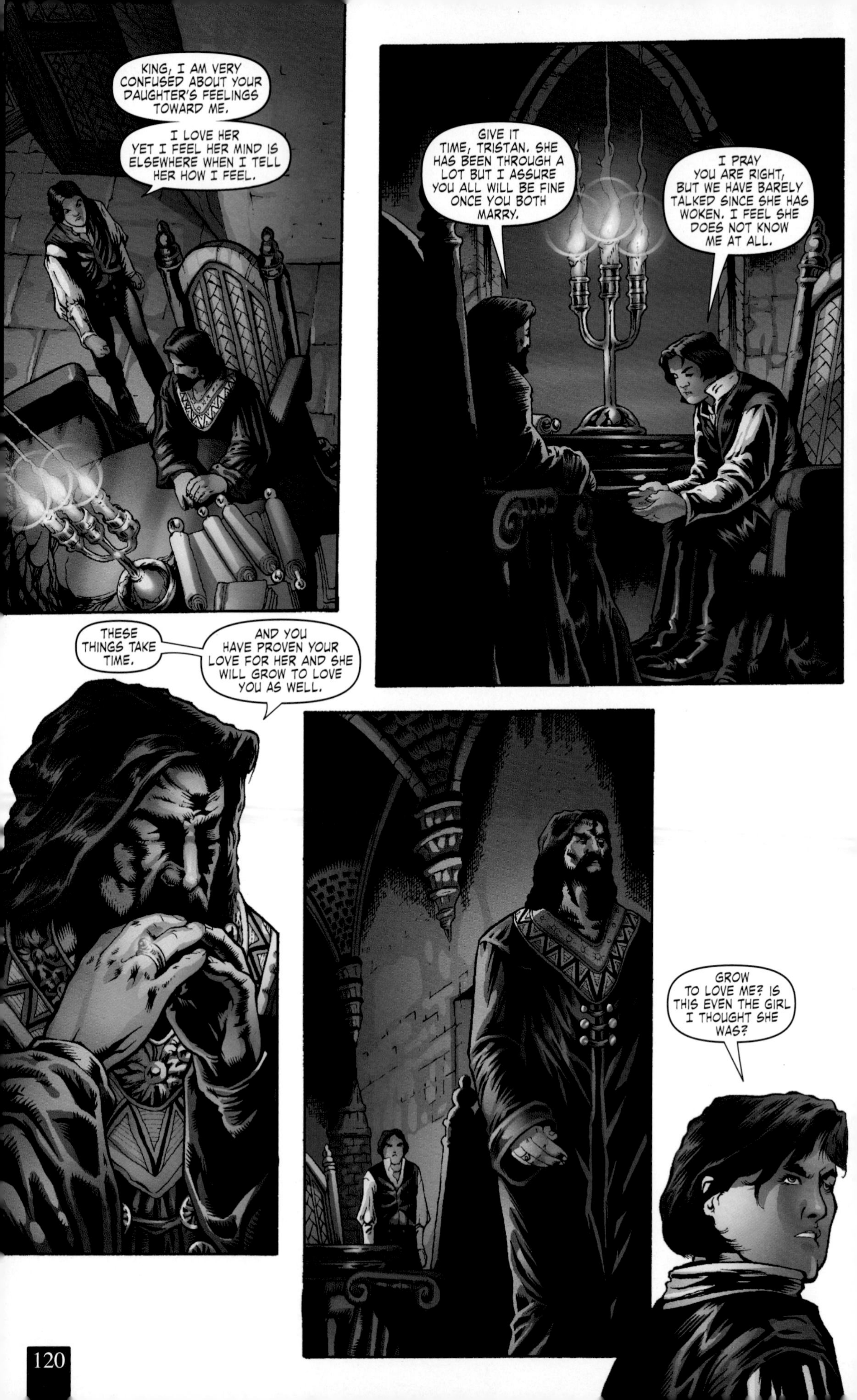
KING, I AM VERY CONFUSED ABOUT YOUR DAUGHTER'S FEELINGS TOWARD ME.
I LOVE HER YET I FEEL HER MIND IS ELSEWHERE WHEN I TELL HER HOW I FEEL.
GIVE IT TIME, TRISTAN. SHE HAS BEEN THROUGH A LOT BUT I ASSURE YOU ALL WILL BE FINE ONCE YOU BOTH MARRY.
I PRAY YOU ARE RIGHT, BUT WE HAVE BARELY TALKED SINCE SHE HAS WOKEN. I FEEL SHE DOES NOT KNOW ME AT ALL.
THESE THINGS TAKE TIME.
AND YOU HAVE PROVEN YOUR LOVE FOR HER AND SHE WILL GROW TO LOVE YOU AS WELL.
GROW TO LOVE ME? IS THIS EVEN THE GIRL I THOUGHT SHE WAS?

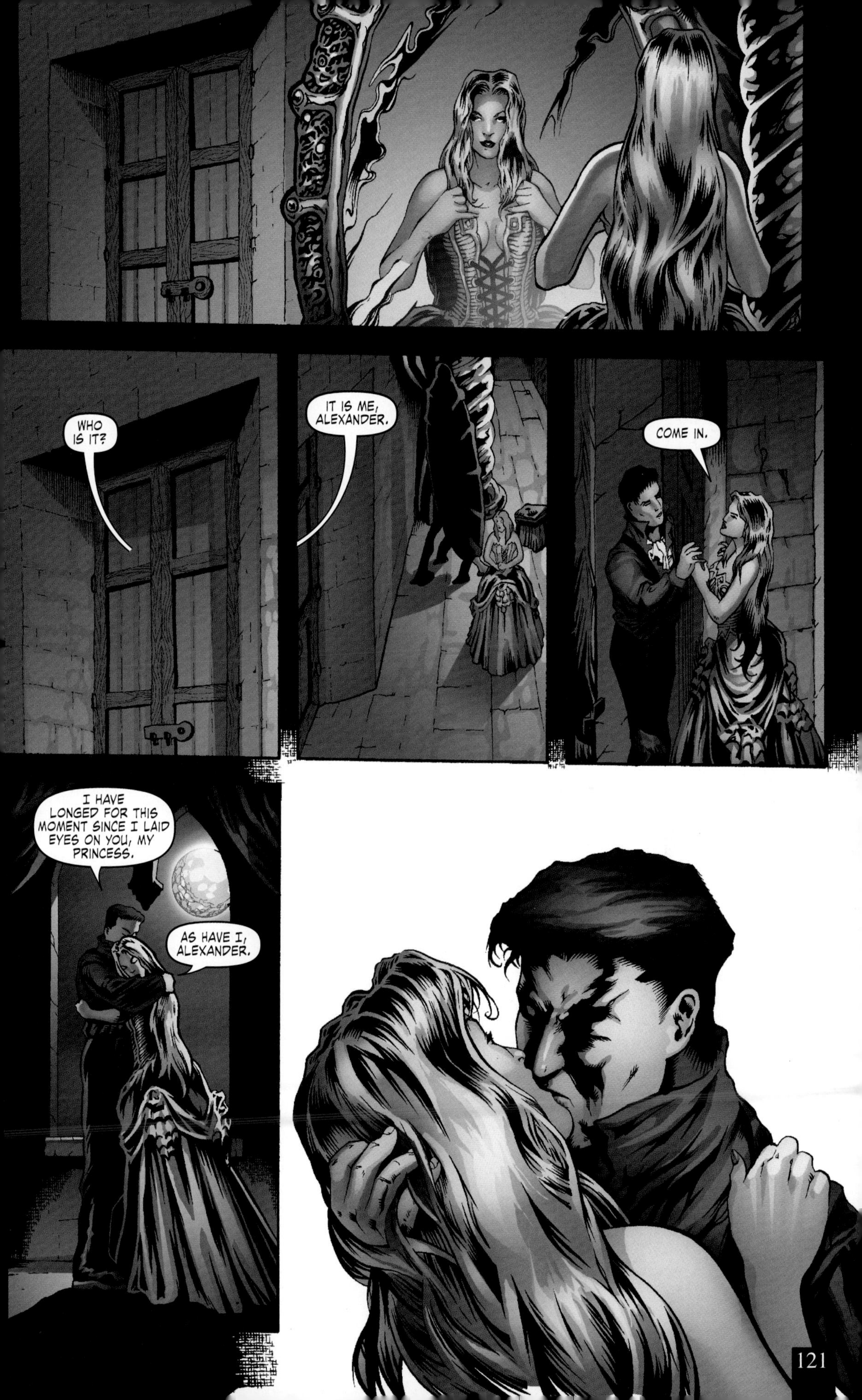
WHO IS IT?
IT IS ME, ALEXANDER.
COME IN.
I HAVE LONGED FOR THIS MOMENT SINCE I LAID EYES ON YOU, MY PRINCESS.
AS HAVE I, ALEXANDER.

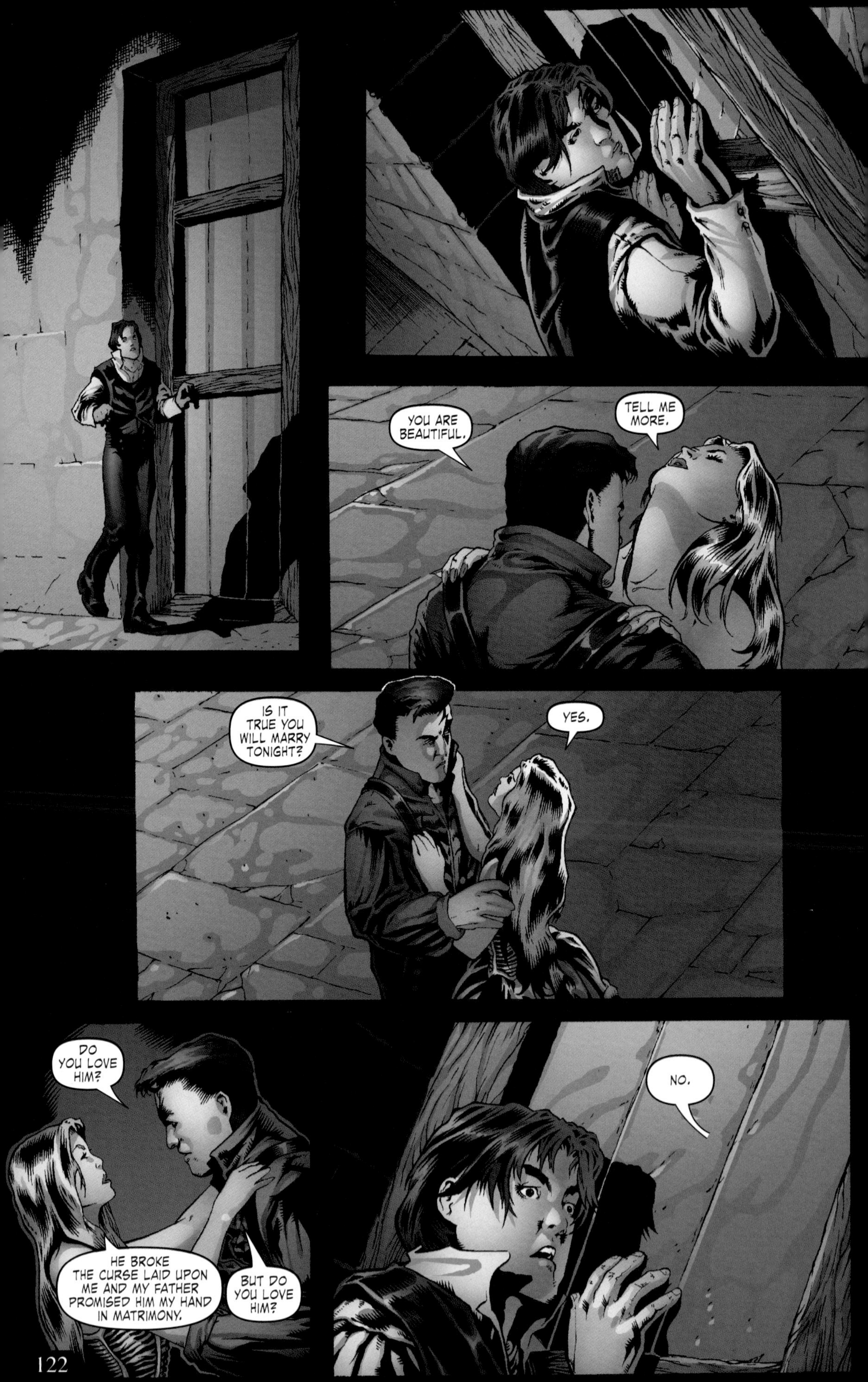
YOU ARE BEAUTIFUL.
TELL ME MORE.
IS IT TRUE YOU WILL MARRY TONIGHT?
YES.
DO YOU LOVE HIM?
HE BROKE THE CURSE LAID UPON ME AND MY FATHER PROMISED HIM MY HAND IN MATRIMONY.
BUT DO YOU LOVE HIM?
NO.

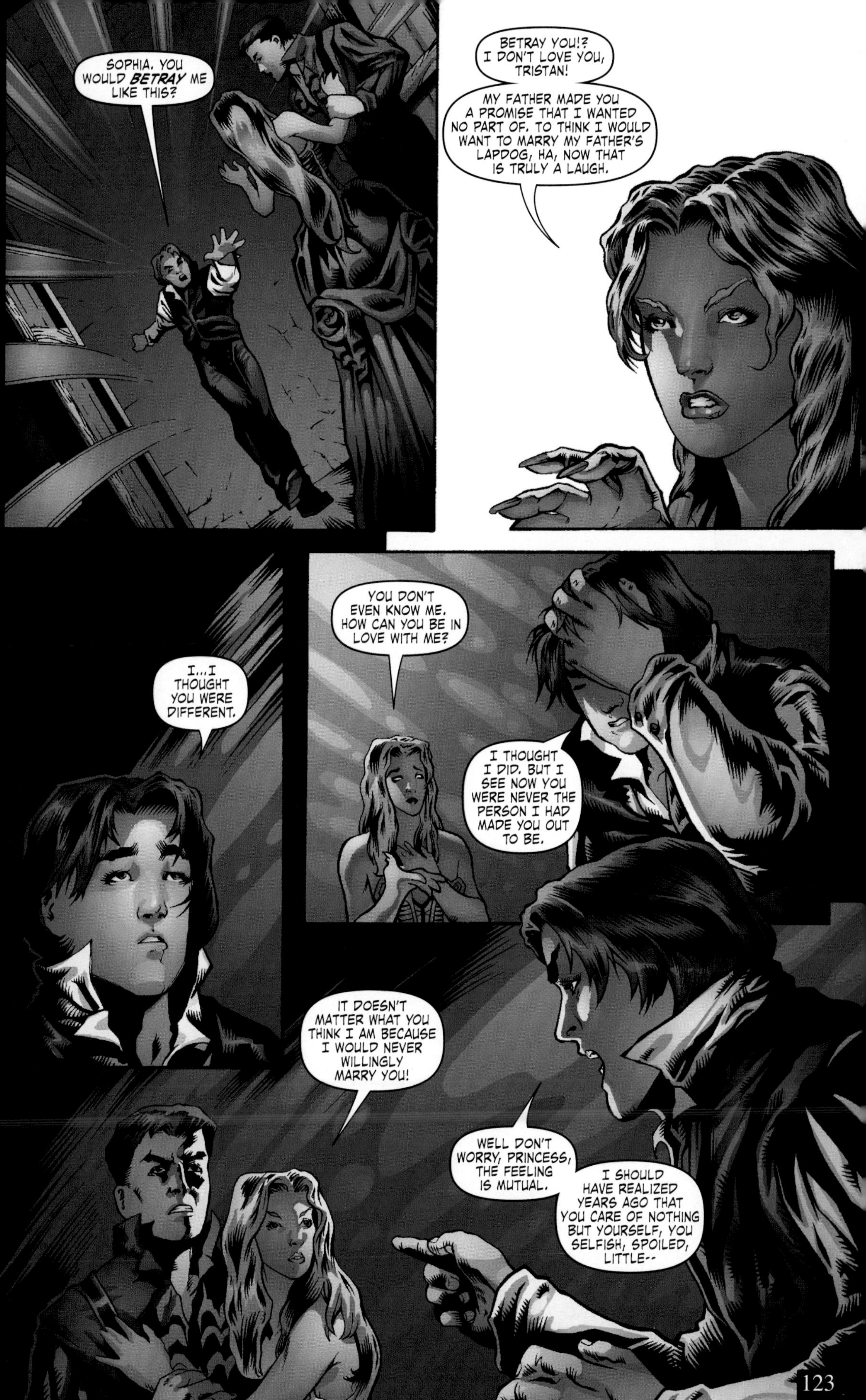
SOPHIA. YOU WOULD BETRAY ME LIKE THIS?
BETRAY YOU!? I DON'T LOVE YOU, TRISTAN!
MY FATHER MADE YOU A PROMISE THAT I WANTED NO PART OF. TO THINK I WOULD WANT TO MARRY MY FATHER'S LAPDOG, HA, NOW THAT IS TRULY A LAUGH.
I...I THOUGHT YOU WERE DIFFERENT.
YOU DON'T EVEN KNOW ME. HOW CAN YOU BE IN LOVE WITH ME?
I THOUGHT I DID. BUT I SEE NOW YOU WERE NEVER THE PERSON I HAD MADE YOU OUT TO BE.
IT DOESN'T MATTER WHAT YOU THINK I AM BECAUSE I WOULD NEVER WILLINGLY MARRY YOU!
WELL DON'T WORRY, PRINCESS, THE FEELING IS MUTUAL.
I SHOULD HAVE REALIZED YEARS AGO THAT YOU CARE OF NOTHING BUT YOURSELF, YOU SELFISH, SPOILED, LITTLE--

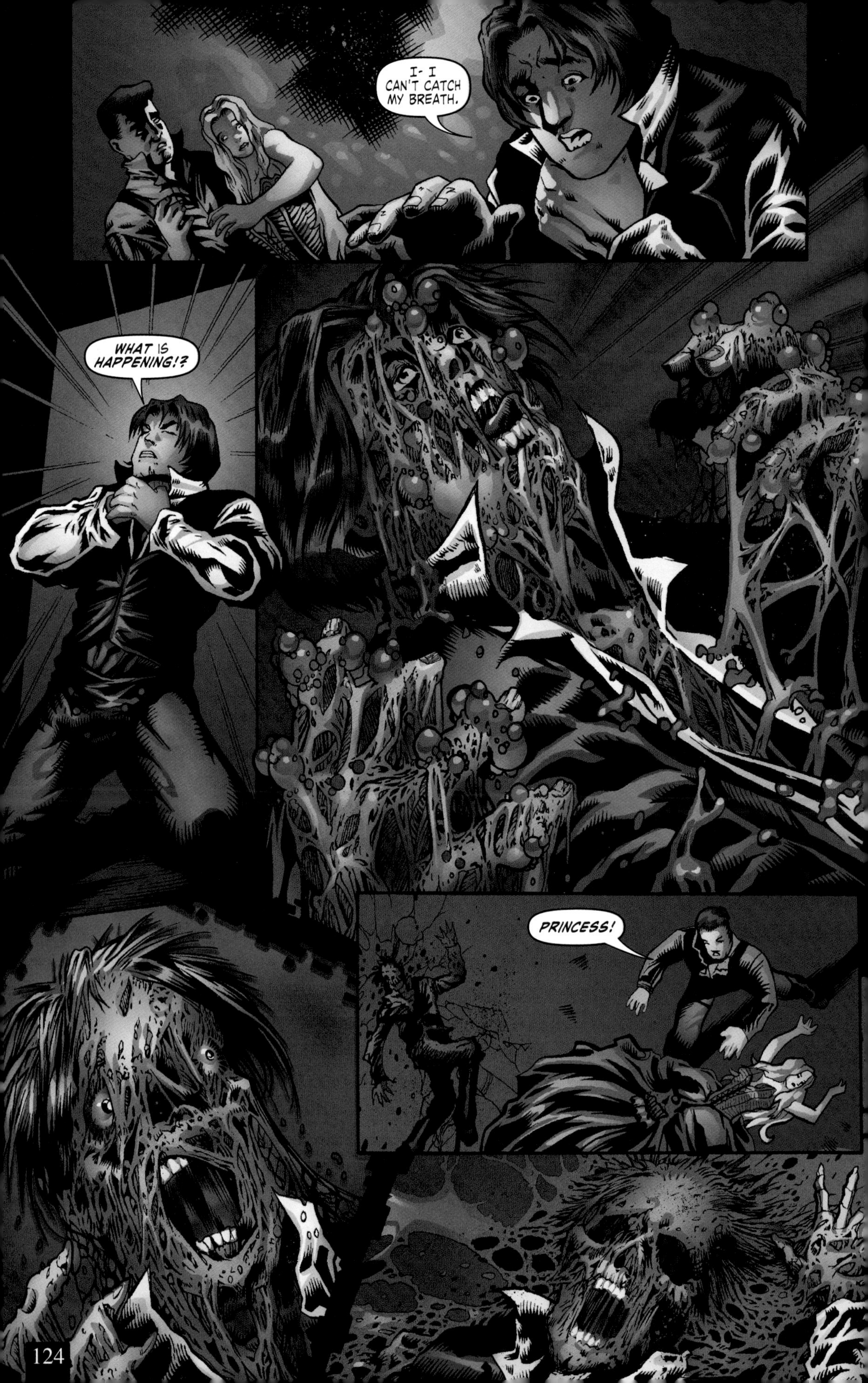
I- I CAN'T CATCH MY BREATH.
WHAT IS HAPPENING!?
PRINCESS!

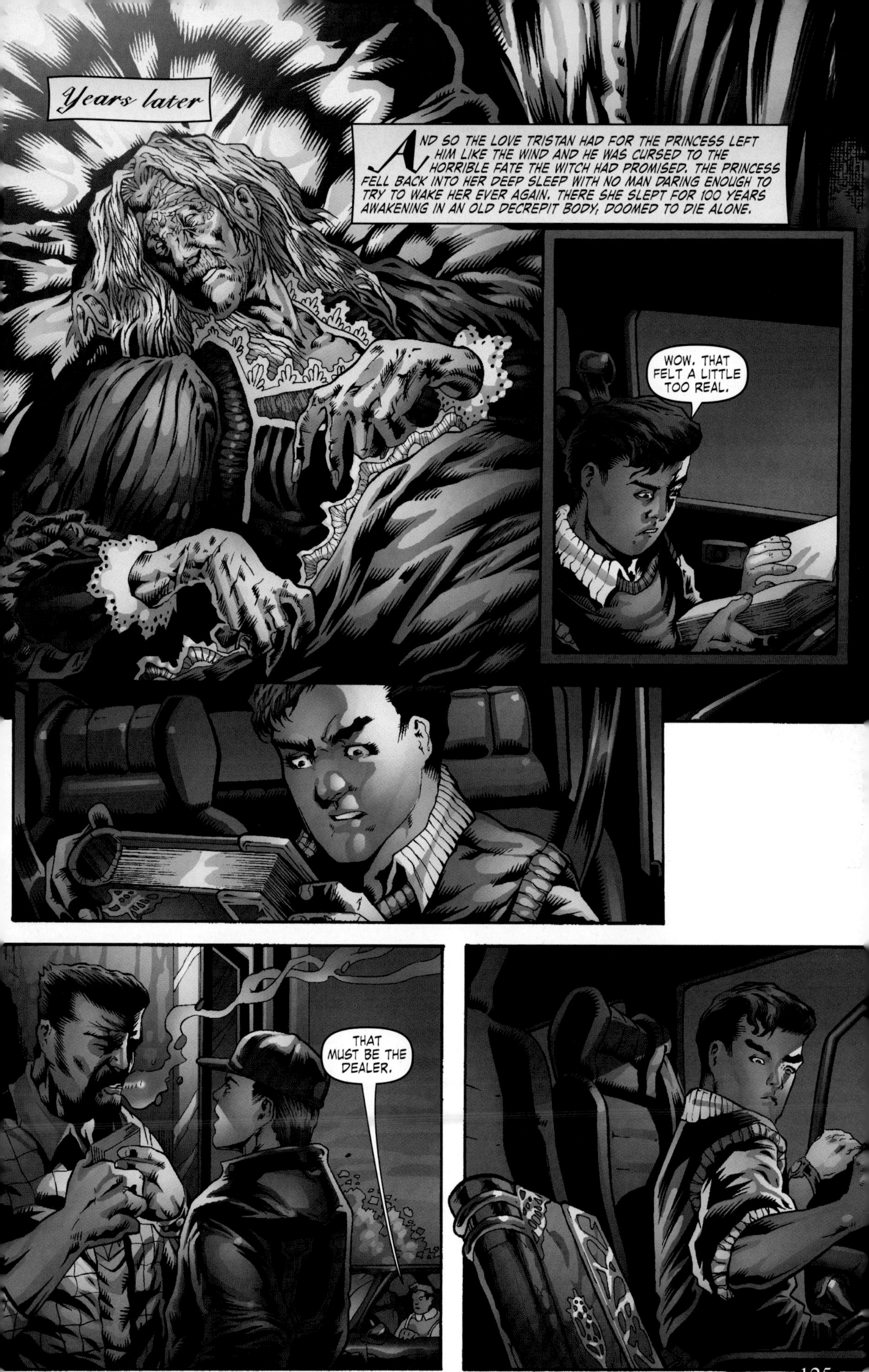

Years later
AND SO THE LOVE TRISTAN HAD FOR THE PRINCESS LEFT HIM LIKE THE WIND AND HE WAS CURSED TO THE HORRIBLE FATE THE WITCH HAD PROMISED. THE PRINCESS FELL BACK INTO HER DEEP SLEEP WITH NO MAN DARING ENOUGH TO TRY TO WAKE HER EVER AGAIN. THERE SHE SLEPT FOR 100 YEARS AWAKENING IN AN OLD DECREPIT BODY, DOOMED TO DIE ALONE.
WOW. THAT FELT A LITTLE TOO REAL.
THAT MUST BE THE DEALER.

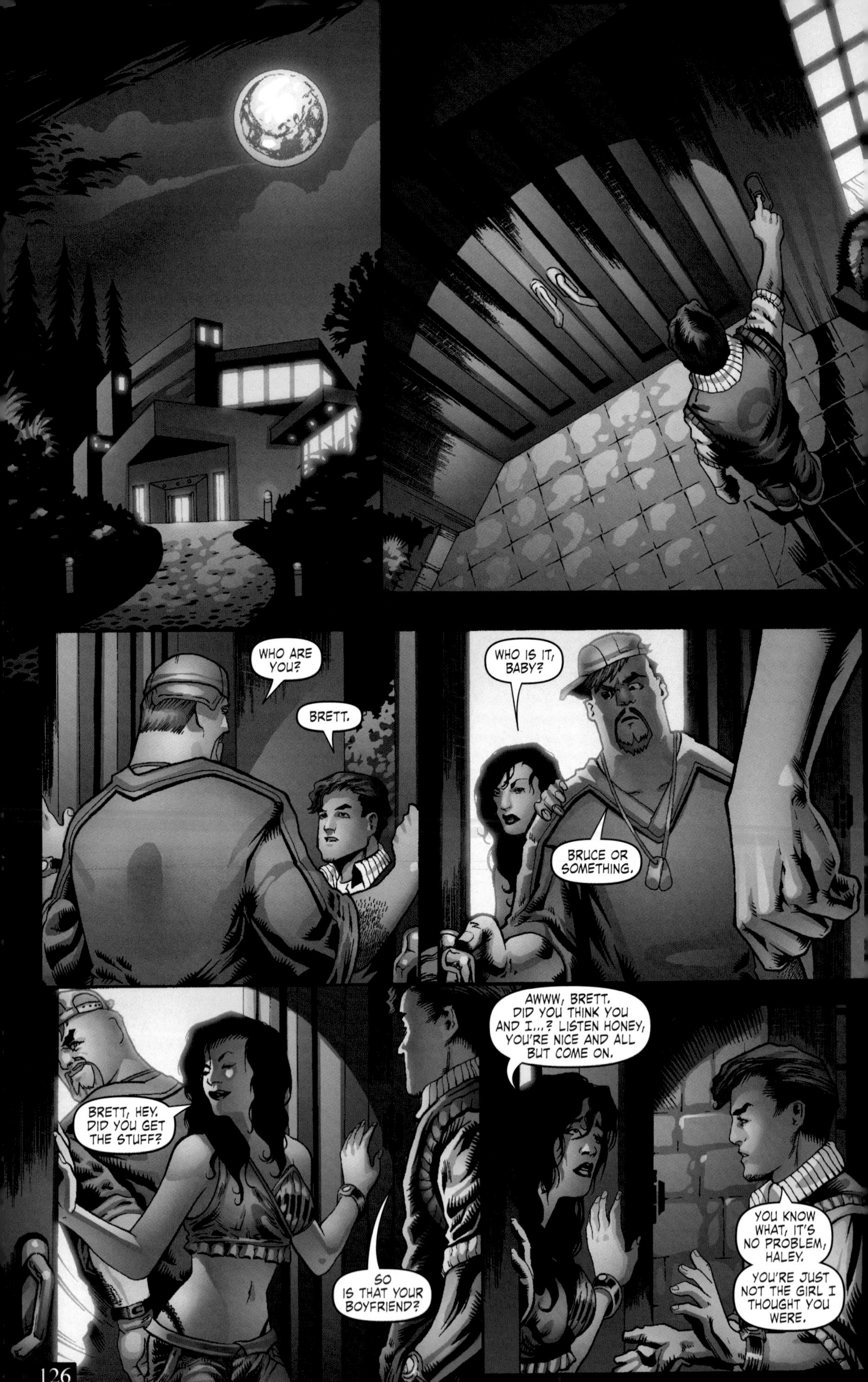
WHO ARE YOU?
BRETT.
WHO IS IT, BABY?
BRUCE OR SOMETHING.
BRETT, HEY. DID YOU GET THE STUFF?
SO IS THAT YOUR BOYFRIEND?
AWWW, BRETT. DID YOU THINK YOU AND I...? LISTEN HONEY, YOU'RE NICE AND ALL BUT COME ON.
YOU KNOW WHAT, IT'S NO PROBLEM, HALEY.
YOU'RE JUST NOT THE GIRL I THOUGHT YOU WERE.

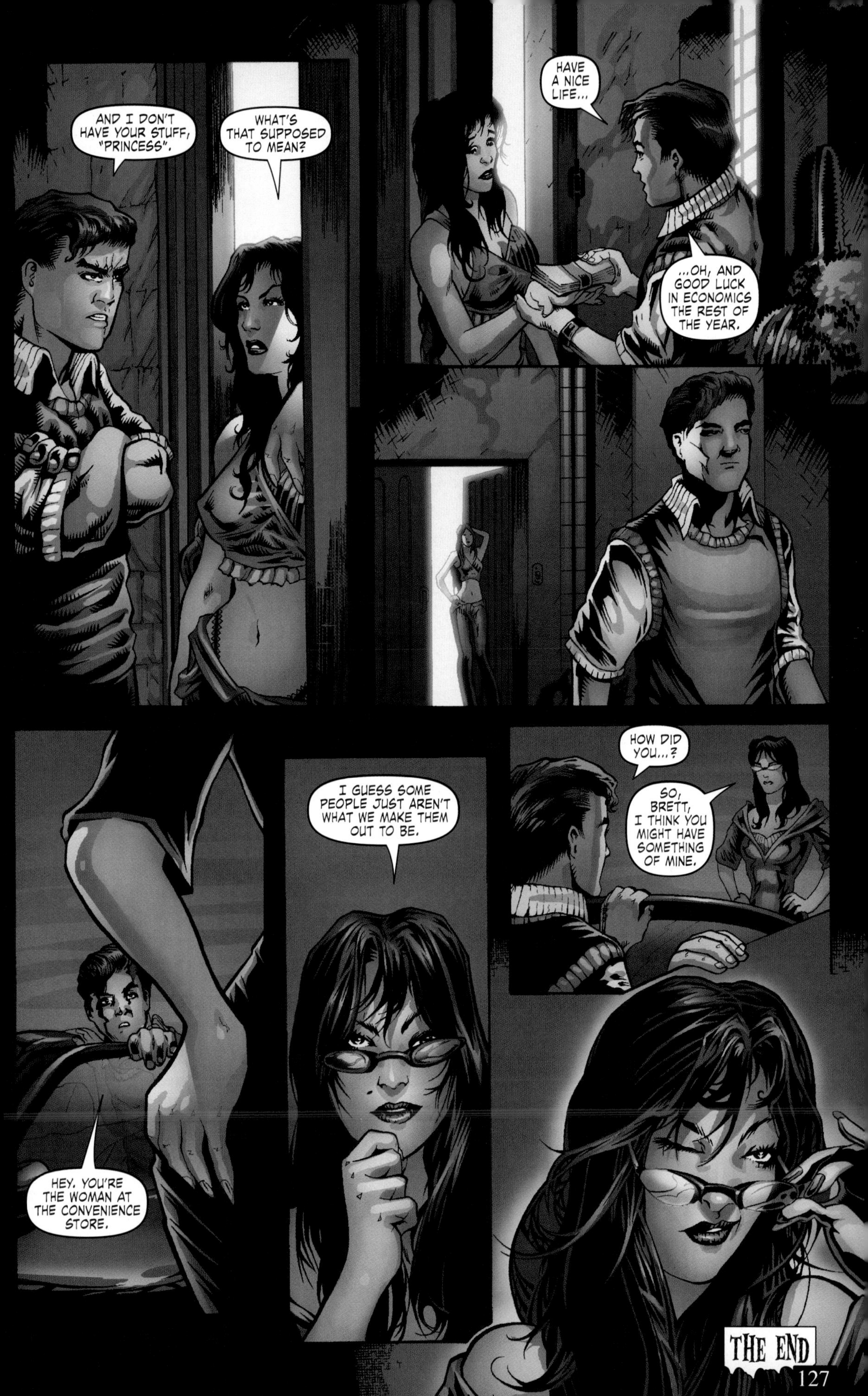
AND I DON'T HAVE YOUR STUFF, "PRINCESS".
WHAT'S THAT SUPPOSED TO MEAN?
HAVE A NICE LIFE...
...OH, AND GOOD LUCK IN ECONOMICS THE REST OF THE YEAR.
HEY. YOU'RE THE WOMAN AT THE CONVENIENCE STORE.
I GUESS SOME PEOPLE JUST AREN'T WHAT WE MAKE THEM OUT TO BE.
HOW DID YOU...?
SO, BRETT, I THINK YOU MIGHT HAVE SOMETHING OF MINE.
THE END

The Robber Bridegroom

Written & Created by
Joe Tyler & Ralph Tedesco

Pencils & Inks Josh Medors
Colors Mark McNabb
Design David Seidman
Lettering Artmonkeys
Cover Nick Marks
Editor Ralph Tedesco

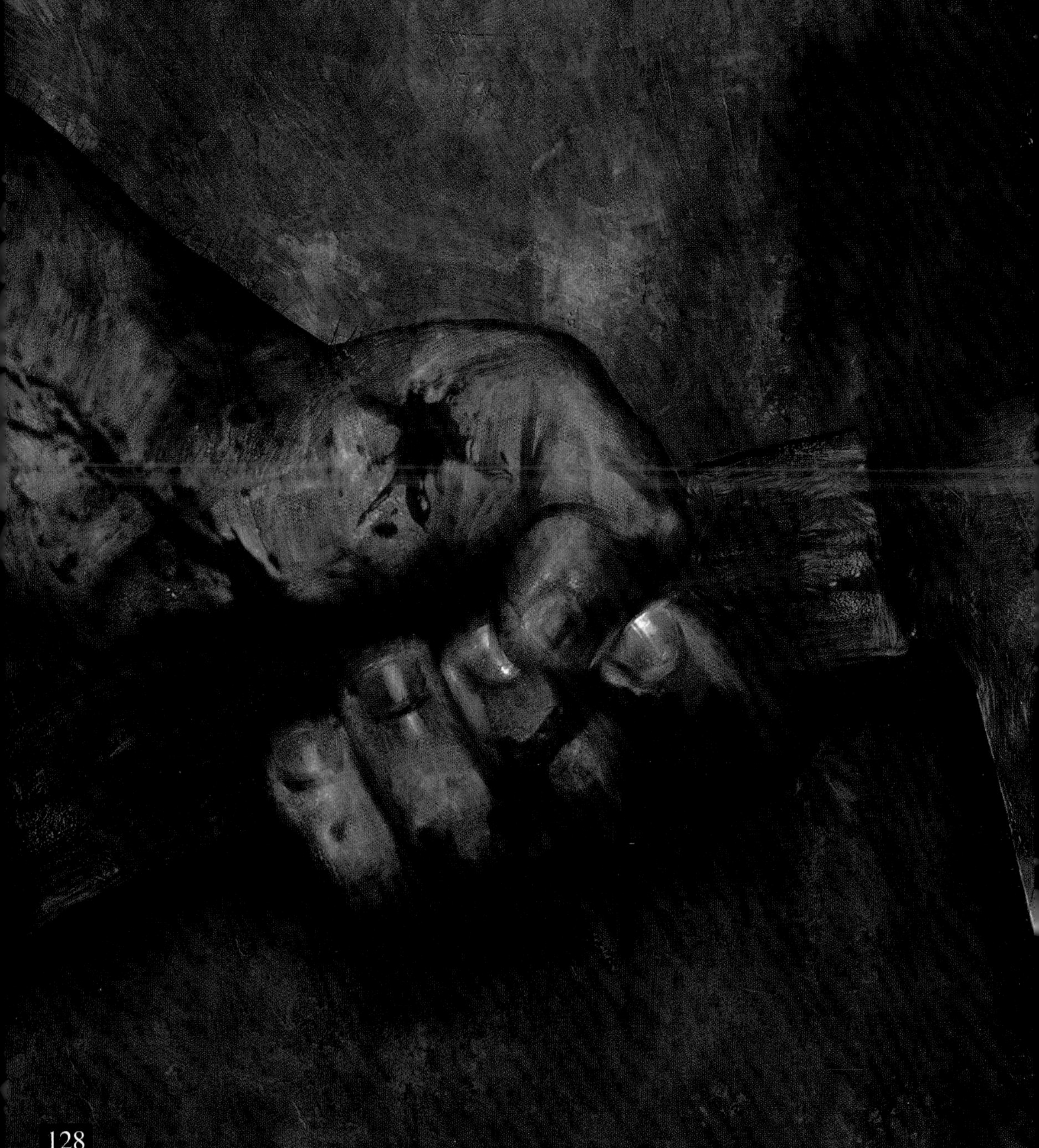

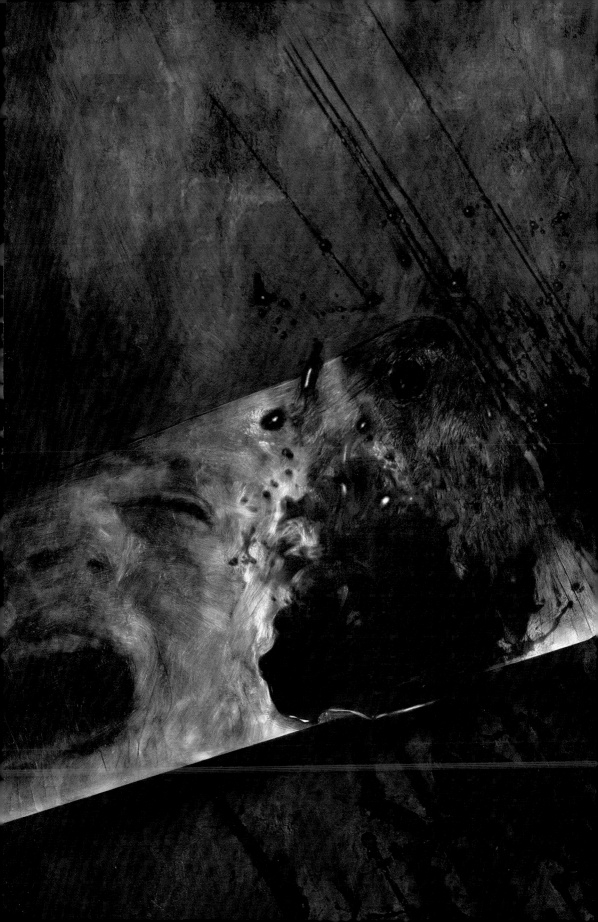

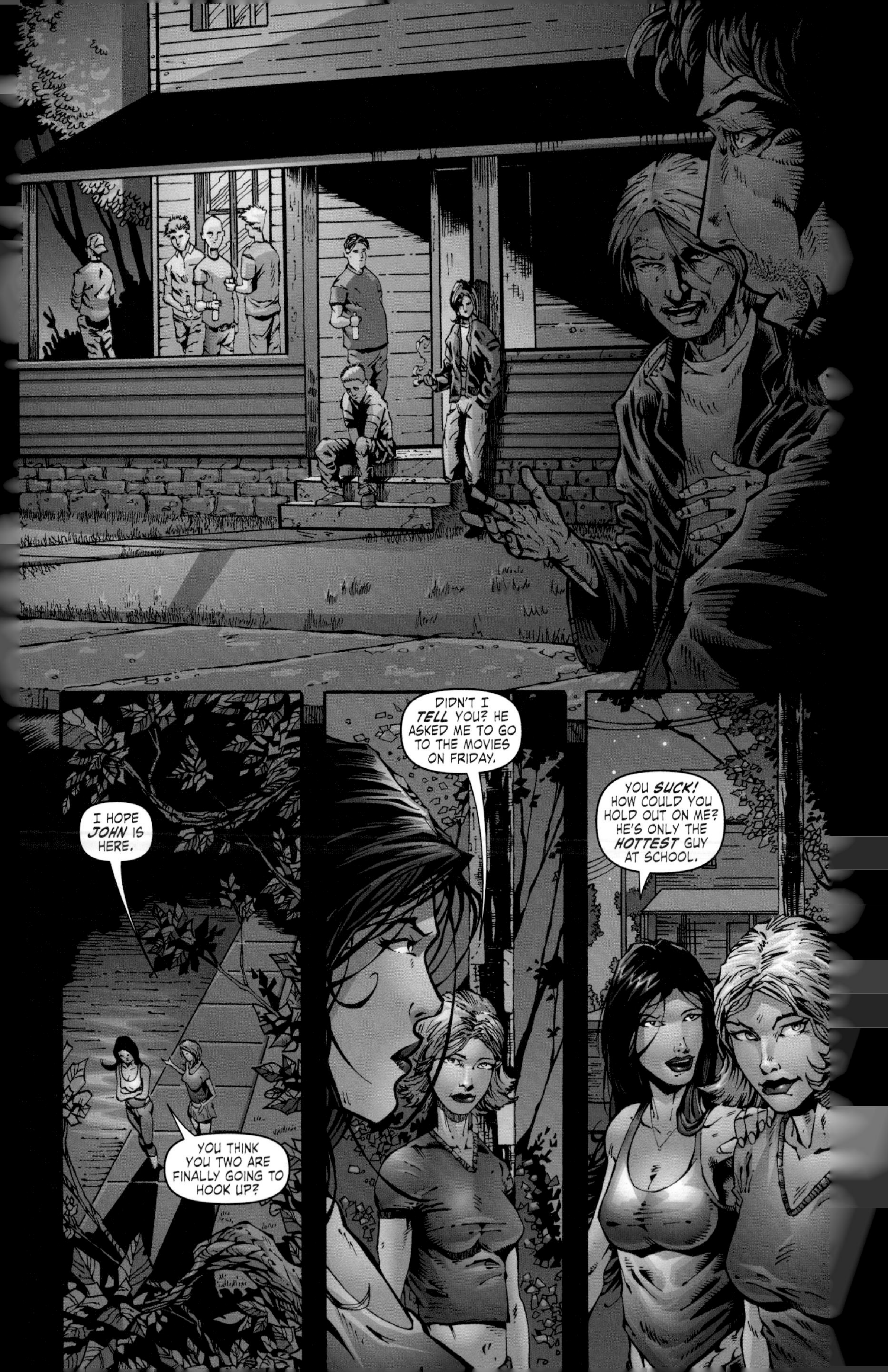
I HOPE JOHN IS HERE.
YOU THINK YOU TWO ARE FINALLY GOING TO HOOK UP?
DIDN'T I TELL YOU? HE ASKED ME TO GO TO THE MOVIES ON FRIDAY.
YOU SUCK! HOW COULD YOU HOLD OUT ON ME? HE'S ONLY THE HOTTEST GUY AT SCHOOL.

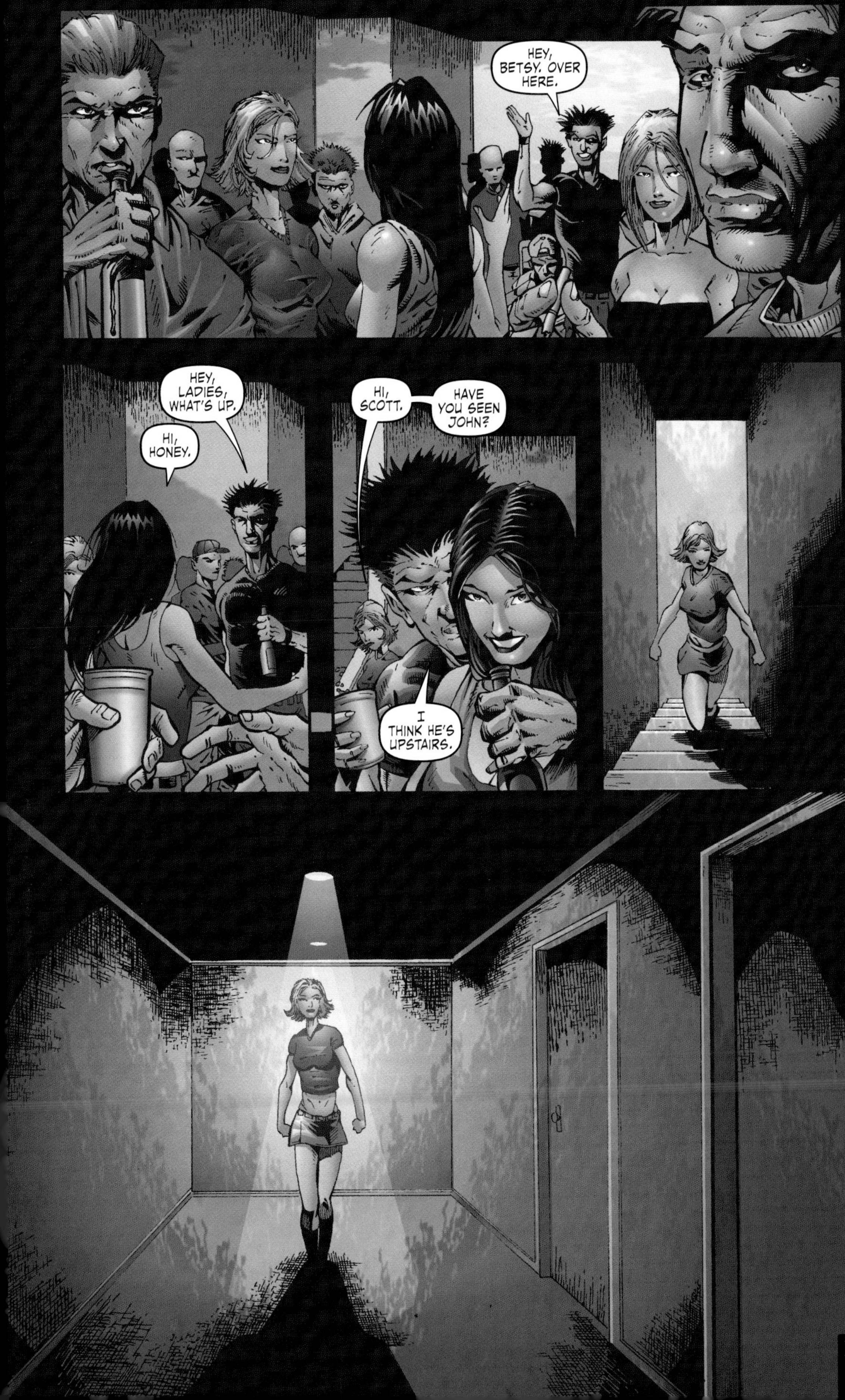
HEY, BETSY. OVER HERE.
HEY, LADIES, WHAT'S UP.
HI, HONEY.
HI, SCOTT.
HAVE YOU SEEN JOHN?
I THINK HE'S UPSTAIRS.

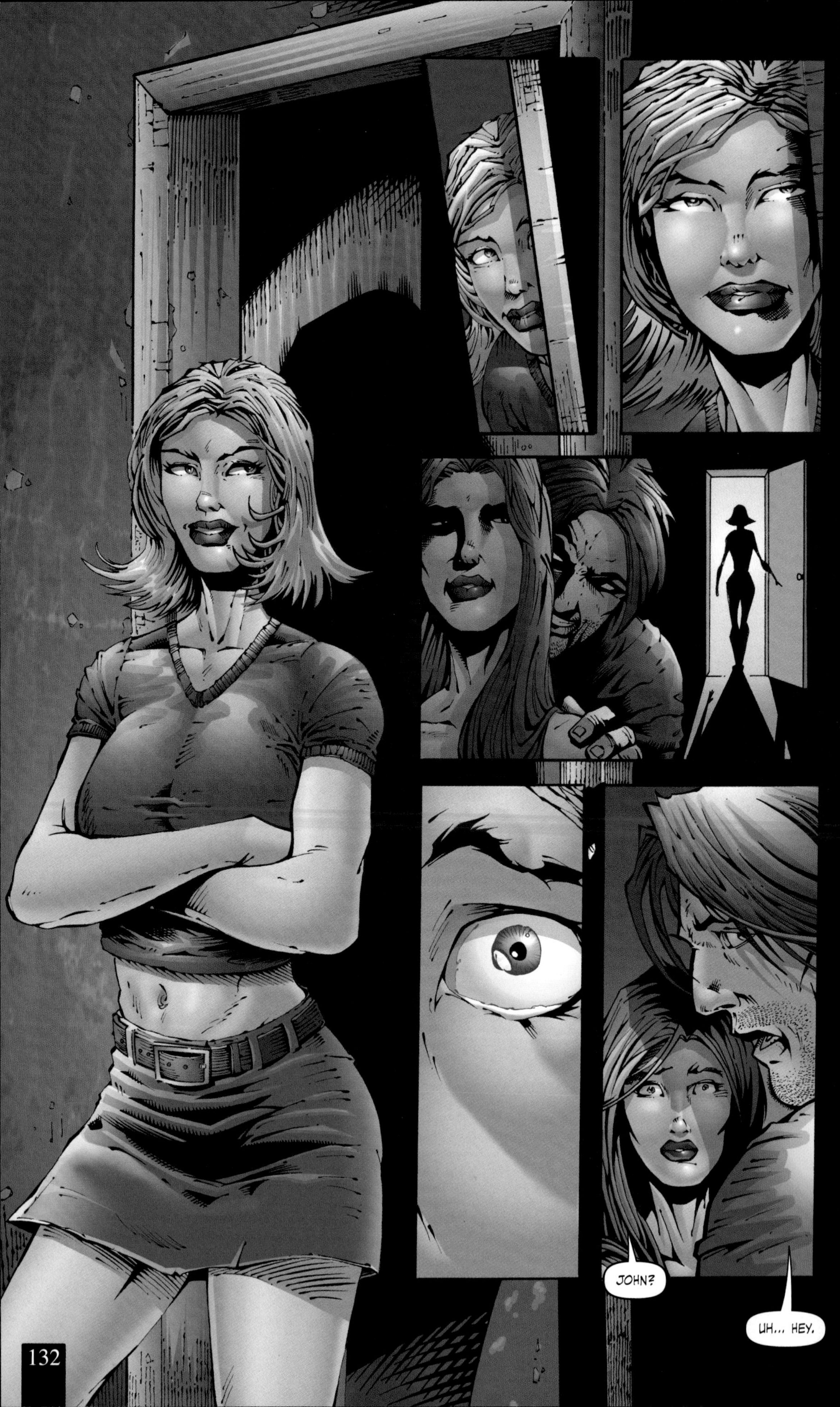
JOHN?
UH... HEY.

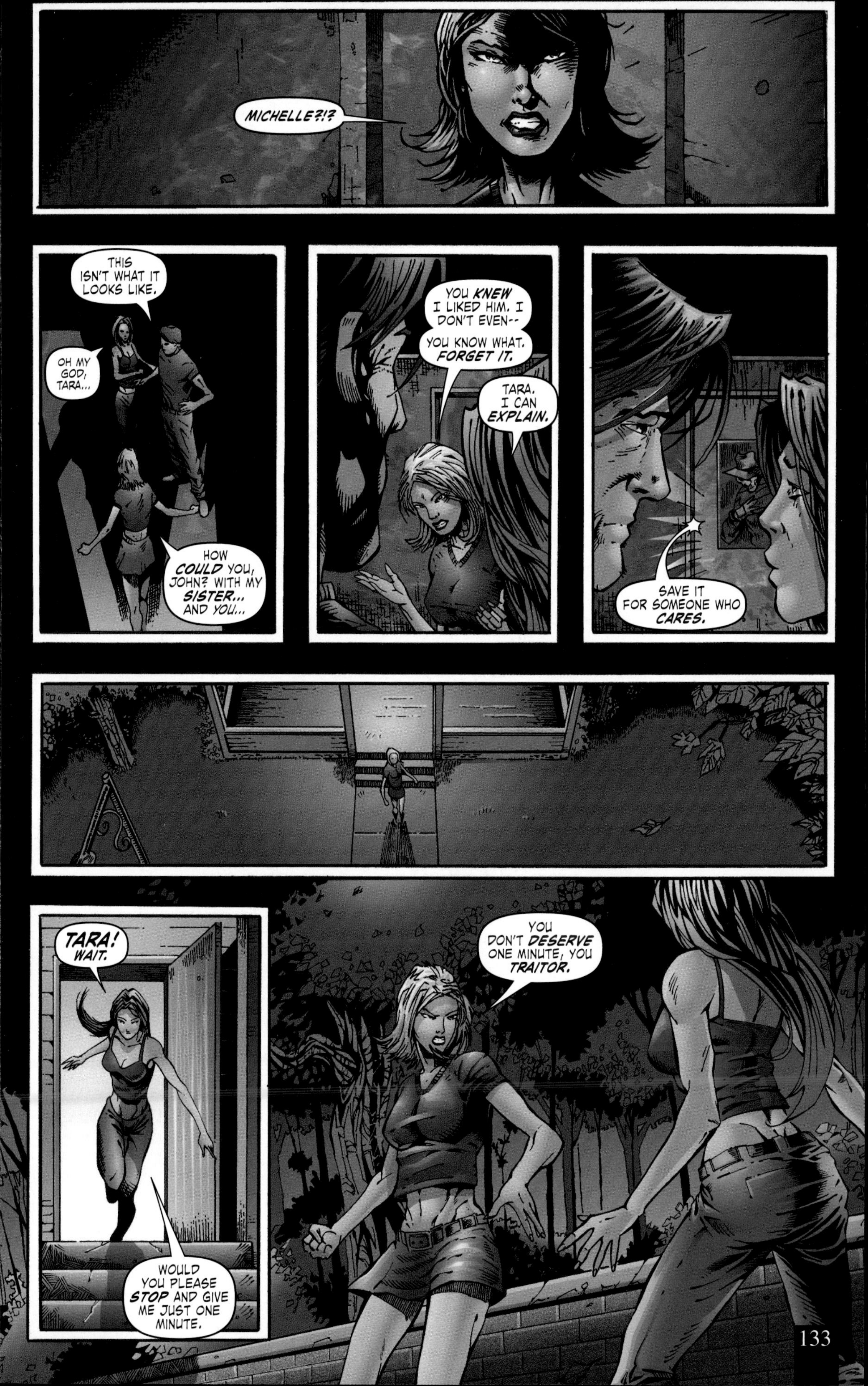
MICHELLE?!?
THIS ISN'T WHAT IT LOOKS LIKE.
OH MY GOD, TARA...
HOW COULD YOU, JOHN? WITH MY SISTER... AND YOU...
YOU KNEW I LIKED HIM. I DON'T EVEN--
YOU KNOW WHAT. FORGET IT.
TARA. I CAN EXPLAIN.
SAVE IT FOR SOMEONE WHO CARES.
TARA! WAIT.
WOULD YOU PLEASE STOP AND GIVE ME JUST ONE MINUTE.
YOU DON'T DESERVE ONE MINUTE, YOU TRAITOR.

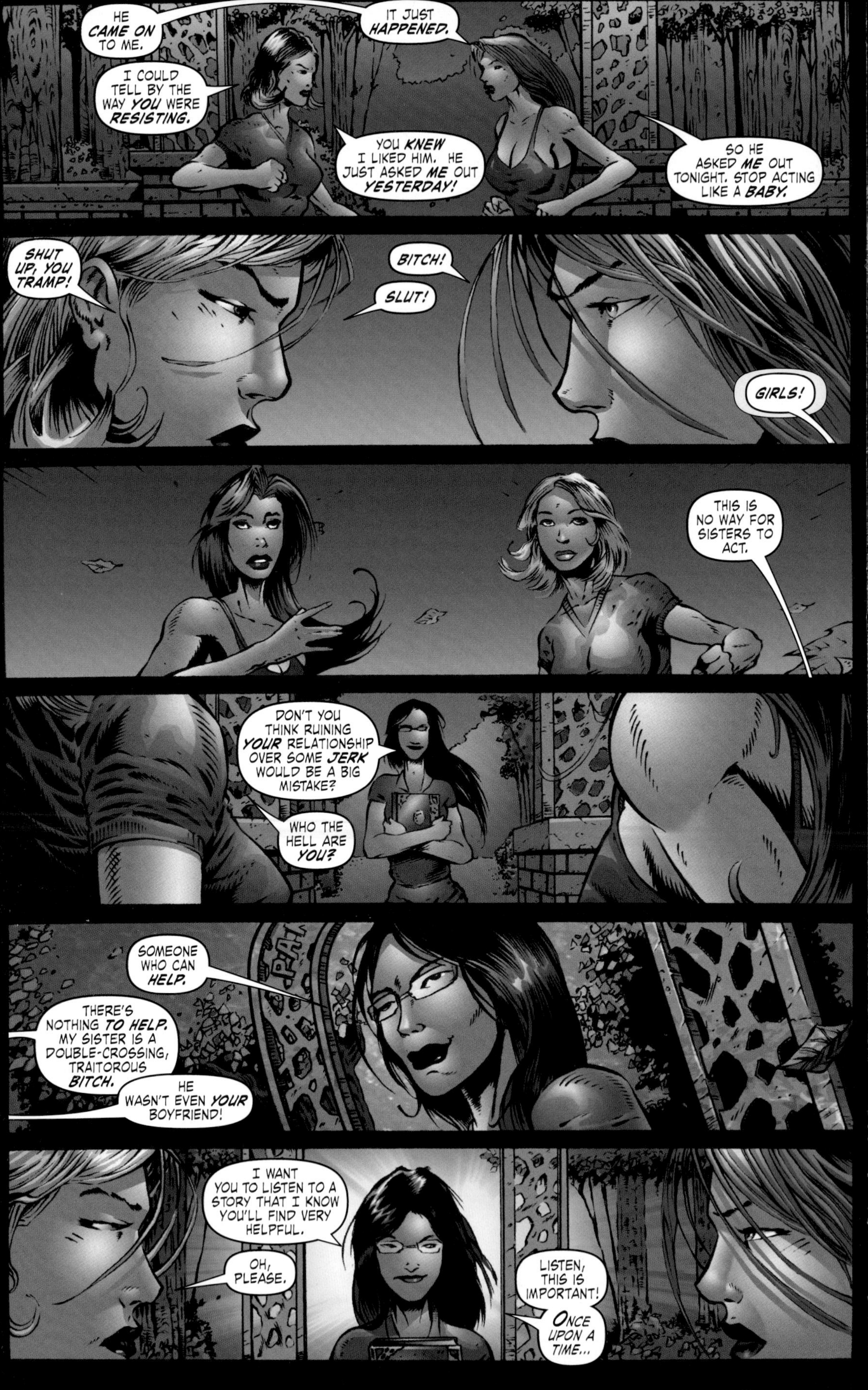
HE CAME ON TO ME.
IT JUST HAPPENED.
I COULD TELL BY THE WAY YOU WERE RESISTING.
YOU KNEW I LIKED HIM. HE JUST ASKED ME OUT YESTERDAY!
SO HE ASKED ME OUT TONIGHT. STOP ACTING LIKE A BABY.
SHUT UP, YOU TRAMP!
BITCH!
SLUT!
GIRLS!
THIS IS NO WAY FOR SISTERS TO ACT.
DON'T YOU THINK RUINING YOUR RELATIONSHIP OVER SOME JERK WOULD BE A BIG MISTAKE?
WHO THE HELL ARE YOU?
SOMEONE WHO CAN HELP.
THERE'S NOTHING TO HELP. MY SISTER IS A DOUBLE-CROSSING, TRAITOROUS BITCH.
HE WASN'T EVEN YOUR BOYFRIEND!
I WANT YOU TO LISTEN TO A STORY THAT I KNOW YOU'LL FIND VERY HELPFUL.
OH, PLEASE.
LISTEN, THIS IS IMPORTANT!
ONCE UPON A TIME...

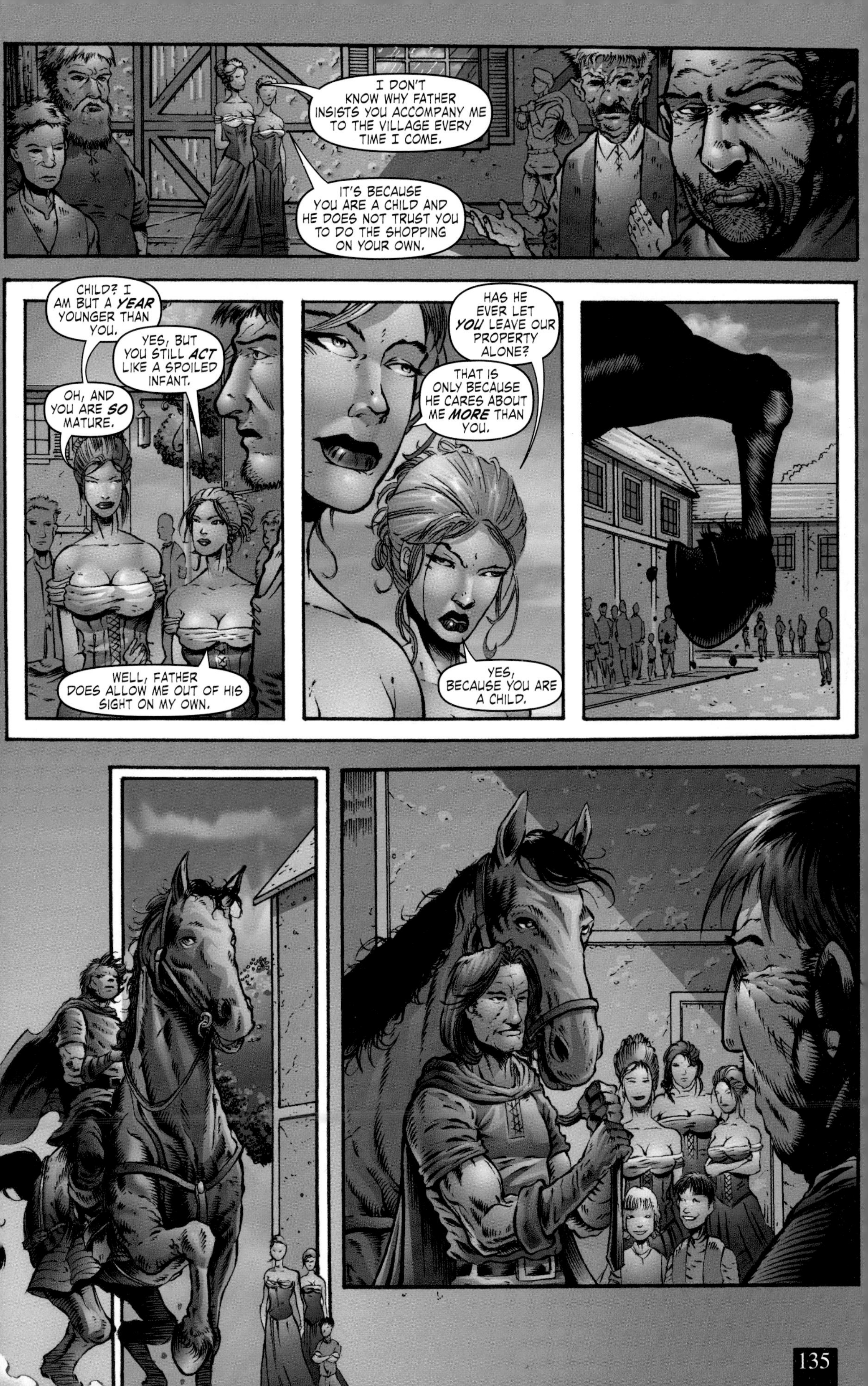
I DON'T KNOW WHY FATHER INSISTS YOU ACCOMPANY ME TO THE VILLAGE EVERY TIME I COME.
IT'S BECAUSE YOU ARE A CHILD AND HE DOES NOT TRUST YOU TO DO THE SHOPPING ON YOUR OWN.
CHILD? I AM BUT A YEAR YOUNGER THAN YOU.
YES, BUT YOU STILL ACT LIKE A SPOILED INFANT.
OH, AND YOU ARE SO MATURE.
WELL, FATHER DOES ALLOW ME OUT OF HIS SIGHT ON MY OWN.
HAS HE EVER LET YOU LEAVE OUR PROPERTY ALONE?
THAT IS ONLY BECAUSE HE CARES ABOUT ME MORE THAN YOU.
YES, BECAUSE YOU ARE A CHILD.

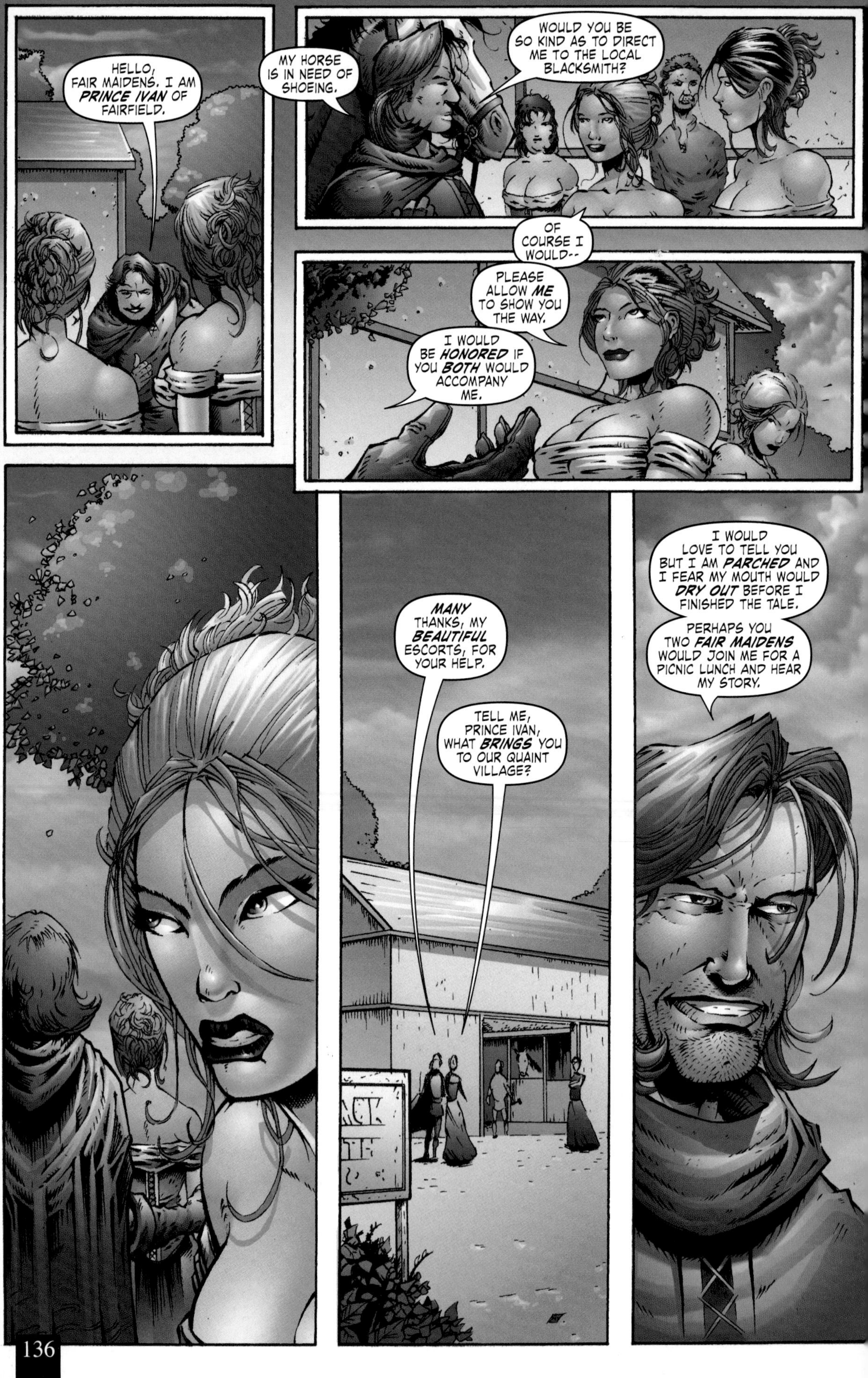
HELLO, FAIR MAIDENS. I AM PRINCE IVAN OF FAIRFIELD.
MY HORSE IS IN NEED OF SHOEING.
WOULD YOU BE SO KIND AS TO DIRECT ME TO THE LOCAL BLACKSMITH?
OF COURSE I WOULD--
PLEASE ALLOW ME TO SHOW YOU THE WAY.
I WOULD BE HONORED IF YOU BOTH WOULD ACCOMPANY ME.
MANY THANKS, MY BEAUTIFUL ESCORTS, FOR YOUR HELP.
TELL ME, PRINCE IVAN, WHAT BRINGS YOU TO OUR QUAINT VILLAGE?
I WOULD LOVE TO TELL YOU BUT I AM PARCHED AND I FEAR MY MOUTH WOULD DRY OUT BEFORE I FINISHED THE TALE.
PERHAPS YOU TWO FAIR MAIDENS WOULD JOIN ME FOR A PICNIC LUNCH AND HEAR MY STORY.

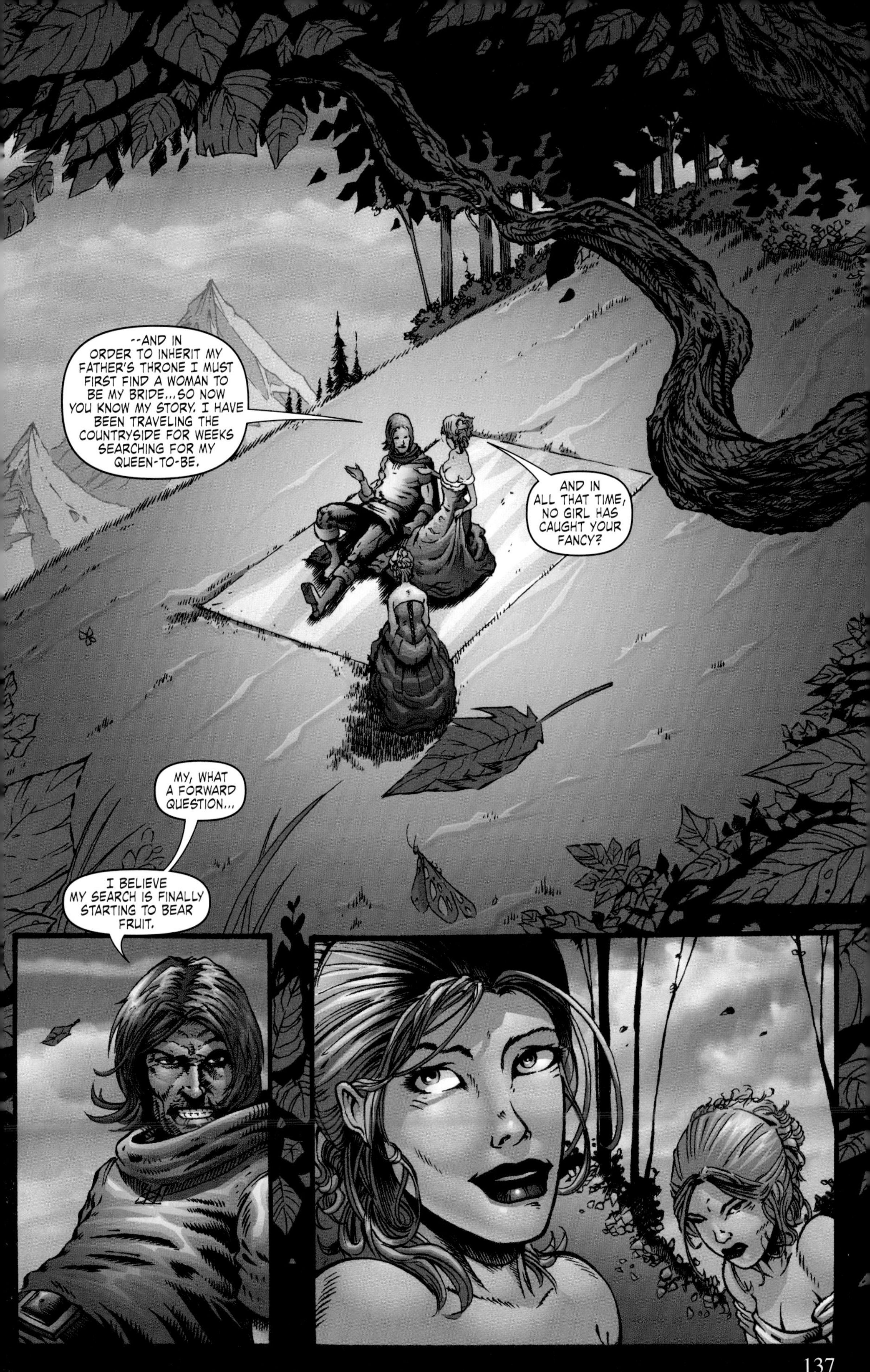

--AND IN ORDER TO INHERIT MY FATHER'S THRONE I MUST FIRST FIND A WOMAN TO BE MY BRIDE...SO NOW YOU KNOW MY STORY. I HAVE BEEN TRAVELING THE COUNTRYSIDE FOR WEEKS SEARCHING FOR MY QUEEN-TO-BE.
AND IN ALL THAT TIME, NO GIRL HAS CAUGHT YOUR FANCY?
MY, WHAT A FORWARD QUESTION...
I BELIEVE MY SEARCH IS FINALLY STARTING TO BEAR FRUIT.

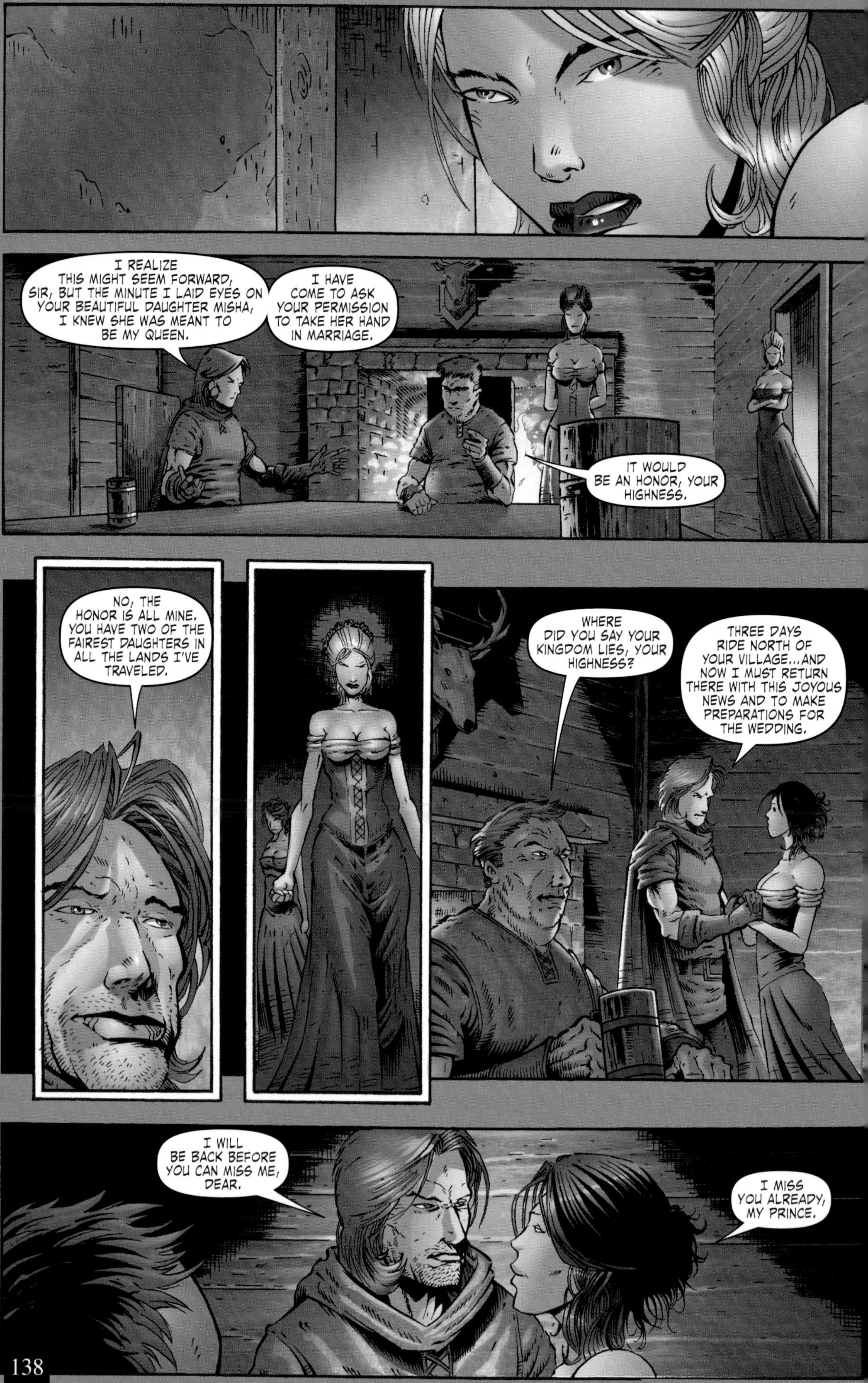
I REALIZE THIS MIGHT SEEM FORWARD, SIR, BUT THE MINUTE I LAID EYES ON YOUR BEAUTIFUL DAUGHTER MISHA, I KNEW SHE WAS MEANT TO BE MY QUEEN.
I HAVE COME TO ASK YOUR PERMISSION TO TAKE HER HAND IN MARRIAGE.
IT WOULD BE AN HONOR, YOUR HIGHNESS.
NO, THE HONOR IS ALL MINE. YOU HAVE TWO OF THE FAIREST DAUGHTERS IN ALL THE LANDS I'VE TRAVELED.
WHERE DID YOU SAY YOUR KINGDOM LIES, YOUR HIGHNESS?
THREE DAYS RIDE NORTH OF YOUR VILLAGE...AND NOW I MUST RETURN THERE WITH THIS JOYOUS NEWS AND TO MAKE PREPARATIONS FOR THE WEDDING.
I WILL BE BACK BEFORE YOU CAN MISS ME, DEAR.
I MISS YOU ALREADY, MY PRINCE.

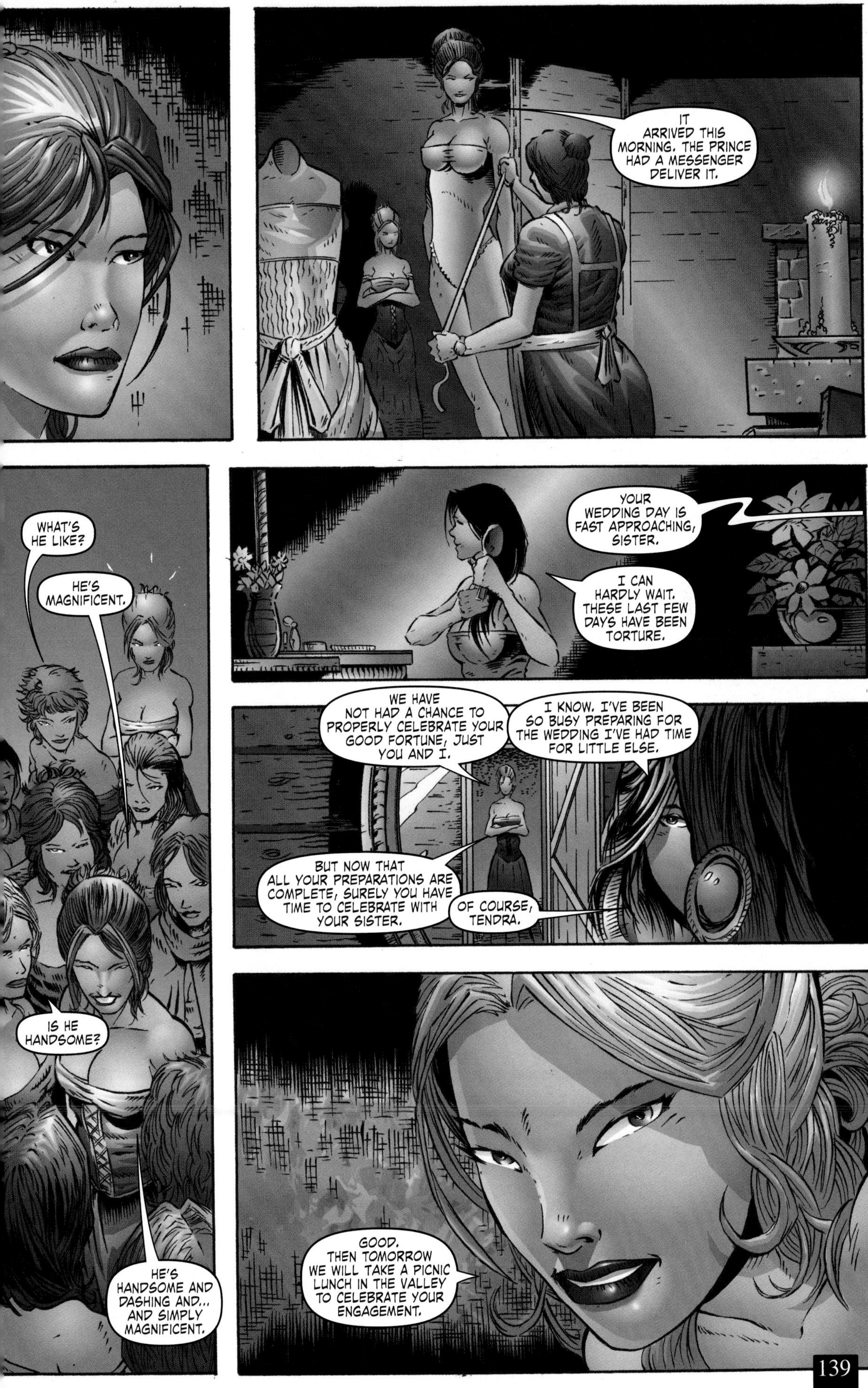
IT ARRIVED THIS MORNING. THE PRINCE HAD A MESSENGER DELIVER IT.
WHAT'S HE LIKE?
HE'S MAGNIFICENT.
IS HE HANDSOME?
HE'S HANDSOME AND DASHING AND... AND SIMPLY MAGNIFICENT.
YOUR WEDDING DAY IS FAST APPROACHING, SISTER.
I CAN HARDLY WAIT. THESE LAST FEW DAYS HAVE BEEN TORTURE.
WE HAVE NOT HAD A CHANCE TO PROPERLY CELEBRATE YOUR GOOD FORTUNE, JUST YOU AND I.
I KNOW. I'VE BEEN SO BUSY PREPARING FOR THE WEDDING I'VE HAD TIME FOR LITTLE ELSE.
BUT NOW THAT ALL YOUR PREPARATIONS ARE COMPLETE, SURELY YOU HAVE TIME TO CELEBRATE WITH YOUR SISTER.
OF COURSE, TENDRA.
GOOD. THEN TOMORROW WE WILL TAKE A PICNIC LUNCH IN THE VALLEY TO CELEBRATE YOUR ENGAGEMENT.

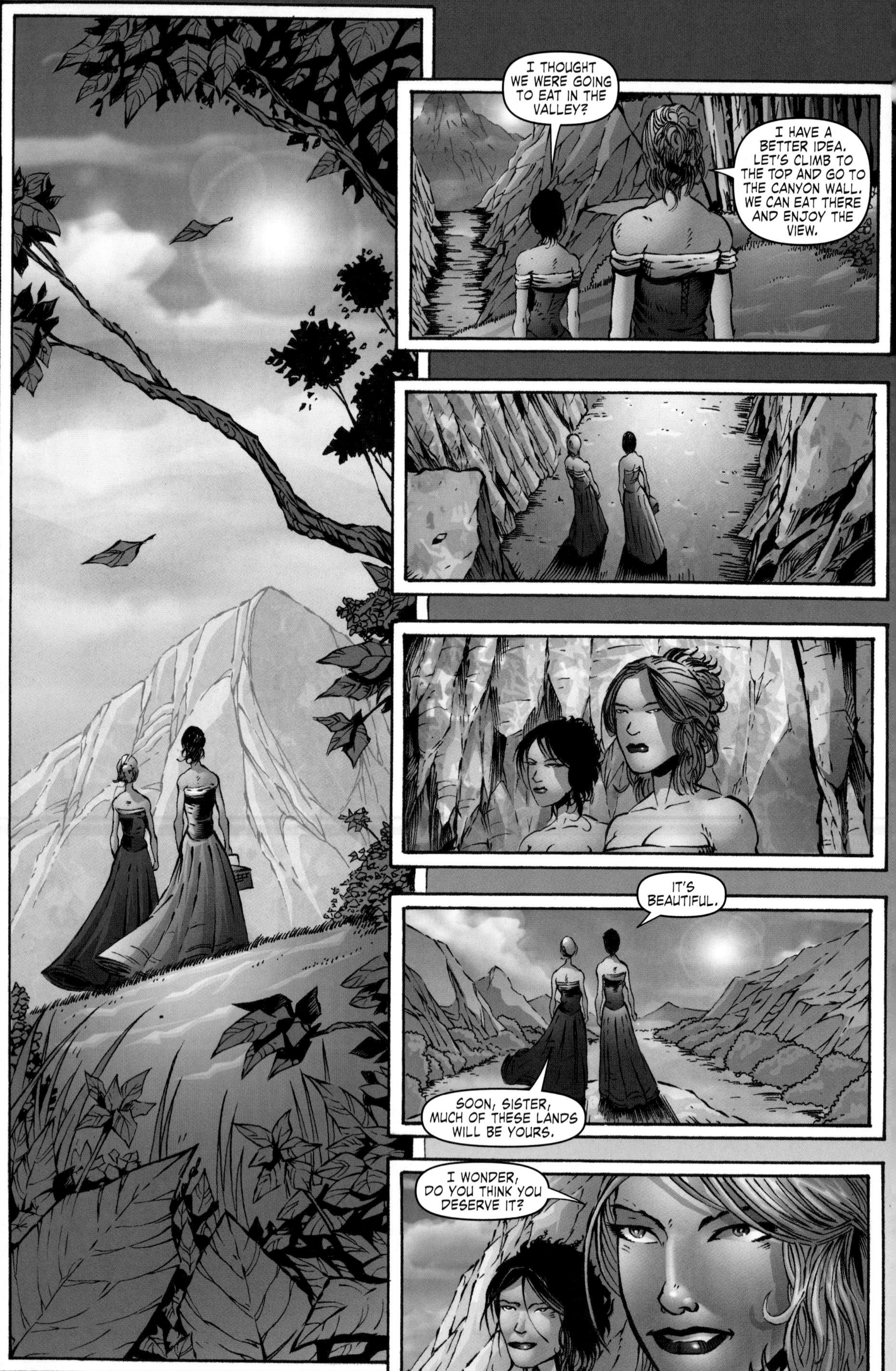
I THOUGHT WE WERE GOING TO EAT IN THE VALLEY?
I HAVE A BETTER IDEA. LET'S CLIMB TO THE TOP AND GO TO THE CANYON WALL. WE CAN EAT THERE AND ENJOY THE VIEW.
IT'S BEAUTIFUL.
SOON, SISTER, MUCH OF THESE LANDS WILL BE YOURS.
I WONDER, DO YOU THINK YOU DESERVE IT?

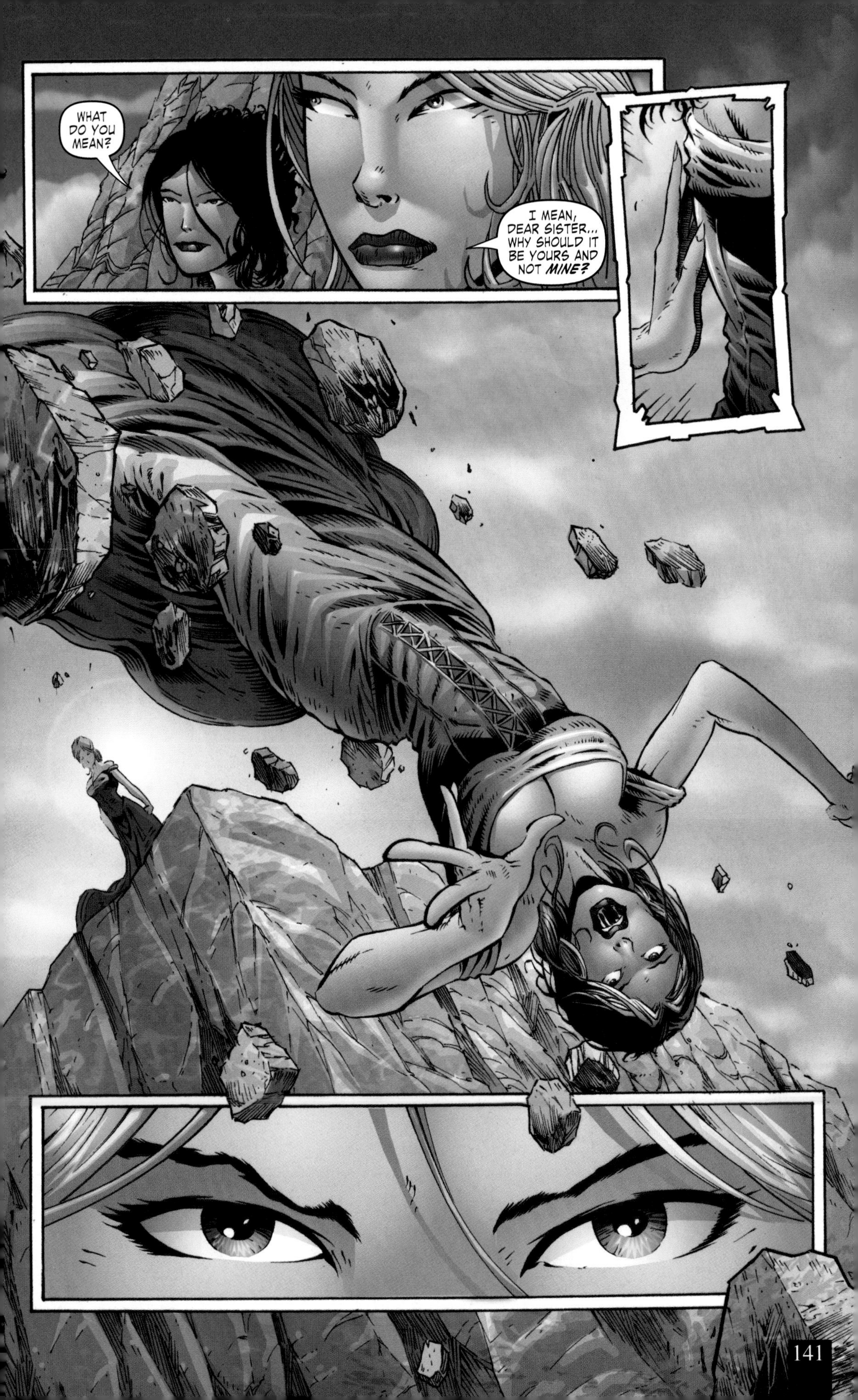
WHAT DO YOU MEAN?
I MEAN, DEAR SISTER... WHY SHOULD IT BE YOURS AND NOT *MINE?*

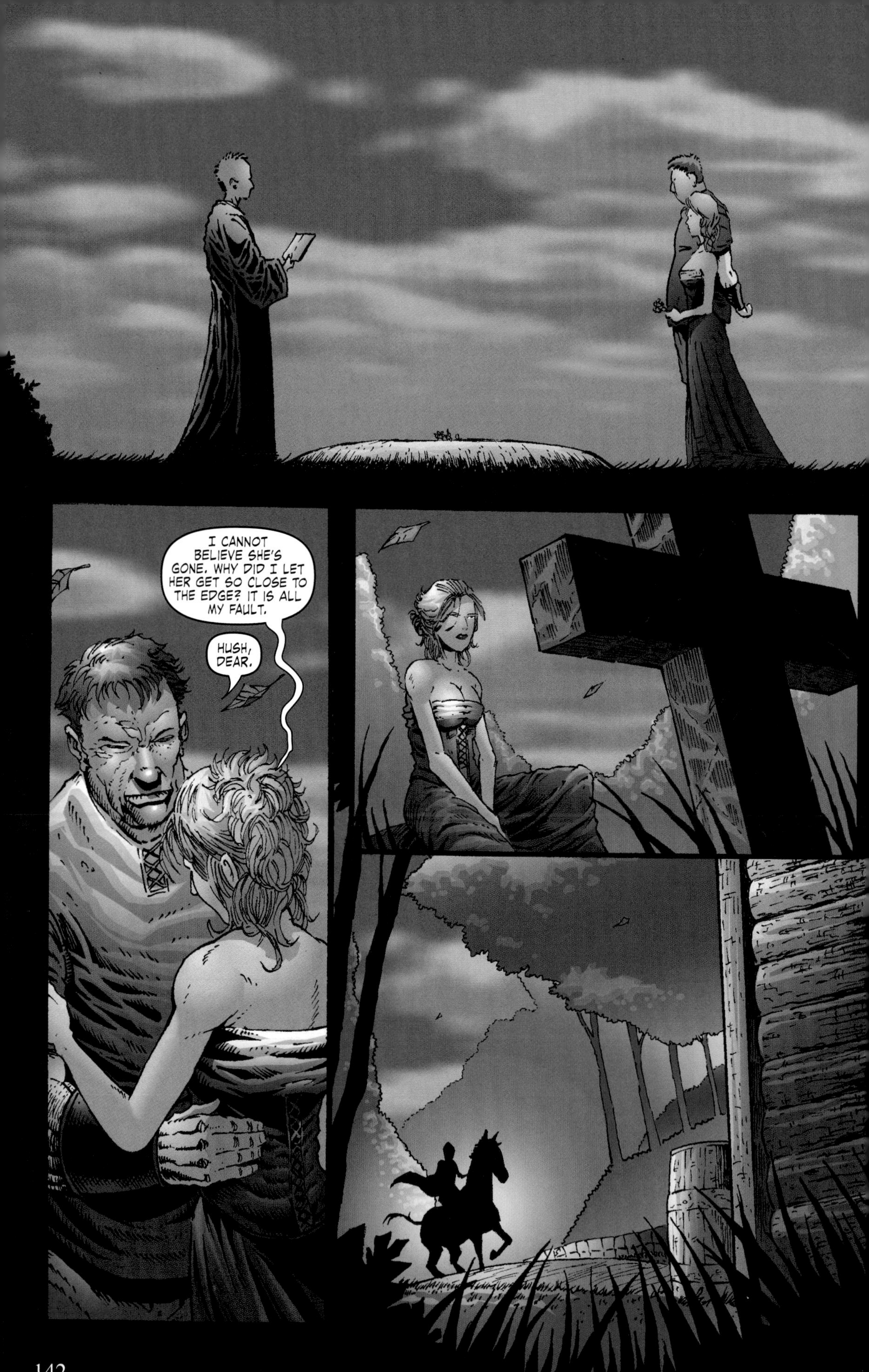
I CANNOT BELIEVE SHE'S GONE. WHY DID I LET HER GET SO CLOSE TO THE EDGE? IT IS ALL MY FAULT.
HUSH, DEAR.

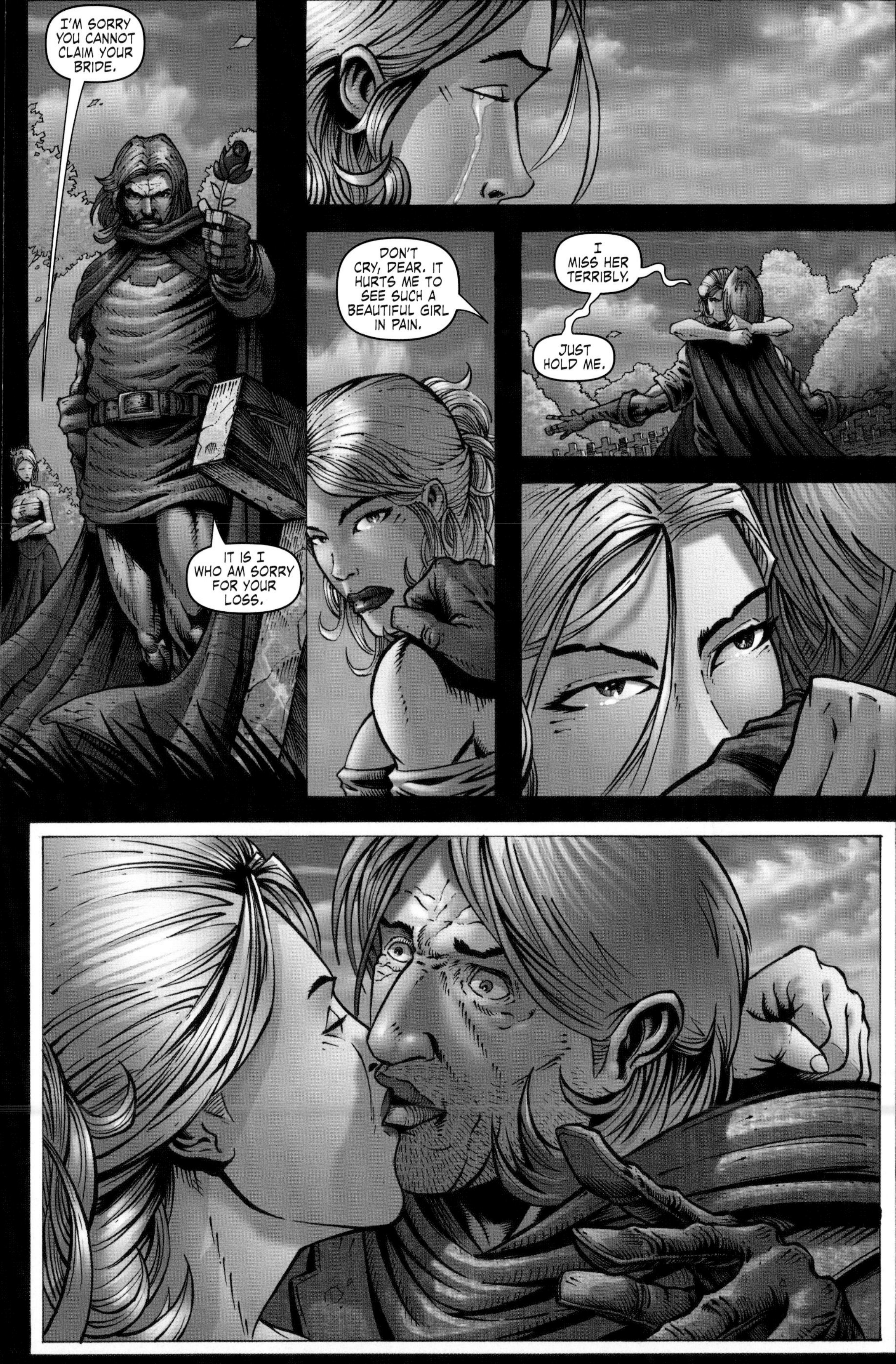
I'M SORRY YOU CANNOT CLAIM YOUR BRIDE.
IT IS I WHO AM SORRY FOR YOUR LOSS.
DON'T CRY, DEAR. IT HURTS ME TO SEE SUCH A BEAUTIFUL GIRL IN PAIN.
I MISS HER TERRIBLY.
JUST HOLD ME.

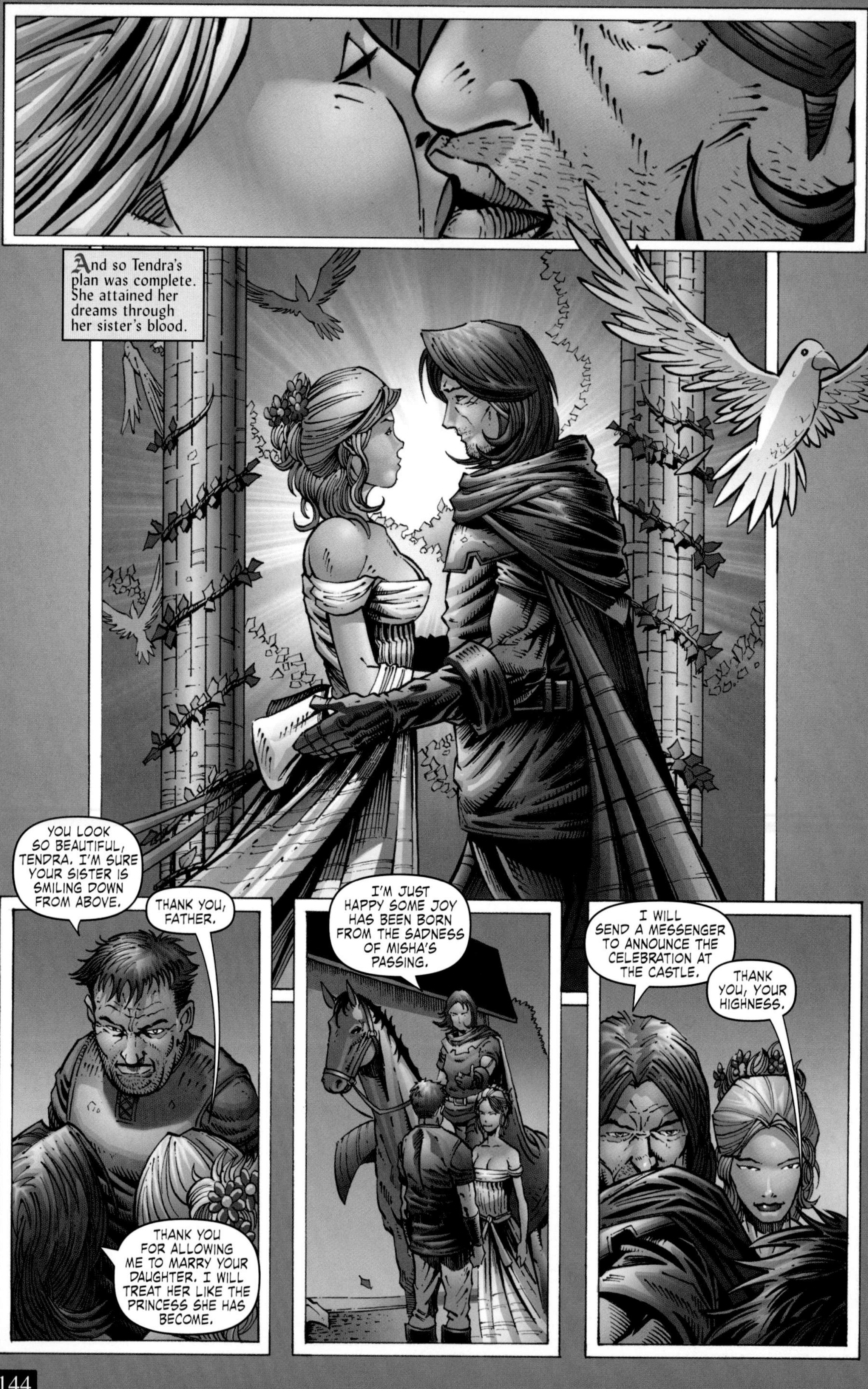
And so Tendra's plan was complete. She attained her dreams through her sister's blood.
YOU LOOK SO BEAUTIFUL, TENDRA. I'M SURE YOUR SISTER IS SMILING DOWN FROM ABOVE.
THANK YOU, FATHER.
THANK YOU FOR ALLOWING ME TO MARRY YOUR DAUGHTER. I WILL TREAT HER LIKE THE PRINCESS SHE HAS BECOME.
I'M JUST HAPPY SOME JOY HAS BEEN BORN FROM THE SADNESS OF MISHA'S PASSING.
I WILL SEND A MESSENGER TO ANNOUNCE THE CELEBRATION AT THE CASTLE.
THANK YOU, YOUR HIGHNESS.

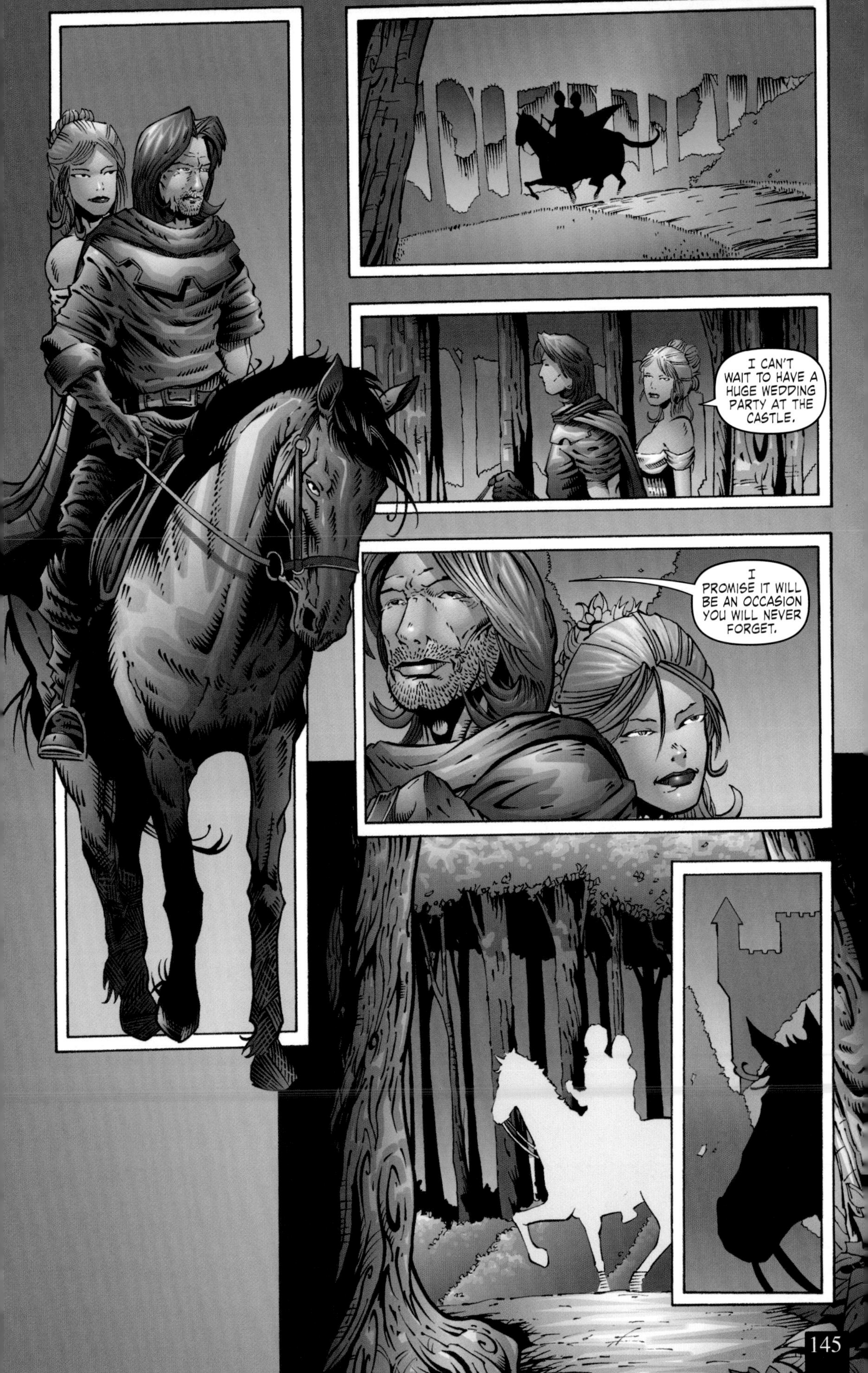
I CAN'T WAIT TO HAVE A HUGE WEDDING PARTY AT THE CASTLE.
I PROMISE IT WILL BE AN OCCASION YOU WILL NEVER FORGET.

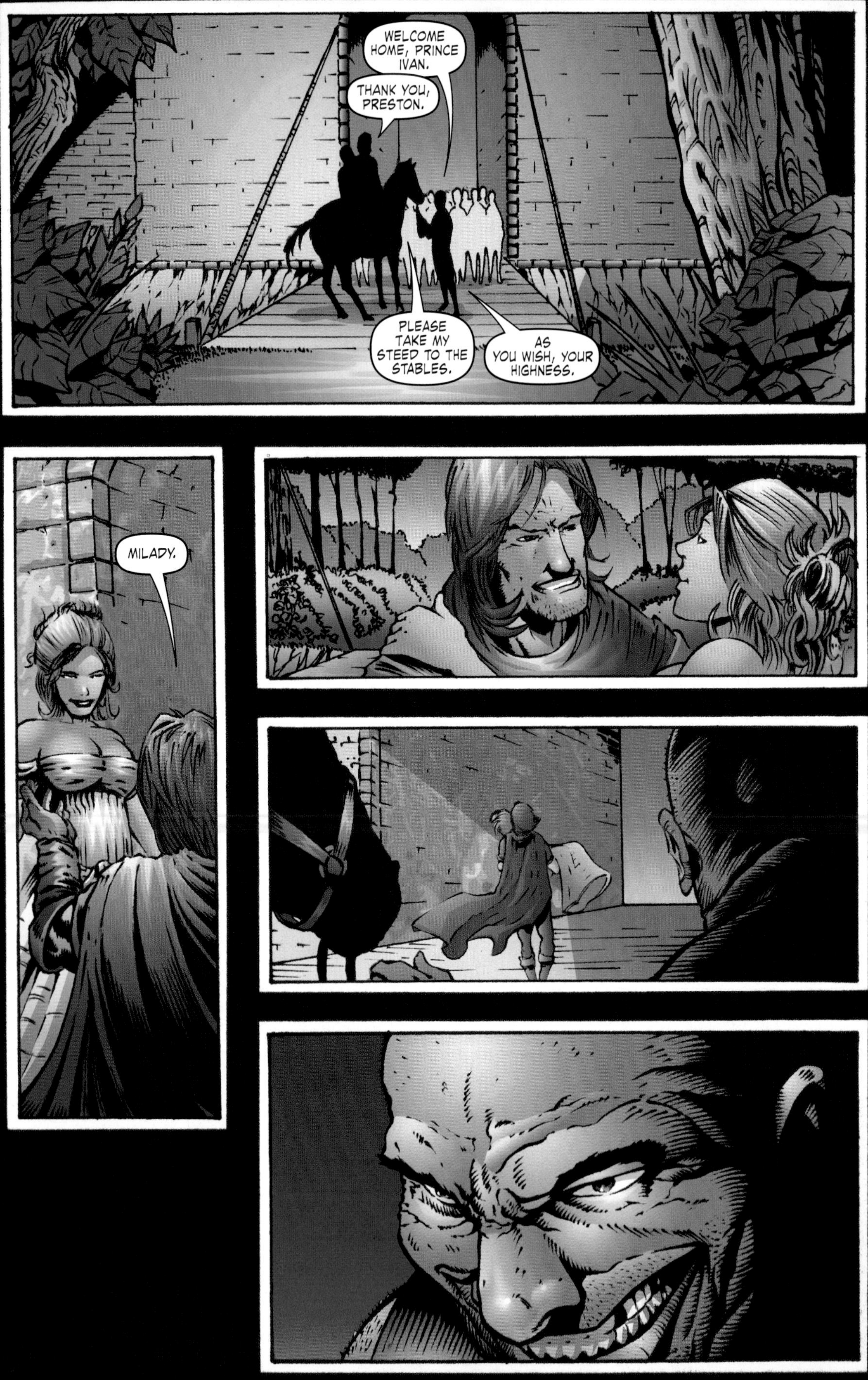
WELCOME HOME, PRINCE IVAN.
THANK YOU, PRESTON.
PLEASE TAKE MY STEED TO THE STABLES.
AS YOU WISH, YOUR HIGHNESS.
MILADY.

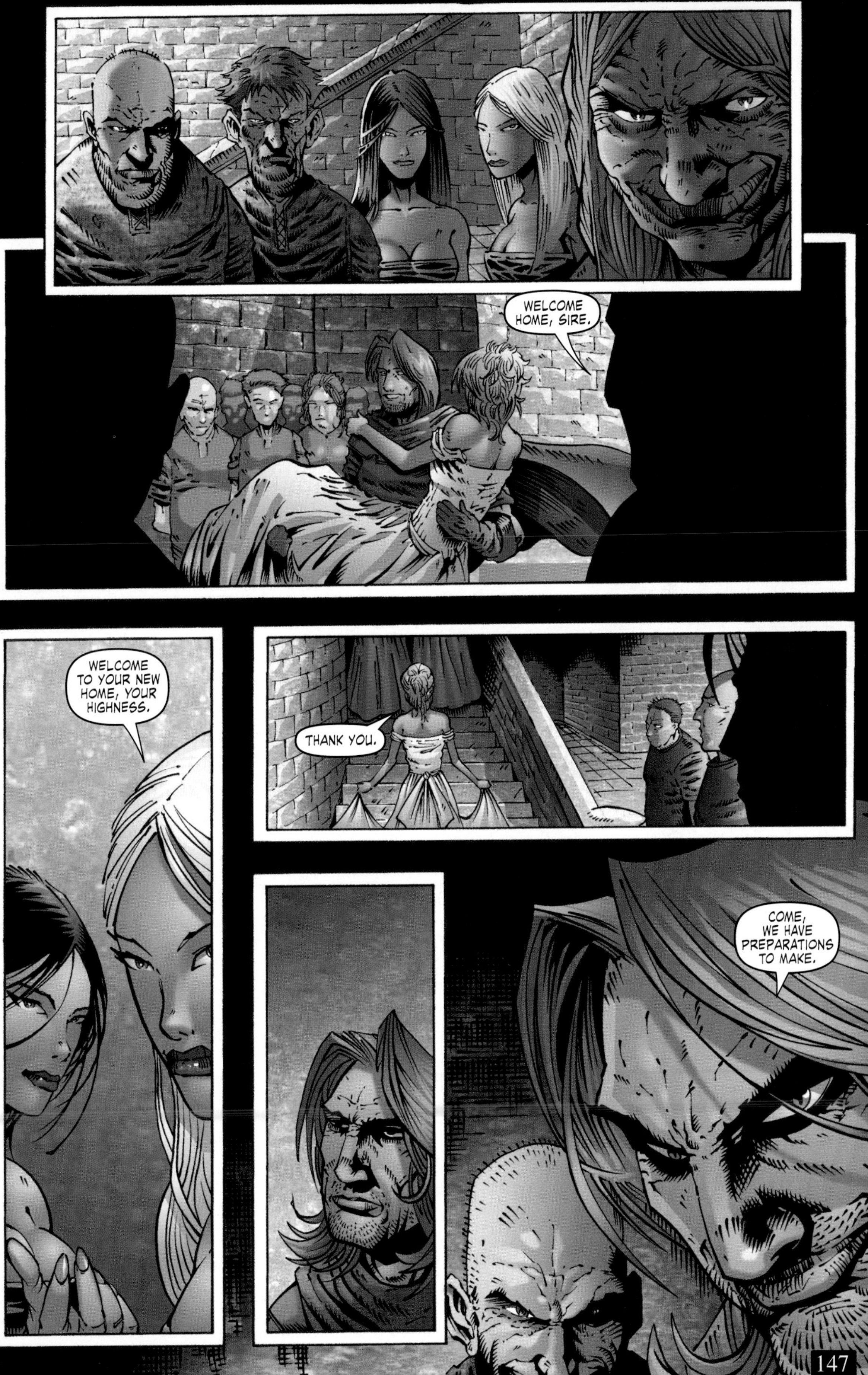
WELCOME HOME, SIRE.
WELCOME TO YOUR NEW HOME, YOUR HIGHNESS.
THANK YOU.
COME, WE HAVE PREPARATIONS TO MAKE.

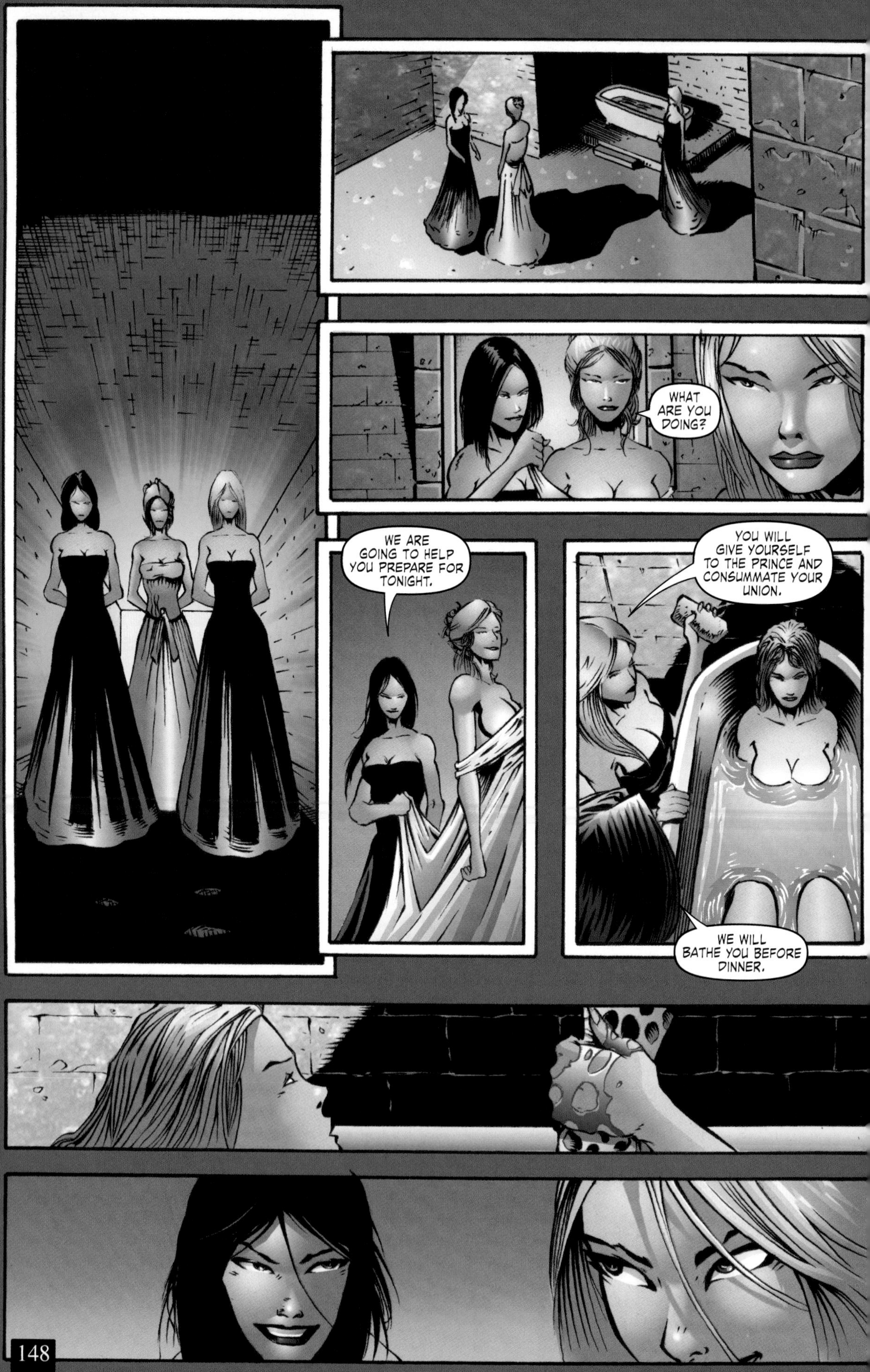
WHAT ARE YOU DOING?
WE ARE GOING TO HELP YOU PREPARE FOR TONIGHT.
YOU WILL GIVE YOURSELF TO THE PRINCE AND CONSUMMATE YOUR UNION.
WE WILL BATHE YOU BEFORE DINNER.

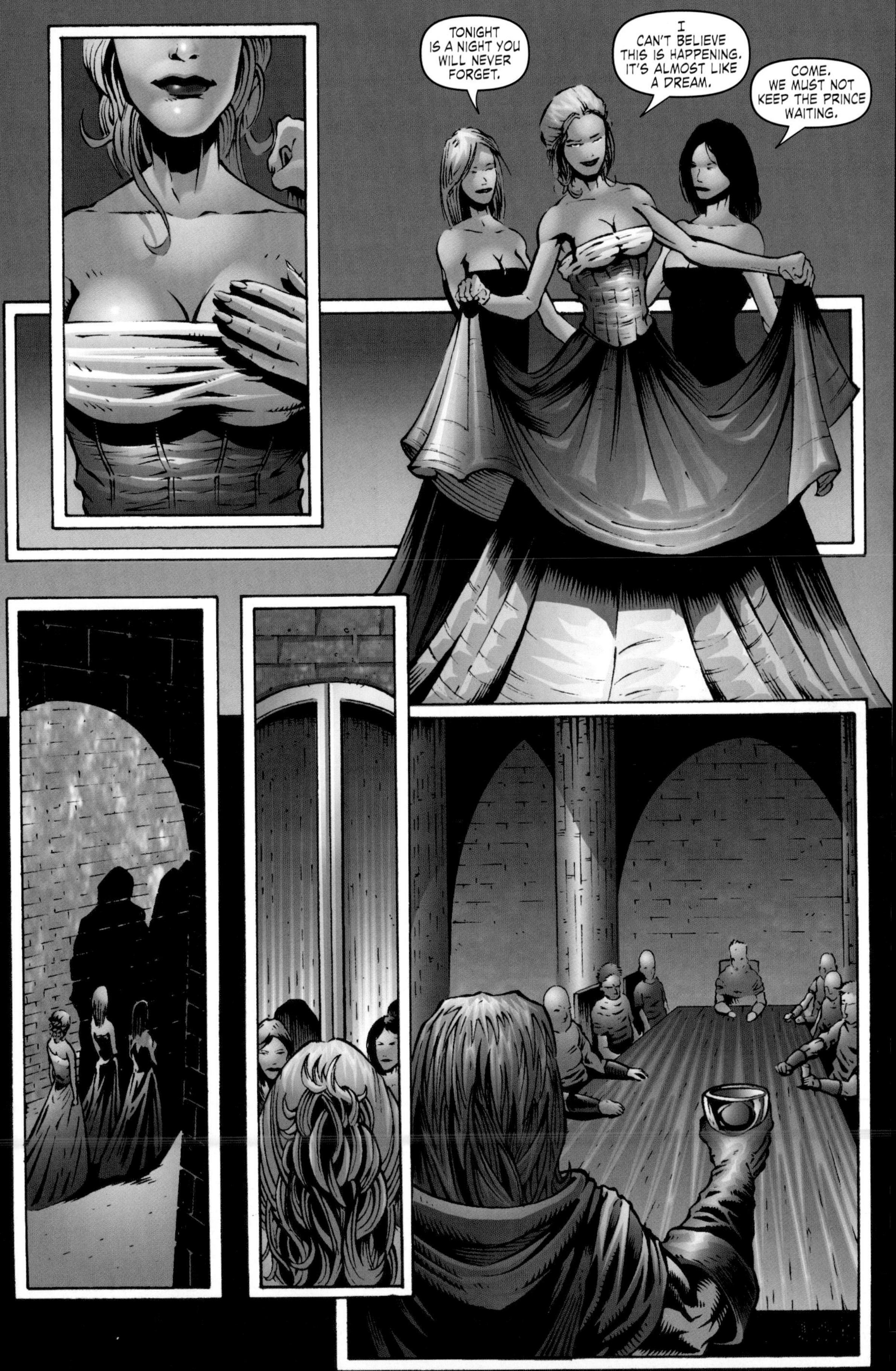
TONIGHT IS A NIGHT YOU WILL NEVER FORGET.
I CAN'T BELIEVE THIS IS HAPPENING. IT'S ALMOST LIKE A DREAM.
COME. WE MUST NOT KEEP THE PRINCE WAITING.

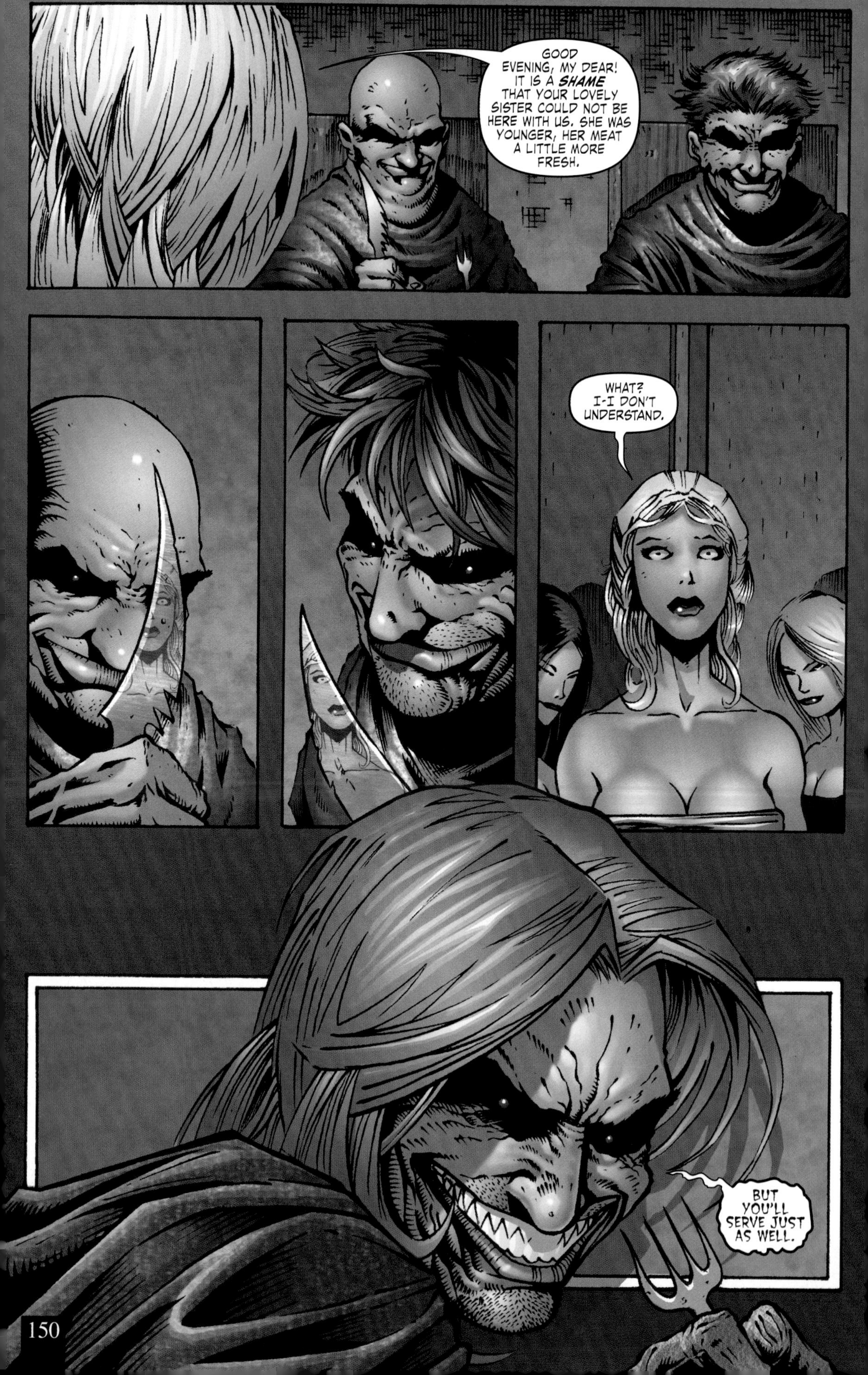
GOOD EVENING, MY DEAR! IT IS A SHAME THAT YOUR LOVELY SISTER COULD NOT BE HERE WITH US. SHE WAS YOUNGER, HER MEAT A LITTLE MORE FRESH.
WHAT? I-I DON'T UNDERSTAND.
BUT YOU'LL SERVE JUST AS WELL.

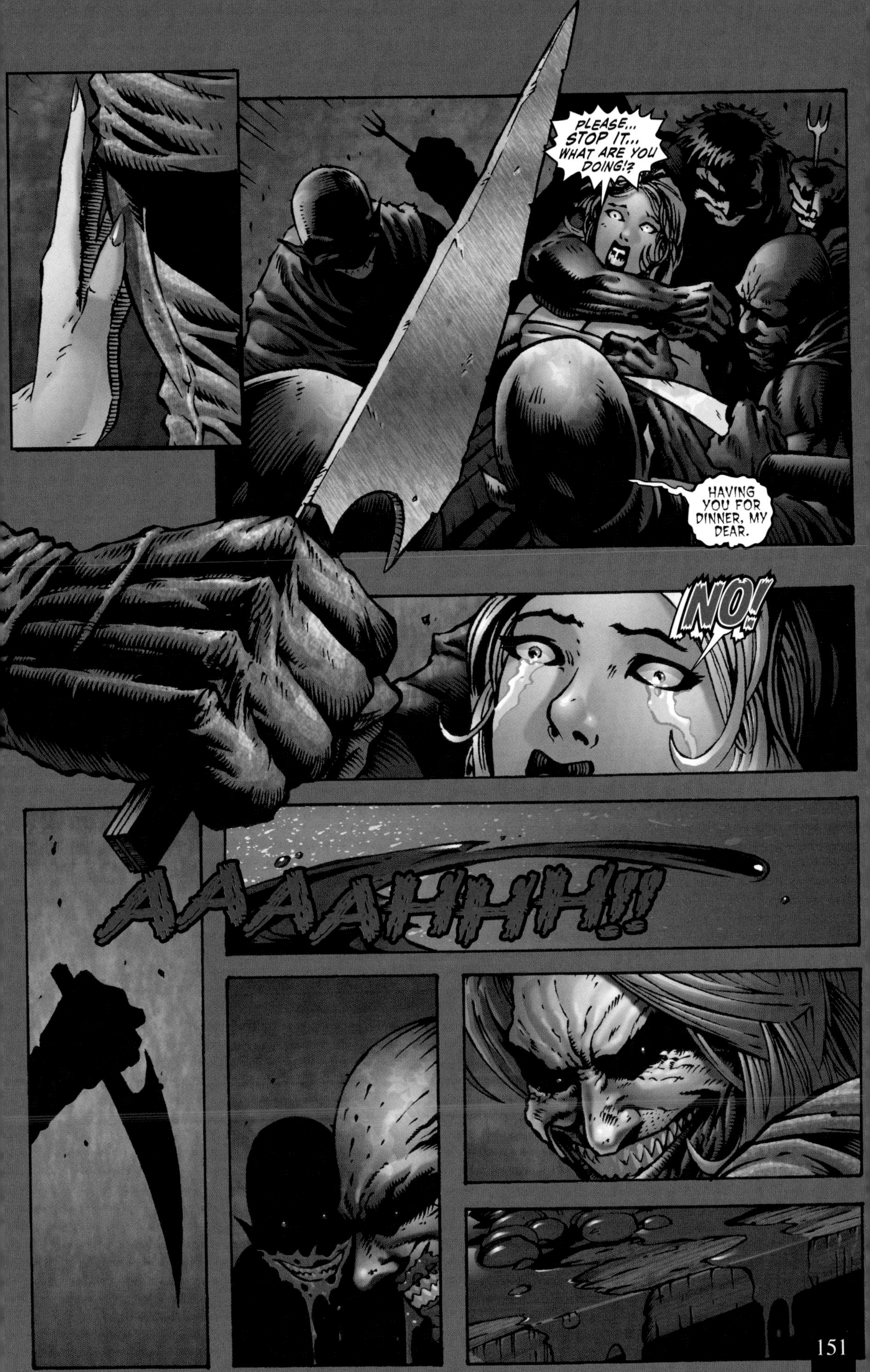
PLEASE... STOP IT... WHAT ARE YOU DOING!?
HAVING YOU FOR DINNER, MY DEAR.
NO!
AAAAHHHH!!

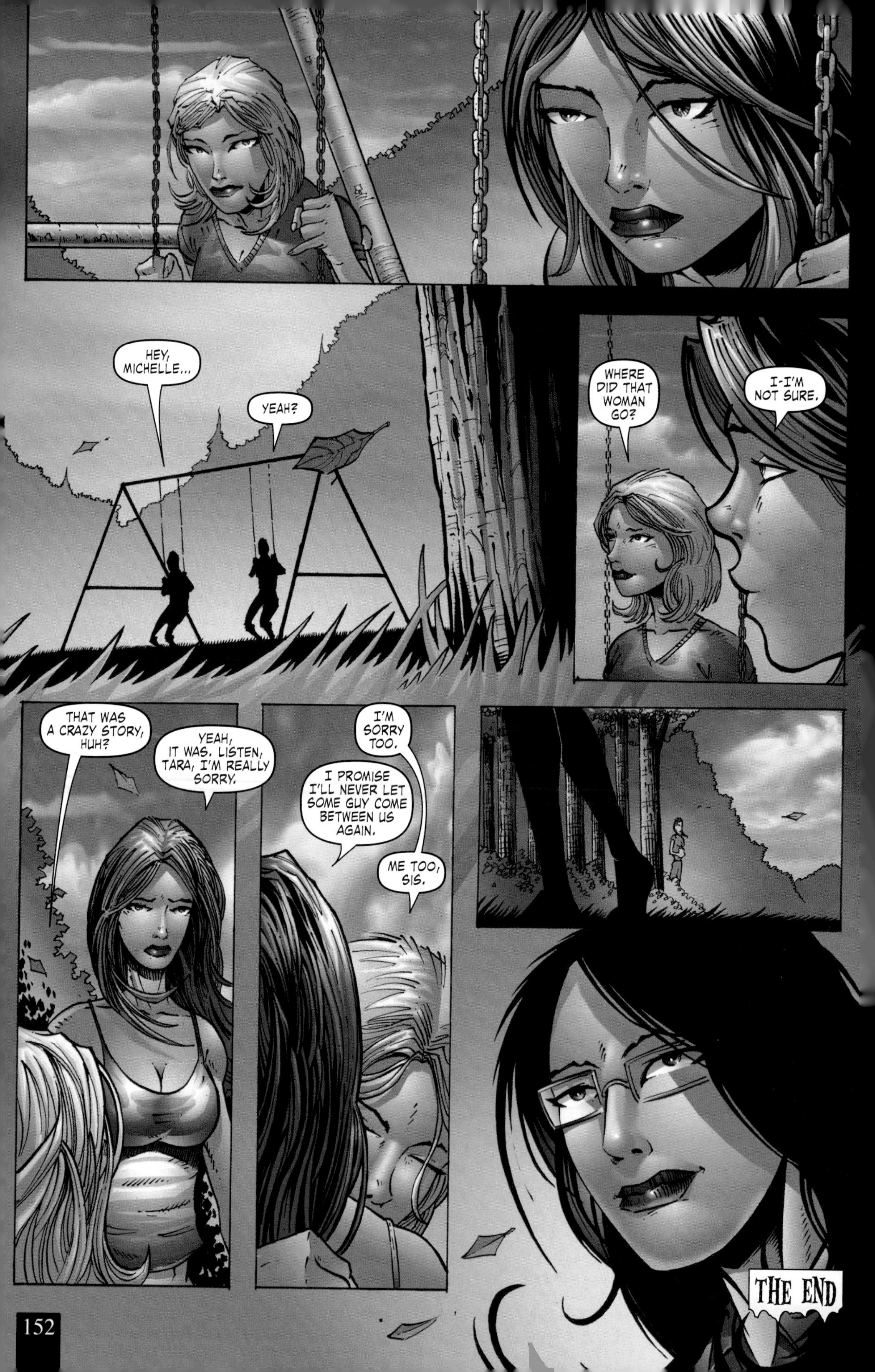
HEY, MICHELLE...
YEAH?
WHERE DID THAT WOMAN GO?
I-I'M NOT SURE.
THAT WAS A CRAZY STORY, HUH?
YEAH, IT WAS. LISTEN, TARA, I'M REALLY SORRY.
I'M SORRY TOO.
I PROMISE I'LL NEVER LET SOME GUY COME BETWEEN US AGAIN.
ME TOO, SIS.
THE END

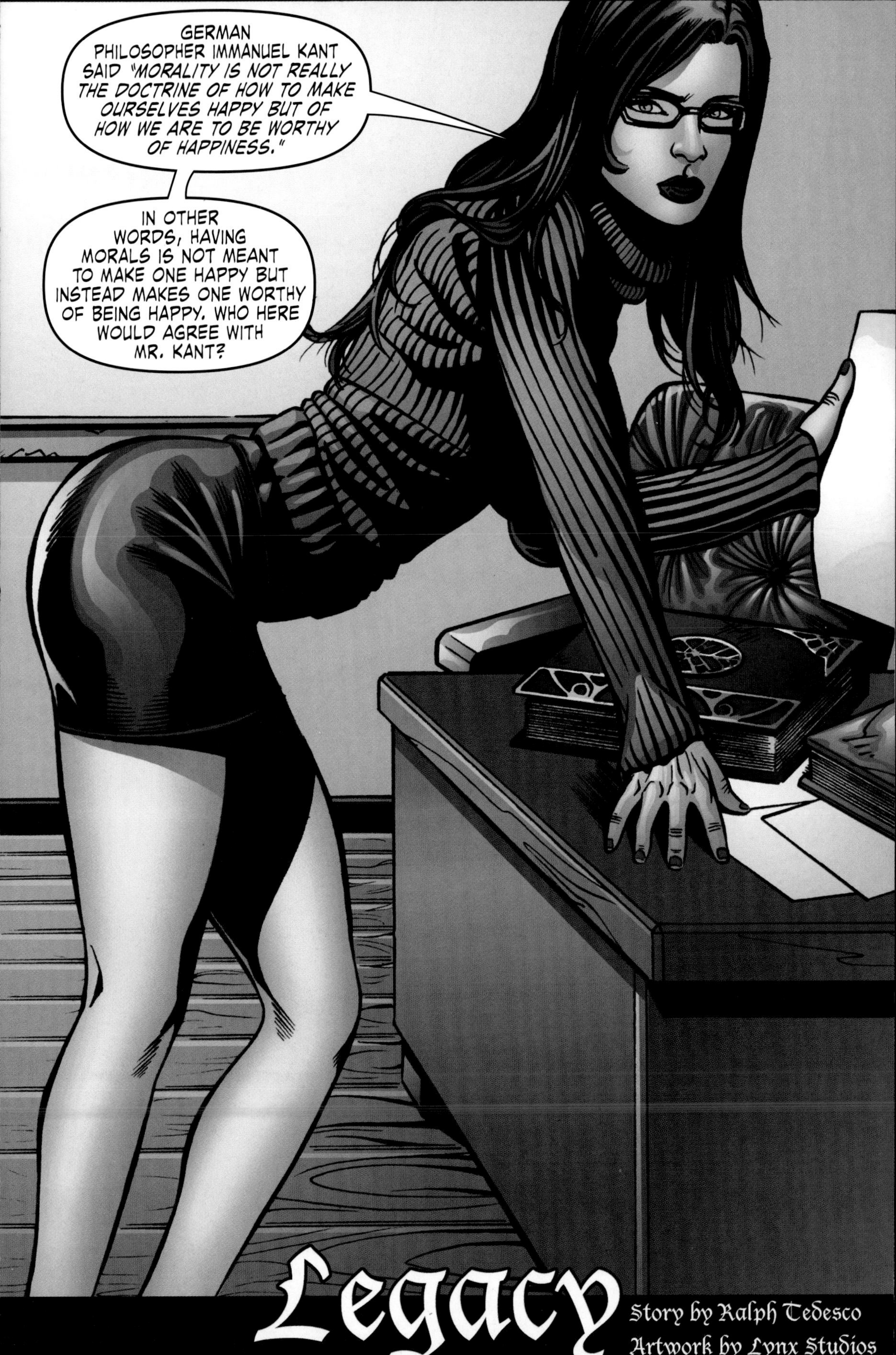
GERMAN PHILOSOPHER IMMANUEL KANT SAID *"MORALITY IS NOT REALLY THE DOCTRINE OF HOW TO MAKE OURSELVES HAPPY BUT OF HOW WE ARE TO BE WORTHY OF HAPPINESS."*
IN OTHER WORDS, HAVING MORALS IS NOT MEANT TO MAKE ONE HAPPY BUT INSTEAD MAKES ONE WORTHY OF BEING HAPPY. WHO HERE WOULD AGREE WITH MR. KANT?

Legacy

Story by Ralph Tedesco
Artwork by Lynx Studios

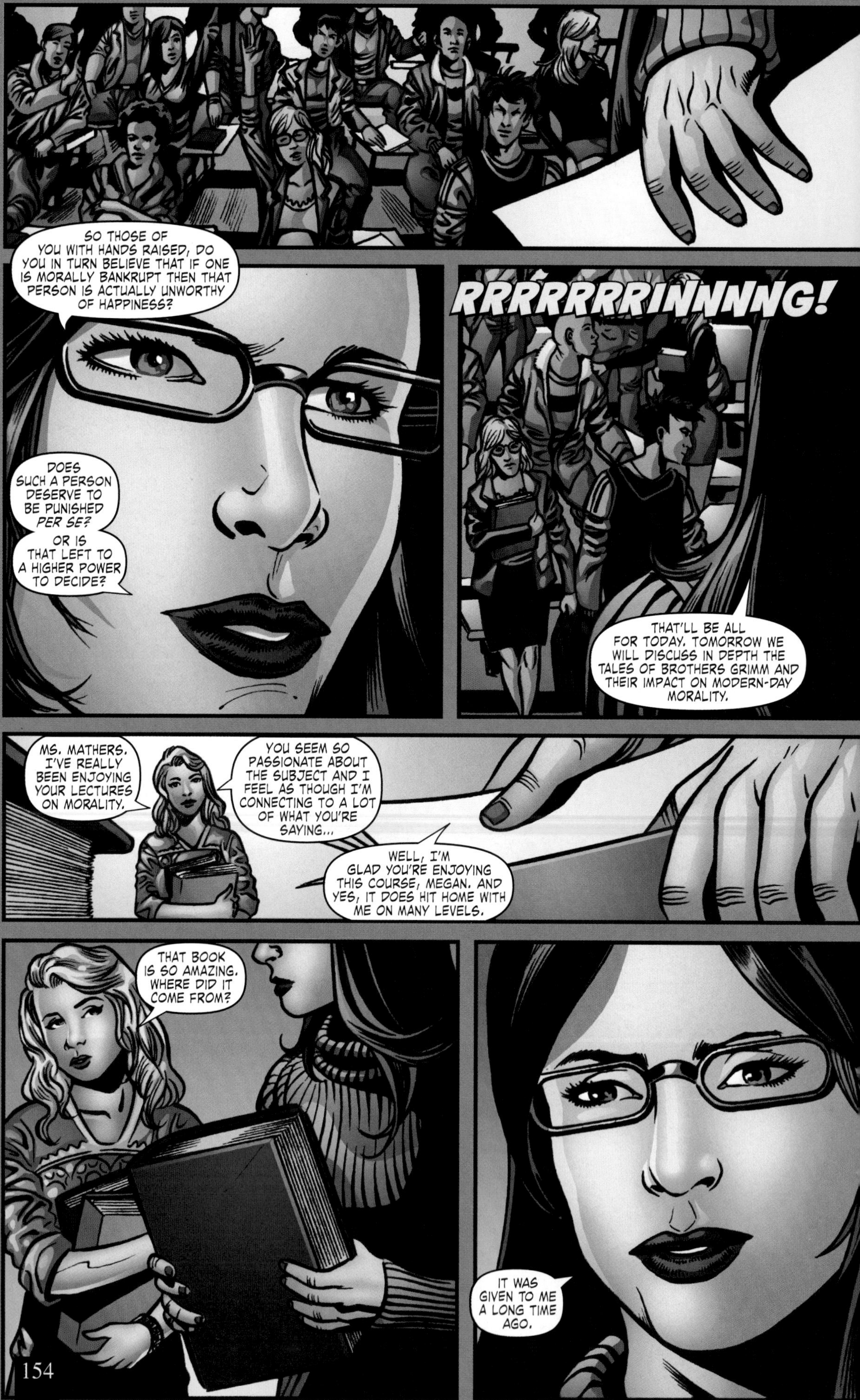
SO THOSE OF YOU WITH HANDS RAISED, DO YOU IN TURN BELIEVE THAT IF ONE IS MORALLY BANKRUPT THEN THAT PERSON IS ACTUALLY UNWORTHY OF HAPPINESS?
DOES SUCH A PERSON DESERVE TO BE PUNISHED *PER SE*?
OR IS THAT LEFT TO A HIGHER POWER TO DECIDE?
RRRRRRRINNNNG!
THAT'LL BE ALL FOR TODAY. TOMORROW WE WILL DISCUSS IN DEPTH THE TALES OF BROTHERS GRIMM AND THEIR IMPACT ON MODERN-DAY MORALITY.
MS. MATHERS. I'VE REALLY BEEN ENJOYING YOUR LECTURES ON MORALITY.
YOU SEEM SO PASSIONATE ABOUT THE SUBJECT AND I FEEL AS THOUGH I'M CONNECTING TO A LOT OF WHAT YOU'RE SAYING...
WELL, I'M GLAD YOU'RE ENJOYING THIS COURSE, MEGAN. AND YES, IT DOES HIT HOME WITH ME ON MANY LEVELS.
THAT BOOK IS SO AMAZING. WHERE DID IT COME FROM?
IT WAS GIVEN TO ME A LONG TIME AGO.

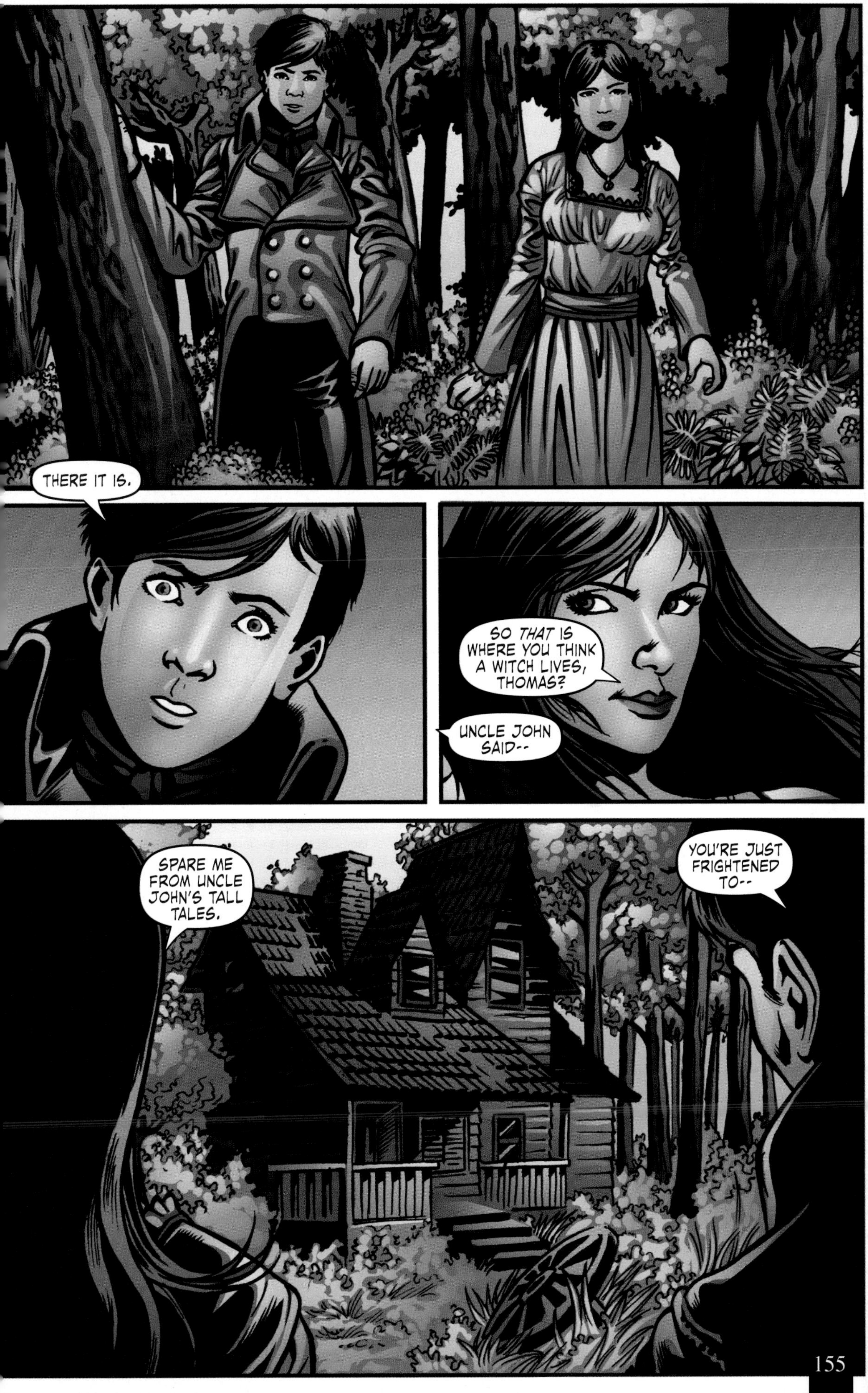
THERE IT IS.
SO THAT IS WHERE YOU THINK A WITCH LIVES, THOMAS?
UNCLE JOHN SAID--
SPARE ME FROM UNCLE JOHN'S TALL TALES.
YOU'RE JUST FRIGHTENED TO--

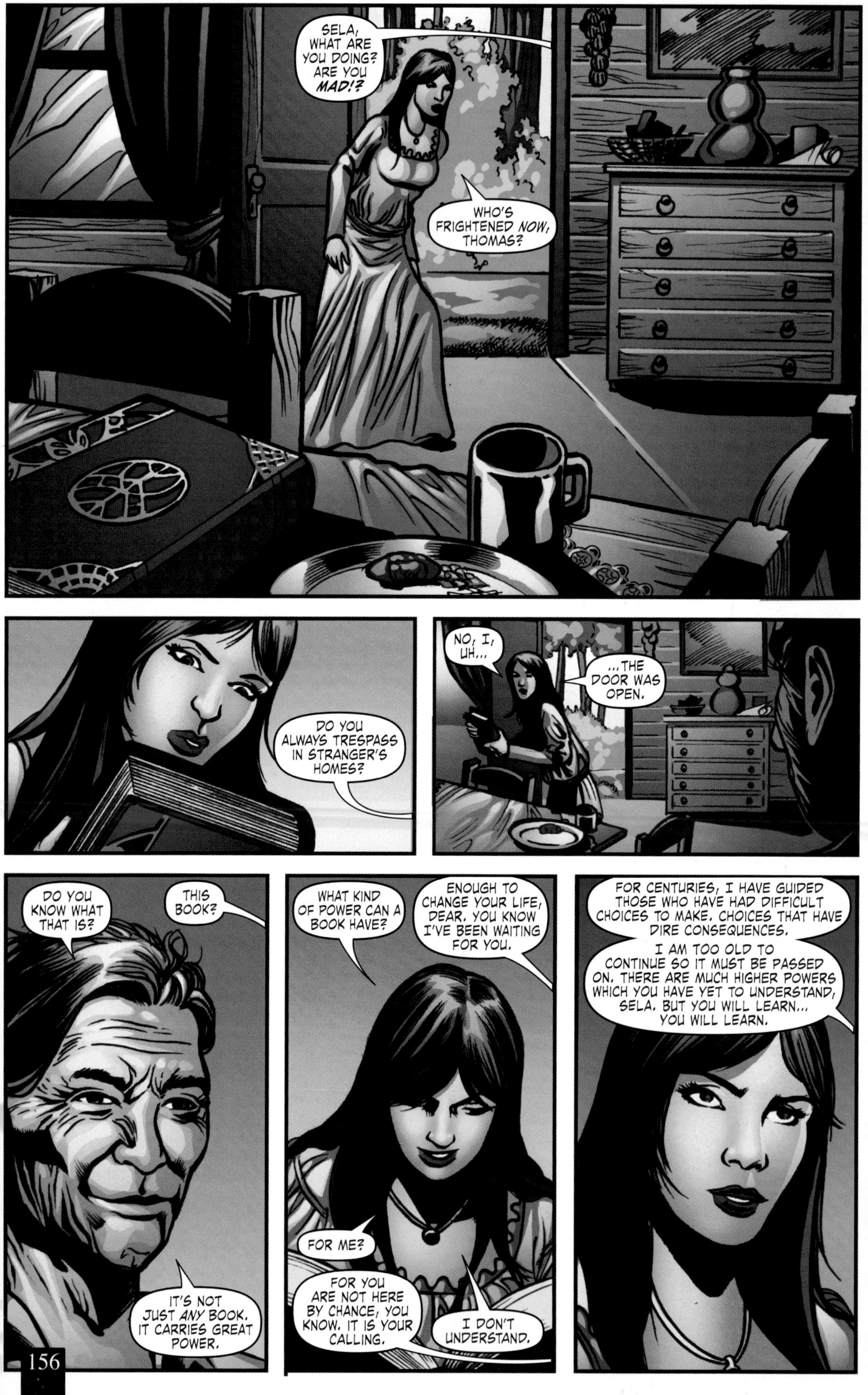
SELA, WHAT ARE YOU DOING? ARE YOU MAD!?
WHO'S FRIGHTENED NOW, THOMAS?
DO YOU ALWAYS TRESPASS IN STRANGER'S HOMES?
NO, I, UH...
...THE DOOR WAS OPEN.
DO YOU KNOW WHAT THAT IS?
THIS BOOK?
IT'S NOT JUST ANY BOOK. IT CARRIES GREAT POWER.
WHAT KIND OF POWER CAN A BOOK HAVE?
ENOUGH TO CHANGE YOUR LIFE, DEAR. YOU KNOW I'VE BEEN WAITING FOR YOU.
FOR ME?
FOR YOU ARE NOT HERE BY CHANCE, YOU KNOW. IT IS YOUR CALLING.
I DON'T UNDERSTAND.
FOR CENTURIES, I HAVE GUIDED THOSE WHO HAVE HAD DIFFICULT CHOICES TO MAKE. CHOICES THAT HAVE DIRE CONSEQUENCES.
I AM TOO OLD TO CONTINUE SO IT MUST BE PASSED ON. THERE ARE MUCH HIGHER POWERS WHICH YOU HAVE YET TO UNDERSTAND, SELA. BUT YOU WILL LEARN... YOU WILL LEARN.

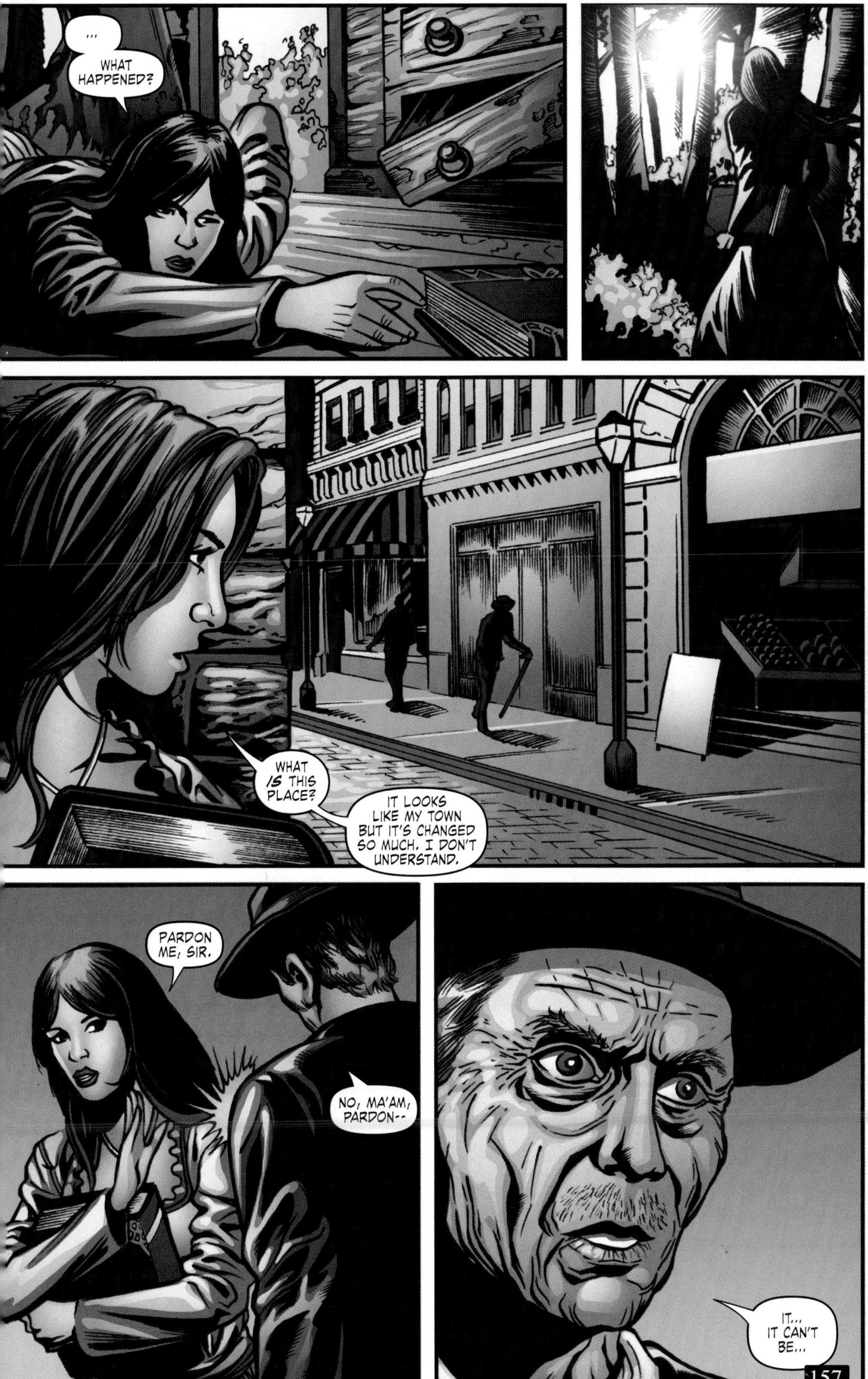
...
WHAT HAPPENED?
WHAT IS THIS PLACE?
IT LOOKS LIKE MY TOWN BUT IT'S CHANGED SO MUCH. I DON'T UNDERSTAND.
PARDON ME, SIR.
NO, MA'AM, PARDON--
IT... IT CAN'T BE...

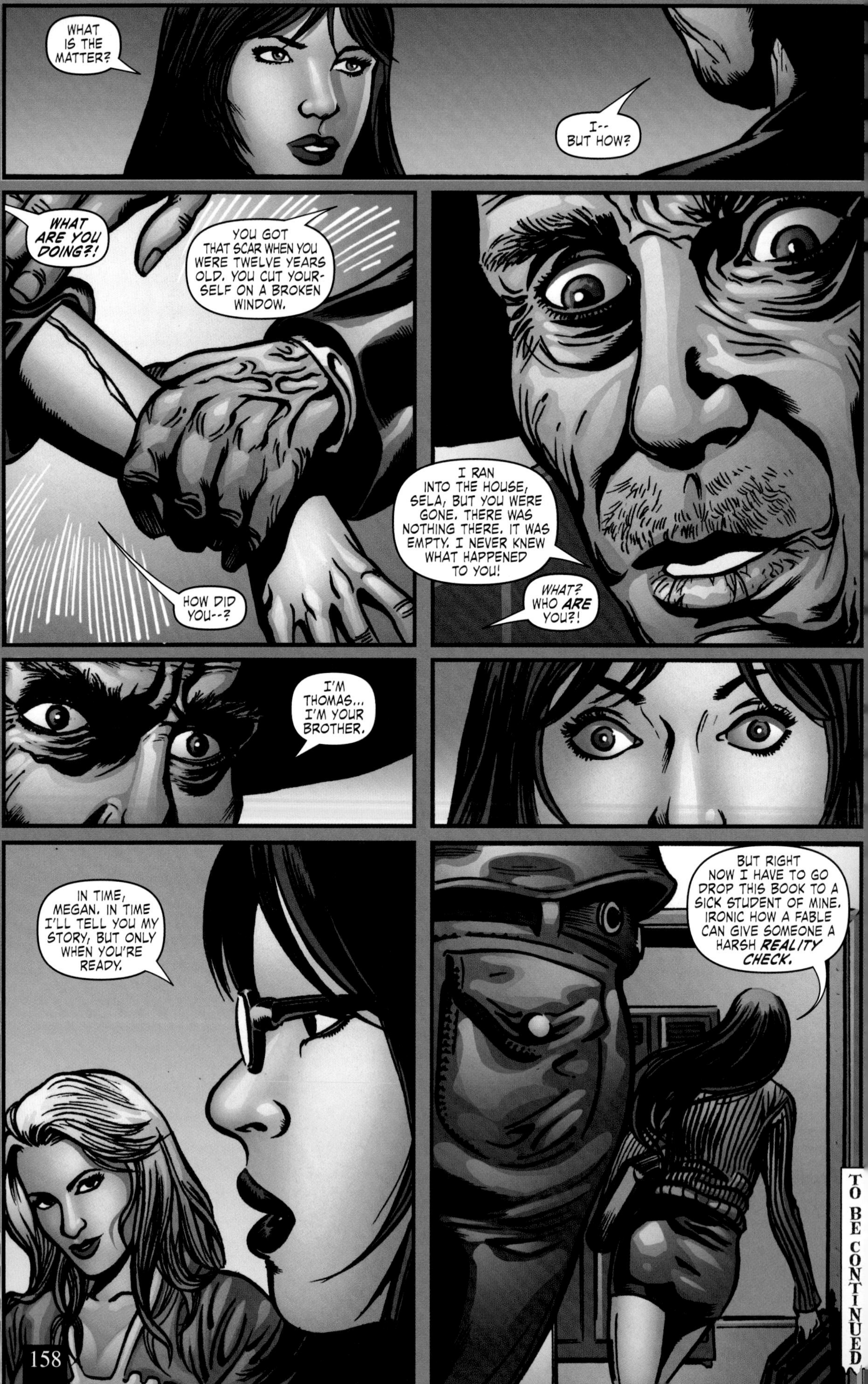
WHAT IS THE MATTER?
I-- BUT HOW?
WHAT ARE YOU DOING?!
YOU GOT THAT SCAR WHEN YOU WERE TWELVE YEARS OLD. YOU CUT YOURSELF ON A BROKEN WINDOW.
HOW DID YOU--?
I RAN INTO THE HOUSE, SELA, BUT YOU WERE GONE. THERE WAS NOTHING THERE. IT WAS EMPTY. I NEVER KNEW WHAT HAPPENED TO YOU!
WHAT? WHO ARE YOU?!
I'M THOMAS... I'M YOUR BROTHER.
IN TIME, MEGAN. IN TIME I'LL TELL YOU MY STORY, BUT ONLY WHEN YOU'RE READY.
BUT RIGHT NOW I HAVE TO GO DROP THIS BOOK TO A SICK STUDENT OF MINE. IRONIC HOW A FABLE CAN GIVE SOMEONE A HARSH REALITY CHECK.
TO BE CONTINUED

Grimm Fairy Tales

Al Rio Cover Gallery

Al Rio lives in Brazil, in the city of Fortaleza in the State of Ceará. He was born May 19, 1962, is married and has three children, a boy and two girls.

Since Al Rio was 6 years old, he dreamed of drawing for American comic companies. After dedicating many years to drawing, this dream came true.

Al Rio has since worked for Marvel, DC Comics, Dark Horse, Image and many other publishers on titles including Gen13, Dv8, Star Wars and of course, the covers of these great Zenescope books.

He loves his fans and is thrilled to be able to share his work through comic books.

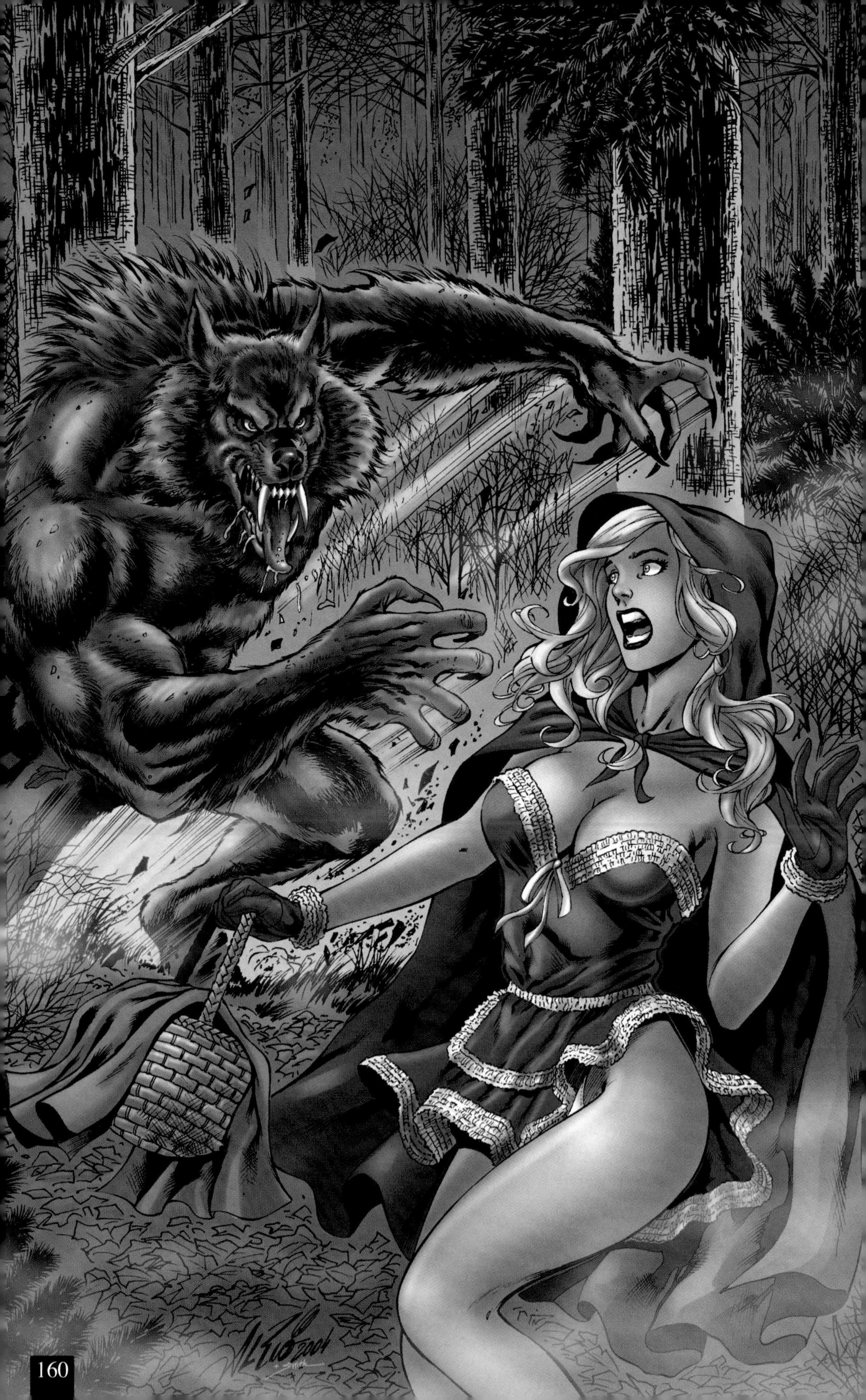

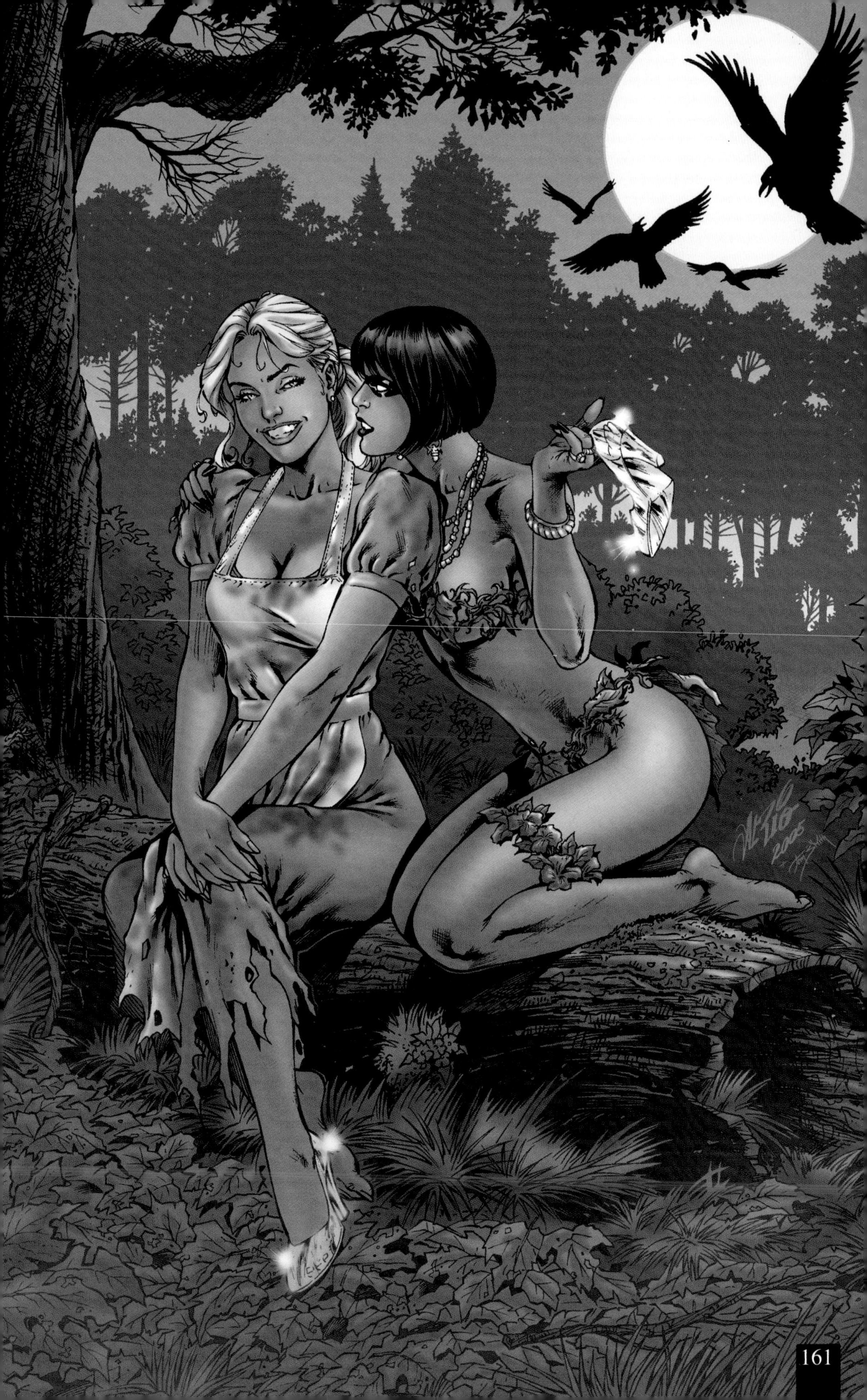

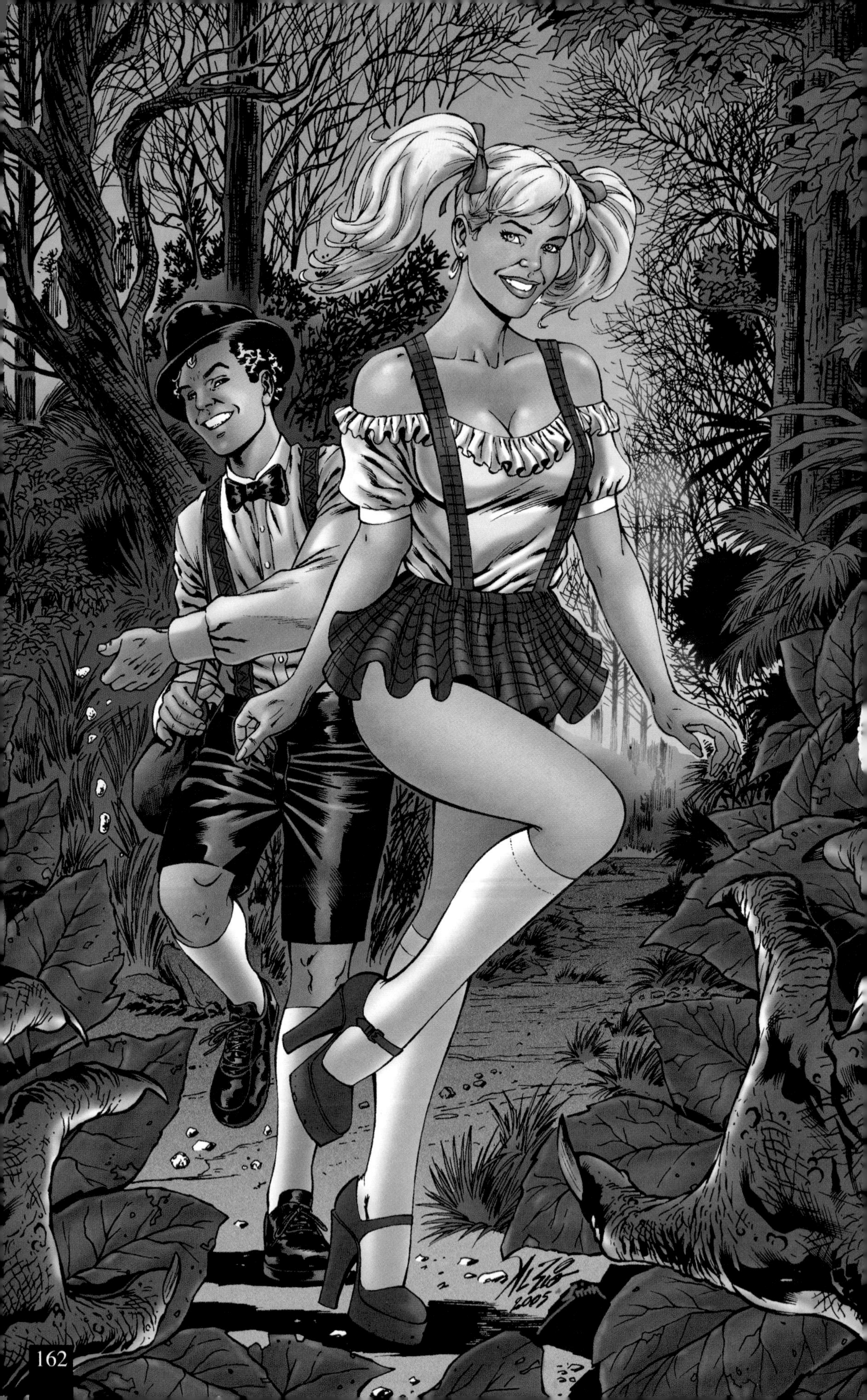

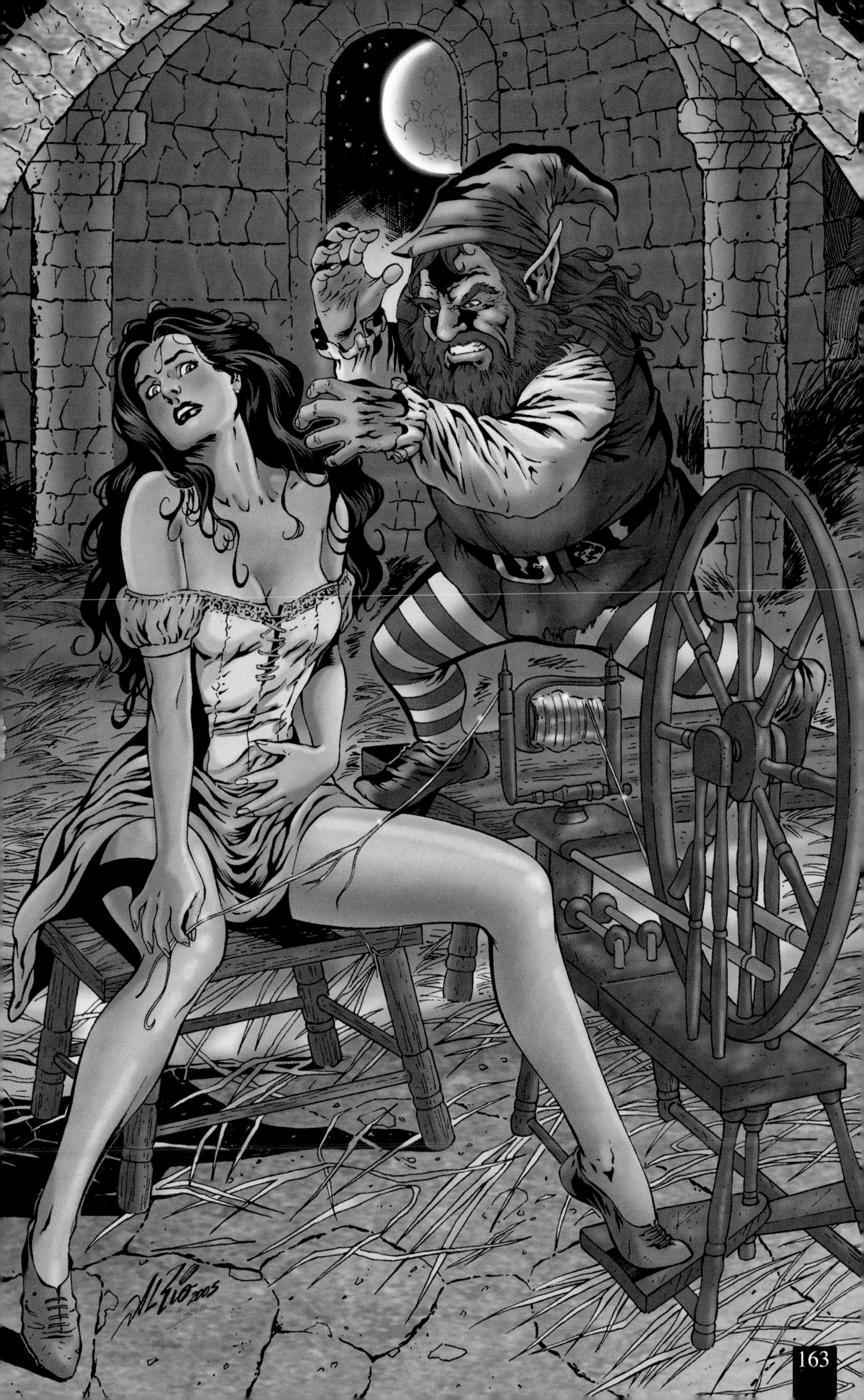

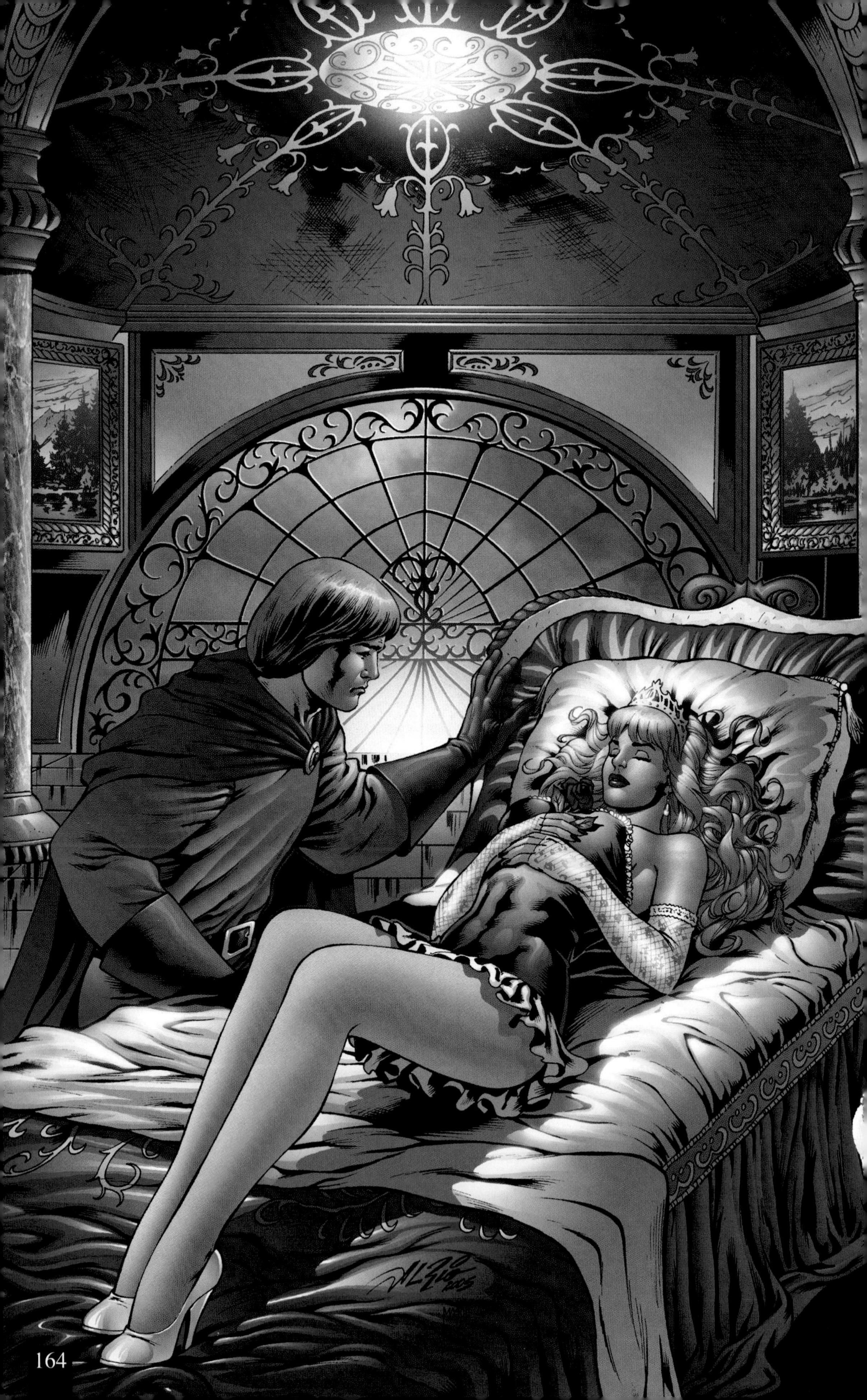

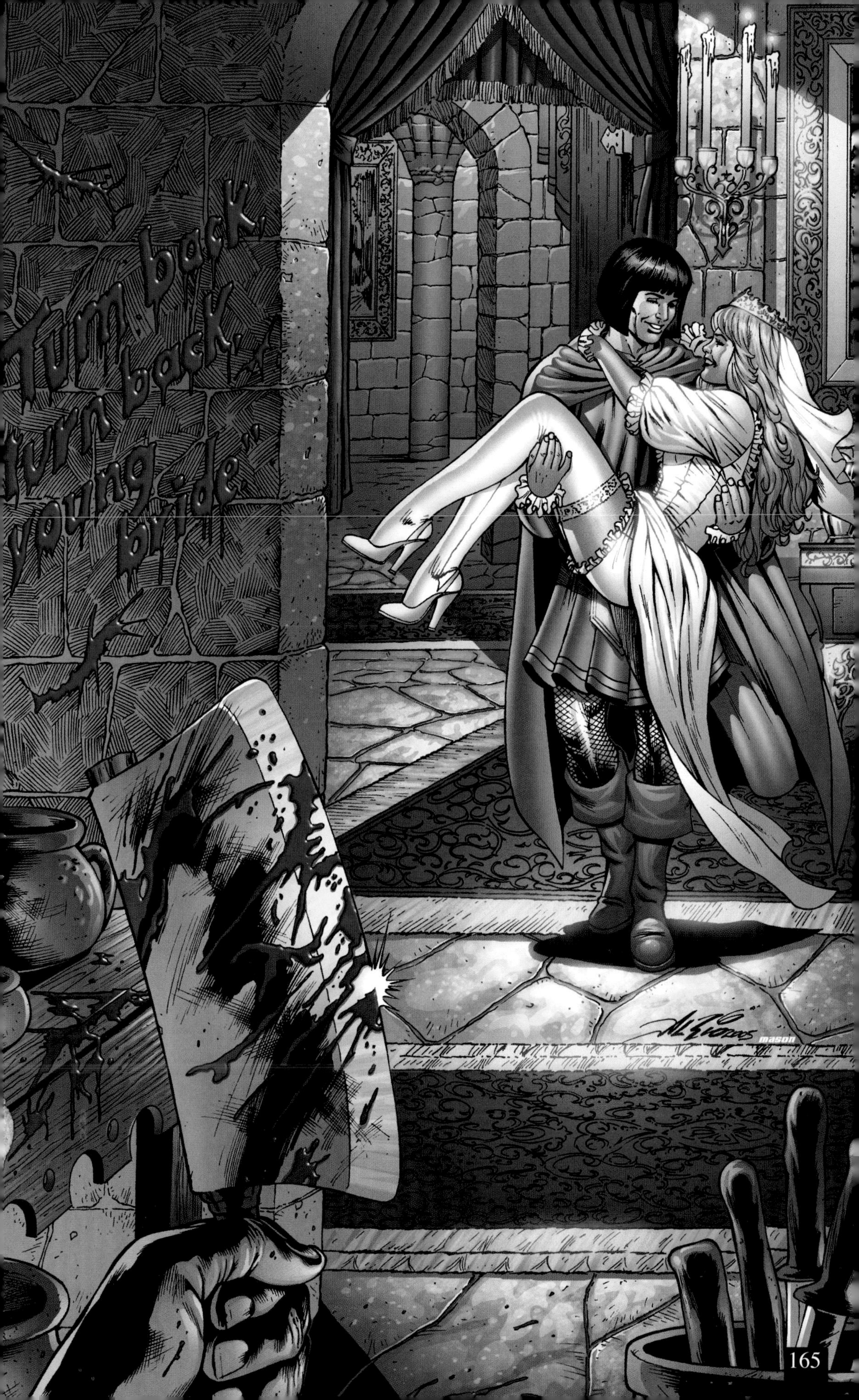
"Turn back,
turn back,
young
bride."

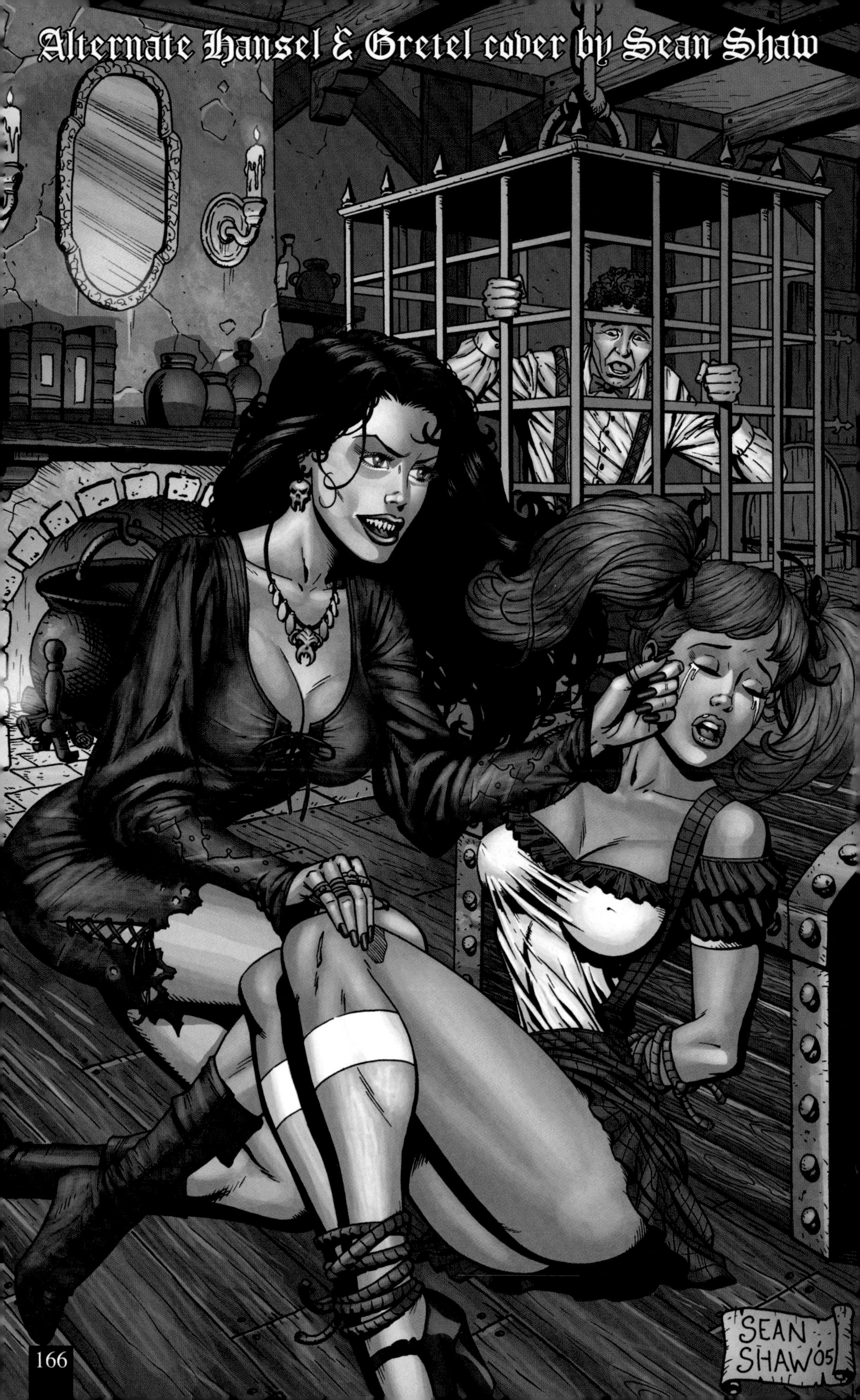
SEAN
SHAW'05

Alternate Hansel & Gretel cover by Sean Shaw

Letter from the Editor...

Fairy tales and comic books have a lot in common. They are universal in their appeal and are found in almost every culture around the world. Fairy tales have been around for hundreds of years, handed down from generation to generation and finally recorded by Wilhelm and Jacob Grimm in the early 1800s. There have been hundreds of adaptations of these popular stories. Walt Disney virtually built an empire on them. Cinderella is widely considered the best-known fictitious story in the history of the world. While fairy tales have been around for centuries, comics, in one form or another, have been around for much longer. Since primitive man drew the first cave paintings, we have used illustrations to tell stories. Comics are found throughout history.

In 1300 B.C., the Egyptians deified their pharos by using hieroglyphics. In 1511, Michelangelo covered the entire ceiling of the Sistine Chapel in a sequential art painting. Since the first newspaper saw print, artists have used cartoons to comment on politics and the state of the world around them. In the modern times, comics bring to life incredible worlds of fantasy and adventure. They can capture any genre: comedy, crime thrillers, romance and even non-fiction. When done right, they can inspire and raise the human spirit as well as any other entertainment medium. Comics have survived the invention of motion pictures, television, home video and video games and are proving to be an excellent compliment to all of these mediums. As long as we continue to imagine, comics will be here to entertain us and help us tell our stories.

Zenescope is happy to help contribute to this dynamic and diverse medium with our first volume of Grimm Fairy Tales. Hopefully you find these stories to be entertaining and compelling and we hope you enjoy reading them as much as we enjoyed re-creating them.

Sincerely,

Joe Brusha

Joe Brusha
President
Zenescope Entertainment